$2.95

The Indian and the White Man

Edited with an introduction by
<u>Wilcomb E. Washburn</u>

The Indian and the White Man

General Editors:
Hennig Cohen and John William Ward

Statement by the General Editors

The Anchor Series, "Documents in American Civilization," provides primary materials for the study of the history of the United States and for the understanding of American culture. In the belief that neither history nor culture can be properly studied without consideration of a variety of sources, the editors have adopted the interdisciplinary approach in the selection of documents. In our sense, a "document" is any idea, institution, or manmade object that provides a clue to the way in which subjective experience is organized at a specific moment in time.

The purpose of the series is twofold: to show the pervasiveness of those themes which are central to particular moments in history; and to underline the significance of cultural documents in their total historical context—and thus to illuminate problems or themes that characterize American society.

HENNIG COHEN is Professor of English at the University of Pennsylvania and editor of *American Quarterly*. He is also editor of *Selected Poems of Herman Melville* (Anchor Books, A375) and co-editor of *Folklore in America*.

JOHN WILLIAM WARD is Professor of History and American Studies at Amherst College. He is the author of *Andrew Jackson: Symbol for an Age* and editor of *Society, Manners, and Politics in the United States* by Michael Chevalier.

WILCOMB E. WASHBURN, although born in the Midwest, was brought up in Hanover, New Hampshire, where his father was Professor of Romance Languages at Dartmouth College. He graduated from Phillips Exeter Academy, received his A.B. from Dartmouth in 1948, and his Ph.D. in the History of American Civilization from Harvard in 1955. During World War II and the Korean War he served as an officer in the U. S. Marine Corps. From 1955 to 1958 he was a Fellow of the Institute of Early American History and Culture in Williamsburg, Virginia, as well as Instructor in History at the College of William and Mary. From 1958 to the present Mr. Washburn has served as Curator of the Division of Political History of the Smithsonian Institution, Washington, D.C. In addition, Mr. Washburn has, since 1961, been associated with the American University, where he is at present an Adjunct Professor. In 1957 he collaborated with William N. Fenton and L. H. Butterfield in a bibliographical study entitled *American Indian and White Relations to 1830: Needs & Opportunities for Study* (Chapel Hill: University of North Carolina Press). He is the author of *The Governor and The Rebel: A History of Bacon's Rebellion in Virginia* (University of North Carolina Press, 1958), and has published articles on Indian-white relations, early maritime exploration, and American colonial history in several journals.

THE INDIAN AND THE WHITE MAN

Edited with an Introduction by
Wilcomb E. Washburn

Anchor Books
Doubleday & Company, Inc.
Garden City, New York

Grateful acknowledgment is made to the following for permission to use excerpts of copyrighted material:

BARNES & NOBLE, INC. for *Narratives of New Netherland, 1609–1664,* edited by J. Franklin Jameson. Reprinted by permission.

ANTHONY BLOND LIMITED, CLARKSON N. POTTER INC. for Bartolomé de las Casas, *The Journal of Christopher Columbus,* translated by Cecil Jane, revised and annotated by L. A. Vigneras. Reprinted by permission.

THE CHAMPLAIN SOCIETY for David Thompson, *Narrative of His Explorations in Western America, 1784–1812,* edited by J. B. Tyrrell. Reprinted by permission.

DARTMOUTH PUBLICATIONS for *Letters of Eleazar Wheelock's Indians,* edited by James Dow McCallum (Hanover, New Hampshire, Dartmouth Publications, 1932). Reprinted by permission of Trustees of Dartmouth College.

GARRETT AND MASSIE, INC. for John Lawson, *History of North Carolina,* taken from the London edition of 1714 and edited by Frances Latham Harriss. Reprinted by permission.

THE HAKLUYT SOCIETY for *The Original Writings & Correspondence of the Two Richard Hakluyts,* with an introduction and notes by E. G. R. Taylor, series II, Vols. 76 & 77, 1935. Reprinted by permission.

INDIAN RIGHTS ASSOCIATION for M. K. Sniffen, "The Meaning of the Ute 'War.'" Reprinted through the courtesy of the Indian Rights Association from its *Publications,* No. 100, Second Series, November 15, 1915.

ALFRED A. KNOPF, INC. for William Bradford, *Of Plymouth Plantation, 1620–1647,* edited by Samuel Eliot Morison. Copyright 1952 by Samuel Eliot Morison. Egon Friedell, *A Cultural History of the Modern Age,* translated by Charles Francis Atkinson, Vol. 1, *Renaissance and Reformation: from the Black Death to the Thirty Years' War.* Both reprinted by permission of the publisher.

MINNESOTA HISTORICAL SOCIETY for *Documents Relating to*

Northwest Missions, 1815–1827, edited by Grace Lee Nute. Reprinted by permission.

OLD SOUTH ASSOCIATION for Old South Leaflet, No. 53: John Cotton, "God's Promise to His Plantations." Reprinted by permission.

PRINCETON UNIVERSITY PRESS for Amerigo Vespucci: *Letter to Piero Soderini, Gonfaloniere*, translated and edited by George Tyler Northup. *The Papers of Thomas Jefferson*, edited by Julian P. Boyd. Reprinted by permission of the publisher.

RANDOM HOUSE, INC., and CHATTO & WINDUS LTD. for excerpts from "The Bear," as it appears in *Go Down, Moses*, by William Faulkner. Copyright 1942 by The Curtis Publishing Co., copyright 1942 by William Faulkner. Reprinted by permission of the publishers.

CHARLES SCRIBNER'S SONS and JONATHAN CAPE LIMITED for the selection from "Fathers and Sons" (copyright 1933 Charles Scribner's Sons; renewal copyright © 1961 Mary Hemingway). Reprinted with the permission of Charles Scribner's Sons and Jonathan Cape Limited from *Winner Take Nothing* by Ernest Hemingway.

PETER SMITH for Morton's *New English Canaan*, reprinted in *Tracts and Other Papers*, compiled by Peter Force. Reprinted by permission.

SOUTH CAROLINA ARCHIVES DEPARTMENT for William L. McDowell, Jr., editor, *Colonial Records of South Carolina*, Series 2, *Documents Relating to Indian Affairs, May 21, 1750–August 7, 1754*. Reprinted by permission.

THE SOUTH CAROLINA HISTORICAL SOCIETY for Frank J. Klinberg, "The Mystery of the Lost Yamassee Prince," in the *South Carolina Historical Magazine*, LXIII (January 1962). Reprinted by permission.

STANFORD UNIVERSITY PRESS for *The Complete Works of Montaigne: Essays, Travel Journal, Letters*, translated by Donald M. Frame. Reprinted with the permission of the publishers, Stanford University Press. Copyright 1947, © 1957, 1958 by the Board of Trustees of the Leland Stanford Junior University.

UNIVERSITY OF CALIFORNIA for Toribio Motolinía, *History of the Indians of New Spain*, translated and edited by Elizabeth Andros Foster (the Cortes Society, Bancroft Library, Berkeley, California, 1950), Book III. Reprinted by permission.

THE UNIVERSITY OF NORTH CAROLINA PRESS for *The Adams–Jefferson Letters: The Complete Correspondence Between Thomas Jefferson and Abigail and John Adams*, edited by Lester J. Cappon. Thomas Jefferson, *Notes on the State of Virginia*, edited by William Peden. Both reprinted by permission.

UNIVERSITY OF OKLAHOMA PRESS for Pierre-Antoine Tabeau, *Narrative of Loisel's Expedition to the Upper Missouri*, edited

For Samuel Eliot Morison

Introduction

This collection of documents is designed to tell a story. It is not a source book for the scholar writing on Indian history. It is not a mere miscellany. The quotations were selected because they illustrate the most important aspects of Indian-white relations, many of which are either little understood or misunderstood. It is hoped that the reader will be attracted from the excerpts to the larger literature mentioned in the introductions to the documents and in the notes.

Historians of the Indian-white relationship tend to fall into the same categories that the people in general assume toward the Indians: that is, they may be hostile, friendly, or indifferent, although each, of course, assumes his viewpoint to be unbiased and impartial. I write from a point of view strongly sympathetic to the American Indian. Whatever their points of view all historians must face the sources equally and try to judge whether their beliefs are well or ill based on fact, logic, and morality. To ferret out the truth is a task more difficult in determining the history of two races in conflict than in narrating the history of one country from its own point of view. And it is not a problem that can be solved by a conventional and unreflecting willingness to "split the difference" between the claims of both parties.

The material in this book is organized around eight themes, which provide the chapter headings. Together they illustrate the larger theme of the Indian as part of the American experience. The American is the product of many forces: the frontier, modern industry, the reform movement, and countless other influences. The influence of the Indian is one of the most difficult to discuss because it represents a competing human tradition, a tradition with values of its own, with problems of its own, and with themes of its own development. The two societies could not, or would not, reconcile themselves to each other. The individualism of the European, for example, would not accommodate itself to the communal character of the original American, nor would the communal Indian society accommodate itself to European individualism. The two human elements fought for the same land base, and the loser might retain his physical existence but almost invariably he lost the culture and the land that gave his life meaning.

I have not, in this book, attempted to create unity where diversity exists. I have not tried to find national or personal themes in the American experience that might do justice to one element of white society but ignore other elements, to say nothing of the Indian himself. Rather, I have tried to point out how the Indian affected the white man in key relationships, and how in turn this experience has been interpreted in opposite and varying ways by all concerned. I have tried to get back to the specific actions and to the specific words that passed between white and Indian, and upon which the themes and interpretations of the experience have been based. For example, I have selected several "first contact" experiences in Chapter I, and several literary views of the "noble savage" in Chapter VIII. I have, in the notes, attempted to show that the writers did not create the "noble savage" just for the sake of supporting pet theories of their own, or out of sheer ignorance, as too many critics assume. Rather, their interpretations were based on the early contact reports combined with their observation of European behavior at home and abroad. I hope that, by the simple device of making the twentieth-century reader look at some of the early explorers' narratives, I may prevent him from jumping blindly into a sophisticated but erroneous literary attitude concerning the so-called "myth of the noble savage."

I have discussed in two separate chapters personal relations and governmental relations. Again I hope to get behind the cliché and to the source material from which later assumptions have been built. One is faced, of course, with the inevitable distortion caused by the limited knowledge or prejudiced point of view of the individual observer in his personal dealings with the Indians. I have tried to select points of view of all types: hostile, friendly, ignorant, perceptive. The twentieth-century reader, who is already surfeited with theories about the Indian-white relationship, will be afforded a chance to match those theories with some specific evidence.

The white man as officeholder is, in many ways, a more perplexing and perverse figure to the Indian than the individual conqueror, or fur trapper, or explorer. Under the panoply of European formality the government representative communicated with the Indian leaders, but too often the form and the spirit were not in close juxtaposition. The Indian, valuing the spirit rather than the recorded form, which in his letterless society was, for the most part, superfluous, could not cope with the legalisms of the white man. Nor could an alien government sympathize with, let alone understand, the plight of a race organized into categories that had no parallels in the white bureaucratic machinery.

Though white society displaced red in dominion of the continent, it was not done without thought or shame. A significant literature was produced by the English in an attempt to justify colonization and conquest in the New World. The morality of expansion was not a subject left to the Catholic theologians of Spain alone, though the greatest literature was produced from that source. Chapter III demonstrates that English theologians and writers were equally as successful as Spanish theorists in defending and justifying dispossession of the Indian. Though the problem is largely academic, it is still alive in the American experience, as is evident from the periodic reappearance in Al Capp's "L'il Abner" comic strip of Indian Joe and his claim to repossess the continent.

The themes of trade and war form, except in Marxist ideology, a balance of opposites. Trade is normally possible only in the absence of war, while war marks the absence of trade. One represents the absence of hatred and passion; the other is its supreme expression. Exchange of goods normally satisfies the needs or desires of both parties; in war victory can be won by only one side. War is a heroic success or a pathetic tragedy. Trade is neither. No one mourns the death of a salesman. Yet both themes alternate throughout the relationship between white and red. The selections in this book attempt to give some sense of the practical and imaginative dimensions of the themes.

All of the European nations accepted the responsibility of converting the natives of America as part of the bargain by which the Almighty in his guiding wisdom provided such a handsome endowment of land. As one English writer put it, the Europeans would exchange "spirituals" for "temporals" with the heathen. But the whites seemed never able to consummate their end of the bargain. For some reason the Indians perversely refused to accept the "spirituals" offered by the Christians, at least in the areas dominated by northern European nations, though this did not prevent the Christians from claiming their full measure of "temporals." The missionary impulse was sincere, if it was not successful. The passages in this book illustrate the high hopes and acute disappointments of the missionaries. According to one's orientation, one can see the dedication or stupidity of those proffering the Christian God and the perversity or subtlety of those refusing it.

Scattered throughout the book are visual documents that attempt to help illuminate the meaning of the Indian-white relationship. Although mechanical limitations required that most visual documents be grouped together, all relate to one or other of the themes discussed in each chapter, and some demonstrate their own themes in addition. For example, those documents that show work made by the hands of the Indian, though limited in number, stand as mute but powerful testimony to the creative spirit of the native inhabitants. Their forms are alien to white culture, but the gap is growing increasingly smaller, as exotic cultures impinge upon our own, and as our modern artists draw inspiration from the insight and power of the misnamed "primitive" artists of the world.

Of one thing the reader can be certain. No one can assure him, without being challenged, that "this is the way it was" with the Indian-white relationship on this continent. Passion and ignorance have been too heavily mixed with fact, both in past centuries and at present, to provide an unquestioned interpretation. Therefore, let the reader start his journey into this book with caution—and with humility.

Wilcomb E. Washburn

Contents

The Indian and the White Man

CHAPTER I

First Contact

How did the Indians receive the first white men? Did they receive them with rejoicing as gods from heaven? Did they receive them with hostility as natural enemies? Did they receive them with curiosity as beings whose capabilities and intentions were unknown? The historian is hard put to say. In the first place it is difficult to say of any recorded "contact" that it was indeed the first. The freebooters and slave raiders who cruised the seas simultaneously with the officially commissioned discoverers did not care to record their deeds for posterity. We sometimes know of their activities only from the hostility shown by the Indians to later explorers whom they suspected of similar missions of plunder and rapine.

And yet it is possible to isolate some original contacts —Columbus', for example. The excerpts from Columbus' journal reveal the openness and kindness of his reception by the inhabitants of the West Indian islands whose fate it was to be deprived of their very being. Whether their hospitality was conditioned by fear can be disputed. The fact is, as Samuel Eliot Morison has pointed out, that the New World surrendered its virginity gracefully, a complaisance which served only to whet the appetite of the Europeans.

The conventional picture of Indians lurking behind every bush waiting to shoot arrows into the sides of European explorers arriving for the first time is hallowed only by the tradition that followed, after some years, the initial contact and, in most cases, bore little relation to it. Our view of Indian-white relations is conditioned by the period in which the European occupants of the American continents were well entrenched and were, indeed, a majority advancing into the yet unappropriated lands of the once proud possessors of the whole. The Indian is known to us mainly as the wicked animal of the French proverb who defends himself when one attacks him. Hence, the lurking Indian is a fit symbol for our later relationship, but not for the earliest period when the white man was welcomed more often than not by people whose views of "human" nature and the future were none too keen. The unhappy fact remains that those Indian groups that reacted to European intrusion with the greatest hostility survived longest.

Document 1

October 12, 1492

The first chapter of the story of Indian-white relations was written in the journal of Christopher Columbus. The day was October 12, 1492, and the island Guanahaní or, as Columbus named it, San Salvador. Columbus imagined himself to have arrived at a small island off the mainland of Asia. He would not have attempted to claim possession had he arrived at any of the great kingdoms of Asia, whose power was a byword in Europe. Indeed, it was the weakness of the natives, their ignorance of weapons of iron, which seems to have made the strongest impression upon him. His actions, and European policy in general, flow in a natural logic from this observation. The original journal of Columbus was lost, and we owe our knowledge of it to the great historian of the Indies, Bartolomé de las Casas, who paraphrased and transcribed it in his *Historia de las Indias*. The following translation is that of Cecil Jane, revised and annotated by L. A. Vigneras, and published under the title *The Journal of Christopher Columbus*, pp. 23–24 (New York: Clarkson N. Potter, 1960).

Two hours after midnight land appeared, at a distance of about two leagues from them. They took in all sail, remaining with the mainsail, which is the great sail without bonnets, and kept jogging, waiting for day, a Friday, on which they reached a small island of the Lucayos, which is called in the language of the Indians "Guanahaní." Immediately they saw naked people, and the admiral [Columbus] went ashore in the armed boat, and Martin Alonso Pinzón and Vicente Yañez, his brother, who was captain of the *Niña*. The admiral brought out the royal standard, and the captains went with two banners of the Green Cross, which the admiral flew on all the ships as a flag, with an F and a Y, and over each letter their crown, one being on one side of the ✠ and the other on the other. When they had landed, they saw very green trees and much water and fruit of various kinds. The admiral called the two captains and the others who had landed, and Rodrigo de Escobedo, secretary of the whole fleet, and Rodrigo Sanchez de Segovia, and said that they should bear witness and testimony how he, before them all, took possession of the island, as in fact he did, for the King and Queen, his Sovereigns, making the declarations which are required, as is contained more at length in the testimonies which were there made in writing. Soon many people of the island gathered there. What follows are the actual words of the admiral, in his book of his first voyage and discovery of these Indies.

"I," he says, "in order that they might feel great amity towards us, because I knew that they were a people to be delivered and converted to our holy faith rather by love than by force, gave to some among them some red caps and some glass beads, which they hung round their necks, and many other things of little value. At this they were greatly pleased and became so entirely our friends that it was a wonder to see. Afterwards they came swimming to the ships' boats, where we were, and brought us parrots and cotton thread in balls, and spears and many other things, and we exchanged for them other things, such as small glass beads and hawks' bells, which we gave to them. In fact, they took all and gave all, such as they had, with good will, but it seemed to me that they were a people very deficient in everything. They all go naked as their mothers bore them, and the women also, although I saw only one very young girl. And all those whom I did see were youths, so that I did not see one who was over thirty years of age; they were very well built, with very handsome bodies and very good faces. Their hair is coarse almost like the hairs of a horse's tail and short; they wear their hair down over their eyebrows, except for a few strands behind, which they wear long and never cut. Some of them are painted black, and they are the colour of the people of the Canaries, neither black nor white, and some of them are painted white and some red and some in any colour that they find. Some of them paint their faces, some their whole bodies, some only the eyes, and some only the nose. They do not bear arms or know them, for I showed to them swords and they took them by the blade and cut themselves through ignorance. They have no iron. Their spears are certain reeds, without iron, and some of these have a fish tooth at the end, while others are pointed in various ways. They are all generally fairly tall, good looking and well proportioned. I saw some who bore marks of wounds on their bodies, and I made signs to them to ask how this came about, and they indicated to me that people came from other islands, which are near, and wished to capture them, and they defended themselves. And I believed and still believe that they come here from the mainland to take them for slaves. They should be good servants and of quick intelligence, since I see that they very soon say all that is said to them, and I believe that they would easily be made Christians, for it appeared to me that they had no creed. Our Lord willing, at the time of my departure I will bring back six of them to Your Highnesses, that they may learn to talk. I saw no beast of any kind in this island, except parrots." All these are the words of the admiral.

DOCUMENT 2

"The Full Extreme of Hospitality"

Amerigo Vespucci, for whom America is named, is one of the most enigmatic and controversial figures in the history of American exploration. Vespucci, a native of Florence, Italy, claimed to have made four voyages to the New World, the first of which left Cadiz on May 10, 1497. The precise locations of Vespucci's explorations are subject to dispute, but the bulk of his accepted activities, in the early years of the sixteenth century, took place along the northern and eastern shores of South America. The following quotation is from Vespucci's letter to Piero Soderini, Gonfaloniere, in 1504, and purports to describe the 1497 voyage. It is taken from *Amerigo Vespucci: Letter to Piero Soderini, Gonfaloniere,* translated and edited by George Tyler Northup (Princeton: Princeton University Press, 1916), pp. 7–10.

The manner of their living is very barbarous, because they do not eat at fixed times, but as often as they please. And it matters little to them that they should be seized with a desire to eat at midnight rather than by day, for at all times they eat. And their eating is done upon the ground, without tablecloth or any other cloth, because they hold their food either in earthen basins which they make or in half gourds. They sleep in certain nets made of cotton, very big, and hung in the air. And although this their way of sleeping may appear uncomfortable, I say that it is a soft way to sleep; [because it was very frequently our lot to sleep] in them, and we slept better in them than in quilts. They are people neat and clean of person, owing to the constant washing they practise. When, begging your pardon, they evacuate the bowels, they do everything to avoid being seen; and just as in this they are clean and modest, the more dirty and shameless are they in making water [both men and women]. Because, even while talking to us, they let fly such filth, without turning around or showing shame, that in this they have no modesty. They do not practise marriage amongst themselves. Each one takes all the wives he pleases; and when he desires to repudiate them, he does repudiate them without it being considered a wrong on his part or a disgrace to the woman; for in this the woman has as much liberty as the man. They are not very jealous, and are libidinous beyond measure, and the women far more than the men; for I refrain out of decency from telling you the trick which they play to satisfy their immoderate lust. They are very fertile women, and in their pregnancies avoid no toil. Their parturitions are so easy that one day after giving birth they go out everywhere, and especially to bathe in the rivers; and they are sound as fish. They are so heartless and cruel that, if they become angry with their husbands, they immediately resort to a trick whereby they kill the child within the womb, and a miscarriage is brought about, and for this reason they kill a great many babies. They are women of pleasing person, very well proportioned, so that one does not see on their bodies any ill-formed feature or limb. And although they go about utterly naked, they are fleshy women, and that part of their privies which he who has not seen them would think to see is invisible; for they cover all with their thighs, save that part [for] which nature made no provision, and which is modestly speaking, the *mons veneris*. In short they are no more ashamed [of their shameful parts] than we are in displaying the nose and mouth. Only exceptionally will you see a woman with drooping breasts, or with belly shrunken through frequent parturition, or with other wrinkles; for all look as though they had never given birth. They showed themselves very desirous of copulating with us Christians. While among these people we did not learn that they had any religion. They can be termed neither Moors nor Jews; and they are

worse than heathen; because we did not see that they offered any sacrifice, nor yet did they have [any] house of
prayer. I deem their manner of life to be Epicurean. Their
dwellings are in common, and their houses built after the
fashion of huts, but stoutly wrought and constructed out
of very large trees and thatched with palm leaves, safe
against tempests and winds, and in some places of such
breadth [and length] that in a single house we found there
were 600 souls; [and we saw towns of only thirteen houses
where there were 4,000 souls]. Every eight to ten years
they shift their towns. And when asked why [they put
themselves to so much trouble, they made us a very plausible answer. They said that] they did so on account of the
soil, which, when once rendered infectious and unhealth-
ful by filth, occasioned disease in their bodies, which
seemed to us a good reason. Their wealth consists of feathers of many-hued birds, or of little rosaries which they
make out of fish bones, or of white or green stones which
they stick through cheeks, lips, and ears, and of many
other things to which we attach no value. They engage in
no barter [whatsoever]; they neither buy nor sell. In short,
they live and are contented with what nature gives them.
The wealth which we affect in this our Europe and elsewhere, such as gold, jewels, pearls, and other riches, they
hold of no value at all; and although they have them in
their lands they do not work to get them, nor do they care
for them. They are so [liberal] in giving that it is the exception when they deny you anything; and, on the other
hand, [they are free] in begging, when they show themselves to be your friends. But the greatest token of friendship which they show you is that they give you their
wives and daughters; and when a father or a mother brings
you the daughter, although she be a virgin, and you sleep
with her, they esteem themselves highly honored; and in
this way they practise the full extreme of hospitality.

DOCUMENT 3

A Renaissance Gentleman in America

Plate 1, following page 134, shows Indian women being offered Amerigo Vespucci on his reported voyage of 1497. It is reproduced from an engraving in Johann Theodore de Bry's *America* published in Frankfurt in 1617 and now in the Rare Book Division of the Library of Congress, Washington, D.C. The prudishness of later centuries tended to obscure the carnal bond that was immediately established between Europeans and Indians, but it is brought out in this engraving as it is in Vespucci's uninhibited narrative.

DOCUMENT 4

Disputed Sovereignty

The practice of the European nations of claiming
sovereignty by the placing of visible symbols on the
lands they "discovered" is here amusingly recounted in
the narrative of the voyage of Jacques Cartier of St.
Malo, who left France on April 20, 1534, and who ex-
plored in the Gulf of St. Lawrence between Newfoundland and the mainland. The passage, and bibliographical information concerning the account, is taken from
Henry S. Burrage, ed., *Early English and French Voyages, Chiefly from Hakluyt, 1534–1608*, pp. 24–26;
Original Narratives of Early American History series
(New York: Charles Scribner's Sons, 1906).

Upon the 25 of the moneth, wee caused a faire high
Crosse to be made of the height of thirty foote, which was
made in the presence of many of them, upon the point
of the entrance of the sayd haven [Gaspé Bay], in the
middest whereof we hanged up a Shield with three Floure
de Luces in it, and in the top was carved in the wood with
Anticke letters this posie, Vive le Roy de France. Then
before them all we set it upon the sayd point. They with
great heed beheld both the making and setting of it up.
So soone as it was up, we altogether kneeled downe before
them, with our hands toward Heaven, yeelding God
thankes: and we made signes unto them, shewing them
the Heavens, and that all our salvation dependeth onely on
him which in them dwelleth: whereat they shewed a great
admiration, looking first one at another, and then upon
the Crosse. And after wee were returned to our ships,
their Captaine clad with an old Beares skin, with three of
his sonnes, and a brother of his with him, came unto us in

one of their boates, but they came not so neere us as they were wont to doe: there he made a long Oration unto us, shewing us the crosse we had set up, and making a crosse with two fingers, then did he shew us all the Countrey about us, as if he would say that all was his, and that wee should not set up any crosse without his leave. His talke being ended, we shewed him an Axe, faining that we would give it him for his skin, to which he listned, for by little and little hee came neere our ships. One of our fellowes that was in our boate, tooke hold on theirs, and suddenly leapt into it, with two or three more, who enforced them to enter into our ships, whereat they were greatly astonished. But our Captain did straightwaies assure them, that they should have no harme, nor any injurie offred them at all, and entertained them very friendly, making them eate and drinke. Then did we shew them with signes, that the crosse was but onely set up to be as a light and leader which wayes to enter into the port, and that wee would shortly come againe, and bring good store of iron wares and other things, but that we would take two of his children with us, and afterward bring them to the sayd port againe: and so wee clothed two of them in shirts, and coloured coates, with red cappes, and put about every ones necke a copper chaine, whereat they were greatly contented: then gave they their old clothes to their fellowes that went backe againe, and we gave to each one of those three that went backe, a hatchet, and some knives, which made them very glad. After these were gone, and had told the newes unto their fellowes, in the afternoone there came to our ships sixe boates of them, with five or sixe men in every one, to take their farewels of those two we had detained to take with us, and brought them some fish, uttering many words which we did not understand, making signes that they would not remove the crosse we had set up.

CHAPTER II

Personal Relations

When cultures meet something has to give. When one culture is physically weaker than the other, most of the "giving" is on the part of the weaker culture, unless it is so obviously superior to its conqueror, even in the latter's eyes, that the conqueror adapts his culture to that of the conquered, as the Romans did, in part, when they conquered the Greeks. Students of the American Indian use the word "acculturation" to describe the process by which the culture of the native races was modified by contact with European culture. Nevertheless, the modifications were not solely on the Indian side. The following selections emphasize the impact of Indian oratory, Indian friendship, and the Indian woman on the men of Europe, influences which powerfully impressed some whites but left others unaffected.

DOCUMENT 5

Captain John Smith

The following passage, concerning Captain John Smith, then "President" or Governor of the English colony in Virginia, and his journey to Pamunkey in the winter of 1608–9, throws a stark light on the nature of the Indian-white relationship in this early period. Smith, bold and aggressive, continued to hold the English colony together by living off the country, i.e., the Indians. Powhatan, the Indian Emperor, grew increasingly restive with the intruders, and it is not difficult to see why the relationship was to culminate in the great Indian massacre of 1622. The passage quoted below was written by Walter Russell and Anas Todkill, two of Smith's men on the trip, and published in Smith's *A Map of Virginia, with a Description of the Countrey, the Commodities, People, Government, and Religion* (London: 1612). The passage is available in Edward Arber, ed., *Travels and Works of Captain John Smith*, Vol. I, pp. 132–36 (Edinburgh: John Grant, 1910), and in Lyon Gardiner Tyler, ed., *Narratives of Early Virginia, 1606–1625*, pp. 163–66; Original Narratives of Early American History series (New York: Charles Scribner's Sons, 1907).

The next night being lodged at Kecoughtan, 6 or 7 daies the extreame wind, raine, frost, and snowe caused us to keepe Christmas amongst the Salvages, where wee were never more merrie, nor fedde on more plentie of good oysters, fish, flesh, wild foule, and good bread, nor never had better fires in England then in the drie warme smokie houses of Kecoughtan. But departing thence, when we found no houses, we were not curious (in any weather) to lie, 3 or 4 nights together, upon any shore, under the trees, by a good fire. 148 fowles, the President, Anth. Bagly, and Edward Pising did kill at 3. shoots. At Kiskiack, the frost forced us 3 or 4 daies, also to suppresse the insolencie of those proud Salvages, to quarter in their houses and guard our barge, and cause them give us what wee wanted; yet were we but 12 with the President, and yet we never wanted harbour where we found any houses.

The 12 of Januarie we arrived at Werawocomoco, where the river was frozen neare halfe a mile from the shore. But to neglect no time, the President with his barge, so farre had approached, by breaking the Ice, as the eb left him amongst those oozie shoules; yet, rather then to lie there frozen to death, by his owne example, hee taught them to march middle deepe, more then a flight shot, through this muddie froye [frozen] ooze. When the barge floted, he appointed 2 or 3 to returne her abord the Pinnace, where, for want of water, in melting the salt ice they made fresh water. But in this march, M. Russell (whome none could perswade to stay behind) being somewhat ill and exceeding heavie, so overtoiled himself, as the rest had much adoe (ere he got a shore) to regain life into his dead benummed spirits. Quartering in the next houses we found, we sent to Powhatan for provision, who sent us plentie of bread, Turkies, and Venison. The next day, having feasted us after his ordinarie manner, he began to aske, when wee would bee gon, faining hee sent not for us, neither had hee any corne, and his people much lesse, yet for 40 swords he would procure us 40 bushels. The President, shewing him the men there present, that brought him the message and conditions, asked him, how it chaunced he became so forgetful; thereat, the king concluded the matter with a merry laughter, asking for our commodities, but none he liked without gunnes and swords, valuing a basket of corne more pretious then a basket of copper, saying he could eate his corne, but not his copper.

Captaine Smith seeing the intent of this subtil Salvage, began to deale with him after this manner.

Powhatan, though I had many courses to have made my provision; yet beleeving your promises to supply my wants, I neglected all, to satisfie your desire; and to testifie my love, I sent you my men for your building, neglecting my owne. What your people had, you have engrossed, forbidding them our trade, and nowe you thinke by consuming the time, wee shall consume for want, not having [wherewith] to fulfill your strange demandes. As for swords and gunnes, I told you long agoe, I had none to spare. And you shall knowe, those I have, can keepe me from want: yet steale, or wrong you, I will not, nor dissolve that friendship wee have mutually promised, except you constraine mee by your bad usage.

The king having attentively listned to this discourse, promised that both hee and his Country would spare him what they could; the which within 2 daies, they should receave. Yet, Captaine Smith, (saith the king)

some doubt I have of your comming hither, that makes me not so kindly seeke to relieve you as I would; for many do informe me, your comming is not for trade, but to invade my people and possesse my Country, who dare not come to bring you corne, seeing you thus armed with your men. To cheere us of this feare, leave abord your weapons, for here they are needlesse, we being all friends and for ever Powhatans.

With many such discourses, they spent the day, quartring that night in the kings houses. . . .

Whilst we expected the comming in of the countrie, we wrangled out of the king 10 quarters of corne for a copper kettle; the which the President perceiving him much to effect, valued it at a much greater rate, but (in regard of his scarcety) hee would accept of as much more the next yeare, or else the country of Monacan. The King exceeding liberall of that hee had not, yeelded him Monacan. Wherewith each seeming well contented, Powhatan began to expostulate the difference betwixt peace and war, after this manner.

Captaine Smith, you may understand that I, having seene the death of all my people thrice, and not one living of those 3 generations but my selfe, I knowe the difference of peace and warre better then any in my Countrie. But now I am old, and ere long must die. My brethren, namely Opichapam, Opechankanough, and Kekataugh, my two sisters, and their two daughters, are distinctly each others successours. I wish their experiences no lesse then mine, and your love to them, no lesse then mine to you: but this brute [noise] from Nansamund, that you are come to destroy my Countrie, so much affrighteth all my people, as they dare not visit you. What will it availe you to take that perforce, you may quietly have with love, or to destroy them that provide you food? What can you get by war, when we can hide our provision and flie to the woodes, whereby you must famish, by wronging us your friends? And whie are you thus jealous of our loves, seeing us unarmed, and both doe, and are willing still to feed you with that you cannot get but by our labours? Think you I am so simple not to knowe it is better to eate good meate, lie well, and sleepe quietly with my women and children, laugh, and be merrie with you, have copper, hatchets, or what I want being your friend; then bee forced to flie from al, to lie cold in the woods, feed upon acorns roots and such trash, and be so hunted by you that I can neither rest eat nor sleepe, but my tired men must watch, and if a twig but breake, everie one crie, there comes Captaine Smith: then must I flie I knowe not whether, and thus with miserable feare end my miserable life, leaving my pleasures to such youths as you, which, through your rash unadvisednesse, may quickly as miserably ende, for want of that you never knowe how to find? Let this therefore assure you of our

loves, and everie yeare our friendly trade shall furnish
you with corne; and now also if you would come in
friendly manner to see us, and not thus with your
gunnes and swords, as to invade your foes.

DOCUMENT 6

Captain John Smith

Plate 2, following page 134, suggests the strength of Virginia's famous leader without whose courage, ruthlessness, and wit the colony would never have survived. Smith is shown in a characteristic pose, taking the King of Pamunkey prisoner in 1608, literally grabbing him by the hair, while in the background English and Indians engage in mortal combat. The engraving is from Smith's *Generall Historie of Virginia, New England, and the Summer Isles* (London: 1624), in the Rare Book Division of the Library of Congress, Washington, D.C.

DOCUMENT 7

"So Intricate a Laborinth"

One of the most celebrated marriages in American
history is that between John Rolfe, the English planter
of Virginia, and Pocahontas, daughter of Powhatan, the
Indian "Emperor" whose power extended throughout
the area the English sought to settle. The following letter, written by Rolfe before his marriage to Pocahontas
in April of 1614, to Sir Thomas Dale, the deputy governor of the colony, sheds a brilliant light on the motives
and attitudes that surrounded the match. In 1616 Rolfe
and his wife went to England, where Pocahontas was
introduced at court and attentions befitting a princess
shown her. Her portrait, done in England possibly prior
to her tragic and unexpected death at Gravesend on
March 21, 1617, when about to return to Virginia, is
illustrated in Document 8. The force of her life and her
legend is demonstrated in the insistence with which so
many Americans attempt to claim descent from her only
son, Thomas Rolfe. The letter, published by Ralph
Hamor in his *A True Discourse of the Present Estate of
Virginia* (London: 1615), is taken from Lyon Gardiner
Tyler, ed., *Narratives of Early Virginia, 1606–1625*,
pp. 239–44; Original Narratives of Early American History series (New York: Charles Scribner's Sons, 1907).

Honourable Sir, and most worthy Governor:
When your leasure shall best serve you to peruse these
lines, I trust in God, the beginning will not strike you into
a greater admiration [surprise], then the end will give you
good content. It is a matter of no small moment, concerning my own particular, which here I impart unto you, and
which toucheth mee so neerely, as the tendernesse of my
salvation. Howbeit I freely subject my selfe to your grave

and mature judgement, deliberation, approbation and determination; assuring my selfe of your zealous admonitions, and godly comforts, either perswading me to desist, or incouraging me to persist therin, with a religious feare and godly care, for which (from the very instant, that this began to roote it selfe within the secret bosome of my brest) my daily and earnest praiers have bin, still are, and ever shall be produced forth with as sincere a godly zeale as I possibly may to be directed, aided and governed in all my thoughts, words and deedes, to the glory of God, and for my eternal consolation. To persevere wherein I never had more neede, nor (till now) could ever imagine to have bin moved with the like occasion.

But (my case standing as it doth) what better worldly refuge can I here seeke, then [than] to shelter my selfe under the safety of your favourable protection? And did not my ease proceede from an unspotted conscience, I should not dare to offer to your view and approved judgement, these passions of my troubled soule, so full of feare and trembling is hypocrisie and dissimulation. But knowing my owne innocency and godly fervor, in the whole prosecution hereof, I doubt not of your benigne acceptance, and clement construction. As for malicious depravers, and turbulent spirits, to whom nothing is tastful, but what pleaseth their unsavory pallat, I passe not for them being well assured in my perswasion (by the often triall and proving of my selfe, in my holiest meditations and praiers) that I am called hereunto by the spirit of God; and it shall be sufficient for me to be protected by your selfe in all vertuous and pious indevours. And for my more happie proceeding herein, my daily oblations [prayers] shall ever be addressed to bring to passe so good effects, that your selfe, and all the world may truely say: This is the worke of God, and it is marvelous in our eies.

But to avoid tedious preambles, and to come neerer the matter: first suffer me with your patence, to sweepe and make cleane the way wherein I walke, from all suspicions and doubts, which may be covered therein, and faithfully to reveale unto you, what should move me hereunto.

Let therefore this my well advised protestation, which here I make betweene God and my own conscience, be a sufficient witnesse, at the dreadfull day of judgement (when the secret of all mens harts shall be opened) to condemne me herein, if my chiefest intent and purpose be not, to strive with all my power of body and minde, in the undertaking of so mightie a matter, no way led (so farre forth as mans weakenesse may permit) with the unbridled desire of carnall affection: but for the good of this plantation, for the honour of our countrie, for the glory of God, for my owne salvation, and for the converting to the true knowledge of God and Jesus Christ, an unbeleeving creature, namely Pokahuntas. To whom my hartie and best thoughts are, and have a long time bin so intangled, and inthralled in so intricate a laborinth, that I was even awearied to unwinde my selfe thereout. But almighty God, who never faileth his, that truely invocate his holy name hath opened the gate, and led me by the hand that I might plainely see and discerne the safe paths wherein to treade.

To you therefore (most noble Sir) the patron and Father of us in this countrey doe I utter the effects of this my setled and long continued affection (which hath made a mightie warre in my meditations) and here I doe truely relate, to what issue this dangerous combate is come unto, wherein I have not onely examined, but throughly tried and pared my thoughts even to the quicke, before I could finde any fit wholesome and apt applications to cure so daungerous an ulcer. I never failed to offer my daily and faithfull praiers to God, for his sacred and holy assistance. I forgot not to set before mine eies the frailty of mankinde, his prones [proneness] to evill, his indulgencie of wicked thoughts, with many other imperfections wherein man is daily insnared, and oftentimes overthrowne, and them compared to my present estate. Nor was I ignorant of the heavie displeasure which almightie God conceived against the sonnes of Levie and Israel for marrying strange wives, nor of the inconveniences which may thereby arise, with other the like good motions which made me looke about warily and with good circumspection, into the grounds and principall agitations, which thus should provoke me to be in love with one whose education hath bin rude, her manners barbarous, her generation accursed, and so discrepant in all nurtriture from my selfe, that oftentimes with feare and trembling, I have ended my private controversie with this: surely these are wicked instigations, hatched by him who seeketh and delighteth in mans destruction; and so with fervent praiers to be ever preserved from such diabolical assaults (as I tooke those to be) I have taken some rest.

Thus when I had thought I had obtained my peace and quietnesse, beholde another, but more gracious tentation hath made breaches into my holiest and strongest meditations; with which I have bin put to a new triall, in a straighter manner then the former: for besides the many passions and sufferings which I have daily, hourely, yea and in my sleepe indured, even awaking mee to astonishment, taxing mee with remisnesse, and carelesnesse, refusing and neglecting to performe the duetie of a good Christian, pulling me by the eare, and crying: why dost not thou indeavour to make her a Christian? And these have happened to my greater wonder, even when she hath bin furthest seperated from me, which in common reason (were it not an undoubted worke of God) might breede forgetfulnesse of a farre more worthie creature. Besides, I say the holy spirit of God hath often demaunded of me, why I was created? If not for transitory pleasures and worldly vanities, but to labour in the Lords vineyard, there to sow and plant, to nourish and increase the fruites thereof, daily adding with the good husband in the Gospell, somewhat to the tallent, that in the end the fruites may be reaped, to the comfort of the laborer in this life, and his salvation in the world to come? And if this be, as undoubtedly this is, the service Jesus Christ requireth of his best servant: wo unto him that hath these instruments of pietie put into his hands, and wilfully despiseth to worke with them. Likewise, adding hereunto her great apparance of love to me, her desire to be taught and instructed in the knowledge of God, her capablenesse of understanding, her aptnesse and willingnesse to receive anie good impression, and also the spirituall, besides her owne incitements stirring me up hereunto.

What should I doe? shall I be of so untoward a disposition, as to refuse to leade the blind into the right way? Shall I be so unnaturall, as not to give bread to the hungrie? or uncharitable, as not to cover the naked? Shall I despise to actuate these pious dueties of a Christian? Shall the base feare of displeasing the world, overpower and with holde mee from revealing unto man these spirituall workes of the Lord, which in my meditations and praiers, I have daily made knowne unto him? God forbid. I assuredly trust hee hath thus delt with me for my eternall felicitie, and for his glorie: and I hope so to be guided by his heavenly graice, that in the end by my faithfull paines, and christianlike labour, I shall attaine to that blessed promise, Pronounced by that holy Prophet Daniell unto the righteous that bring many unto the knowledge of God. Namely, that they shall shine like the starres forever and ever. A sweeter comfort cannot be to a true Christian, nor a greater incouragement for him to labour all the daies of his life, in the performance thereof, nor a greater gaine of consolation, to be desired at the hower of death, and in the day of judgement.

Againe by my reading, and conference with honest and religious persons, have I received no small encouragement, besides *serena mea conscientia,* the cleerenesse of my conscience, clean from the filth of impurity, *quae est instar muri ahenei,* which is unto me, as a brasen wall. If I should set down at large, the perturbations and godly motions, which have striven within mee, I should but make a tedious and unnecessary volume. But I doubt not these shall be sufficient both to certifie you of my tru intents, in discharging of my dutie to God, and to your selfe, to whose gracious providence I humbly submit my selfe, for his glory, your honour, our Countreys good, the benefit of this Plantation, and for the converting of one unregenerate, to regeneration; which I beseech God to graunt, for his deere Sonne Christ Jesus his sake.

Now if the vulgar sort, who square [measure] all mens actions by the base rule of their own filthinesse, shall taxe or taunt me in this my godly labour: let them know, it is not any hungry appetite, to gorge my selfe with incontinency; sure (if I would, and were so sensually inclined) I might satisfie such desire, though not without a seared conscience, yet with Christians more pleasing to the eie, and lesse fearefull in the offence unlawfully committed. Nor am I in so desperate an estate, that I regard not what becommeth of mee; nor am I out of hope but one day to see my Country, nor so void of friends, nor mean in birth, but there to obtain a mach [match] to my great content: nor have I ignorantly passed over my hopes there, or regardlesly seek to loose the love of my friends, by taking this course: I know them all, and have not rashly overslipped any.

But shal it please God thus to dispose of me (which I earnestly desire to fulfill my ends before sette down) I will heartely accept of it as a godly taxe appointed me, and I will never cease, (God assisting me) untill I have accomplished, and brought to perfection so holy a worke, in which I will daily pray God to blesse me, to mine, and her eternall happines. And thus desiring no longer to live, to enjoy the blessings of God, then [than] this my resolution doth tend to such godly ends, as are by me before declared: not doubting of your favourable acceptance, I take my leave, beseeching Almighty God to raine downe upon you, such plenitude of his heavenly graces, as your heart can wish and desire, and so I rest, At your commaund most willing to be disposed off

JOHN ROLFE.

DOCUMENTS 8, 9, 10

Three Views of Pocahontas

The story of Pocahontas has become a part of the myth of America, both in its truth and in its fancy. Pictorial representations of Powhatan's daughter from three different centuries are shown in Plates 3, 4, and 5 following page 134. In the first we see a painting, now in the National Gallery of Art, Washington, D.C., done by an anonymous English artist, presumably at the time Pocahontas was in England in 1616–17, prior to her tragic death there. In the second we see a portrait of Pocahontas, now in the Massachusetts Historical Society, Boston, apparently done at a young ladies' finishing school in Boston by Mary Woodbury of Beverly who later, on March 3, 1737, married Dr. Benjamin Jones. In the third the romanticism of the nineteenth century has obviously taken over and, in the portrait of Pocahontas by Robert Matthew Sully (1803–55), now in the State Historical Society of Wisconsin, Madison, we pause to consider how far away we are from the seventeenth century.

These three versions of a single person suggest that it is as difficult to get at the truth of Indian-white relations through the artist's delineation of form as it is through the written work of the missionary or explorer. It is hard enough to describe one's own society; harder still to describe another's. Similarly, one is sometimes hard put to tell whether the contemporary observer or the later historian is more awry in his depiction of an alien society. A portrait, whether done in words, with the painter's brush, or with the photographer's lens, can reflect the training, the whims, the ignorance, the hatred, and the love of the artist. Artists of the period, from the time of John White, who accompanied the earliest English settlers in the New World, may have been influenced by their classical training, their European interests, and their human prejudices. The assertion that the European artists painted Indians as Romans and Greeks because of an incurable romanticism, however, has been carried beyond all logical bounds. The assertion of the sixteenth- and seventeenth-century artists' "fallacy" frequently rests on the critics' twentieth-century assumption that the sixteenth- and seventeenth-century Indian was the innately hostile and squalid "savage" known to the nineteenth- and twentieth-century reader of casual literature—a fallacy in its own right.

DOCUMENT 11

Thomas Morton of Merrymount
(In Pilgrim Eyes)

The following critical view of Thomas Morton of
Merrymount is from the pen of William Bradford,
Governor of Plymouth Plantation, in his *Of Plymouth
Plantation, 1620–1647*, pp. 204–10, edited by Samuel
Eliot Morison (New York: Alfred A. Knopf, 1952).
Bradford's severest blows fall on the lasciviousness of
Morton's men, and on their willingness to trade arms
and ammunition to the Indians. Two editorial notes
have been omitted in reprinting this passage.

[Thomas Morton of Merrymount]

About some three or four years before this time, there
came over one Captain Wollaston (a man of pretty parts)
and with him three or four more of some eminency, who
brought with them a great many servants, with provisions
and other implements for to begin a plantation. And
pitched themselves in a place within the Massachusetts
which they called after their Captain's name, Mount Wollaston. Amongst whom was one Mr. Morton, who it should
seem had some small adventure of his own or other men's
amongst them, but had little respect amongst them, and
was slighted by the meanest servants. Having continued
there some time, and not finding things to answer their
expectations nor profit to arise as they looked for, Captain
Wollaston takes a great part of the servants and transports
them to Virginia, where he puts them off at good rates,
selling their time to other men; and writes back to one
Mr. Rasdall (one of his chief partners and accounted their
merchant) to bring another part of them to Virginia like-

wise, intending to put them off there as he had done the rest. And he, with the consent of the said Rasdall, appointed one Fitcher to be his Lieutenant and govern the remains of the Plantation till he or Rasdall returned to take further order thereabout. But this Morton abovesaid, having more craft than honesty (who had been a kind of pettifogger of Furnival's Inn) in the others' absence watches an opportunity (commons being but hard amongst them) and got some strong drink and other junkets and made them a feast; and after they were merry, he began to tell them he would give them good counsel. "You see," saith he, "that many of your fellows are carried to Virginia, and if you stay till this Rasdall return, you will also be carried away and sold for slaves with the rest. Therefore I would advise you to thrust out this Lieutenant Fitcher, and I, having a part in the Plantation, will receive you as my partners and consociates; so may you be free from service, and we will converse, plant, trade, and live together as equals and support and protect one another," or to like effect. This counsel was easily received, so they took opportunity and thrust Lieutenant Fitcher out o' doors, and would suffer him to come no more amongst them, but forced him to seek bread to eat and other relief from his neighbours till he could get passage for England.

After this they fell to great licentiousness and led a dissolute life, pouring out themselves into all profaneness. And Morton became Lord of Misrule, and maintained (as it were) a School of Atheism. And after they had got some goods into their hands, and got much by trading with the Indians, they spent it as vainly in quaffing and drinking, both wine and strong waters in great excess (and, as some reported) £10 worth in a morning. They also set up a maypole, drinking and dancing about it many days together, inviting the Indian women for their consorts, dancing and frisking together like so many fairies, or furies, rather; and worse practices. As if they had anew revived and celebrated the feasts of the Roman goddess Flora, or the beastly practices of the mad Bacchanalians. Morton likewise, to show his poetry composed sundry rhymes and

verses, some tending to lasciviousness, and others to the
detraction and scandal of some persons, which he affixed
to this idle or idol maypole.[1] They changed also the name
of their place, and instead of calling it Mount Wollaston
they call it Merry-mount, as if this jollity would have
lasted ever. But this continued not long, for after Morton
was sent for England (as follows to be declared) shortly
after came over that worthy gentleman Mr. John Endecott,
who brought over a patent under the broad seal for the
government of the Massachusetts. Who, visiting those
parts, caused that maypole to be cut down and rebuked
them for their profaneness and admonished them to look
there should be better walking. So they or others now
changed the name of their place again and called it Mount
Dagon.[2]

Now to maintain this riotous prodigality and profuse
excess, Morton, thinking himself lawless, and hearing what
gain the French and fishermen made by trading of pieces,
powder and shot to the Indians, he as the head of this
consortship began the practice of the same in these parts.
And first he taught them how to use them, to charge and
discharge, and what proportion of powder to give the

---

[1] Morton gives some of the verses, which he says "puzzled the
Separatists most pitifully to expound," in his New English Canaan (the book which he wrote to get even with the Pilgrims),
pp. 277–81. The best is a drinking song, of which one verse goes:

    Give to the Nymph that's free from scorn
    No Irish stuff nor Scotch over-worn.
    Lasses in beaver coats, come away,
    Ye shall be welcome to us night and day.
        Then drink and be merry, merry, merry boys,
        Let all your delight be in Hymen's joys;
        Io! to Hymen, now the day is come,
        About the merry Maypole take a room.

It perhaps should be explained that the "Irish stuff" and "Scotch"
were not whisky but woolens. Neither whisky nor rum had as yet
appeared in New England; the only strong liquors known were
aqua vitae and brandy.

[2] After the god of the Philistines—Judges xvi.23. The site of
Merrymount or Mount Wollaston is marked on Route 3, in
Quincy.

piece, according to the size or bigness of the same; and
what shot to use for fowl and what for deer. And having
thus instructed them, he employed some of them to hunt
and fowl for him, so as they became far more active in
that employment than any of the English, by reason of
their swiftness of foot and nimbleness of body, being also
quick-sighted and by continual exercise well knowing the
haunts of all sorts of game. So as when they saw the execution that a piece would do, and the benefit that might
come by the same, they became mad (as it were) after
them and would not stick to give any price they could attain to for them; accounting their bows and arrows but
baubles in comparison of them.

And here I may take occasion to bewail the mischief
that this wicked man began in these parts, and which
since, base covetousness prevailing in men that should
know better, has now at length got the upper hand and
made this thing common, notwithstanding any laws to the
contrary. So as the Indians are full of pieces all over, both
fowling pieces, muskets, pistols, etc. They have also their
moulds to make shot of all sorts, as musket bullets, pistol
bullets, swan and goose shot, and of smaller sorts. Yea
some have seen them have their screw-plates to make
screw-pins themselves when they want them, with sundry
other implements, wherewith they are ordinarily better
fitted and furnished than the English themselves. Yea, it
is well known that they will have powder and shot when
the English want it nor cannot get it; and that in a time of
war or danger, as experience hath manifested, that when
lead hath been scarce and men for their own defense
would gladly have given a groat a pound, which is dear
enough, yet hath it been bought up and sent to other
places and sold to such as trade it with the Indians at 12d
the pound. And it is like they give 3s or 4s the pound, for
they will have it at any rate. And these things have been
done in the same times when some of their neighbours
and friends are daily killed by the Indians, or are in danger thereof and live but at the Indians' mercy. Yea some,
as they have acquainted them with all other things, have

told them how gunpowder is made, and all the materials in it, and that they are to be had in their own land; and I am confident, could they attain to make saltpeter, they would teach them to make powder.

O, the horribleness of this villainy! How many both Dutch and English have been lately slain by those Indians thus furnished, and no remedy provided; nay, the evil more increased, and the blood of their brethren sold for gain (as is to be feared) and in what danger all these colonies are in is too well known. O that princes and parliaments would take some timely order to prevent this mischief and at length to suppress it by some exemplary punishment upon some of these gain-thirsty murderers, for they deserve no better title, before their colonies in these parts be overthrown by these barbarous savages thus armed with their own weapons, by these evil instruments and traitors to their neighbours and country! But I have forgot myself and have been too long in this digression; but now to return.

This Morton having thus taught them the use of pieces, he sold them all he could spare, and he and his consorts determined to send for many out of England and had by some of the ships sent for above a score. The which being known, and his neighbours meeting the Indians in the woods armed with guns in this sort, it was a terror unto them who lived stragglingly and were of no strength in any place. And other places (though more remote) saw this mischief would quickly spread over all, if not prevented. Besides, they saw they should keep no servants, for Morton would entertain any, how vile soever, and all the scum of the country or any discontents would flock to him from all places, if this nest was not broken. And they should stand in more fear of their lives and goods in short time from this wicked and debased crew than from the savages themselves.

So sundry of the chief of the straggling plantations, meeting together, agreed by mutual consent to solicit those of Plymouth (who were then of more strength than them all) to join with them to prevent the further growth of this mischief, and suppress Morton and his consorts before they grew to further head and strength. Those that joined in this action, and after contributed to the charge of sending him for England, were from Piscataqua, Naumkeag, Winnisimmet, Wessagusset, Nantasket and other places where any English were seated. Those of Plymouth being thus sought to by their messengers and letters, and weighing both their reasons and the common danger, were willing to afford them their help though themselves had least cause of fear or hurt. So, to be short, they first resolved jointly to write to him, and in a friendly and neighbourly way to admonish him to forbear those courses, and sent a messenger with their letters to bring his answer.

But he was so high as he scorned all advice, and asked who had to do with him, he had and would trade pieces with the Indians, in despite of all, with many other scurrilous terms full of disdain. They sent to him a second time and bade him be better advised and more temperate in his terms, for the country could not bear the injury he did. It was against their common safety and against the King's proclamation. He answered in high terms as before; and that the King's proclamation was no law, demanding what penalty was upon it. It was answered, more than he could bear—His Majesty's displeasure. But insolently he persisted and said the King was dead and his displeasure with him, and many the like things. And threatened withal that if any came to molest him, let them look to themselves for he would prepare for them.

Upon which they saw there was no way but to take him by force; and having so far proceeded, now to give over would make him far more haughty and insolent. So they mutually resolved to proceed, and obtained of the Governor of Plymouth to send Captain Standish and some other aid with him, to take Morton by force. The which accordingly was done. But they found him to stand stiffly in his defense, having made fast his doors, armed his consorts, set divers dishes of powder and bullets ready on the table; and if they had not been over-armed with drink, more hurt might have been done. They summoned him to yield, but he kept his house and they could get nothing but scoffs and scorns from him. But at length, fearing they would do some violence to the house, he and some of his crew came out, but not to yield but to shoot; but they were so steeled with drink as their pieces were too heavy for them. Himself with a carbine, overcharged and almost half filled with powder and shot, as was after found, had thought to have shot Captain Standish; but he stepped to him and put by his piece and took him. Neither was there any hurt done to any of either side, save that one was so drunk that he ran his own nose upon the point of a sword that one held before him, as he entered the house; but he lost but a little of his hot blood.

Morton they brought away to Plymouth, where he was kept till a ship went from the Isle of Shoals for England, with which he was sent to the Council of New England, and letters written to give them information of his course and carriage. And also one was sent at their common charge to inform their Honours more particularly and to prosecute against him. But he fooled of the messenger, after he was gone from hence, and though he went for England yet nothing was done to him, not so much as rebuked, for aught was heard, but returned the next year. Some of the worst of the company were dispersed and some of the more modest kept the house till he should be heard from. But I have been too long about so unworthy a person, and bad a cause.

Thomas Morton of Merrymount
(In His Own Eyes)

A glimpse of the attitude that enraged the Pilgrim Fathers is evident in Morton's praise of the way of life of the Indians he so much admired and with whom he dealt so intimately. Had New England gone the way of Morton, it is not impossible to imagine a quite different United States. It went, instead, the way of the grave Pilgrim Separatists and their later associates, the Puritans of Massachusetts Bay. The society created by these men could not embrace the Indian warmly to its heart. The following passage is taken from Morton's *New English Canaan* (London: 1632), reprinted in Peter Force, comp., *Tracts and Other Papers, Relating Principally to the Origin, Settlement, and Progress of the Colonies in North America, from the Discovery of the Country to the Year 1776*, Vol. II, pp. 10, 38–40 (reprinted, New York: Peter Smith, 1947).

NEW ENGLISH CANAAN,
OR
NEW CANAAN.

The Authors Prologue.

If art & industry should doe as much
As Nature hath for Canaan, not such
Another place, for benefit and rest,
In all the universe can be possest,
The more we proove it by discovery,
The more delight each object to the eye
Procures, as if the elements had here
Bin reconcil'd, and pleas'd it should appeare,

Like a faire virgin, longing to be sped,
And meete her lover in a Nuptiall bed,
Deck'd in rich ornaments t' advaunce her state
And excellence, being most fortunate,
When most enjoy'd, so would our Canaan be
If well employ'd by art and industry
Whose offspring, now shewes that her fruitfull wombe
Not being enjoy'd, is like a glorious tombe,
Admired things producing which there dye,
And ly fast bound in darck obscurity,
The worth of which in each particuler,
Who list to know, this abstract will declare.

Chap. XIX.
Of their inclination to Drunkenesse.

Although Drunkennesse be justly termed a vice, which
the Salvages are ignorant of, yet the benefit is very great
that comes to the planters by the sale of strong liquor to
the Salvages, who are much taken with the delight of it,
for they will pawne their wits, to purchase the acquaintance of it, yet in al the commerce that I had with them, I
never proffered them any such thing; nay I would hardly
let any of them have a drame unless hee were a Sachem,
or a Winnaytue, that is a rich man, or a man of estimation, next in degree to a Sachem, or Sagamore: I alwayes
tould them it was amongst us the Sachems drinke. But
they say if I come to the Northerne parts of the Country,
I shall have no trade, if I will not supply them with lusty
liquors, it is the life of the trade, in all those parts, for it
so happened, that thus a Salvage desperately killed himselfe, when hee was drunke, a gunne being charged and
the cock up, hee sets the mouth to his brest, and putting
back the tricker with his foote, shot himselfe dead.

Chap. XX.
That the Salvages live a contented life.

A gentleman and a traveller, that had bin in the parts of New England for a time, when hee retorned againe in his discourse of the Country, wondered (as hee said,) that the natives of the land lived so poorely, in so rich a Country, like to our Beggers in England: Surely that Gentleman had not time or leasure whiles hee was there, truely to informe himselfe of the state of that Country, and the happy life the Salvages would leade weare they once brought to Christianity.

I must confesse they want the use and benefit of Navigation (which is the very sinnus of a flourishing Commonwealth,) yet are they supplied with all manner of needfull things, for the maintenance of life and lifelyhood, Foode and rayment are the cheife of all that we make true use of; and of these they finde no want, but have, them in a most plentifull manner.

If our beggers of England should with so much ease (as they,) furnish themselves with foode, at all seasons, there would not be so many starved in the streets, neither would so many gaoles be stuffed, or gallouses furnished with poore wretches, as I have seene them.

But they of this sort of our owne nation, that are fitt to goe to this Canaan are not able to transport themselves, and most of them unwilling to goe from the good ale tap; which is the very loadstone of the lande by which our English beggers steere theire Course: it is the Northpole to which the flowre-deluce of their compasse points; the more is the pitty that the Commonalty of oure Land are of such leaden capacities, as to neglect so brave a Country, that doth so plentifully feede Maine lusty and a brave, able men, women, and children that have not the meanes that a Civilized Nation hath to purchase foode and rayment: which that Country with a little industry will yeeld a man in a very comfortable measure; without overmuch carking.

I cannot deny but a civilized Nation, hath the preheminence of an uncivilized, by meanes of those instruments that are found to be common amongst civile people, and the uncivile want the use of, to make themselves masters of those ornaments, that make such a glorious shew, that will give a man occasion to cry, *sic transit gloria Mundi*.

Now since it is but foode and rayment that men that live needeth (though not all alike,) why should not the Natives of New England be sayd to live richly having no want of either: Cloaths are the badge of sinne, and the more variety of fashions is but the greater abuse of the Creature, the beasts of the forrest there doe serve to furnish them at any time, when they please: fish and flesh they have in greate abundance which they both roast and boyle.

They are indeed not served in dishes of plate with variety of Sauces to procure appetite, that needs not there. The rarity of the aire begot by the medicinable quality of the sweete herbes of the Country, alwayes procures good stomakes to the inhabitants.

I must needs commend them in this particular, that though they buy many commodities of our Nation, yet they keepe but fewe, and those of speciall use.

They love not to bee cumbered with many utensilles, and although every proprietor knowes his owne, yet all things (so long as they will last,) are used in common amongst them: A bisket cake given to one; that one breakes it equally into so many parts, as there be persons in his company, and distributes it. Platoes Commonwealth is so much practised by these people.

According to humane reason guided onely by the light of nature, these people leades the more happy and freer life, being voyde of care, which torments the mindes of so many Christians: They are not delighted in baubles, but in usefull things.

Their naturall drinke is of the Christall fountaine, and this they take up in their hands, by joyning them close together. They take up a great quantity at a time, and drinke at the wrists. It was the sight of such a feate, which made

Diogenes hurle away his dishe, and like one that would have this principall confirmed. *Natura paucis contentat*, used a dish no more.

I have observed that they will not be troubled with superfluous commodities. Such things as they finde, they are taught by necessity to make use of they will make choise of; and seeke to purchase with industry so that in respect, that their life is so voyd of care, and they are so loving also that they make use of those things they enjoy (the wife onely excepted) as common goods, and are therein, so compassionate that rather than one should starve through want, they would starve all, thus doe they passe away the time merrily, not regarding our pompe (which they see dayly before their faces) but are better content with their owne, which some men esteeme so meanely of.

They may be rather accompted to live richly wanting nothing that is needefull; and to be commended for leading a contented life, the younger being ruled by the Elder, and the Elder ruled by the Powahs, and the Powahs are ruled by the Devill, and then you may imagin what good rule is like to be amongst them.

DOCUMENT 13

The Pipe of Peace

The role of the calumet, or pipe of peace, is clearly described in the following account of the explorations of the French explorer La Salle along the western shore of Lake Michigan in 1679. The account, written by Father Louis Hennepin, a Recollect missionary who accompanied the expedition, was first published in Utrecht, in 1697, in French. The following quotation is taken from Hennepin's *A New Discovery of a Vast Country in America*, edited by Reuben Gold Thwaites from the second London issue of 1698, 2 vols; Vol. I, pp. 124–27 (Chicago: A. C. McClurg & Co., 1903). Thwaites' editorial notes are omitted.

As we had no manner of Acquaintance with the Savages of the Village near which we landed, our Men prepar'd themselves to make a vigorous Defence in case they were attack'd; and in order to it, possessed our selves of a rising Ground, where we could not be surpriz'd, and where we might make head against a great number of Savages. We sent afterwards three Men to buy Provisions in the Village with the Calumet or Pipe of Peace, which the *Poutouatami's* of the Island had given us. I had forgot to mention that when they made us that Present, they observ'd a great many Ceremonies; and because that *Calumet* of Peace is the most sacred Thing amongst the Savages, I think fit to describe the same in the next Chapter.

Chap. XXIV
A *Description of the* Calumet, *or Great Pipe.*

This *Calumet* is the most mysterious Thing in the World among the Savages of the Continent of the North-

ern *America*; for it is us'd in all their important Transaction: However, it is nothing else but a large Tobacco-Pipe
made of Red, Black, or White Marble: The Head is finely
polish'd, and the *Quill*, which is commonly two Foot and
a half long; is made of a pretty strong Reed, or Cane,
adorn'd with Feathers of all Colours, interlac'd with Locks
of Womens Hair. They tie to it two Wings of the most
curious Birds they find, which makes their *Calumet* not
much unlike *Mercury's* Wand, or that Staff Ambassadors
did formerly carry when they went to treat of Peace. They
sheath that Reed into the Neck of Birds they call *Huars*,
[loons] which are as big as our Geese, and spotted with
Black and White; or else of a sort of Ducks who make
their Nests upon Trees, though Water be their ordinary
Element, and whose Feathers are of many different Colours. However, every Nation adorns the *Calumet* as they
think fit according to their own Genius and the Birds they
have in their Country.

A Pipe, such as I have describ'd it, is a Pass and safe
Conduct amongst all the Allies of the Nation who has
given it; and in all Embassies, the Ambassadors carry that
Calumet as the Symbol of Peace, which is always respected; for the Savages are generally persuaded, that a
great Misfortune would befal 'em, if they violated the
Publick Faith of the *Calumet*. All their Enterprizes, Declarations of War, or Conclusion of Peace, as well as all the
rest of their Ceremonies, are sealed, if I may be permitted
to say so, with this *Calumet*. They fill that Pipe with the
best Tobacco they have, and then present it to those with
whom they have concluded any great Affair, and smoak
out of the same after them. I had certainly perish'd in my
Voyage, had it not been for this *Calumet* or Pipe, as the
Reader will observe in perusing the following Account.

Our three Men, provided with this Pipe as a Pass, and
very well Arm'd, went to the little Village of the Savages,
which was about three Leagues from the place where we
landed; but they found no body therein; for the Savages
having heard that we had refus'd to land at the other Village, thought we were Enemies, and therefore had left

their Habitation. Our Men finding no body in their Cabins, took some *Indian* Corn, and left in stead of it some Goods, to let them see that we were no Robbers, nor their Enemies. However, the Savages, to the number of twenty Men, arm'd with Axes, small Guns, Bows, and a sort of Club, which in their Language they call *Breakheads* [In French, *casse-tête*, war-club] advanc'd near the Place where we stood; whereupon M. *la Salle*, with four Men very well arm'd, went toward them to speak with them, and desir'd them to come near us, for fear, as he said, a Party of our Men, who were gone a Hunting, should meet with them and kill them. They were persuaded to sit down at the foot of the Eminence where we were posted, and M. *la Salle* spoke to them all the while of the subject matter of his Voyage, which he had undertaken for their good and advantage, as he told them. This was only to amuse them till our three Men return'd; who appearing with the *Calumet* of Peace, the Savages made a great Shout, and rose, and began to dance. We made them some Excuse because of our Men having taken some of their Corn, and told them they had left the true Value of it in Goods; which they took so well, that they sent immediately for more, and gave us the next Day as much as we could conveniently carry in our Canou's. They retir'd towards the Evening; and M. *la Salle* order'd some Trees to be cut down, and laid cross the way, to prevent any Surprize from the Savages.

The next Morning about ten a Clock, the Oldest of them came to us with their *Calumet* of Peace, and entertain'd us with some wild Goats they had taken. We return'd them our Thanks, and presented them with some Axes, Knives, and several little Toys for their Wives, with which they were very much pleas'd.

DOCUMENT 14

Peace Pipes

Plate 6, following page 134, shows two decorated
"Catlinite" stone pipes. The one without feathers is
Sioux; the one with feathers is Mandan. Both are in the
Smithsonian Institution, Washington, D.C.

"They Never Love beyond Retrieving"

In 1709, John Lawson, gentleman and surveyor, published in London his history of North Carolina under the title *A New Voyage to Carolina*. Two years later, while on a surveying expedition in the Indian country, he was seized by the jealous Indians and put to death. His knowledge and understanding of the Indians is evident in the following passage concerning the women he knew in his travels among the native villages of North Carolina. The passage is taken from Lawson's *History of North Carolina: containing the Exact Description and Natural History of that Country, together with the present state thereof and a Journal of a Thousand Miles Traveled through several Nations of Indians, giving a Particular Account of their Customs, Manners, etc.*, taken from the London edition of 1714, and edited by Frances Latham Harriss, pp. 194–99 (Richmond, Va.: Garrett & Massie, 1937, reprinted 1952).

As for the Indian Women which now happen in my Way, when young, and at Maturity, they are as fine shaped Creatures, (take them generally,) as any in the Universe. They are of a tawny Complexion, their Eyes very brisk and amorous, their Smiles afford the finest Composure a Face can possess, their Hands are of the finest Make, with small, long Fingers, and as soft as their Cheeks, and their whole Bodies of a smooth Nature. They are not so uncouth or unlikely as we suppose them, nor are they Strangers or not Proficients in the soft Passion. They are, most of them, mercenary, except the married Women, who sometimes bestow their Favours also to some or other, in their Husband's Absence; for which they never ask any Re-

ward. As for the Report, that they are never found uncon-
stant, like the Europeans, it is wholly false; for were the old
World and the new one put into a Pair of Scales (in point
of constancy) it would be a hard Matter to discern which
was the heavier. As for the Trading Girls, which are those
designed to get Money by their Natural Parts, these are
discernable by the Cut of their Hair; their tonsure differing from all others of that Nation, who are not of their
Profession, which Method is intended to prevent Mistakes;
for the Savages of America are desirous (if possible) to
keep their Wives to themselves, as well as those in other
Parts of the World. When any Addresses are made to one
of these Girls, she immediately acquaints her Parents
therewith, and they tell the King of it, (provided he that
courts her be a Stranger) his Majesty commonly being the
principal Bawd of the Nation he rules over, and there
seldom being any of these Winchester-Weddings agreed on
without his Royal Consent. He likewise advises her what
Bargain to make, and if it happens to be an Indian Trader
that wants a Bed-fellow and has got Rum to sell, be sure
the King must have a large Dram for a Fee to confirm the
Match. These Indians that are of the elder sort, when any
such Question is put to them, will debate the Matter
amongst themselves with all the Sobriety and Seriousness
imaginable, every one of the Girl's Relations arguing the
Advantage or Detriment that may ensue such a Night's
Encounter; all which is done with as much Steadiness and
Reality as if it was the greatest Concern in the World, and
not so much as one Person shall be seen to smile, so long
as the Debate holds, making no Difference betwixt an
Agreement of this Nature and a Bargain of any other. If
they comply with the Men's Desire, then a particular Bed
is provided for them, either in a Cabin by themselves or
else all the young people turn out to another Lodging,
that they may not spoil Sport, and if the old People are
in the same Cabin along with them all Night, they lie as
unconcerned as if they were so many Logs of Wood. If it
be an Indian of their own Town or Neighborhood, that
wants a Mistress, he comes to none but the Girl, who re-

ceives what she thinks fit to ask him, and so lies all Night
with him, without the Consent of her Parents.

The Indian Traders are those which travel and abide
amongst the Indians for a long space of time; sometimes
for a Year, two, or three. These Men have commonly their
Indian Wives, whereby they soon learn the Indian Tongue,
keep a Friendship with the Savages; and, besides the
Satisfaction of a She-Bed-Fellow, they find these Indian
Girls very serviceable to them, on Account of dressing
their Victuals, and instructing them in the Affairs and
Customs of the Country. Moreover, such a Man gets a
great Trade with the Savages; for when a Person that lives
amongst them, is reserved from the Conversation of their
Women, tis impossible for him ever to accomplish his
Designs amongst that People.

But one great Misfortune which often times attends
those that converse with these Savage Women, is, that
they get Children by them, which are seldom educated
any otherwise than in a State of Infidelity; for it is a certain Rule and Custom, amongst all the Savages of America, that I was ever acquainted withal, to let the Children
always fall to the Woman's Lot; for it often happens, that
two Indians that have lived together, as Man and Wife, in
which Time they have had several Children; if they part,
and another Man possesses her, all the Children go along
with the Mother, and none with the Father. And therefore, on this Score it ever seems impossible for the Christians to get their Children (which they have by these
Indian Women) away from them; whereby they might
bring them up in the Knowledge of the Christian Principles. Nevertheless, we often find, that English Men, and
other Europeans that have been accustomed to the Conversation of these Savage Women and their Way of Living,
have been so allured with that careless sort of Life, as to
be constant to their Indian Wife, and her Relations, so
long as they lived, without ever desiring to return again
amongst the English, although they had very fair Opportunities of Advantages amongst their Countrymen; of
which sort I have known several.

As for the Indian Marriages, I have read and heard of a great deal of Form and Ceremony used, which I never saw; nor yet could learn in the Time I have been amongst them, any otherwise than I shall here give you an Account of, which is as follows:

When any young Indian has a Mind for such a Girl to his Wife, he, or some one for him, goes to the young Woman's Parents, if living; if not, to her nearest Relations, where they make Offers of the Match betwixt the Couple. The Relations reply, they will consider of it; which serves for a sufficient Answer, till there be a second Meeting about the Marriage, which is generally brought into Debate before all the Relations, (that are old People) on both Sides, and sometimes the King with all his great Men, give their Opinions therein. If it be agreed on, and the young Woman approve thereof, (for these Savages never give their Children in Marriage without their own Consent) the Man pays so much for his Wife; and the handsomer she is the greater Price she bears. Now, it often happens, that the Man has not so much of their Money ready as he is to pay for his Wife; but if they know him to be a good Hunter, and that he can raise the Sum agreed for, in some few Moons, or any little time they agree, she shall go along with him as betrothed, but he is not to have any Knowledge of her till the utmost Payment is discharged; all which is punctually observed. Thus they lie together under one Covering for several Months, and the Woman remains the same as she was when she first came to him. I doubt our Europeans would be apt to break this Custom, but the Indian Men are not so vigorous and impatient in their Love as we are. Yet the Women are quite contrary, and those Indian Girls that have conversed with the English and other Europeans, never care for the Conversation of their own Countrymen afterwards.

They never marry so near as a first Cousin, and although there is nothing more coveted amongst them than to marry a Woman of their own Nation, yet when the Nation consists of a very few People, (as nowadays it often happens) so that they are all of them related to one another, then they look out for Husbands and Wives amongst Strangers. For if an Indian lies with his Sister, or any very near Relation, his Body is burnt, and his Ashes thrown into the River, as unworthy to remain on Earth; yet an Indian is allowed to marry two Sisters, or his Brother's Wife. Although these People are called Savages, yet Sodomy is never heard of amongst them, and they are so far from the Practice of that beastly and loathsome Sin, that they have no Name for it in their Language.

The Marriages of these Indians are no farther binding than the Man and Woman agree Together. Either of them has Liberty to leave the other upon any frivolous Excuse they can make, yet whosoever takes the Woman that was another Man's before, and bought by him, as they all are, must certainly pay to her former Husband whatsoever he gave for her. Nay, if she be a Widow, and her Husband died in Debt, whosoever takes her to Wife pays all her Husband's Obligations, though never so many; yet the Woman is not required to pay anything, (unless, she is willing) that was owing from her Husband, so long as she keeps Single. But if a Man courts her for a Night's Lodging and obtains it, the Creditors will make him pay her Husband's Debts, and he may, if he will take her for his Money, or sell her to another for his Wife. I have seen several of these Bargains driven in a day; for you may see Men selling their Wives as Men do Horses in a Fair, a Man being allowed not only to change as often as he pleases, but likewise to have as many Wives as he is able to maintain. I have often seen that very old Indian Men, (that have been Grandees in their own Nation) have had three or four very likely young Indian Wives, which I have much wondered at, because, to me, they seemed incapacitated to make good Use of one of them.

The young Men will go in the Night from one House to another to visit the young Women, in which sort of Rambles they will spend the whole Night. In their Addresses they find no Delays, for if she is willing to entertain the Man, she gives him Encouragement and grants him Admittance; otherwise she withdraws her Face from him, and says, I cannot see you, either you or I must leave this Cabin and sleep somewhere else this Night.

They are never to boast of their Intrigues with the Women. If they do, none of the Girls value them ever after, or admit of their Company in their Beds. This proceeds not on the score of Reputation, for there is no such thing, (on that account) known amongst them; and although we may reckon them the greatest Libertines and most extravagant in their Embraces, yet they retain and possess a Modesty that requires those Passions never to be divulged.

The Trading Girls, after they have led that Course of Life, for several Years, in which time they scarce ever have a Child; (for they have an Art to destroy the Conception, and she that brings a Child in this Station, is accounted a Fool, and her Reputation is lessened thereby) at last they grow weary of so many, and betake themselves to a married State, or to the Company of one Man; neither does their having been common to so many any wise lessen their Fortunes, but rather augment them.

The Woman is not punished for Adultery, but tis the Man that makes the injured Person Satisfaction, which is the Law of Nations practised amongst them all; and he that strives to evade such Satisfaction as the Husband demands, lives daily in Danger of his Life; yet when discharged, all Animosity is laid aside, and the Cuckold is very well pleased with his Bargain, whilst the Rival is laughed at by the whole Nation, for carrying on his intrigue with no better Conduct, than to be discovered and pay so dear for his Pleasure.

The Indians say, that the Woman is a weak Creature, and easily drawn away by the Man's Persuasion; for which Reason, they lay no Blame upon her, but the Man (that ought to be Master of his Passion) for persuading her to it.

They are of a very hale Constitution; their Breaths are as Sweet as the Air they breathe in, and the Woman seems to be of that tender Composition, as if they were designed rather for the Bed than Bondage. Yet their Love is never of that Force and Continuance, that any of them ever runs Mad, or makes away with themselves on that score. They never love beyond Retrieving their first Indifferency, and when slighted, are as ready to untie the Knot at one end, as you are at the other.

Yet I knew an European Man that had a Child or two by one of these Indian Women, and afterwards married a Christian, after which he came to pass away a Night with his Indian Mistress; but she made Answer that she then had forgot she ever knew him, and that she never lay with another Woman's Husband, so fell a crying and took up the Child she had by him, and went out of the Cabin (away from him) in great Disorder.

DOCUMENT 16

The False Face Ceremony

The following description of an Iroquois mask, used in the Iroquois purification rite in which evil spirits are driven from the houses of the village (see Document 17 for illustration), is taken from John Bartram's *Observations on the Inhabitants, Climate, Soil, Rivers, Productions, Animals, and Other Matters Worthy of Notice* (London, 1751), pp. 43–44, and is based on an experience that occurred on July 21, 1743.

At night, soon after we were laid down to sleep, and our fire almost burnt out, we were entertained by a comical fellow, disguised in as odd a dress as *Indian* folly could invent; he had on a clumsy vizard of wood colour'd black, with a nose 4 or 5 inches long, a grining mouth set awry, furnished with long teeth, round the eyes circles of bright brass, surrounded by a larger circle of white paint, from his forehead hung long tresses of buffaloes hair, and from the catch part of his head ropes made of the plated husks of *Indian* corn; I cannot recollect the whole of his dress, but that it was equally uncouth: he carried in one hand a long staff, in the other a calabash with small stones in it, for a rattle, and this he rubbed up and down his staff; he would sometimes hold up his head and make a hideous noise like the braying of an ass; he came in at the further end, and made this noise at first, whether it was because he would not surprise us too suddenly I can't say: I ask'd *Conrad Weiser*, who as well as myself lay next the alley, what noise that was? and *Shickalamy* the *Indian* chief, our companion, who I supposed, thought me somewhat scared, called out, lye still *John*, I never heard him speak so much

plain *English* before. The jack-pudding presently came up
to us, and an *Indian* boy came with him and kindled our
fire, that we might see his glittering eyes and antick pos-
tures as he hobbled round the fire, sometimes he would
turn the Buffaloes hair on one side that we might take the
better view of his ill-favoured phyz, when he had tired
himself, which was sometime after he had well tired us,
the boy that attended him struck 2 or 3 smart blows on
the floor, at which the hobgoblin seemed surprised and
on repeating them he jumped fairly out of doors and dis-
appeared. I suppose this was to divert us and get some
tobacco for himself, for as he danced about he would hold
out his hand to any he came by to receive this gratifica-
tion which as often as any one gave him he would return
an awkward compliment. By this I found it no new diver-
sion to any one but my self. In my whim I saw a vizard
of this kind hang by the side of one of their cabins to
another town. After this farce we endeavoured to compose
ourselves to sleep but towards morning was again disturbed by a drunken *Squaw* coming into the cabin frequently complimenting us and singing.

DOCUMENT 17

An Iroquois "False Face"

Plate 7, following page 134, depicts an Iroquois wooden mask similar to that described in the foregoing document. The mask, from the Six Nations Reserve, Grand River, Ontario, Canada, is in the Smithsonian Institution, Washington, D.C.

DOCUMENT 18

Forest Diplomacy

In 1751, Jean-Bernard Bossu, a French naval officer, was sent to North America where he spent almost twelve years dealing with the Indian nations allied to the French. His contemporary letters concerning those activities were published in Paris in 1768 under the title of *Nouveaux Voyages aux Indes occidentales*. The following passage is taken from the eighteenth-century English edition of that work, entitled *Travels through that Part of North America Formerly Called Louisiana*, translated by John Reinhold Forster (2 vols.; Vol. I. pp. 237–46 [London: 1771]), and concerns Bossu's mission to the Alabama Indians in 1759. The notes are Bossu's except for that of Forster identified by the letter "F". A modern English edition, under the title, *Travels in the Interior of North America, 1751–1762*, translated and edited by Seymour Feiler, has been published by the University of Oklahoma Press (Norman: 1962).

The Indians are very hospitable towards strangers with whom they are in peace, and kind to their allies and friends, but cruel and unmerciful to their enemies. They are surprised and even scandalized to see a number of Englishmen at *New Orleans*, drawn thither in time of war, for the sake of trading under the specious pretence of coming to exchange prisoners[1]. A cacique lately re-

[1] Here our author inserts a long invective against the English, who come in vessels to *New Orleans* with prisoners of war on board, which they offer to exchange, and that under this cloak, they get information of the strength and situation of the colony, and buy up all the furs they can get. Some allowance must be made for national prejudice and French pertness. F.

turned from *New Orleans* freely owned to me, that he had a great mind to break their heads for killing the *French* in the north, that is, during the siege of Quebec, and that he was tempted to take his revenge upon those that were at *New Orleans*. He added, that in his country they spoke to their enemies with the club in their hands, as soon as *the hatchet is dug up*; a phrase which denotes, that nobody ought to have any commerce or correspondence with the enemy, directly or indirectly, under any pretence whatsoever, after war is declared, unless he will prove a traitor to his country, and be punished accordingly.

When peace is concluded they bury the hatchet or the club under ground, signifying thereby that all their hatred towards their enemies is buried in oblivion, that the horrors of war are at an end, and that friendship and good understanding are growing again between them and their friends, like the white flowers of their tree of peace, (which is the white laurel), that ought to spread its branches over the *white* ground; which is a metaphorical expression which means the ground of peace.

The cacique I mentioned before, is called *Tamathlemingo*, and he is very warm in the French interest. I know that he has scornfully rejected the presents which some Englishmen would have loaded him with, and he had a great mind to break their heads for making him such a proposition. He wears a silver medal fastened round his neck by a leather thong. He often told me, he would be buried together with the image of his father (that is, the king's portrait) which he wears on his breast; and having always been faithful to him he hoped to shake hands with him in the land of the souls, where he expected to see him one day. After this worthy chief had shewn me these fine sentiments which parted from his heart, I gave him a bottle of brandy to drink the health of his father and mine. Such little *douceurs* when given on proper occasions, have a great effect upon these people; thus they were greatly moved when I pulled off my shirt and gave it them in the name of their father, telling them that he pitied them, because he knew by means of the *speaking substance*[2] that his children were naked.

These nations have no idea of the political systems which are known among the European powers. In their opinion, the allies of a nation must assist them, when they are in war, and have no correspondence with their enemies. I have had a long and serious conference with one *Allexi Mingo*, who is a juggler and likewise the chief of a district among them, and pretends to have been abused by some *Spanish* soldiers of the garrison of *Pensacola*: this Indian owned that he had formed a design in order to be revenged of them, to make a general incursion with his warriors into *Florida*, to the very gates of *Pensacola*. This Indian would pay me a compliment, and make me approve of his design, by telling me, that he was partly drawn into it, because the Spaniards lay still upon their mats; i. e. they were at peace with the English, whom they received into their ports, though at that time, they were our enemies.

I answered this discourse of the Cacique in express terms and such as were most capable of making him desist from his enterprize, as I was willing to prevent a massacre of the Spaniards who were our allies and neighbours: accordingly I spoke to him in a manner analogous to the genius and character of the nation.

Alexi Mingo, said I, prepare thy heart, open thy ears to hear the force of my words, for it will bring back to thee thy wits, which thou hast lost to-day.

I tell thee, then that the grand chief sovereign of the *Spaniards*, who lives on the other side of the great salt-water lake, in the old world that swarms with inhabitants is the brother[3] of the father of the red men, i. e. of the king of *France*, and accordingly, I must say, I disapprove very much of thy bold design. I fairly declare to thee, that if thou persistest in it, thou canst do no better than to begin with breaking my head. The Cacique answered,

---

[2] Paper, or letters.
[3] The Indians call their allies brothers.

"Thy blood is as dear to me as my own; besides, the *French* have never done me any harm, and I am ready to give my life for them; thou canst assure our father of that. Oh that I had the speaking substance which thou hast, to let him know my words, but no, I rather wish I had a hundred mouths which he might hear[4]."

After this protestation of friendship he gave me his *Calumet*, and when I had smoked a little I returned it to him, as having made peace for the *Spaniards*, by whom he pretended to have been ill-used; and as a ratification I gave him a bottle of the fiery water, that is of brandy, saying, this I give thee to clean thy mouth, that it may not utter any more bad words against the Spaniards our allies: and to strengthen my discourse I gave a great roll of tobacco, for his warriors to smoke out of the great *Calumet* of peace. After my harangue was at an end, the young people came one after another to squeeze me by the hand, as a mark of friendship, which is customary among them.

I wished, however, to persuade this Cacique, who was piqued at the *Spaniards*, who receive English vessels at *Pensacola*, because they are at peace: for he said they came to inform themselves of the situation and strength of these coasts.

By way of appeasing the Indian, I told him, that the governor daily waited for the arrival of a great piragua[5], which should bring him some of the speaking substance, wherein the great chief of the Spaniards should order him to dig up the hatchet of war, and to lift up his club against the English.

This discourse satisfied my Cacique; and as he had drank a good portion of brandy, he was very talkative, and I took the opportunity of questioning him concerning the grudge he bore the *Spaniards* in *Florida*. He told me,

[4] Some time after the author's departure, the Indians of these parts massacred several Englishmen, that were come within two leagues of fort *Toulouse*, where M. *de Grand-Maison* then commanded, who is now Major of the troops at *New Orleans*.

[5] An European ship.

that he had heard by tradition, that the first *warriors of fire*[6] who came into this country had committed hostilities in it, and violated the law of nations; and, that ever since that period, the ancestors of his nation had always recommended it to their posterity to revenge the blood which had been unjustly shed. I told the juggling Cacique, that the Lord of life had revenged them sufficiently, by the death of *Ferdinand Soto*, and almost all his warriors.

I added, that they had no further reason to hate the *Spaniards*; that *Philip* II, grand chief of the *Spaniards*, had disavowed all the mischief which his generals had done in these climates, as being contrary to his intentions.

I told this American prince part of the story, of *Don Francis de Toledo*, viceroy of *Peru*, who publicly hanged the presumptive heir to the crown, and ordered all the princes of the royal family of the *Yncas* to be killed, not even excepting the Spaniards, who from their mother's side were descended from *Atahualipa*. Don *Francis*, after such an execution, expected to be raised to the greatest dignities of the state on his return to Spain; but he was very ill received by the grand chief of the nation, who ordered him with a harsh voice to get out of his presence, saying, I have not appointed thee to be the executioner of princes, but to serve me and assist the unhappy. These words stuck the viceroy dumb, and caused him such an illness that he died a few days after. The same king caused the death of one of his ministers that had imposed upon him, merely by saying the word *Hoolabè*, which in the Indian language, signifies, *What, dost thou lye?* The Cacique very gravely replied, "But if the grand chief of the men of fire, appeared, as thou sayest, so angry at the viceroy, on account of the cruelties which he had committed against his will, why did he not put him in the

---

[6] History informs us, that in 1544, *Ferdinand Soto* made incursions into this country; the Indians there, who had never seen any Europeans, called the Spaniards warriors of fire, because they were armed with guns and pistols: they said, that the cannon was thunder, and that it caused the earth to tremble, by killing people at a great distance.

frame[7]? or why did he not cut off his head, and send it back to *Peru?* This example of severity and justice would in part have satisfied the people whom this general had ill-treated, by hanging on a gibbet, like a thief, the heir of a great empire, who depended only from the *Lord of life*, or the Supreme Being. Thus we red men, whom the Europeans call savages and barbarians would act towards the wicked and the murderers, who ought to be treated like the fiercest beasts of the forest."

I again replied to this Indian chief in the following terms, "Thou must know that the grand chiefs of the white men that live in the old country, are despotic and absolute, and that when they drive from their presence their generals or warriors, who have abused their subjects without cause, this affront is much more sensibly felt by those proud chiefs, who are hated by the *Great Spirit*, or by God, on account of their misdeeds, than the punishment of the frame, or a hundred blows with the club upon the head, would be by a red man."

At last I succeeded in softening the hatred which these people had conceived against the *Spaniards*, and I imagine every hostile intention is suppressed now; for my explication was very satisfactory to my juggler.

[7] A punishment which the Indians adjudge to those that have committed cruelties, and are taken at war: they are put into a kind of frame, composed of two posts, and a pole laid across them, and burnt alive.

DOCUMENT 19

"Send Us Your Children, and We Will Make Men of Them"

The attractions of Indian life to the English and the unsuitability of English education to the Indians are nowhere better brought out than in Benjamin Franklin's letter to Peter Collinson of May 9, 1753. The story of the Indian rejection of the English offer to educate their children was used by Franklin in other writings, but seems to have been first stated in this letter. The letter, only a portion of which is printed below, is taken from *The Papers of Benjamin Franklin,* Leonard W. Labaree, et al., eds., Vol. IV, pp. 481–83 (New Haven: Yale University Press, 1961).

The proneness of human Nature to a life of ease, of freedom from care and labour appears strongly in the little success that has hitherto attended every attempt to civilize our American Indians, in their present way of living, almost all their Wants are supplied by the spontaneous Productions of Nature, with the addition of very little labour, if hunting and fishing may indeed be called labour when Game is so plenty, they visit us frequently, and see the advantages that Arts, Sciences, and compact Society procure us, they are not deficient in natural understanding and yet they have never shewn any Inclination to change their manner of life for ours, or to learn any of our Arts; When an Indian Child has been brought up among us, taught our language and habituated to our Customs, yet if he goes to see his relations and make one Indian Ramble with them, there is no perswading him ever to return, and that this is not natural [to them] merely as Indians, but as men, is plain from this, that when white persons of either sex have been taken prisoners young by the Indians, and lived a while among them, tho' ransomed by their Friends, and treated with all imaginable tenderness to prevail with them to stay among the English, yet in a Short time they become disgusted with our manner of life, and the care and pains that are necessary to support it, and take the first good Opportunity of escaping again into the Woods, from whence there is no reclaiming them. One instance I remember to have heard, where the person was brought home to possess a good Estate; but finding some care necessary to keep it together, he relinquished it to a younger Brother, reserving to himself nothing but a gun and a match-Coat, with which he took his way again to the Wilderness.

Though they have few but natural wants and those easily supplied. But with us are infinite Artificial wants, no less craving than those of Nature, and much more difficult to satisfy; so that I am apt to imagine that close Societies subsisting by Labour and Arts, arose first not from choice, but from necessity: When numbers being driven by war from their hunting grounds and prevented by seas or by other nations were crowded together into some narrow Territories, which without labour would not afford them Food. However as matters [now] stand with us, care and industry seem absolutely necessary to our well being; they should therefore have every Encouragement we can invent, and not one Motive to diligence be subtracted, and the support of the Poor should not be by maintaining them in Idleness, But by employing them in some kind of labour suited to their Abilities of body &c. as I am informed of late begins to be the practice in many parts of England, where work houses are erected for that purpose. If these were general I should think the Poor would be more careful and work voluntarily and lay up something for themselves against a rainy day, rather than run the risque of being obliged to work at the pleasure of others for a bare subsistence and that too under confinement. The little value Indians set on what we prize so highly under the name of Learning appears from a pleasant passage that happened some years since at a Treaty between one of our Colonies and the Six Nations; when every thing had been settled to the Satisfaction of both sides, and nothing remained but a mutual exchange of civilities, the English Commissioners told the Indians, they had in their Country a College for the instruction of Youth who were there taught various languages, Arts, and Sciences; that there was a particular foundation in favour of the Indians to defray the expense of the Education of any of their sons who should desire to take the Benefit of it. And now if the Indians would accept of the Offer, the English would take half a dozen of their brightest lads and bring them up in the Best manner; The Indians after consulting on the proposal replied that it was remembered some of their Youths had formerly been educated in that College, but it had been observed that for a long time after they returned to their Friends, they were absolutely good for nothing being neither acquainted with the true methods of killing deer, catching Beaver or surprizing an enemy. The Proposition however, they looked on as a mark of the kindness and good will of the English to the Indian Nations which merited a grateful return; and therefore if the English Gentlemen would send a dozen or two of their Children to Onondago the great Council would take care of their Education, bring them up in really what was the best manner and make men of them.

DOCUMENT 20

"The Grass Which Grows Out of the Earth Is Common to All"

The Indian attitude toward land use and personal relations is suggested in the following anecdote of the Reverend John Heckewelder, a Moravian missionary, in his *Account of the History, Manners, and Customs of the Indian Nations, Who Once Inhabited Pennsylvania and the Neighbouring States*, pp. 85–87 (Philadelphia: American Philosophical Society, 1819).

Not satisfied with paying this first of duties to the Lord of all, in the best manner they are able, the Indians also endeavour to fulfil the views which they suppose he had in creating the world. They think that he made the earth and all that it contains for the common good of mankind; when he stocked the country that he gave them with plenty of game, it was not for the benefit of a few, but of all. Every thing was given in common to the sons of men. Whatever liveth on the land, whatsoever groweth out of the earth, and all that is in the rivers and waters flowing through the same, was given jointly to all, and every one is entitled to his share. From this principle, hospitality flows as from its source. With them it is not a virtue but a strict duty. Hence they are never in search of excuses to avoid giving, but freely supply their neighbour's wants from the stock prepared for their own use. They give and are hospitable to all, without exception, and will always share with each other and often with the stranger, even to their last morsel. They rather would lie down themselves on an empty stomach, than have it laid to their charge that they had neglected their duty, by not satisfying the wants of the stranger, the sick or the needy. The stranger has a claim to their hospitality, partly on account of his being at a distance from his family and friends, and partly because he has honoured them by his visit, and ought to leave them with a good impression upon his mind; the sick and the poor because they have a right to be helped out of the common stock: for if the meat they have been served with, was taken from the woods, it was common to all before the hunter took it; if corn or vegetables, it had grown out of the common ground, yet not by the power of man, but by that of the Great Spirit. Besides, on the principle, that all are descended from one parent, they look upon themselves as but one great family, who therefore ought at all times and on all occasions, to be serviceable and kind to each other, and by that means make themselves acceptable to the head of the universal family, the great and good Mannitto. Let me be permitted to illustrate this by an example.

Some travelling Indians having in the year 1777, put their horses over night to pasture in my little meadow, at Gnadenhutten on the Muskingum, I called on them in the morning to learn why they had done so. I endeavoured to make them sensible of the injury they had done me, especially as I intended to mow the meadow in a day or two. Having finished my complaint, one of them replied: "My friend, it seems you lay claim to the grass my horses have eaten, because you had enclosed it with a fence: now tell me, who caused the grass to grow? Can *you* make the grass grow? I think not, and no body can except the great Mannitto. He it is who causes it to grow both for my horses and for yours! See, friend! the grass which grows out of the earth is common to all; the game in the woods is common to all. Say, did you never eat venison and bear's meat?—"Yes, very often."—Well, and did you ever hear me or any other Indian complain about that? No; then be not disturbed at my horses having eaten only once, of what you call *your* grass, though the grass my horses did eat, in like manner as the meat you did eat, was given to the Indians by the Great Spirit. Besides, if you will but consider, you will find that my horses did not eat *all* your grass. For friendship's sake, however, I shall never put my horses in your meadow again."

The Indians are not only just, they are also in many respects a generous people, and cannot see the sick and the aged suffer for want of clothing. To such they will give a blanket, a shirt, a pair of leggings, mocksens, &c. Otherwise, when they make presents, it is done with a view to receive an equivalent in return, and the receiver is given to understand what that ought to be. In making presents to strangers, they are content with some trifle in token of remembrance; but when they give any thing to a trader, they at least expect double the value in return, saying that he can afford to do it, since he had cheated them so often.

They treat each other with civility, and shew much affection on meeting after an absence. When they meet in the forenoon, they will compliment one another with saying, "a good morning to you!" and in the afternoon "a good evening." In the act of shaking hands with each other, they strictly attend to the distinguishing names of relations, which they utter at the time; as for instance, "a good morning, father, grandfather, uncle, aunt, cousin," and so down to a small grandchild. They are also in the habit of saluting old people no ways related to them, by the names of grandfather and grandmother, not in a tone of condescending superiority or disguised contempt, but as a genuine mark of the respect which they feel for age. The common way of saluting where no relationship exists, is that of "friend;" when, however, the young people meet, they make use of words suitable to their years or stage in life; they will say "a good morning, comrade, favourite, beloved, &c." Even the children salute each other affectionately. "I am glad to see you," is the common way in which the Indians express themselves to one another after a short absence; but on meeting after a long absence, on the return of a messenger or a warrior from a critical or dangerous expedition, they have more to say; the former is saluted in the most cordial manner with some such expression: "I thank the Great Spirit, that he has preserved our lives to this time of our happily meeting again. I am, indeed, very glad to see you." To which the other will reply: "you speak the truth; it is through the favour of the great and good Spirit that we are permitted to meet. I am equally glad to see you," To the latter will be said: "I am glad that the Great Spirit has preserved your life and granted you a safe return to your family."

DOCUMENT 21

"Get an Indian Ear!"

The problem of truly understanding the Indian is a monumental one. It is difficult for the modern ethnologist. It was a task of backbreaking difficulty to the early observers of Indian life. The first requisite to understanding is a knowledge of the language. The pitfalls in acquiring that command are amusingly related in this passage from the Moravian missionary John Heckewelder's *Account of the History, Manners, and Customs of the Indian Nations, Who Once Inhabited Pennsylvania and the Neighbouring States*, pp. 316–20 (Philadelphia: American Philosophical Society, 1819).

The first and most important thing for a traveller is a competent knowledge of the language of the people among whom he is. Without this knowledge it is impossible that he can acquire a correct notion of their manners and customs and of the opinions which prevail among them. There is little faith to be placed in those numerous vocabularies of the languages of distant nations which are to be found in almost every book of voyages or travels; they are generally full of the most ridiculous mistakes; at least (for I must speak only of what I know) those which relate to the Indian languages of North America. I was some years ago shewn a vocabulary of the idiom of the Indians who inhabited the banks of the Delaware, while Pennsylvania was under the dominion of the Swedes, which idiom was no other than the pure Unami dialect of the Lenape, and I could hardly refrain from laughing at the numerous errors that I observed in it; for instance, the Indian word given for *hand*, in fact means *finger*. This is enough to shew how carelessly those vocabularies are made, and how little their authors are acquainted with the languages that they pretend to teach.

The cause of these mistakes may be easily accounted for. When pointing to a particular object you ask an Indian how it is called, he never will give you the name of the *genus*, but always that of the *species*. Thus if you point to a tree, and ask for its name, the answer will be oak, beech, chesnut, maple, &c. as the case may be. Thus the Swedish author of the vocabulary that I have mentioned, probably happened to point to a *finger*, when he asked what was the Indian word for *hand*, and on receiving the answer, without further enquiry enriched his work with this notable specimen of Indian learning.

When I first went to reside among the Indians, I took great care to learn by heart the words *Kœcu k'delloundamen yun?* which mean *What do you call this?* Whenever I found the Indians disposed to attend to my enquiries, I would point to particular objects and repeat my formulary, and the answers that they gave I immediately wrote down in a book which I kept for the purpose; at last when I had written about half a dozen sheets, I found that I had more than a dozen names for "*tree,*" as many for "*fish,*" and so on with other things and yet I had not a single generic name. What was still worse, when I pointed to something, repeating the name or one of the names by which I had been taught to call it, I was sure to excite a laugh; and when in order to be set right I put the question *Kœcu,* &c. I would receive for answer a new word or name which I had never heard before. This began to make me believe that every thing was not as it should be, and that I was not in the right way to learn the Indian language.

It was not only in substantives or the proper names of things that I found myself almost always mistaken. Those who are not acquainted with the copiousness of the Indian languages, can hardly form an idea of the various shades and combinations of ideas that they can express. For instance, the infinitive *Mitzin,* signifies *to eat,* and so does *Mohoan.* Now although the first of these words is sufficiently expressive of the act of eating something, be it what it may, yet the Indians are very attentive to expressing in one word what and how they have eaten, that is to say whether they have been eating something which needed no chewing, as pottage, mush or the like, or something that required the use of the teeth. In the latter case the proper word is *mohoan*, and in the former *guntammen*. If an Indian is asked *k'dapi mitzi?* have you eaten? he will answer *n'dapi guntammen*, or *n'dapi mohoa*, according as what he has eaten did or did not require the aid of chewing. If he has eaten of both kinds of provisions at his meal he will then use the generic word, and say, *n'dapi mitzi*, which means generally, *I have eaten*.

These niceties of course escaped me, and what was worse, few of the words I had taken down were correctly written. Essential letters or syllables, which in the rapidity of pronunciation had escaped my ear, were almost every where omitted. When I tried to make use of the words which I had so carefully collected, I found I was not understood, and I was at a loss to discover the cause to which I might attribute my want of success in the earnest endeavours that I was making to acquire the Indian tongue.

At last there came an Indian, who was conversant with the English and German, and was much my friend. I hastened to lay before him my learned collection of Indian words, and was very much astonished when he advised me immediately to burn the whole, and write no more. "The first thing" said he, "that you are to do to learn our language is to get an Indian *ear*; when that is obtained, no sound, no syllable will ever escape your hearing it, and you will at the same time learn the true pronunciation and how to accent your words properly; the rest will come of itself." I found he was right. By listening to the natives, and repeating the words to myself as they spoke them, it was not many months before I ventured to converse with them and finally understood every word they said. The Indians are very proud of a white man's endeavouring to learn their language; they help him in every thing that they can, and it is not their fault if he does not succeed.

The language, then, is the first thing that a traveller ought to endeavour to acquire, at least, so as to be able to make himself understood and to understand others. Without this indispensible requisite he may write about the soil, earth and stones, describe trees and plants that grow on the surface of the land, the birds that fly in the air and the fishes that swim in the waters, but he should by no means attempt to speak of the disposition and characters of the human beings who inhabit the country, and even of their customs and manners, which it is impossible for him to be sufficiently acquainted with. And indeed, even with the advantage of the language, this knowledge is not to be acquired in a short time, so different is the impression which new objects make upon us at first sight, and that which they produce on a nearer view. I could speak the Delaware language very fluently but I was yet far from being well acquainted with the character and manners of the Lenape.

The Indians are very ready to answer the enquiries that are made respecting the usages of their country. But they are very much disgusted with the manner which they say some white people have of asking them questions on questions, without allowing them time to give a proper answer to any one of them. They, on the contrary, never ask a second question until they have received a full answer to the first. They say of those who do otherwise, that they seem as if they wished to know a thing, yet cared not whether they knew it correctly or properly. There are some men who before the Indians have well understood the question put to them, begin to write down their answers; of these they have no good opinion, thinking that they are writing something unfavourable of them.

There are men who will relate incredible stories of the Indians, and think themselves sufficiently warranted because they have Indian authority for it. But these men ought to know that all that an Indian says is not to be relied upon as truth. I do not mean to say that they are addicted to telling falsehoods, for nothing is farther from their character; but they are fond of the marvellous, and when they find a white man inclined to listen to their tales of wonder, or credulous enough to believe their superstitious notions, there are always some among them ready to entertain him with tales of that description, as it gives them an opportunity of diverting themselves in their leisure hours, by relating such fabulous stories, while they laugh at the same time at their being able to deceive a people who think themselves so superior to them in wisdom and knowledge. They are fond of trying white men who come among them, in order to see whether they can act upon them in this way with success. Travellers who cannot speak their language, and are not acquainted with their character, manners and usages, should be more particularly careful not to ask them questions that touch in any manner upon their superstitious notions, or, as they are often considered even by themselves "fabulous amusements." Nor should a stranger ever display an anxiety to witness scenes of this kind, but rather appear indifferent about them. In this manner he cannot be misled by interested persons or those who have formed a malicious design to deceive him. Whenever such a disposition appears (and it is not difficult to be discovered) questions of this kind should be reserved for another time, and asked in a proper manner before other persons, or of those who would be candid and perhaps let the enquirer into the secret.

DOCUMENT 22

Friend and Foe

The attitude of the Indian toward friend and foe is vividly painted in this passage from the Moravian missionary John Heckewelder's *Account of the History, Manners, and Customs of the Indian Nations, Who Once Inhabited Pennsylvania and the Neighbouring States*, pp. 272–86 (Philadelphia: American Philosophical Society, 1819). Compare the account of Colonel Crawford's capture, plea for mercy, and death by torture, with the comments of Hugh Henry Brackenridge on pp. 111–17.

Those who believe that no faith is to be placed in the friendship of an Indian are egregiously mistaken, and know very little of the true character of those men of nature. They are, it is true, revengeful to their enemies, to those who wilfully do them an injury, who insult, abuse, or treat them with contempt. It may be said, indeed, that the passion of revenge is so strong in them that it knows no bounds. This does not, however, proceed from a bad or malicious disposition, but from the violence of natural feelings, unchecked by social institutions, and unsubdued by the force of revealed religion. The tender and generous passions operate no less powerfully on them than those of an opposite character, and they are as warm and sincere in their friendship, as vindictive in their enmities. Nay, I will venture to assert that there are those among them who on an emergency would lay down their lives for a friend: I could fill many pages with examples of Indian friendship and fidelity, not only to each other, but to men of other nations and of a different colour than themselves. How often, when wars were impending between them and the whites, have they not forewarned those among our frontier settlers whom they thought well disposed towards them, that dangerous times were at hand, and advised them to provide for their own safety, regardless of the jealousy which such conduct might excite among their own people? How often did they not even guard and escort them through the most dangerous places until they had reached a secure spot? How often did they not find means to keep an enemy from striking a stroke, as they call it, that is to say from proceeding to the sudden indiscriminate murder of the frontier whites, until their friends or those whom they considered as such were out of all danger?

These facts are familiar to every one who has lived among Indians or in their neighbourhood, and I believe it will be difficult to find a single case in which they betrayed a real friend or abandoned him in the hour of danger, when it was in their power to extricate or relieve him. The word "Friend" to the ear of an Indian does not convey the same vague and almost indefinite meaning that it does with us; it is not a mere complimentary or social expression, but implies a resolute determination to stand by the person so distinguished on all occasions, and a threat to those who might attempt to molest him; the mere looking at two persons who are known or declared friends, is sufficient to deter any one from offering insult to either. When an Indian believes that he has reason to suspect a man of evil designs against his friend, he has only to say emphatically: "This is *my friend*, and if any one tries to hurt him, I will do to him *what is in my mind*." It is as much as to say that he will stand in his defence at the hazard of his own life. This language is well understood by the Indians, who know that they would have to combat with a spirited warrior, were they to attempt any thing against his friend. By this means much bloodshed is prevented; for it is sufficiently known that an Indian never proffers his friendship in vain. Many white men and myself among others have experienced the benefit of their powerful as well as generous protection.

When in the spring of the year 1774, a war broke out
between the Virginians and the Shawanese and Mingoes,
on account of murders committed by the former on the
latter people, and the exasperated friends of those who
had suffered had determined to kill every white man in
their country, the Shawano chief *Silver-heels*, taking another Indian with him, undertook out of friendship to
escort several white traders from thence to Albany, a distance of near two hundred miles; well knowing at the
time that he was running the risk of his own life, from
exasperated Indians and vagabond whites, if he should
meet with such on the road, as in fact he did on his
return. . . .

In the year 1779, the noted Girty with his murdering
party of Mingoes, nine in number, fell in with the Missionary Zeisberger, on the path leading from Goschacking
to Gnadenhütten; their design was to take that worthy
man prisoner, and if they could not seize him alive, to
murder him and take his scalp to Detroit. They were on
the point of laying hold of him, when two young spirited
Delawares providentially entered the path at that critical
moment and in an instant presented themselves to defend
the good Missionary at the risk of their lives. Their determined conduct had the desired success, and his life
was saved. His deliverers afterwards declared that they
had no other motive for thus exposing themselves for his
sake than that he was a friend to their nation and was
considered by them as a good man.

But why should I speak of others when I have myself
so often experienced the benefits of Indian protection and
friendship. Let me be permitted to corroborate my as-
sertions on this subject by my own personal testimony.

In the year 1777, while the revolutionary war was raging, and several Indian tribes had enlisted on the British
side, and were spreading murder and devastation along
our unprotected frontier, I rather rashly determined to
take a journey into the country on a visit to my friends.
Captain White Eyes, the Indian hero, whose character I

have already described, resided at that time at the distance of seventeen miles from the place where I lived. Hearing of my determination, he immediately hurried up to me, with his friend Captain Wingenund, (whom I shall presently have occasion further to mention) and some of his young men, for the purpose of escorting me to Pittsburg, saying, "that he would not suffer me, to go, while the Sandusky warriors were out on war excursions, without a proper escort and *himself* at my side." He insisted on accompanying me and we set out together. One day, as we were proceeding along, our spies discovered a suspicious track. White Eyes, who was riding before me, enquired whether I felt afraid? I answered that while he was with me, I entertained no fear. On this he immediately replied, "You are right; for until I am laid prostrate at your feet, no one shall hurt you." "And even not then," added Wingenund, who was riding behind me; "before this happens, I must be also overcome, and lay by the side of our friend *Koguethagechton*."[1] I believed them, and I believe at this day that these great men were sincere, and that if they had been put to the test, they would have shewn it, as did another Indian friend by whom my life was saved in the spring of the year 1781. From behind a log in the bushes where he was concealed, he espied a hostile Indian at the very moment he was levelling his piece at me. Quick as lightning he jumped between us, and exposed his person to the musket shot just about to be fired, when fortunately the aggressor desisted, from fear of hitting the Indian whose body thus effectually protected me, at the imminent risk of his own life. Captain White Eyes, in the year 1774, saved in the same manner the life of David Duncan, the peace-messenger, whom he was escorting. He rushed, regardless of his own life, up to an inimical Shawanese, who was aiming at our ambassador from behind a bush, and forced him to desist.

I could enumerate many other similar acts, but I think I have shewn enough for my purpose. Mr. Zeisberger fully

[1] The Indian name of Capt. White Eyes.

agreed with me in the opinion, that it is impossible to deny to the Indians the praise of firm attachment and sincere friendship. It is not meant to say, that all will carry that feeling to the same pitch of heroism; but it is certain that there are many among them, whose strong attachments and a manly pride will induce to risk their lives in the defence of their friends. And, indeed, there is no Indian, who would not blush at being reproached that after boasting that a particular person was his friend, he had acted the coward when his friendship was put to the test, and had shrunk from venturing his own life, when there was even a chance of saving that of the man whom he professed to love.

It is not true, as some have supposed, that an Indian's friendship must be purchased by presents, and that it lasts only so long as gifts continue to be lavished upon them. Their attachments, on the contrary, are perfectly disinterested. I admit that they receive with pleasure a present from a friend's hand. They consider presents as marks of the giver's good disposition towards them. They cannot, in their opinion, proceed from an enemy, and he who befriends them, they think must love them. Obligations to them are not burdensome, they love to acknowledge them, and whatever may be their faults, ingratitude is not among the number.

Indeed, the friendship of an Indian is easily acquired, provided it is sought in good faith. But whoever chooses to obtain it must be sure to treat them on a footing of perfect equality. They are very jealous of the whites, who, they think affect to consider themselves as beings of a superior nature and too often treat them with rude undeserved contempt. This they seldom forgive, while on the other hand, they feel flattered when a white man does not disdain to treat them as children of the same Creator. Both reason and humanity concur in teaching us this conduct, but I am sorry to say that reason and humanity are in such cases too little attended to. I hope I may be permitted to expatiate a little on this subject; perhaps it may be beneficial to some white persons hereafter.

The Indians are, as I have already observed before, excellent physiognomists. If they are accosted by or engaged in business with a number of whites, though they may not understand the language that is spoken, they will pretty accurately distinguish by the countenance, those who despise their colour from those who are under the influence of a more generous feeling, and in this they are seldom mistaken. They fix their eyes on the whole party round, and read as it were in the souls of the individuals who compose it. They mark those whom they consider as their friends, and those whom they think to be their enemies, and are sure to remember them ever after. But what must those expect, if a war or some other circumstance should put them into the power of the Indians, who, relying on their supposed ignorance of our idiom, do not scruple even in their presence to apply to them the epithets of *dogs, black d—ls,* and the like? Will not these poor people be in some degree justifiable in considering those persons as decidedly hostile to their race? such cases have unfortunately too frequently happened, and the savages have been blamed for treating as enemies those who had so cruelly wounded their most delicate feelings! many white men have been thus put to death, who had brought their fate on themselves by their own imprudence. On the other hand the Indians have not failed to mark those who at the time reprobated such indecent behaviour and reproached their companions for using such improper language. In the midst of war these benevolent Christians have been treated as friends, when perhaps, they had forgotten the humane conduct to which they were indebted for this kind usage.

Their reasoning in such cases is simple, but to them always conclusive. They merely apply their constant maxim, which I believe I have already noticed, that "good can never proceed from evil or evil from good, and that good and evil, like heterogeneous substances, can never combine or coalesce together." How far this maxim is founded in a profound knowledge of human nature, it is not my business to determine; what is certain is that they adhere to it in almost every occasion. If a person treats them ill, they ascribe it invariably to his bad heart; it is the bad spirit within him that operates; he is, therefore, a bad man. If on the contrary one shews them kindness, they say he is prompted so to act by "the good spirit within him," and that he has a *good heart*; for if he had not, he would not do good. It is impossible to draw them out of this circle of reasoning, and to persuade them that the friendship shewn to them may be dissembled and proceed from motions of interest; so convinced are they of the truth of their general principle "that good cannot proceed from an evil source."

The conduct of the Europeans towards them, particularly within the last fifty or sixty years, has, however, sufficiently convinced them that men may dissemble, and that kind speeches and even acts of apparent friendship do not always proceed from friendly motives, but that the bad spirit will sometimes lurk under the appearance of the good. Hence, when they speak of the whites in general, they do not scruple to designate them as a false, deceitful race; but it is nevertheless true that with individuals, they frequently forget this general impression, and revert to their own honest principle; and if a white man only behaves to them with common humanity, it is still easy to get access to their simple hearts. Such are those brutes, those savages, from whom, according to some men, no faith is to be expected, and with whom no faith is to be kept; such are those *barbarous* nations, as they are called, whom God, nevertheless, made the lawful owners and masters of this beautiful country; but who, at no very remote time, will probably live, partially live, only in its history.

My object in this chapter is to prove that those men are susceptible of the noblest and finest feelings of genuine friendship. It is not enough that by a long residence among them, I have acquired the most complete conviction of this truth; facts and not opinions, I know, are expected from me. Perhaps I might rest satisfied with the proofs that I have already given, but I have only shewn the strength and have yet to display the *constancy* of their attachments; and although in the story which I am going to relate, a friend was forced to see his friend perish miserably without having it in his power to save him from the most terrible death that vengeance and cruelty could inflict, we shall not be the less astonished to see him persevere in his friendly sentiments, under circumstances of all others the most calculated, (particularly to an Indian) not only to have entirely extinguished, but converted those sentiments into feelings of hatred and revenge.

I am sorry to be so often obliged to revert to the circumstance of the cruel murder of the Christian Indians on the Sandusky river in the year 1782, by a gang of banditti, under the command of one Williamson. Not satisfied with this horrid outrage, the same band, not long afterwards marched to Sandusky, where it seems they had been informed that the remainder of that unfortunate congregation had fled, in order to perpetrate upon them the same indiscriminate murder. But Providence had so ordered it that they had before left that place, where they had found that they could not remain in safety, their ministers having been taken from them and carried to Detroit by order of the British government, so that they had been left entirely unprotected. The murderers, on their arrival, were much disappointed in finding nothing but empty huts. They then shaped their course towards the hostile Indian villages, where being, contrary to their expectations, furiously attacked, Williamson and his band took the advantage of a dark night and ran off, and the whole party escaped, except one Colonel Crawford and another, who being taken by the Indians, were carried in triumph to their village, where the former was condemned to death by torture, and the punishment was inflicted with all the cruelty that rage could invent. The latter was demanded by the Shawanese and sent to them for punishment.

While preparations were making for the execution of this dreadful sentence, the unfortunate Crawford recollected that the Delaware chief Wingenund,[2] of whom I have spoken in the beginning of this chapter, had been his friend in happier times; he had several times entertained him at his house, and shewed him those marks of attention which are so grateful to the poor despised Indians. A ray of hope darted through his soul, and he requested that Wingenund, who lived at some distance from the village, might be sent for. His request was granted, and a messenger was despatched for the chief, who, reluctantly, indeed, but without hesitation, obeyed the summons, and immediately came to the fatal spot.

This great and good man was not only one of the bravest and most celebrated warriors, but one of the most amiable men of the Delaware nation. To a firm undaunted mind, he joined humanity, kindness and universal benevolence; the excellent qualities of his heart had obtained for him the name of *Wingenund*, which in the Lenape language signifies *the well beloved*. He had kept away from the tragical scene about to be acted, to mourn in silence and solitude over the fate of his guilty friend, which he well knew it was not in his power to prevent. He was now called upon to act a painful as well as difficult part: the eyes of his enraged countrymen were fixed upon him; he was an Indian and a Delaware; he was a leader of that nation, whose defenceless members had been so cruelly murdered without distinction of age or sex, and whose innocent blood called aloud for the most signal revenge. Could he take the part of a chief of the base murderers? Could he forget altogether the feelings of ancient fellowship and give way exclusively to those of the Indian and the patriot? Fully sensible that in the situation in which he was placed the latter must, in appearance, at least, predominate, he summoned to his aid the firmness and dignity of an Indian warrior, approached Colonel Crawford and waited in silence for the communications

[2] This name, according to the English orthography, should be written *Winganoond* or *Wingaynoond*, the second syllable accented and long, and the last syllable short.

he had to make. The following dialogue now took place between them.

CRAWF. Do you recollect me, Wingenund?

WINGEN. I believe I do; are you not Colonel Crawford?

CRAWF. I am. How do you do? I am glad to see you, Captain.

WINGEN. (embarrassed) So! yes, indeed.

CRAWF. Do you recollect the friendship that always existed between us, and that we were always glad to see each other?

WINGEN. I recollect all this. I remember that we have drunk many a bowl of punch together. I remember also other acts of kindness that you have done me.

CRAWF. Then I hope the same friendship still subsists between us.

WINGEN. It would, of course, be the same, were you in your proper place and not here.

CRAWF. And why not here, Captain? I hope you would not desert a friend in time of need. Now is the time for you to exert yourself in my behalf, as I should do for you, were you in my place.

WINGEN. Colonel Crawford! you have placed yourself in a situation which puts it out of my power and that of others of your friends to do any thing for you.

CRAWF. How so, Captain Wingenund?

WINGEN. By joining yourself to that execrable man, Williamson and his party; the man, who, but the other day murdered such a number of the Moravian Indians, knowing them to be friends; knowing that he ran no risk in murdering a people who would not fight, and whose only business was praying.

CRAWF. Wingenund, I assure you, that had I been with him at the time, this would not have happened; not I alone but all your friends and all good men, wherever they are, reprobate acts of this kind.

WINGEN. That may be; yet these friends, these good men did not prevent him from going out again, to kill the remainder of those inoffensive, yet *foolish* Moravian Indians! I say *foolish*, because they believed the whites in preference to us. We had often told them that they would be one day so treated by those people who called themselves their friends! We told them that there was no faith to be placed in what the white men said; that their fair promises were only intended to allure us, that they might the more easily kill us, as they have done many Indians before they killed these Moravians.

CRAWF. I am sorry to hear you speak thus; as to Williamson's going out again, when it was known that he was determined on it, I went out with him to prevent him from committing fresh murders.

WINGEN. This, Colonel, the Indians would not believe, were even I to tell them so.

CRAWF. And why would they not believe it?

WINGEN. Because it would have been out of your power to prevent his doing what he pleased.

CRAWF. Out of my power! Have any Moravian Indians been killed or hurt since we came out?

WINGEN. None; but you went first to their town, and finding it empty and deserted you turned on the path towards us? If you had been in search of warriors only, you would not have gone thither. Our spies watched you closely. They saw you while you were embodying yourselves on the other side of the Ohio; they saw you cross that river; they saw where you encamped at night; they saw you turn off from the path to the deserted Moravian town; they knew you were going out of your way; your steps were constantly watched, and you were suffered quietly to proceed until you reached the spot where you were attacked.

CRAWF. What do they intend to do with me? Can you tell me?

WINGEN. I tell you with grief, Colonel. As Williamson and his whole cowardly host, ran off in the night at the whistling of our warrior's balls, being satisfied that now he had no Moravians to deal with, but men who could fight, and with such he did not wish to have any thing to do; I say, as he escaped, and they have taken you, they will take revenge on you in his stead.

CRAWF. And is there no possibility of preventing this? Can you devise no way to get me off? You shall, my friend, be well rewarded if you are instrumental in saving my life.

WINGEN. Had Williamson been taken with you, I and some friends, by making use of what you have told me, might perhaps, have succeeded to save you, but as the matter now stands, no man would dare to interfere in your behalf. The king of England himself, were he to come to this spot, with all his wealth and treasures could not effect this purpose. The blood of the innocent Moravians, more than half of them women and children, cruelly and wantonly murdered calls aloud for *revenge*. The relatives of the slain, who are among us, cry out and stand ready for *revenge*. The nation to which they belonged will have *revenge*. The Shawanese, our grandchildren, have asked for your fellow prisoner; on him they will take *revenge*. All the nations connected with us cry out *Revenge! revenge!* The Moravians whom you went to destroy having fled, instead of avenging their brethren, the offence is become national, and the nation itself is bound to take REVENGE!

CRAWF. Then it seems my fate is decided, and I must prepare to meet death in its worst form?

WINGEN. Yes, Colonel!—I am sorry for it; but cannot do any thing for you. Had you attended to the Indian principle, that as good and evil cannot dwell together in the same heart, so a good man ought not to go into evil company; you would not be in this lamentable situation. You see, now, when it is too late, after Williamson has deserted you, what a bad man he must be! Nothing now remains for you but to meet your fate like a brave man. Farewel, Colonel Crawford! they are coming;[3] I will retire to a solitary spot.

I have been assured by respectable Indians that at the close of this conversation, which was related to me by

---

[3] The people were at that moment advancing, with shouts and yells, to torture and put him to death.

Wingenund himself as well as by others, both he and Crawford burst into a flood of tears; they then took an affectionate leave of each other, and the chief immediately *hid himself in the bushes*, as the Indians express it, or in his own language, retired to a solitary spot. He never, afterwards, spoke of the fate of his unfortunate friend without strong emotions of grief, which I have several times witnessed. Once, it was the first time that he came into Detroit after Crawford's sufferings, I heard him censured in his own presence by some gentlemen who were standing together for not having saved the life of so valuable a man, who was also his particular friend, as he had often told them. He listened calmly to their censure, and first turning to me, said in his own language: "These men talk like fools," then turning to them, he replied in English: "If king George himself, if your king had been on the spot with all his ships laden with goods and treasures, he could not have ransomed my friend, nor saved his life from the rage of a *justly* exasperated multitude." He made no further allusion to the act that had been the cause of Crawford's death, and it was easy to perceive that on this melancholy subject, grief was the feeling that predominated in his mind. He felt much hurt, however, at this unjust accusation, from men who, perhaps, he might think, would have acted very differently in his place. For, let us consider in what a situation he found himself, at that trying and critical moment. He was a Delaware Indian and a highly distinguished character among his nation. The offence was national, and of the most atrocious kind, as it was wanton and altogether unprovoked. He might have been expected to partake with all the rest of his countrymen in the strong desire which they felt for *revenge*. He had been Crawford's friend, it is true, and various acts of sociability and friendship had been interchanged between them. But, no doubt, at that time, he believed him, at least, not to be an enemy, to his nation and colour, and if he was an enemy, he might have expected him to be, like himself, a fair, open generous foe. But when he finds him enlisted with those who are waging a war of extermination against the Indian race, murdering in cold blood, and without distinction of age or sex, even those who had united their fate to that of the whites, and had said to the Christians: "Your people shall be *our* people, and your God *our* God,"[4] was there not enough here to make him disbelieve all the former professions of such a man, and to turn his abused friendship into the most violent enmity and the bitterest rage. Instead of this we see him persevering to the last in his attachment to a person, who, to say the least, had ceased to be deserving of it; we see him in the face of his enraged countrymen avow that friendship, careless of the jealousy that he might excite; we see him not only abstain from participating in the national revenge, but deserting his post, as it were, seek a solitary spot to bewail the death of him, whom, in spite of all, he still loved, and felt not ashamed to call his *friend*.

It is impossible for friendship to be put to a severer test, and the example of Wingenund proves how deep a root this sentiment can take in the mind of an Indian, when even such circumstances as those under which the chief found himself, fail to extinguish it.

[4] Ruth, i. 16.

DOCUMENT 23

The Call of the Wild

One of the significant but little-known aspects of the Indian-white relationship was the sexual one. Though unreported on the whole, enough evidence exists to show that the sexual attraction of the dark-haired native was one of the major forces inducing whites to push on into the interior. Sometimes the liaisons were casual, sometimes formal and solemn. One example of the psychology involved is demonstrated in the following passage from David Thompson's *Narrative of His Explorations in Western America, 1784–1812*, pp. 234–37, edited by J. B. Tyrrell (Toronto: The Champlain Society, 1916).

The curse of the Mandanes is an almost total want of chastity: this, the men with me knew, and I found it was almost their sole motive for their journey hereto: The goods they brought, they sold at 50 to 60 per cent above what they cost; and reserving enough to pay their debts, and buy some corn; [they] spent the rest on Women. Therefore we could not preach chastity to them, and by experience they informed me that siphylis was common and mild. These people annually, at least once in every summer, have the following detestable ceremony, which lasts three days. The first day both sexes go about within and without the Village, but mostly on the outside, as if in great distress, seeking for persons they cannot find, for a few hours, then sit down and cry as if for sorrow, then retire to their houses. The next day the same is repeated, with apparent greater distress accompanied with low singing. The third day begins with both sexes crying (no tears) and eagerly searching for those they wish to find, but cannot; at length tired with this folly; the sexes separate, and the Men sit down on the ground in one line, with their elbows resting on their knees, and their heads resting on their hands as in sorrow; The Women standing and crying heartily, with dry eyes, form a line opposite the Men; in a few minutes, several Women advance to the Men, each of them takes the Man she chooses by the hand, he rises and goes with her to where she pleases, and they lie down together. And thus until none remain, which finishes this abominable ceremony. No woman can choose her own husband; but the women who love their husbands lead away aged Men. Messrs Jussomme and McCrachan said they had often partaken of the latter part of the third day; and other men said the same. Manoah strongly denied that either himself, or his wife had ever taken part in these rights of the devil.

The white men who have hitherto visited these Villages, have not been examples of chastity; and of course religion is out of the question; and as to the white Men who have no education, and who therefore cannot read, the little religion they ever had is soon forgotten when there is no Church to remind them of it.

Fall Indians who also have Villages, are strictly confederate with the Mandanes, they speak a distinct language; and it is thought no other tribe of Natives speak it: very few of the Mandanes learn it; the former learn the language of the latter, which is a dialect of the Pawnee language. The Fall Indians are now removed far from their original country, which was the Rapids of the Saskatchewan river, northward of the Eagle Hill; A feud arose between them, and their then neighbours, the Nahathaways and the Stone Indians confederates, and [they were] too powerful for them, they then lived wholly in tents, and removed across the Plains to the Missisourie; became confederate with the Mandanes, and from them have learned to build houses, form villages and cultivate the ground; The architecture of their houses is in every respect the same as that of the Mandanes, and their cultivation is the same: Some of them continue to live in tents and are in friendship with the Chyenne Indians, whose village was lately destroyed, and now live in tents to the westward of them. Another band of these people now dwell in tents near the head of this River in alliance with the Peeagans and their allies; The whole tribe of these people may be estimated at 2200 to 2500 souls. They are not as fair as the Mandanes; but somewhat taller. Their features, like those of the plains have a cast of sterness, yet they are cheerful, very hospitable and friendly to each other, and to strangers. What has been said of the Mandanes may be said of them; except in regard to Women. The Fall Indians exact the strictest chastity of their wives; adultry is punishable with death to both parties; though the Woman escapes this penalty more often than the man: who can only save his life by absconding which, if the woman does not do, she suffers a severe beating, and becomes the drudge of the family. But those living in the Villages I was given to understand have relaxed this law to the man in favor of a present of a Horse, and whatever else can be got from him. As they do not suffer the hardships of the Indians of the Plains, the Men are nearly equal to the Women in number, and few have more than two wives, more frequently only one. It always appeared to me that the Indians of the Plains did not regard the chastity of their wives as a moral law, but as an unalienable right of property to be their wives and the mothers of their own children; and not to be interfered with by another Man. The morality of the Indians, may be said to be founded on it's [sic] necessity to the peace and safety of each other, and although they profess to believe in a Spirit of great power, and that the wicked are badly treated after death; yet this seems to have no effect on their passions and desires. The crimes they hold to be avoided are, theft, treachery and murder.

Christianity alone by it's holy doctrines and precepts, by it's promises of a happy immortality, and dreadful punishments to the wicked, can give force to morality. It alone can restrain the passions and desires and guide them to fulfil the intentions of a wise, and benevolent Providence. As the Missisourie River with all it's Villages and population are within the United States, it is to be hoped Missionaries will soon find their way to these Villages, and give them a knowledge of christianity, which they will gladly accept.

DOCUMENT 24

The Fair Sex

Ernest Hooton, the physical anthropologist, used to say that when races meet they usually fight, but they always interbreed. The form of these unions varied with the character of the whites and the character of the Indians, as with the time, place, and situation. Sometimes force was used, sometimes love, sometimes money. The following account of the Arikara Indians of the Upper Missouri in 1803–5 was written by Pierre-Antoine Tabeau, who accompanied Régis Loisel in his expedition for the Spanish Company of Commerce for the Discovery of the Nations of the Upper Missouri. The passage is from Tabeau's *Narrative of Loisel's Expedition to the Upper Missouri,* edited by Annie Heloise Abel, translated from the French by Rose Abel Wright, pp. 178–81 (Norman, Okla.: University of Oklahoma Press, 1939). Editorial notes have been omitted.

The Sioux women, although not very strict, are more reserved than the Ricara women. It could be said that the latter do justice to themselves and know the value of their favors, if their facility in granting them is any criterion. The most inflexible is not proof against a prize of vermilion and of twenty strands of blue beads. There are, nevertheless, a few prudes who greatly wish to pass for cautious ones; but who surrender themselves, moreover, with discretion and secrecy. All are generally hostile to ceremony and, to avoid the embarrassment of an intrigue, they ordinarily make the first advances in a less equivocal manner and it is here where one truly takes the romance by the tail. The most peculiar thing is that all goes on often in the presence of and even by order of a jealous husband. This paradox will be no longer a paradox when it is understood that a Sioux, as a Ricara, is alive to this affront only when his wife, by a secret infidelity, departs from his house. Therefore, all that which meets with his approval, being in order, is not offensive and such a man, who would kill or at least turn out his wife upon the slightest suspicion, prostitutes her himself for a very small reward and it is seen that a wife has not yet been chastised for having failed in submission in like case.

I have seen among the Bois Brulés a secret infidelity punished and a husband order his wife to be unfaithful. Here are the two cases: The 6th. of August a man surprises his better half in flagrant wrongdoing and, in order to avoid all proceedings, he takes it upon himself to pronounce and to execute sentence. He commences by removing her hair from the nape of the neck up to brow and, stopping near the ears, he allows the hair and skin to hang down each side. He continues his work by mutilating her arms and hands and ends by a cut of the knife on the shoulder-blade. The wife having wholly recovered from the wounds, he said that if she did wrong again he would regard her as incorrigible. A Savage regards the infidelity of his wife in favor of a white man less of a sin, in that she is won by the allurement of gain and he does not dream that this rival presumes to think that he is preferred to himself. This opinion, elsewhere, is perhaps often the hidden cause of jealousy and it cannot be otherwise among the Savages, who know neither love nor delicacy.

A Sioux brave, wishing to prove that he is brave-hearted, comes, in open daylight, to find a Frenchman at the Isle of Cedars. He is followed by his young wife, one of the prettiest of the village and, moreover, reputed discreet. He offers the favors of this well-beloved, demanding only a few small articles in return. The cavalier, although surprised, is not the man to give up his cloak and offers at first a fine knife, a prize of vermilion, and about six inches of tobacco. As the present appeared small because of her attractions, the husband pulls off the robe in which the Venus is wrapped through modesty and, in spite of some affected manners, increased, of course, the price of his goods by exposing it. The cavalier still hesitated, when the victim to whom the sacrifice was doubtless painful, but who feared, nevertheless, to lose the occasion of proving her submissiveness, remarked that knives with a green handle were not common; that the vermilion was a beautiful red; that the tobacco—in short, well, what else? At least, she speaks so well that they agree and the husband firmly holds the door.

This politeness is carried out every day among the Ricaras, and always the more readily in the case of the whites; but infidelities, unavowed, are not always punished severely and the braves ordinarily content themselves with repudiating the wives. This is, often, only a momentary divorce. Besides, the intrigues are so common that they are generally made light of. Furthermore, reciprocation of injury suffices in a nation, where immodesty is carried to its highest pitch.

The word, modesty, is not even known among the Ricaras. The Chayennes and the Caninanbiches are reserved in this respect, even in their conversation. The Sioux are, at least, modestly covered; but the Ricara men are absolutely nude. Through force of habit, though, no notice is taken of it. The women and the young girls mingle with the men and laugh, inconsequently, at the most obscene things. The men, nevertheless, would think it immodest to be without a loin cloth made of blades of curled grass. To neglect this is here a great fault. The 2nd. of August I saw all the women and girls of the village, spectators of a comic dance, where the men, attached thus, two by two, drew backwards and offered, in their gambols, attitudes which drew great applause. After that, it would surely astonish one to hear it said that the girls are virtuous before marriage and that there are virgins, eighteen to twenty years old. Truth exceeds probability here. It is true that the mothers and all the relatives watch with the greatest care and that they carry watchfulness up to the point of fastening at night the petticoats of the girls who lie thus tied down. Nevertheless, these bonds are not proof against a lover who pleases; but, according to their law, that is a marriage and, even if it last only an hour, the girl becomes, none the less, an honest widow.

DOCUMENT 25

The Founding Fathers and the Indian

It is worthy of note that the four outstanding American Revolutionary leaders, George Washington, Thomas Jefferson, Benjamin Franklin, and John Adams, had close knowledge of, and frequent dealings with, American Indian groups. Knowledge of different cultures is the foundation stone of wisdom, and it is not improbable that these gentlemen, particularly Jefferson and Franklin, profited by their relationship with the Red Man. The following exchange between Thomas Jefferson and John Adams, at the onset of the War of 1812, reflects their sincere interest in the American Indian. The quotations are taken from *The Adams-Jefferson Letters: The Complete Correspondence Between Thomas Jefferson and Abigail and John Adams*, edited by Lester J. Cappon, Vol. II, pp. 307–8, 310–11 (Chapel Hill: University of North Carolina Press, 1959). The first letter is from Jefferson to Adams; the second from Adams to Jefferson.

So much in answer to your enquiries concerning Indians, a people with whom, in the very early part of my life, I was very familiar, and acquired impressions of attachment and commiseration for them which have never been obliterated. Before the revolution they were in the habit of coming often, and in great numbers to the seat of our government, where I was very much with them. I knew much the great Outassete [Outacity], the warrior and orator of the Cherokees. He was always the guest of my father, on his journeys to and from Williamsburg. I was in his camp when he made his great farewell oration to his people, the evening before his departure for England. The moon was in full splendor, and to her he seemed to address himself in his prayers for his own safety on the voyage, and that of his people during his absence. His sounding voice, distinct articulation, animated action, and the solemn silence of his people at their several fires, filled me with awe and veneration, altho' I did not understand a word he uttered. That nation, consisting now of about 2000. wariors, and the Creeks of about 3000. are far advanced in civilisation. They have good Cabins, inclosed fields, large herds of cattle and hogs, spin and weave their own clothes of cotton, have smiths and other of the most necessary tradesmen, write and read, are on the increase in numbers, and a branch of the Cherokees is now instituting a regular representative government. Some other tribes were advancing in the same line. On those who have made any progress, English seductions will have no effect. But the backward will yield, and be thrown further back. These will relapse into barbarism and misery, lose numbers by war and want, and we shall be obliged to drive them, with the beasts of the forest into the Stony mountains. They will be conquered however in Canada. The possession of that country secures our women and children for ever from the tomahawk and scalping knife, by removing those who excite them: and for this possession, orders I presume are issued by this time; taking for granted that the doors of Congress will re-open with a Declaration of war. That this may end in indemnity for the past, security for the future, and compleat emancipation from Anglomany, Gallomany, and all the manias of demoralized Europe, and that you may live in health and happiness to see all this, is the sincere prayer of Yours affectionately.

Th: Jefferson

Monticello June 11. 1812.

I also have felt an Interest in the Indians and a Commiseration for them from my Childhood. Aaron Pomham the Priest and Moses Pomham the King of the Punkapaug and Neponsit Tribes, were frequent Visitors at my Fathers house at least seventy Years ago. I have a distinct remembrance of their Forms and Figures. They were very aged, and the tallest and stoutest Indians I have ever seen. The titles of King and Priest, and the names of Moses and Aaron were given them no doubt by our Massachusetts Divines and Statesmen. There was a numerous Family in this Town, whose Wigwam was within a Mile of this House. This Family were frequently at my Fathers house, and I in my boyish Rambles used to call at their Wigwam, where I never failed to be treated with Whortle Berries, Blackberries, Strawberries or Apples, Plumbs, Peaches, etc., for they had planted a variety of fruit Trees about them. But the Girls went out to Service and the Boys to Sea, till not a Soul is left. We scarcely see an Indian in a year. I remember the Time when Indian Murders, Scalpings, Depredations and conflagrations were as frequent on the Eastern and Northern Frontier of Massachusetts as they are now in Indiana, and spread as much terror. But since the Conquest of Canada, all this has ceased; and I believe with you that another Conquest of Canada will quiet the Indians forever and be as great a Blessing to them as to Us.

. . . .

I am, Sir, with an affectionate Respect, yours.
John Adams

Quincy, June 28 1812

DOCUMENT 26

The Way West

As the settlers trekked west minor skirmishes with the Indians took place and often went unreported except, occasionally, in the work of an artist of the trail who might record his impressions (factual or fanciful) on a handy surface such as that of his powderhorn. Plate 8, following page 134, is a reproduction of a photograph of a powderhorn, possibly carried by one of the '49ers, with engraved scenes of a fight between Indians and whites, and varied views of the emigrants as they moved west. The powderhorn is in the possession of Mr. Theodore T. Dorman of Washington, D.C.

DOCUMENT 27

Never the Twain Shall Meet

Lieutenant Colonel Elwell S. Otis, U. S. Army, in his *The Indian Question*, pp. 231–32 (New York: 1878), reflects the combination of admiration and disgust often held by those who dealt with the Indian in an official capacity.

The Indian is sometimes called a statesman and an orator. His dignified bearing in council, the beautiful metaphors and rich imagery with which his efforts at oratory often abound, challenge admiration. Language is the embodiment of thought. It mirrors the mind, though it does not reveal intention nor morals. While, therefore, manifestations of the highest excellence which the red man has attained may be witnessed in the proceedings of their great tribal gatherings, no correct opinion of their moral condition can be gained. He is a keen observer of nature, and its objects supply him with figures to illustrate and impress his primitive ideas. Oratory, says a distinguished scholar, seems to have made but little advancement since the days of Homer. If it consists in simple illustration rather than in the employment of abstract terms, the statement is correct, for barbarous and semi-civilized nations excel in the first particular. With the Indian it is an art, the result of study and repeated practice. Few acquire it and they become the leading spirits of the tribe. The maiden speeches of the young chiefs about to assume control of the movements of their people, are generally miserable failures. After a few years of trial some become fluent declaimers and fervent exhorters. Fortunately for their reputations, their ideas are few and simple, and they can by their labor, be frequently reproduced with increased adornment.

The efforts of years secure a dress which is rich and oftentimes brilliant. Still it must be remembered that before the speech obtains our criticism, it is embellished by the imagination of the poetical interpreter.

We think that a progress towards civilization has a tendency to weaken the charms of Indian oratory. The wild savage is more eloquent than his half-tamed brother. He who has seen him as he comes from the excitement of battle to name conditions of peace, when every word is vehemently uttered, when passion, strangely visible in his countenance, finds vent in words, and in his peerless gesticulation, will agree in this assertion. So also he might do the same who has observed him as he rises in council, flings back from off his shoulders his pictured buffalo robe, shakes back his waving hair, and with a haughtiness more befitting a conqueror, proclaims the fancied wrongs of his race, and defiantly refuses the requests of the Great Father's commissioners. But should the savage be followed from the council to the feast or the dance, the respect which his talents had inspired would be lost, because of the sudden transition from superior dignity of manner to abasement or degradation of deportment. Within the same hour he may be seen carrying himself with proud nobility as he indulges in flowing declamation, or with rude song keeping time to the beating of the tom-tom, while sitting in the dust and filth of camp.

CHAPTER III

Justification for Dispossession

The Age of Discovery was an age of power as well as an age of faith. Both the practical and the moral aspects of the problems facing man were more clearly outlined than in our own day, though this is not to say that they were correctly outlined. In any event, the Europeans went to the New World feeling a need to justify their actions which was almost as intense as their desire to conquer and to settle. Both Catholic Spain and Protestant England concerned themselves not only with the royal conscience, but with the consciences of the colonists. Most of the disquisitions on the justice of expansion into the New World come from the hands of religious leaders, particularly in the seventeenth century. That the issue was not ignored in later centuries is evident from the vehemence of the statements of lay leaders such as Theodore Roosevelt in the passage quoted in doc. 34. For a general statement on the entire problem, see Wilcomb E. Washburn, "The Moral and Legal Justifications for Dispossessing the Indian," in *Seventeenth-Century America: Essays in Colonial History*, edited by James Morton Smith, pp. 15–32 (Chapel Hill: University of North Carolina Press, 1959).

DOCUMENT 28

God's Promise to His Plantation

When John Winthrop's company departed South-ampton, England, in 1630, to found the Massachusetts Bay colony, the Reverend John Cotton, who later joined his Puritan compatriots in America, preached a farewell sermon from the text (2 Sam. 7:10) "Moreover I will appoint a place for my people Israell, and I will plant them, that they may dwell in a place of their owne, and move no more." Cotton played a role similar to that of John Robinson, who bid farewell to his Pilgrim flock going to Plymouth ten years earlier. (See Robinson's letter, p. 176). Cotton's sermon, entitled "God's Promise to His Plantations," laid the moral basis for the settlement, and established a framework within which the relations between Indians and whites might be worked out. The sermon was printed in London in 1630, and has been conveniently reprinted as an Old South Leaflet, No. 53, by the Old South Association in Boston at Washington and Milk Streets. The following passage is from pp. 5–8.

Now God makes room for a people 3 wayes:
First, when he casts out the enemies of a people before them by lawfull warre with the inhabitants, which God cals them unto: as in *Ps. 44. 2. Thou didst drive out the heathen before them.* But this course of warring against others, & driving them out without provocation, depends upon speciall Commission from God, or else it is not imitable.

Secondly, when he gives a forreigne people favour in the eyes of any native people to come and sit downe with them either by way of purchase, as *Abraham* did obtaine

the field of *Machpelah*; or else when they give it in cour-
tesie, as *Pharaoh* did the land of *Goshen* unto the sons of
Jacob.

Thirdly, when hee makes a Countrey though not altogether void of inhabitants, yet voyd in that place where
they reside. Where there is a vacant place, there is liberty
for the sonne of *Adam* or *Noah* to come and inhabite,
though they neither buy it, nor aske their leaves. *Abraham*
and *Isaac*, when they sojourned amongst the Philistines,
they did not buy that land to feede their cattle, because
they said There is roome enough. And so did *Jacob* pitch
his Tent by *Sechem*, *Gen.* 34. 21. There was *roome enough*
as *Hamor* said, *Let them sit down amongst us*. And in
this case if the people who were former inhabitants did
disturbe them in their possessions, they complained to the
King, as of wrong done unto them: As *Abraham* did because they took away his well, in *Gen.* 21, 25. For his
right whereto he pleaded not his immediate calling from
God, (for that would have seemed frivolous amongst the
Heathen) but his owne industry and culture in digging
the well, verse 30. Nor doth the King reject his plea, with
what had he to doe to digge wells in their soyle? but ad-
mitteth it as a Principle in Nature, That in a vacant soyle,
hee that taketh possession of it, and bestoweth culture
and husbandry upon it, his Right it is. And the ground
of this is from the grand Charter given to *Adam* and his
posterity in Paradise, *Gen.* 1. 28. *Multiply, and replenish
the earth, and subdue it.* If therefore any sonne of *Adam*
come and finde a place empty, he hath liberty to come,
and fill, and subdue the earth there. This Charter was renewed to *Noah*, *Gen.* 9. 1. *Fulfill the earth and multiply*:
So that it is free from that comon Grant for any to take
possession of vacant Countries. Indeed no Nation is to
drive out another without speciall Commission from
heaven, such as the Israelites had, unless the Natives do
unjustly wrong them, and will not recompence the wrongs
done in peaceable sort, & then they may right themselves
by lawfull war, and subdue the Countrey unto themselves.

This placeing of people in this or that Countrey, is

from Gods soveraignty over all the earth, and the inhabitants thereof: as in *Psal.* 24. 1. *The earth is the Lords,
and the fulnesse thereof.* And in *Ier.* 10. 7. God is there
called, *The King of Nations:* and in *Deut.* 10. 14. Therefore it is meete he should provide a place for all Nations
to inhabite, and haue all the earth replenished. Onely in
the Text here is meant some more speciall appointment,
because God tells them it by his owne mouth; he doth
not so with other people, he doth not tell the children of
Sier, that hee hath appointed a place for them: that is, He
gives them the land by promise; others take the land by
his providence, but Gods people take the land by promise: And therefore the land of *Canaan* is called a land of
promise. Which they discerne, first, by discerning themselves to be in Christ, in whom all the promises are yea,
and amen.

Secondly, by finding his holy presence with them, to
wit, when he plants them in the holy Mountaine of his
Inheritance: *Exodus.* 15. 17. And that is when he giveth
them the liberty and purity of his Ordinances. It is a
land of promise, where they have provision for soule as well
as for body. *Ruth* dwelt well for outward respects while
shee dwelt in *Moab*, but when shee cometh to dwell in
Israel, shee is said to come under the wings of God: *Ruth*
2. 12. When God wrappes us in with his Ordinances, and
warmes us with the life and power of them as with wings,
there is a land of promise.

This may teach us all where we doe now dwell, or where
after wee may dwell, be sure you looke at every place appointed to you, from the hand of God: wee may not rush
into any place, and never say to God, By your leave; but we
must discerne how God appoints us this place. There is
poore comfort in sitting down in any place, that you cannot say, This place is appointed me of God. Canst thou
say that God spied out this place for thee, and there hath
setled thee above all hindrances? didst thou finde that
God made roome for thee either by lawfull descent, or
purchase, or gift, or other warrantable right? Why then
this is the place God hath appointed thee; here hee hath

made roome for thee, he hath placed thee in *Rehoboth*, in a peaceable place: This we must discerne, or els we are but intruders upon God. And when wee doe withall discerne, that God giveth us these outward blessings from his love in Christ, and maketh comfortable provision as well for our soule as for our bodies, by the meanes of grace, then doe we enjoy our present possession as well by gracious promise, as by the common, and just, and bountifull providence of the Lord. Or if a man doe remove, he must see that God hath espied out such a Countrey for him.

DOCUMENT 29

Indian Title

When the Glorious Revolution broke out in England in 1688–89, bringing the Protestant William of Orange and his consort Mary to the throne of England, and discarding the Catholic James II, New England reacted sympathetically and imprisoned the royal governor Sir Edmund Andros. Numerous pamphlets were published to justify the action, among them *The Revolution in New-England Justified*, published in 1691 and probably written by Edward Rawson, from which the following dissertation on Indian title is taken. The exchange between the minister, John Higginson, of Salem, and Governor Andros, brings out clearly the point of view of the colonists that their right derived from the occupation and use of the soil and from their purchase of the land from the Indians rather than from the grant of the English King. While this argument was designed primarily for use against the London authorities, it does, nevertheless, represent a sincerely held viewpoint on the part of many of New England's leaders. The quotation is from pp. 17–20 of the pamphlet as reproduced in Peter Force, comp., *Tracts and Other Papers, Relating Principally to the Origin, Settlement, and Progress of the Colonies in North America, from the Discovery of the Country to the Year 1776*, Vol. IV, no. 9 (reprinted, New York: Peter Smith, 1947).

That those who were in confederacy with Sir *Edmund Androsse* for the enriching themselves on the ruins of *New-England*, did *invade the property* as well as liberty of the subject, is in the next place to be cleared, and we trust will be made out beyond dispute. When they little imagined that there should ever be such a *revolution* in *England* as that which by means of his present majesty this nation is blest with, they feared not to declare their sentiments to the inexpressible exasperation of the people whom they were then domineering over. They gave out, that *now their charter was gone, all their lands were the king's*, that themselves did represent the king, and that therefore men that would have any legal title to their lands must take *patents* of them, on such terms as they should see meet to impose. What people that had the spirits of Englishmen, could endure this? That when they had at *vast charges of their own conquered a wilderness*, and been in possession of their estates forty, nay sixty years, that now a parcel of strangers, some of them indigent enough, must come and inherit all that the people now in *New-England* and their fathers before them, had laboured for! Let the whole nation judge, whether these men were not driving on a French design, and had not fairly erected a French government. And that our adversaries may not insult and say, these are words without proof, we shall here subjoin the testimonies of the reverend Mr. *Higginson*, and several other worthy persons, given in upon oath, concerning this matter.

Being called by those in present authority to give my testimony to the discourse between Sir *Edmund Androsse* and myself, when he came from the Indian war, as he passed through *Salem* going for *Boston* in *March* 1688–9, I cannot refuse it, and therefore declare as followeth, what was the substance of that discourse. Sir *Edmund Androsse* then governor being accompanied with the attorney-general *Graham*, secretary *West*, judge *Palmer*, the room being also full of other people, most of them his attendants, he was pleased to tell me, he would have my judgment about this question; *Whether all the lands in* New-England *were not the king's?* I told him I was surprized with such a question, and was not willing to speak to it; that being a minister, if it was a question about a matter of religion, I should not be averse, but this being a state matter, I did not look upon it as proper for me to declare my mind in it, therefore entreated again and again that I might be excused. Sir *Edmund Androsse* replied and urged me with much importunity, saying, Because you are a minister, therefore we desire to know your judgment in it, then I told him, if I must speak to it, I would only speak as a minister from scripture and reason, not medling with the law. He said, the king's attorney was present there to inform what was law. I then said, I did not understand that the lands of *New-England* were the king's, but the king's subjects, who had for more than sixty years had the possession and use of them by a twofold right warranted by the word of God. 1. By a right of just occupation from the grand charter in *Genesis* 1st and 9th chapters, whereby God gave the earth to the sons of *Adam* and *Noah*, to be subdued and replenished. 2. By a right of purchase from the Indians, who were native inhabitants, and had possession of the land before the English came hither, and that having lived here sixty years, I did certainly know that from the beginning of these plantations our fathers entered upon the land, partly as a wilderness and V*acuum Domicilium*, and partly by the consent of the Indians, and therefore care was taken to treat with them, and to gain their consent, giving them such a valuable consideration as was to their satisfaction, and this I told them I had the more certain knowledge of, because having learned the Indian language in my younger time, I was at several times made use of by the government, and by divers particular plantations as an interpreter in treating with the Indians about their lands, which being done and agreed on, the several townships and proportions of lands of particular men were ordered and settled by the government of the country, and therefore I did believe that the lands of *New-England* were the subjects properties, and not the king's lands. Sir *Edmund Androsse* and the rest replied, that the lands were the king's, and that he gave the lands within such limits to his subjects by a charter upon such conditions as were not performed, and therefore all the lands of *New-England* have returned to the king, and that the attorney general then present could tell what was law, who spake divers things to the same purpose as Sir *Edmund Androsse* had done, slighting what I had said, and vilifying the Indian title, saying, they were brutes, &c. and if we had possessed and used the land, they said we were the king's subjects, and what land the king's subjects have, they are the king's, and one of them used such an expression, *where-ever an Englishman sets his foot, all that he hath is the king's,* and more to the same purpose. I told them that so far as I understood, we received only the right and power of government from the king's charter within such limits and bounds, but the right of the land and soil we had received from God according to his grand charter to the sons of *Adam* and *Noah,* and with the consent of the native inhabitants as I had expressed before. They still insisted on the king's right to the land as before, whereupon I told them, I had heard it was a standing principle in law and reason, *nil dat qui non habet;* and from thence I propounded this argument, he that hath no right, can give no right to another, but the king had no right to the lands of *America* before the English came hither, therefore he could give no right to them. I told them, I knew not of any that could be pleaded but from a Popish principle, that christians have a right to the lands of heathen, upon which the Pope as the head of the christians had given the *West-Indies* to the king of *Spain,* but this was disowned by all protestants. Therefore I left it to them to affirm and prove the king's title. They replied and insisted much upon that, that the king had a right by his subjects coming and taking possession of this land. And at last Sir *Edmund Androsse* said with indignation, either you are subjects or you are rebels, intimating, as I understood him, according to the whole scope and tendency of his speeches and actions, that if we would not yield all the lands of *New-England* to be the king's, so as to take patents for lands, and to pay rent for the same, then we should not be accounted subjects but rebels, and treated accordingly.

There were many other various replies and answers on both sides, but this is the sum and substance of that discourse.

> JOHN HIGGINSON, aged seventy-four years.
> STEPHEN SEAWALL, aged thirty-two years.

John Higginson, minister in *Salem*, personally appeared before me, *December*, 24, 1689, and made oath to the truth of the abovesaid evidence.

> JOHN HATHORNE, assistant.

Captain *Stephen Seawall* of *Salem* appeared before me, *December* 24, 1689, and made oath to the truth of the abovesaid evidence.

> JOHN HATHORNE, assistant.

DOCUMENT 30

"The Animals, Vulgarly Called Indians"

West of the Alleghanies, the attitude toward the Indian in the eighteenth century was similar to that east of the mountains in the seventeenth. The Indian was a direct threat and disputed the entrance of the white man onto his territory. Representative of the western sentiment in the late eighteenth century was Hugh Henry Brackenridge, a resident of Pittsburgh and early literary figure of the young republic. The following quotation is from a letter written by Brackenridge transmitting the narratives of Dr. Knight, a physician, and John Slover, a frontiersman, who had been captured by the Indians following the defeat of Colonel Crawford's punitive expedition against the Indians on the Sandusky River in 1782, to the editor of the *Freeman's Journal or North American Intelligencer*. The narratives were printed serially in the *Freeman's Journal* and reprinted several times thereafter in pamphlet form. The present text of Brackenridge's letter is taken from the 1867 edition of the narratives published in Cincinnati under the title: *Indian Atrocities: Narratives of the Perils and Sufferings of Dr. Knight and John Slover, among the Indians, during the Revolutionary War*, pp. 62–72.

With the narrative enclosed, I subjoin some observations with regard to the animals, vulgarly called Indians. It is not my intention to write any labored essay; for at so great a distance from the city, and so long unaccustomed to write, I have scarcely resolution to put pen to paper. Having an opportunity to know something of the character of this race of men, from the deeds they perpetrate daily round me, I think proper to say something on the subject. Indeed, several years ago, and before I left your city, I had thought different from some others with respect to the right of soil, and the propriety of forming treaties and making peace with them.

In the United States Magazine in the year 1777, I published a dissertation denying them to have a right in the soil. I perceive a writer in your very elegant and useful paper, has taken up the same subject, under the signature of "Caractacus," and unanswerably shown, that their claim to the extensive countries of America, is wild and inadmissible. I will take the liberty in this place, to pursue this subject a little.

On what is their claim founded?—Occupancy. A wild Indian with his skin painted red, and a feather through his nose, has set his foot on the broad continent of North and South America; a second wild Indian with his ears cut in ringlets, or his nose slit like a swine or a malefactor, also sets his foot on the same extensive tract of soil. Let the first Indian make a talk to his brother, and bid him take his foot off the continent, for he being first upon it, had occupied the whole, to kill buffaloes, and tall elks with long horns. This claim in the reasoning of some men would be just, and the second savage ought to depart in his canoe, and seek a continent where no prior occupant claimed the soil. Is this claim of occupancy of a very early date? When Noah's three sons, Shem, Ham, and Japhet, went out to the three quarters of the old world, Ham to Africa, Shem to Asia, Japhet to Europe, did each claim a quarter of the world for his residence? Suppose Ham to have spent his time fishing or gathering oysters in the Red Sea, never once stretching his leg in a long walk to see his vast dominions, from the mouth of the Nile, across the mountains of Ethiopia and the river Niger to the Cape of Good Hope, where the Hottentots, a cleanly people, now stay; or supposing him, like a Scots pedlar, to have traveled over many thousand leagues of that country; would this give him a right to the soil? In the opinion of some men it would establish an exclusive right. Let a man in more modern times take a journey or voyage like Patrick Kennedy and others to the heads of the Mississippi or Missouri rivers, would he gain a right ever after to exclude all persons from drinking the waters of these streams? Might not a second Adam make a talk to them and say, is the whole of this water necessary to allay your thirst, and may I also drink of it?

The whole of this earth was given to man, and all descendants of Adam have a right to share it equally. There is no right of primogeniture in the laws of nature and of nations. There is reason that a tall man, such as the chaplain in the American army we call the High Priest, should have a large spot of ground to stretch himself upon; or that a man with a big belly, like a goodly alderman of London, should have a larger garden to produce beans and cabbage for his appetite, but that an agile, nimble runner, like an Indian called the Big Cat, at Fort Pitt, should have more than his neighbors, because he has traveled a great space, I can see no reason.

I have conversed with some persons and found their mistakes on this subject, to arise from a view of claims by individuals in a state of society, from holding a greater proportion of the soil than others; but this is according to the laws to which they have consented; an individual holding one acre, cannot encroach on him who has a thousand, because he is bound by the law which secures property in this unequal manner. This is the municipal law of the state under which he lives. The member of a distant society is not excluded by the laws from a right to the soil. He claims under the general law of nature, which gives a right, equally to all, to so much of the soil as is necessary for subsistence. Should a German from the closely peopled country of the Rhine, come into Pennsylvania, more thinly peopled, he would be justifiable in demanding a settlement, though his personal force would not be sufficient to effect it. It may be said that the cultivation or melioration of the earth, gives a property in it. No—if an individual has engrossed more than is necessary to produce grain for him to live upon, his useless gardens, fields and pleasure walks, may be seized upon by the person who, not finding convenient ground else-where, choose to till them for his support.

It is a usual way of destroying an opinion by pursuing it to its consequence. In the present case we may say, that if the visiting one acre of ground could give a right to it, the visiting of a million would give a right on the same principle; and thus a few surly ill natured men, might in the earlier ages have excluded half the human race from a settlement, or should any have fixed them-selves on a territory, visited before they had set a foot on it, they must be considered as invaders of the rights of others.

It is said that an individual, building a house or fabri-cating a machine has an exclusive right to it, and why not those who improve the earth? I would say, should man build houses on a greater part of the soil, than falls to his share, I would, in a state of nature, take away a proportion of the soil and the houses from him, but a machine or any work of art, does not lessen the means of subsistence to the human race, which an extensive oc-cupation of the soil does.

Claims founded on the first discovery of soil are futile. When gold, jewels, manufactures, or any work of men's hands is lost, the finder is entitled to some reward, that is, he has some claims on the thing found, for a share of it.

When by industry or the exercise of genius, something unusual is invented in medicine or in other matters, the author doubtless has a claim to an exclusive profit by it, but who will say the soil is lost, or that any one can found a claim by discovering it. The earth with its woods and rivers still exist, and the only advantage I would allow to any individual for having cast his eye first on any partic-ular part of it, is the privilege of making the first choice of situation. I would think the man a fool and unjust, who would exclude me from drinking the waters of the Mississippi river, because he had first seen it. He would be equally so who would exclude me from settling in the country west of the Ohio, because in chasing a buffalo he had been first over it.

The idea of an exclusive right to the soil in the natives had its origin in the policy of the first discoverers, the kings of Europe. Should they deny the right of the natives from their first treading on the continent, they would take away the right of discovery in themselves, by sailing on the coast. As the vestige of the moccasin in one case gave a right, so the cruise in the other was the foundation of a claim.

Those who under these kings, derived grants were led to countenance the idea, for otherwise why should kings grant or they hold extensive tracts of country. Men become enslaved to an opinion that has been long entertained. Hence it is that many wise and good men will talk of the right of savages to immense tracts of soil.

What use do these ring, streaked, spotted and speckled cattle make of the soil? Do they till it? Revelation said to man, "Thou shalt till the ground." This alone is human life. It is favorable to population, to science, to the information of a human mind in the worship of God. Warburton has well said, that before you can make an Indian a christian you must teach him agriculture and reduce him to a civilized life. To live by tilling is *more humano*, by hunting is *more bestiarum*. I would as soon admit a right in the buffalo to grant lands, as in Killbuck, the Big Cat, the Big Dog, or any of the ragged wretches that are called chiefs and sachems. What would you think of going to a big lick or place where the beasts collect to lick saline nitrous earth and water, and addressing yourself to a great buffalo to grant you land? It is true he could not make the mark of the stone or the mountain reindeer, but he could set his cloven foot to the instrument like the great Ottomon, the father of the Turks, when he put his signature to an instrument, he put his large hand and spreading fingers in the ink and set his mark to the parchment. To see how far the folly of some would go, I had once a thought of supplicating some of the great elks or buffaloes that run through the woods, to make me a grant of a hundred thousand acres of land and prove he had brushed the weeds with his tail, and run fifty miles.

I wonder if Congress or the different States would recognize the claim? I am so far from thinking the Indians have a right to the soil, that not having made a better use of it for many hundred years, I conceive they have forfeited all pretence to claim, and ought to be driven from it.

With regard to forming treaties or making peace with this race, there are many ideas:

They have the shapes of men and may be of the human species, but certainly in their present state they approach nearer the character of Devils; take an Indian, is there any faith in him? Can you bind him by favors? Can you trust his word or confide in his promise? When he makes war upon you, when he takes you prisoner and has you in his power will he spare you? In this he departs from the law of nature, by which, according to baron Montesquieu and every other man who thinks on the subject, it is unjustifiable to take away the life of him who submits; the conqueror in doing otherwise becomes a murderer, who ought to be put to death. On this principle are not the whole Indian nations murderers?

Many of them may have not had an opportunity of putting prisoners to death, but the sentiment which they entertain leads them invariably to this when they have it in their power or judge it expedient; these principles constitute them murderers, and they ought to be prevented from carrying them into execution, as we would prevent a common homicide, who should be mad enough to conceive himself justifiable in killing men.

The tortures which they exercise on the bodies of their prisoners, justify extermination. Gelo of Syria made war on the Carthaginians because they oftentimes burnt human victims, and made peace with them on conditions they would cease from this unnatural and cruel practice. If we could have any faith in the promises they make we could suffer them to live, provided they would only make war amongst themselves, and abandon their hiding or lurking on the pathways of our citizens, emigrating unarmed and defenceless inhabitants; and murdering men, women and children in a defenceless situation; and on their ceasing in the meantime to raise arms no more among the American Citizens.

DOCUMENT 31

John Marshall and the Cherokees

The momentous judicial decisions by which the diminishing power of the Indians was adjusted to the framework of American law are largely the work of John Marshall, Chief Justice of the United States. Below are quotations from Marshall's opinions in two of the most significant cases: *The Cherokee Nation* v. *The State of Georgia* (1831) and *Samuel A. Worcester* v. *The State of Georgia* (1832). They are found in U. S. Supreme Court *Reports,* 5 Peters 15–18, and 6 Peters 559–61. The attempt of Marshall to frustrate the effort of Georgia to exert its power over the Cherokee Nation was ignored by the Chief Executive, Andrew Jackson.

[*Cherokee Nation* v. *State of Georgia*]

Mr. Chief Justice *Marshall* delivered the opinion of the court:

This bill is brought by the Cherokee Nation, praying an injunction to restrain the State of Georgia from the execution of certain laws of that State, which as it is alleged, go directly to annihilate the Cherokees as a political society, and to seize, for the use of Georgia, the lands of the nation which have been assured to them by the United States in solemn treaties repeatedly made and still in force.

If the courts were permitted to indulge their sympathies, a case better calculated to excite them can scarcely be imagined. A people once numerous, powerful, and truly independent, found by our ancestors in the quiet and uncontrolled possession of an ample domain, gradually sinking beneath our superior policy, our arts and our arms, have yielded their lands by successive treaties, each of which contains a solemn guarantee of the residue, until they retain no more of their formerly extensive territory than is deemed necessary to their comfortable subsistence. To preserve this remnant the present application is made.

Before we can look into the merits of the case, a preliminary inquiry presents itself. Has this court jurisdiction of the cause?

The third article of the Constitution describes the extent of the judicial power. The second section closes an enumeration of the cases to which it is extended, with "controversies" "between the State or the citizens thereof, and foreign states, citizens, or subjects." A subsequent clause of the same section gives the Supreme Court original jurisdiction in all cases in which a state shall be a party. The party defendant may then unquestionably be sued in this court. May the plaintiff sue in it? Is the Cherokee Nation a foreign state in the sense in which that term is used in the Constitution?

The counsel for the plaintiffs have maintained the affirmative of this proposition with great earnestness and ability. So much of the argument as was intended to prove the character of the Cherokees as a State, as a distinct political society separated from others, capable of managing its own affairs and governing itself, has, in the opinion of a majority of the judges, been completely successful. They have been uniformly treated as a State from the settlement of our country. The numerous treaties made with them by the United States recognize them as a people capable of maintaining the relations of peace and war, of being responsible in their political character for any violation of their engagements, or for any aggression committed on the citizens of the United States by any individual of their community. Laws have been enacted in the spirit of these treaties. The acts of our government plainly recognize the Cherokee Nation as a State, and the courts are bound by those acts.

A question of much more difficulty remains. Do the

Cherokees constitute a foreign state in the sense of the Constitution?

The counsel have shown conclusively that they are not a State of the Union, and have insisted that individually they are aliens, not owing allegiance to the United States. An aggregate of aliens composing a State must, they say be a foreign state. Each individual being foreign, the whole must be foreign.

This argument is imposing, but we must examine it more closely before we yield to it. The condition of the Indians in relation to the United States is perhaps unlike that of any other two people in existence. In the general, nations not owing a common allegiance are foreign to each other. The term "foreign nation" is, with strict propriety, applicable by either to the other. But the relation of the Indians to the United States is marked by peculiar and cardinal distinctions which exist nowhere else.

The Indian Territory is admitted to compose part of the United States. In all our maps, geographical treaties, histories and laws, it is so considered. In all our intercourse with foreign nations, in our commercial regulations, in any attempt at intercourse between Indians, and foreign nations, they are considered as within the jurisdictional limits of the United States, subject to many of those restraints which are imposed upon our own citizens. They acknowledge themselves in their treaties to be under the protection of the United States; they admit that the United States shall have the sole and exclusive right of regulating the trade with them, and managing all their affairs as they think proper; and the Cherokees in particular were allowed by the treaty of Hopewell, which preceded the Constitution, "to send a deputy of their choice, whenever they think fit, to Congress." Treaties were made with some tribes by the State of New York under a then unsettled construction of the confederation, by which they ceded all their lands to that State, taking back a limited grant to themselves, in which they admit their dependence.

Though the Indians are acknowledged to have an unquestionable, and, heretofore, unquestioned right to the lands they occupy until that right shall be extinguished by a voluntary cession to our government, yet it may well be doubted whether those tribes which reside within the acknowledged boundaries of the United States can, with strict accuracy, be denominated foreign nations. They may, more correctly, perhaps, be denominated domestic dependent nations. They occupy a territory to which we assert a title independent of their will, which must take effect in point of possession when their right of possession ceases. Meanwhile they are in a state of pupilage. Their relation to the United States resembles that of a ward to his guardian.

They look to our government for protection; rely upon its kindness and its power; appeal to it for relief to their wants; and address the President as their great father. They and their country are considered by foreign nations, as well as by ourselves, as being so completely under the sovereignty and dominion of the United States, that any attempt to acquire their lands, or to form a political connection with them, would be considered by all as an invasion of our territory, and an act of hostility.

These considerations go far to support the opinion that the framers of our Constitution had not the Indian tribes in view when they opened the courts of the Union to controversies between a State or the citizens thereof, and foreign states.

In considering this subject, the habits and usages of the Indians in their intercourse with their white neighbors ought not to be entirely disregarded. At the time the Constitution was framed, the idea of appealing to an American court of justice for an assertion of right or a redress of wrong, had perhaps never entered the mind of an Indian or of his tribe. Their appeal was to the tomahawk, or to the government. This was well understood by the statesmen who framed the Constitution of the United States, and might furnish some reason for omitting to enumerate them among the parties who might sue in the courts of the Union. Be this as it may, the peculiar relations be-

tween the United States and the Indians occupying our
territory are such that we should feel much difficulty
in considering them as designated by the term "foreign
State," were there no other part of the Constitution which
might shed light on the meaning of these words. But we
think that in construing them, considerable aid is furnished by that clause in the eighth section of the third
article, which empowers Congress to "regulate commerce
with foreign nations, and among the several States, and
with the Indian tribes."

In this clause they are as clearly contradistinguished by
a name appropriate to themselves from foreign nations as
from the several States composing the Union. They are
designated by a distinct appellation; and as this appellation can be applied to neither of the others, neither can
the appellation distinguishing either of the others be in
fair construction applied to them. The objects to which
the power of regulating commerce might be directed, are
divided into three distinct classes—foreign nations, the
several States, and Indian tribes. When forming this article, the convention considered them as entirely distinct.
We cannot assume that the distinction was lost in fram-
ing a subsequent article, unless there be something in its
language to authorize the assumption.

[Worcester v. Georgia]

The Indian nations had always been considered as distinct, independent political communities, retaining their
original natural rights, as the undisputed possessors of the
soil from time immemorial, with the single exception of
that imposed by irresistible power, which excluded them
from intercourse with any other European potentate than
the first discoverer of the coast of the particular region
claimed: and this was a restriction which those European
potentates imposed on themselves, as well as on the Indians. The very term "nation," so generally applied to
them, means "a people distinct from others." The Constitution, by declaring treaties already made, as well as those

to be made, to be the supreme law of the land, has adopted and sanctioned the previous treaties with the Indian nations, and consequently admits their rank among those powers who are capable of making treaties. The words "treaty" and "nation" are words of our own language, selected in our diplomatic and legislative proceedings, by ourselves, having each a definite and well understood meaning. We have applied them to Indians, as we have applied them to the other nations of the earth. They are applied to all in the same sense.

Georgia herself has furnished conclusive evidence that her former opinions on this subject concurred with those entertained by her sister States, and by the government of the United States. Various acts of her Legislature have been cited in the argument, including the contract of cession made in the year 1802, all tending to prove her acquiescence in the universal conviction that the Indian nations possessed a full right to the lands they occupied, until that right should be extinguished by the United States, with their consent; that their territory was separated from that of any State within whose chartered limits they might reside, by a boundary line, established by treaties; that, within their boundary, they possessed rights with which no State could interfere, and that the whole power of regulating the intercourse with them was vested in the United States. A review of these acts, on the part of Georgia, would occupy too much time, and is the less necessary because they have been accurately detailed in the argument at the bar. Her new series of laws, manifesting her abandonment of these opinions, appears to have commenced in December, 1828.

In opposition to this original right, possessed by the undisputed occupants of every country; to this recognition of that right, which is evidenced by our history, in every change through which we have passed, is placed the charters granted by the monarch of a distant and distinct region, parceling out a territory in possession of others whom he could not remove and did not attempt to re-

move, and the cession made of his claims by the Treaty
of Peace.

The actual state of things at the time, and all history
since, explain these charters; and the King of Great Britain, at the Treaty of Peace, could cede only what belonged
to his crown. These newly asserted titles can derive no aid
from the articles so often repeated in Indian treaties; extending to them, first, the protection of Great Britain,
and afterwards that of the United States. These articles
are associated with others, recognizing their title to self-
government. The very fact of repeated treaties with them
recognizes it; and the settled doctrine of the law of nations is that a weaker power does not surrender its independence—its right to self-government, by associating with
a stronger and taking its protection. A weak State in order
to provide for its safety, may place itself under the protection of one more powerful without stripping itself of
the right of government, and ceasing to be a State. Examples of this kind are not wanting in Europe. "Tributary
and feudatory states," says Vattel, "do not thereby cease
to be sovereign and independent states so long as self-
government and sovereign and independent authority are
left in the administration of the state." At the present
day, more than one State may be considered as holding
its right of self-government under the guaranty and protection of one or more allies.

The Cherokee nation, then, is a distinct community,
occupying its own territory, with boundaries accurately
described, in which the laws of Georgia can have no force,
and which the citizens of Georgia have no right to enter
but with the assent of the Cherokees themselves or in con-
formity with treaties and with the acts of Congress. The
whole intercourse between the United States and this nation is, by our Constitution and laws, vested in the government of the United States.

The act of the State of Georgia under which the plaintiff
in error was prosecuted is consequently void, and the
judgment a nullity.

Westward the Star of Empire

One of the earliest writers to make the youthful
United States of America conscious of its manifest destiny was Timothy Flint, a Massachusetts missionary
who published the *Western Monthly Review*, 1827–
30, in an attempt to interpret the West to the East, and
who wrote romantic stories of frontier life. In his
*Indian Wars of the West; containing Biographical
Sketches of Those Pioneers who Headed the Western
Settlers in Repelling the Attacks of the Savages*, pp. 36–
37 (Cincinnati: 1833), Flint commented upon the role
of the Indian in the destiny of the American nation.

A dreary uniformity of incident marks all the story of
the commencing settlements in every part of our country,
from Plymouth to Jamestown, and from the lakes to the
Balize. There are examples, indeed, which present the
French forming colonies among the Indians, and remaining in profound peace. But it was by amalgamating with
them, losing their own identity, and becoming savages.
The case of the colony of William Penn, presents only a
seeming exception. It grew out of circumstances, that
never occurred before or since; and, when analyzed, will
be found to be no anomaly from the general aspect.

In the whole history of the incipient settlement of our
country, not one solitary instance of an attempt to settle
an unoccupied tract, claimed by the natives, is to be
found, which was not succeeded by all the revolting details of Indian warfare. It is of little importance to en-
quire, which party was the aggressor. The natives were not
sufficient civilians to distinguish between the right of
empire and the right of soil. Beside a repulsion of nature,

an incompatability of character and pursuit, they constantly saw in every settler a new element to effect their expulsion from their native soul. Our industry, fixed residences, modes, laws, institutions, schools, religion, rendered an union with them as incompatible as with animals of another nature. The crime of aggression, force, and final extinction, charged upon the whites, in relation to the natives, and discussed on the narrow principles of crimination and recrimination, has only been discussed hitherto in a manner worthy of congress wranglers, and in a style of narrow puerility. In the unchangeable order of things, two such races can not exist together, each preserving its co-ordinate identity. Either this great continent, in the order of Providence, should have remained in the occupancy of half a million of savages, engaged in everlasting conflicts of their peculiar warfare with each other, or it must have become, as it has, the domain of civilized millions. It is in vain to charge upon the latter race results, which grew out of the laws of nature, and the universal march of human events. Let the same occupancy of the American wilderness by the municipal European be repeated, if it could be, under the control of the most philanthropic eulogists of the savages, and every reasoning mind will discover, that in the gradual ascendency of the one race, the decline of the other must have been a consequence, and that substantially the same annals would be repeated, as the dark and revolting incidents which we have to record. We do not say, that the aggression has not been in innumerable instances on the part of the whites. We do not deny, that the white borderers have too often been more savage, than the Indians themselves. We abhor injustice as much when practiced towards the whites as the Indians; and we affirm an undoubting belief, from no unfrequent nor inconsiderable means of observation, that aggression has commenced in the account current of mutual crime, as a hundred to one on the part of the Indians. It has been the intercourse of a race more calculating, more wise, with ampler means, it is admitted, but without the instinct of gratuitous cruelty, or a natural

propensity to war as a pursuit, with another race organized
to the love of the horrible excitement of war and murder
for their own sake. Circumstances, fear, impotence may
restrain them. But still in the Indian animal and moral
structure, their ancient propensities would be found, we
doubt not, as vigorous as ever among those remnants the
most subdued and modified by our institutions. Give
them scope, development, and an object, place them in
view of an equal or inferior enemy, and their instinctive
nature would again raise the war-hoop, and wield the
scalping knife, and renew the Indian warfare of the by-
gone days.

DOCUMENT 33

"American Progress"

Interest in the Great West was stimulated by a number of publishers, among whom was George A. Crofutt of New York, who in 1873 published the chromolithograph reproduced in Plate 9, following page 134. The explanatory text printed on the reverse side of the lithograph, giving a clear explanation of the metaphysical assumptions underlying westward expansion, is reproduced below. The document, issued from the offices of Crofutt's *Western World*, is in the Prints and Photographs Division, Library of Congress, Washington, D.C.

American Progress!

Subject, *The United States of America*

This rich and wonderful country—the progress of which at the present time, is the wonder of the old world—was, until recently, inhabited exclusively by the lurking savage and wild beasts of prey. If the rapid progress of the "Great West" has surprised our people, what will those of other countries think of the "*Far* West," which is destined, at an early day, to be the vast granary, as it is now the great treasure chamber of our country? How this change has been wrought, and by whom, is illustrated by our Chromo,

"AMERICAN PROGRESS."

Purely National in design, this beautiful painting represents the United States' portion of the American continent in its beauty and variety, from the Atlantic to the Pacific Ocean, illustrating at a glance the grand drama of Progress in the civilization, settlement and history of our own happy land.

In the foreground the central and principal figure, a beautiful and charming Female, is floating Westward through the air bearing on her forehead the "Star of Empire." She has left the cities of the East far behind, crossed the Alleghanies and the "Father of Waters," and still her march is Westward. In her right hand she carries a book —Common Schools—the emblem of Education and the testimonial of our National enlightenment, while with the left hand she unfolds and stretches the slender wires of the Telegraph, that are to flash intelligence throughout the land. On the right of the picture is a city, steamships, manufactories, schools and churches, over which beams of light are streaming and filling the air—indicative of civilization. The general tone of the picture on the left declares darkness, waste and confusion. From the city proceed the three great continental lines of railway, passing the frontier settlers' rude cabin, and tending toward the Western Ocean. Next to these are the transportation wagons, overland stage, hunters, gold seekers, pony express, the pioneer emigrant and the war-dance of the "noble red man." Fleeing from "Progress," and towards the blue waters of the Pacific, which shows itself on the left of the picture beyond the snow-capped summits of the Sierra Nevadas, are the Indians, buffaloes, wild horses, bears, and other game, moving Westward—ever Westward the Indians, with their squaws, papooses, and "pony lodges," turn their despairing faces towards, as they flee from the presence of, the wondrous vision. The "Star" is *too much for them.*

What American man, woman or child, does not feel a heart-throb of exultations as they think of the glorious achievements of *Progress* since the landing of the Pilgrim Fathers, on stanch old Plymouth Rock! What home, from the miner's humble cabin to the stately marble mansion of the capitalist, should be without this *Great* National Picture, which illustrates in the most artistic manner all the gigantic results of American Brains and Hands! Who would not have such a beautiful token to remind them of our country's grandeur and enterprise which have caused the mighty wilderness to blossom like the rose!!! One of the best art critics has pronounced this picture *"one of the grandest conceptions of the age."*

"American Progress" is 12 × 16 inches in size, painted in 19 colors, in the best manner, and is as richly worth $10 each, as any chromo that has ever been offered for sale in this country.

DOCUMENT 34

"These Foolish Sentimentalists . . ."

Theodore Roosevelt occupies a special place in the story of Indian-white relations not only as a statesman, but as a historian and also as a representative of the vigorous, self-confident America of the turn of the century. Roosevelt pulls no punches in denouncing "sentimentalists" such as Helen Hunt Jackson for what he asserts is their ignorance of the facts of white treatment of the Indian. Nor is he less positive in his conviction that the Indians never "owned" the land they occupied, an occupation Roosevelt persisted in referring to as a nomadic existence based on hunting. Roosevelt would take the lot: Indian, white hunter, and Eastern humanitarian, give them a sound thrashing, and get on with the real business of living. The following passage is from Roosevelt's history, *The Winning of the West*, 4 vols.; Vol. I, pp. 331–35 (Appendix A to Chapter iv) (New York: 1889–96).

It is greatly to be wished that some competent person would write a full and true history of our national dealings with the Indians. Undoubtedly the latter have often suffered terrible injustice at our hands. A number of instances, such as the conduct of the Georgians to the Cherokees in the early part of the present century, or the whole treatment of Chief Joseph and his Nez Percés, might be mentioned, which are indelible blots on our fair fame; and yet, in describing our dealings with the red men as a whole, historians do us much less than justice.

It was wholly impossible to avoid conflicts with the weaker race, unless we were willing to see the American continent fall into the hands of some other strong power;

and even had we adopted such a ludicrous policy, the Indians themselves would have made war upon us. It cannot be too often insisted that they did not own the land; or, at least, that their ownership was merely such as that claimed often by our own white hunters. If the Indians really owned Kentucky in 1775, then in 1776 it was the property of Boon and his associates; and to dispossess one party was as great a wrong as to dispossess the other. To recognize the Indian ownership of the limitless prairies and forests of this continent—that is, to consider the dozen squalid savages who hunted at long intervals over a territory of a thousand square miles as owning it outright—necessarily implies a similar recognition of the claims of every white hunter, squatter, horse-thief, or wandering cattle-man. Take as an example the country round the Little Missouri. When the cattle-men, the first actual settlers, came into this land in 1882, it was already scantily peopled by a few white hunters and trappers. The latter were extremely jealous of intrusion; they had held their own in spite of the Indians, and, like the Indians, the inrush of settlers and the consequent destruction of the game meant their own undoing; also, again like the Indians, they felt that their having hunted over the soil gave them a vague prescriptive right to its sole occupation, and they did their best to keep actual settlers out. In some cases, to avoid difficulty, their nominal claims were bought up; generally, and rightly, they were disregarded. Yet they certainly had as good a right to the Little Missouri country as the Sioux have to most of the land on their present reservations. In fact, the mere statement of the case is sufficient to show the absurdity of asserting that the land really belonged to the Indians. The different tribes have always been utterly unable to define their own boundaries. Thus the Delawares and Wyandots, in 1785, though entirely separate nations, claimed and, in a certain sense, occupied almost exactly the same territory.

Moreover, it was wholly impossible for our policy to be always consistent. Nowadays we undoubtedly ought to break up the great Indian reservations, disregard the tribal governments, allot the land in severalty (with, however, only a limited power of alienation), and treat the Indians as we do other citizens, with certain exceptions, for their sakes as well as ours. But this policy, which it would be wise to follow now, would have been wholly impracticable a century since. Our central government was then too weak either effectively to control its own members or adequately to punish aggressions made upon them; and even if it had been strong, it would probably have proved impossible to keep entire order over such a vast, sparsely-peopled frontier, with such turbulent elements on both sides. The Indians could not be treated as individuals at that time. There was no possible alternative, therefore, to treating their tribes as nations, exactly as the French and English had done before us. Our difficulties were partly inherited from these, our predecessors, were partly caused by our own misdeeds, but were mainly the inevitable result of the conditions under which the problem had to be solved; no human wisdom or virtue could have worked out a peaceable solution. As a nation, our Indian policy is to be blamed, because of the weakness it displayed, because of its shortsightedness, and its occasional leaning to the policy of the sentimental humanitarians; and we have often promised what was impossible to perform; but there has been little wilful wrong-doing. Our government almost always tried to act fairly by the tribes; the governmental agents (some of whom have been dishonest, and others foolish, but who, as a class, have been greatly traduced), in their reports, are far more apt to be unjust to the whites than to the reds; and the Federal authorities, though unable to prevent much of the injustice, still did check and control the white borderers very much more effectually than the Indian sachems and war-chiefs controlled their young braves. The tribes were warlike and bloodthirsty, jealous of each other and of the whites; they claimed the land for their hunting grounds, but their claims all conflicted with one another; their knowledge of their own boundaries was so indefinite that they were always willing, for inadequate compensation, to sell land to which they had merely the vaguest title; and yet, when once they had received the goods, were generally reluctant to make over even what they could; they coveted the goods and scalps of the whites, and the young warriors were always on the alert to commit outrages when they could do it with impunity. On the other hand, the evil-disposed whites regarded the Indians as fair game for robbery and violence of any kind; and the far larger number of well-disposed men, who would not willingly wrong any Indian, were themselves maddened by the memories of hideous injuries received. They bitterly resented the action of the government, which, in their eyes, failed to properly protect them, and yet sought to keep them out of waste, uncultivated lands which they did not regard as being any more the property of the Indians than of their own hunters. With the best intentions, it was wholly impossible for any government to evolve order out of such a chaos without resort to the ultimate arbitrator—the sword.

The purely sentimental historians take no account of the difficulties under which we labored, nor of the countless wrongs and provocations we endured, while grossly magnifying the already lamentably large number of injuries for which we really deserve to be held responsible. To get a fair idea of the Indians of the present day, and of our dealings with them, we have fortunately one or two excellent books, notably "Hunting Grounds of the Great West," and "Our Wild Indians," by Col. Richard I. Dodge (Hartford, 1882), and "Massacres of the Mountains," by J. P. Dunn (New York, 1886). As types of the opposite class, which are worse than valueless, and which nevertheless might cause some hasty future historian, unacquainted with the facts, to fall into grievous error, I may mention, "A Century of Dishonor," by H. H. (Mrs. Helen Hunt Jackson), and "Our Indian Wards," (Geo. W. Manypenny). The latter is a mere spiteful diatribe against various army officers, and neither its manner nor its matter warrants more than an allusion. Mrs. Jackson's book is capable of doing more harm because it is written in good English, and because the author, who had lived a pure and

PLATE 1. *A Renaissance Gentleman in America.* Courtesy of the Library of Congress.

C.Smith taketh the King of Pamavnkee prisoner 1608

PLATE 2. Captain John Smith. Courtesy of the Library of Congress.

Ætatis suæ 21. Aᵒ.1616.

Matoaks als Rebecka daughter to the mighty Prince
Powhatan Emperour of Attanoughkomouck als Virginia
converted and baptized in the Christian faith, and
Wife to the worᵗʰ Mʳ Tho: Rolff.

PLATE. 3. *Pocahontas*, seventeenth century. Courtesy of the National Gallery of Art, Washington, D.C.

PLATE 4. *Pocahontas*, eighteenth-century painting by Mary Woodbury. Courtesy of the Massachusetts Historical Society.

PLATE 5. *Pocahontas*, nineteenth-century painting by Robert Matthew Sully. Courtesy of the State Historical Society of Wisconsin.

PLATE 6. *Peace Pipes.* Courtesy of the Smithsonian Institution, Washington, D.C.

PLATE 7. *An Iroquois "False Face."* Courtesy of the Smithsonian Institution, Washington, D.C.

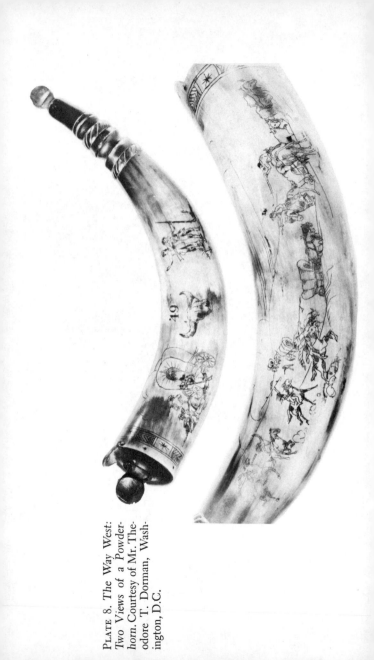

PLATE 8. *The Way West: Two Views of a Powderhorn.* Courtesy of Mr. Theodore T. Dorman, Washington, D.C.

PLATE 9. "American Progress." Courtesy of the Library of Congress.

PLATE 10. Trading with the Indians. Courtesy of the Library of Congress.

PLATE 11. *Indian Weather Vane* by Shem Drowne, 1742. Courtesy of the Massachusetts Historical Society.

PLATE 12. The *Paxton Boys at Work.* Courtesy of the Library of Congress.

PLATE 13. *Thayendanegea (Joseph Brant)*, by Gilbert Stuart. Photograph by courtesy of the New York State Historical Association, Cooperstown, New York.

PLATE 14. *Captured by Indians.* Courtesy of the Library of Congress.

PLATE 15. Captured by Indians. Courtesy of the Library of Congress.

PLATE 16. *The Battle of the Little Big Horn.* Courtesy of the Library of Congress.

noble life, was intensely in earnest in what she wrote, and had the most praiseworthy purpose—to prevent our committing any more injustice to the Indians. This was all most proper; every good man or woman should do whatever is possible to make the government treat the Indians of the present time in the fairest and most generous spirit, and to provide against any repetition of such outrages as were inflicted upon the Nez Percés and upon part of the Cheyennes, or the wrongs with which the civilized nations of the Indian territory are sometimes threatened. The purpose of the book is excellent, but the spirit in which it is written cannot be called even technically honest. As a polemic, it is possible that it did not do harm (though the effect of even a polemic is marred by hysterical indifference to facts.) As a history it would be beneath criticism, were it not that the high character of the author and her excellent literary work in other directions have given it a fictitious value and made it much quoted by the large class of amiable but maudlin fanatics concerning whom it may be said that the excellence of their intentions but indifferently atones for the invariable folly and ill effect of their actions. It is not too much to say that the book is thoroughly untrustworthy from cover to cover, and that not a single statement it contains should be accepted without independent proof; for even those that are not absolutely false, are often as bad on account of so much of the truth having been suppressed. One effect of this is of course that the author's recitals of the many real wrongs of Indian tribes utterly fail to impress us, because she lays quite as much stress on those that are non-existent, and on the equally numerous cases where the wrong-doing was wholly the other way. To get an idea of the value of the work, it is only necessary to compare her statements about almost any tribe with the real facts, choosing at random; for instance, compare her accounts of the Sioux and the plains tribes generally, with those given by Col. Dodge in his two books; or her recital of the Sandy Creek massacre with the facts as stated by Mr. Dunn—who is apt, if any thing, to lean to the Indian's side.

These foolish sentimentalists not only write foul slanders about their own countrymen, but are themselves the worst possible advisers on any point touching Indian management. They would do well to heed General Sheridan's bitter words, written when many Easterners were clamoring against the army authorities because they took partial vengeance for a series of brutal outrages: "I do not know how far these humanitarians should be excused on account of their ignorance; but surely it is the only excuse that can give a shadow of justification for aiding and abetting such horrid crimes."

Chapter IV

The Trade Nexus

"There'll always be a huckster" is, perhaps, as appropriate a phrase for the seventeenth century as for the twentieth. The economic motive may not always be the dominating motive of human affairs, but it is certainly always present. It was present with the first explorers, prepared as they were with mirrors, glass beads, colored cloth, and other materials that had been found attractive in Africa. It was present with the English promoters, like Hakluyt, who saw the New World as a vast market for English cloth and manufactured goods. Trade continued to provide the basis for meeting the needs of the explorers for food and exportable wealth until the gradual extermination of the fur-bearing animals and the shifts of European fashion reduced the enormous importance of the fur trade in the nineteenth century. Some of the varied aspects of the commercial bonds between white and Indian are detailed in the following excerpts.

Trading in the Bay of Chaleur, July 8, 1534

The following passage is from the account of the voyage of Jacques Cartier of St. Malo who, with royal support, left France on April 20, 1534, with two vessels, to continue the discoveries begun by Verrazano in 1524. The caution of the Indians of the area derives, in part, from the firing of cannon and use of lances which the French had employed four days earlier to frighten away the great numbers of natives who surrounded their boat. The passage, and bibliographical information concerning the account, is taken from Henry S. Burrage, ed., *Early English and French Voyages, Chiefly from Hakluyt, 1534–1608*, pp. 20–22; Original Narratives of Early American History series (New York: Charles Scribner's Sons, 1906).

The next day part of the saide wilde men with nine of their boates came to the point and entrance of the Creeke, where we with our ships were at road. We being advertised of their comming, went to the point where they were with our boates: but so soone as they saw us, they began to flee, making signes that they came to trafique with us, shewing us such skinnes as they cloth themselves withall, which are of small value. We likewise made signes unto them, that we wished them no evill: and in signe thereof two of our men ventured to go on land to them, and carry them knives with other Iron wares, and a red hat to give unto their Captaine. Which when they saw, they also came on land, and brought some of their skinnes, and so began to deale with us, seeming to be very glad to have our iron ware and other things, stil dancing with many other ceremonies, as with their hands to cast Sea water on their heads. They gave us whatsoever they had, not keeping any thing, so that they were constrained to go back againe naked, and made signes that the next day they would come againe, and bring more skinnes with them.

How that we having sent two of our men on land with wares, there came about 300. wilde men with great gladnesse. Of the qualitie of the countrey, what it bringeth forth, and of the Bay called Baie du Chaleur, or The Bay of heat.

Upon Thursday being the eight of the moneth, because the winde was not good to go out with our ships, we set our boates in a readinesse to goe to discover the said Bay, and that day wee went 25. leagues within it. The next day the wind and weather being faire, we sailed until noone, in which time we had notice of a great part of the said Bay, and how that over the low lands, there were other lands with high mountaines: but seeing that there was no passage at all, wee began to turne back againe, taking our way along the coast: and sayling, we saw certaine wilde men that stood upon the shoare of a lake, that is among the low grounds, who were making fires and smokes: wee went thither, and found that there was a channel of the sea that did enter into the lake, and setting our boats at one of the banks of the chanell, the wilde men with one of their boates came unto us, and brought up pieces of Seales ready sodden, putting them upon pieces of wood: then retiring themselves, they would make signes unto us, that they did give them us. We sent two men unto them with hatchets, knives, beads, and other such like ware, whereat they were very glad, and by and by in clusters they came to the shore where wee were, with their boates, bringing with them skinnes and other such things as they had, to have of our wares. They were more than 300. men, women, and children: Some of the women which came not over, wee might see stand up to the knees in water, singing and dancing: the other that had passed the river where we were, came very friendly to us, rubbing our armes with their owne handes, then would they lift them up toward heaven, shewing many signes of gladnesse: and in such

wise were wee assured one of another, that we very famil-
iarly began to trafique for whatsoever they had, til they
had nothing but their naked bodies; for they gave us all
whatsoever they had, and that was but of small value. We
perceived that this people might very easily be converted
to our Religion. They goe from place to place. They live
onely with fishing. They have an ordinarie time to fish for
their provision. The countrey is hotter than the countrey of
Spaine, and the fairest that can possibly be found, altogether smooth, and level. There is no place be it never so
little, but it hath some trees (yea albeit it be sandie) or
else is full of wilde corne, that hath an eare like unto Rie:
the corne is like oates, and smal peason as thicke as if they
had bene sowen and plowed, white and red gooseberies,
strawberies, blackberies, white and red Roses, with many
other floures of very sweet and pleasant smell. There be
also many goodly medowes full of grasse, and lakes wherein
great plentie of salmons be. They call a hatchet in their
tongue Cochi, and a knife Bacon: we named it The bay of
heat.

DOCUMENT 36

Hakluyt's Plan of Settlement

Richard Hakluyt, by his tireless efforts to record *The Principal Navigations, Voiages, Traffiques and Discoveries of the English Nation,* published in various editions in London in the late sixteenth century, helped bring on the settlement of North America by the English. In his "Discourse of Western Planting," written in 1584 at the request of Sir Walter Raleigh, Hakluyt gave ample instructions as to how the "planting" of colonies should proceed. In the following passage he discusses how best to achieve the ends of "traficque"—that is, trade—in the New World. The excerpt is taken from *The Original Writings & Correspondence of the Two Richard Hakluyts,* with an introduction and notes by E. G. R. Taylor; 2 vols. (Hakluyt Society Works, Series II, nos. 76 and 77), Document 46, pp. 274–75 (London: 1935).

Havinge by gods goodd guidinge and mercifull direction atchieved happely this presente westerne discoverye, after the seekinge the advauncemente of the kingedome of Christe, the seconde chefe and principall ende of the same is traficque, which consisteth in the vent [sale] of the masse of our clothes and other commodities of England, and in receivinge backe of the nedeful commodities that wee nowe receave from all other places of the worlde. But forasmoche as this is a matter of greate ymportaunce and a thinge of so greate gaine as forren princes will stomacke at [resent], this one thing is to be don, withoute which it were in vaine to goe aboute this, and that is the matter of plantinge and fortificacion, withoute due consideracion whereof in vaine were it to thinck of the former. And

therefore upon the firste said viewe taken, by the shippes
that are to be sente thither, wee are to plante upon the
mouthes of the greate navigable Rivers which are there,
by stronge order of fortification, and there to plante our
Colonies. And so beinge firste setled in strengthe with
men, armour and munition, and havinge our navy within
our Bayes, havens, and Roades, wee shall be able to lett
[prevent] the entraunce of all subjectes of forren princes,
and so with our freshe powers to encounter their shippes at
the sea, and to renewe the same withe freshe men as the
soodden feightes shall require. And by our fortes shalbe
able to holde faste our firste footinge, and readily to annoye suche weary power of any other that shall seke to
arryve. And shalbe able with our navye to sende advertise-
mente into England upon every soodden [emergency]
whatsoever shall happen. And these fortifications shall
kepe the naturall people of the Contrye in obedience and
goodd order. And these fortes at the mowthes of those
greate portable and navigable Ryvers, may at all tymes
sende upp their shippes, Barkes, Barges, and boates into
the Inland with all the commodities of England, and returne unto the said fortes all the commodities of the In-
landes that wee shall receave in exchange, and thence at
pleasure convey the same into England: And thus settled
in those fortes yf the nexte neighboures shall attempte any
annoye to our people, wee are kepte safe by our fortes;
and wee may upon violence and wronge offred by them,
ronne upon the Rivers with our shippes, pynnesses, Barkes
and boates and enter into league with the petite princes
their neighboures that have alwayes lightly warres one with
an other, and so entringe league nowe with the one, and
then with the other wee shall purchase our owne safetie
and make ourselves Lordes of the whole.

DOCUMENT 37

Trading with the Indians

This graphic scene of trading activities between the English and the Indians (Plate 10, following page 134) is reproduced from an engraving in Theodor de Bry, *America*, Pt. 13 (Frankfurt: 1634), from the copy in Rare Book Division of the Library of Congress, Washington, D.C.

DOCUMENT 38

France and England Compete
for the Fur Trade

Perhaps the most important trade in the colonial period, particularly in the early period, was the fur trade.
The competition between European powers for the
skins of fur-bearing animals, useful for the manufacture
of hats and other garments popular in Europe, was keen.
Below is the initial section of a proposal by Cadwallader Colden, in 1724, to put the English of New
York in a better trading position vis-à-vis the French in
Canada. Colden lists the articles of the fur trade and
the comparative advantages accruing to France and England by virtue of their geographical positions, efficient
manufactures, and the like. The passage is from Colden's *The History of the Five Indian Nations of Canada,
Which are dependent on the Province of New-York in
America, and are the Barrier between the English and
French in that Part of the World*, published in London,
1747, and reprinted (New York: New Amsterdam
Book Company, 1902), Vol. II, pp. 33–47.

*A Memorial concerning the Furr-Trade of the
Province of New-York.*

*Presented to his Excellency William Burnet, Esq; Captain
General and Governor, &c. by Cadwallader Colden,
Surveyor General of the said Province, the 10th of No-
vember 1724.*

It has of late been generally believed, that the Inhabitants of the Province of New-York are so advantageously
situated, with respect to the Indian Trade, and enjoy so
many Advantages as to Trade in general, that it is in their
Power not only to rival the French of Canada, who have

almost entirely engrossed the Furr-Trade of America, but that it is impossible for the French to carry on that Trade in Competition with the People of this Province. The enquiring into the Truth of this Proposition, may not only be of some Consequence, as to the Riches and Honour of the British Nation, (for it is well known how valuable the Furr-Trade of America is) but likewise as to the Safety of all the British Colonies in North-America. New-France (as the French now claim) extends from the Mouth of the River Misissippi, to the Mouth of the River St. Lawrence, by which the French plainly show their Intention of enclosing the British Settlements, and cutting us off from all Commerce with the numerous Nations of Indians, that are every where settled over the vast Continent of North-America. The English in America have too good Reason to apprehend such a Design, when they see the French King's Geographer publish a Map, by which he has set Bounds to the British Empire in America, and has taken in many of the English Settlements both in South-Carolina and New-York, within these Boundaries of New-France. And the good Services they intend us, with the Indians, but too plainly appears at this Day, by the Indian War now carried on against New-England.

I have therefore for some Time past, endeavoured to inform myself, from the Writings of the French, and from others who have travelled in Canada, or among the Indians, how far the People of this Province may carry on the Indian Trade, with more Advantage than the French can; or what Disadvantages they labour under, more than the French do. As all Endeavours for the good of ones Country are excusable, I do not doubt but my Intention in this will be acceptable to your Excellency, though I be not capable of treating the Subject as it deserves.

I shall begin with Canada, and consider what Advantages they have either by their Situation, or otherwise. Canada is situated upon the River of St. Lawrence, by which the five great Lakes (which may properly be called, The five Inland Seas of North-America) empty themselves into the Ocean. The Mouth of this great River is in the

Lat. of 50 Degrees, overagainst the Body of Newfoundland. It rises from the Cataracui Lake, (the Easternmost of the five great Lakes) about the Lat. of 44 Degrees, and runs from thence about North-East to the Ocean, and is about nine hundred Miles in Length, from that Lake to the Ocean. The five great Lakes which communicate with each other, and with this River, extend about one thousand Miles Westward, further into the Continent. So far the French have already discovered, and their Discoveries make it probable, that an Inland Passage may be found to the South-Sea, by the Rivers which run into these Lakes, and Rivers which run into the South-Sea.

The Method of carrying Goods upon the Rivers of North-America, into all the small Branches, and over Land, from the Branches of one River to the Branches of another, was learned from the Indians, and is the only Method practicable through such large Forests and Deserts as the Traders pass thro', in carrying from one Nation to another, it is this; the Indians make a long narrow Boat, made of the Bark of the Birch-tree, the Parts of which they join very neatly. One of these Canoes that can carry a Dozen Men, can itself be easily carried upon two Men's Shoulders; so that when they have gone as far by Water as they can (which is further than is easily to be imagined, because their loaded Canoes don't sink six Inches into the Water) they unload their Canoes, and carry both Goods and Canoes upon their Shoulders over Land, into the nearest Branch of the River they intend to follow. Thus, the French have an easy Communication with all the Countries bordering upon the River of St. Lawrence, and its Branches, with all the Countries bordering upon these Inland Seas, and the Rivers which empty themselves into these Seas, and can thereby carry their Burdens of Merchandize thro' all these large Countries, which could not by any other means than Water-carriage be carried thro' so vast a Tract of Land.

This, however, but half finishes the View the French have, as to their Commerce in North-America. Many of the Branches of the River Misissippi come so near to the

Branches of several of the Rivers which empty themselves into the great Lakes, that in several Places there is but a short Land-Carriage from the one to the other. As soon as they have got into the River Misissippi, they open to themselves as large a Field for Traffick in the southern Parts of North-America, as was before mentioned with respect to the northern Parts. If one considers the Length of this River, and its numerous Branches, he must say, That by means of this River, and the Lakes, there is opened to his View such a Scene of inland Navigation as cannot be parallel'd in any other Part of the World.

The French have, with much Industry, settled small Colonies, and built stockaded Forts at all the considerable Passes between the Lakes, except between Cataracui Lake (called by the French Ontario) and Lake Erie, one of our Five Nations of Indians, whom we call Sennekas, (and the French Sonontouans) having hitherto refused them leave to erect any Buildings there.

The French have been indefatigable in making Discoveries, and carrying on their Commerce with Nations, of whom the English know nothing but what they see in the French Maps and Books. The Barrenness of the Soil, and the Coldness of the Climate of Canada, obliges the greatest number of the Inhabitants to seek their living by travelling among the Indians, or by trading with those that do travel. The Governor, and other Officers, have but a scanty Allowance from the King, and could not subsist were it not by the Perquisites they have from this Trade; neither could their Priests find any means to satisfy their Ambition and Luxury without it: So that all Heads and Hands are employ'd to advance it, and the Men of best Parts think it the surest way to advance themselves by travelling among the Indians, and learning their Languages; even the Bigotry and Enthusiasm of some hot Heads has not been a little useful in advancing this Commerce; for that Government having prudently turn'd the Edge of the Zeal of such hot Spirits upon converting the Indians, many of them have spent their Lives under the greatest Hardships, in endeavouring to gain the Indians to their Religion, and to

love the French Nation, while, at the same time, they are
no less industrious to represent the English as the Enemies
of Mankind. So that the whole Policy of that Government, both civil and religious, is admirably turn'd to the
general Advancement of this Trade. Indeed the Art and
Industry of the French, especially that of their religious
Missions, has so far prevail'd upon all the Indians in
North-America, that they are every where directed by
French Councils. Even our own Five Nations, (the Iroquois) who formerly were mortal Enemies of the French,
and have always liv'd in the strictest Amity with the English, have, of late, (by the Practices of the French Priests)
been so far gain'd, that several of the Mohawks, who live
nearest the English, have left their Habitations, and are
gone to settle near Monreal in Canada; and all the rest discover a Dread of the French Power. That much of this is
truly owing to the Priests, appears from many of the
Sachems of the Iroquois wearing Crucifixes when they
come to Albany: And those Mohawk Indians that are gone
to Canada, are now commonly known, both to the French
and English, by the Name of The Praying Indians, it being
customary for them to go through the Streets of Monreal
with their Beads, praying and begging Alms.

But notwithstanding all these Advantages, the French
labour under Difficulties that no Art or Industry can remove. The Mouth of the River of St. Lawrence, and more
especially the Bay of St. Lawrence, lies so far North, and
is thereby so often subject to tempestuous Weather and
thick Fogs, that the Navigation there is very dangerous,
and never attempted but during the Summer Months.
The Wideness of this Bay, together with the many strong
Currents that run in it, the many Shelves, and sunken
Rocks that are every where spread over both the Bay and
River, and the want of Places for anchoring in the Bay,
all increase the Danger of this Navigation; so that a Voyage
to Canada is justly esteem'd much more dangerous than to
any other Part of America. The many Shipwrecks that happen in this Navigation, are but too evident Proofs of the
Truth of this, particularly the Miscarriage of the last Ex-

pedition against Canada. The Channel is so difficult, and the Tides so strong, that after their Shipping get into the River, they never attempt to sail in the Night, tho' the Wind be fair, and the Weather good. These Difficulties are so considerable, that the French never attempt above one Voyage in a Year to Europe, or the West-Indies, tho' it be really nearer Europe than any of the English Colonies, where the Shipping that constantly use the Trade, always make two Voyages in the Year.

The Navigation between Quebeck and Monreal is likewise very dangerous and difficult: The Tide rises about 18 or 20 Feet at Quebeck, which occasions so strong a Stream, that a Boat of six Oars cannot make way against it: The River in many Places very wide, and the Channel at the same time narrow and crooked; there are many Shelves and sunken Rocks, so that the best Pilots have been deceived; for which reason the Vessels that carry Goods to Monreal are always obliged to anchor before Night, tho' both Wind and Tide be fair. The Flood goes no further than Trois Rivieres, half way to Monreal, and about ninety Miles from Quebeck: After they pass this Place they have a strong Stream always against them, which requires a fair Wind and a strong Gale to carry the Vessels against the Stream. And they are obliged in this Part of the River, as well as under the Trois Rivieres, to come to an anchor at Night, though the Wind be good. These Difficulties make the common Passages take up three or four Weeks, and sometimes six Weeks; tho' if they have the chance of a Wind to continue so long, they may run it in five or six Days.

After they pass Monreal they have a strong Stream against them till they come near the Lakes; so that in all that, which is about one hundred and fifty Miles in Length, they force their Canoes forward with setting Poles, or drag them with Ropes along shoar; and at five or six different Places in that way the River falls over Rocks with such Force, that they are obliged to unload their Canoes, and carry them upon their Shoulders. They never make this Voyage from Monreal to Cataracui in less than twenty Days, and frequently, twice that Time is necessary.

Now we are come so far as the Lake, my Design leads me no further, for at this Lake all the far Indians, that go to Canada, must pass by our Traders. And from thence the Road to the Indian Countries is the same from Albany that it is from Monreal.

Besides these Difficulties in the Transportation, the French labour under greater in the purchasing of the principal Goods proper for the Indian Market; for the most considerable and most valuable Part of their Cargo consists in Strouds, Duffils, Blankets, and other Woollens, which are bought at a much cheaper Rate in England than in France. The Strouds (which the Indians value more than any other Cloathing) are only made in England, and must be transported into France before they can be carried to Canada. Rum is another considerable Branch of the Indian Trade, which the French have not, by reason they have no Commodities in Canada fit for the West India Market. This they supply with Brandy, at a much dearer Rate than Rum can be purchased at New-York, tho' of no more Value with the Indians. Generally, all the Goods used in the Indian Trade, except Gun-Powder, and a few Trinkets, are sold at Monreal for twice their Value at Albany. To this likewise must be added, the necessity they are under of laying the whole Charge of supporting their Government on the Indian Trade. I am not particularly informed of their Duties or Imposts, but I am well assured, that they commonly give six or seven hundred Livres for a Licence for one Canoe, in proportion to her Largeness, to go with her Loading into the Indian Country to trade.

I shall next consider the Advantages the Inhabitants of New-York have in carrying on this Trade. In the first place, the Ships that constantly use the Trade to England perform their Voyage to and from London twice every Year; and those that go to Bristol (the Port from whence the greatest part of the Goods for the Indian Trade are exported) frequently return in four Months. These Goods are bought much cheaper in England than in France: They are transported in less Time, with less Charge, and much less Risque, as appears by the Premio for Insurance between London and New-York, being only Two per Cent. Goods are easily carried from New-York to Albany, up Hudson's River, the Distance being only 140 Miles, the River very strait all the way, and bold, and very free from Sandbanks, as well as Rocks; so that the Vessels always sail as well by Night as by Day, and have the Advantage of the Tide upwards as well as downwards, the Flood flowing above Albany. It may therefore be safely concluded, that all sorts of Goods can be carried to Albany at a cheaper Rate than they can be to Quebeck, which is also three times further from the Indian Country than Albany is. To put the Truth of this out of all dispute, I need only observe what is well known both at New-York and Albany, viz. That almost all the Strouds carried by the French into the Indian Countries, as well as large Quantities of other Goods, for the Use of the French themselves, are carried from Albany to Monreal. There has been an Account kept of nine hundred Pieces of Strouds transported thither in one Year, besides other Commodities of very considerable Value. The Distance between Albany and Monreal is about two hundred Miles, all by Water, except twelve Miles between Hudson's River and the Wood-Creek, where they carry their Bark Canoes over Land, and about sixteen Miles between Chambly and La Prairie, overagainst Monreal. And tho' the Passage be so short and easy, these Goods are generally sold at double their Value in Albany.

But as this Path has been thought extremely prejudicial to the Interest of this Colony, I shall leave it, and go on to another, that leads directly from Albany into the Cataracui or Ontario Lake, without going near any of the French Settlements.

From Albany the Indian Traders commonly carry their Goods sixteen Miles over Land, to the Mohawks River at Schenechtady, the Charge of which Carriage is Nine Shillings New-York Money, or Five Shillings Sterling each Waggon-Load. From Schenechtady they carry them in

Canoes up the Mohawks River, to the Carrying-place between the Mohawks River, and the River which runs into the Oneida Lake; which Carrying-place between is only three Miles long, except in very dry Weather, when they are obliged to carry them two Miles further. From thence they go with the Current down the Onondaga River to the Cataracui Lake. The Distance between Albany and the Cataracui Lake (this Way) is nearly the same with that between Albany and Monreal; and likewise with that between Monreal and the Cataracui Lake, and the Passage much easier than the last, because the Stream of the Mohawks River is not near so strong as the Cataracui River between the Lake and Monreal, and there is no Fall in the River, save one short one; whereas there are (as I have said) at least five in the Cataracui River, where the Canoes must be unloaded. Therefore it plainly follows, that the Indian Goods may be carried at as cheap a Rate from Albany to the Cataracui Lake, as from Albany to Monreal. So that the People of Albany plainly save all the Charge of carrying Goods two hundred Miles from Monreal to that Part of the Cataracui Lake, which the French have to carry before they bring them to the same Place from Monreal, besides the Advantage which the English have in the Price of their Goods.

I have said, That when we are in the Cataracui Lake, we are upon the Level with the French, because here we can meet with all the Indians that design to go to Monreal. But besides this Passage by the Lakes, there is a River which comes from the Country of the Sennekas, and falls into the Onondaga River, by which we have an easy Carriage into that Country, without going near the Cataracui Lake. The Head of this River goes near to Lake Erie, and probably may give a very near Passage into that Lake, much more advantageous than the Way the French are obliged to take by the great Fall of Jagara, because narrow Rivers are much safer for Canoes than the Lakes, where they are obliged to go ashore if there be any Wind upon the Water. But as this Passage depends upon a further Discovery, I shall say nothing more of it at this time.

Whoever then considers these Advantages New-York has of Canada, in the first buying of their Goods, and in the safe, speedy, and cheap Transportation of them from Britain to the Lakes, free of all manner of Duty or Imposts, will readily agree with me, that the Traders of New-York may sell their Goods in the Indian Countries at half the Price the People of Canada can, and reap twice the Profit they do. This will admit of no Dispute with those that know that Strouds (the Staple Indian Commodity) this Year are sold for Ten Pounds apiece at Albany, and at Monreal for Twenty-five Pounds, notwithstanding the great Quantity of Strouds said to be brought directly into Quebeck from France, and the Great Quantities that have been clandestinely carried from Albany. It cannot therefore be denied that it is only necessary for the Traders of New-York to apply themselves heartily to this Trade, in order to bring it wholly into their own Hands; for in every thing besides Diligence, Industry, and enduring Fatigues, the English have much the Advantage of the French. And all the Indians will certainly buy, where they can, at the cheapest Rate.

DOCUMENT 39

Trade and the Flag

The influence of the trader in determining the nature of political relations between white and Indian is well brought out in the following letter from the fur trader Manuel Lisa to General William Clark, of Lewis and Clark expedition fame, then Governor of Missouri Territory. Lisa, in his defense of his conduct as Indian agent, attempts to demonstrate how the Indians of the Missouri River area were won to a closer relationship with the Americans by his honest and politic approach. It is to be noted that Lisa, at the time he wrote, had both a European wife and an Indian wife. The letter is printed in Hiram Martin Chittenden, *The American Fur Trade of the Far West,* 3 vols.; Vol. III, pp. 899–902 (New York: 1902).

ST. LOUIS, July 1st, 1817.

To His Excellency, Governor Clark:

SIR:—I have the honor to remit to you the commission of sub-agent, which you were pleased to bestow upon me, in the summer of 1814, for the Indian nations who inhabit the Missouri river above the mouth of the Kansas, and to pray you to accept my resignation of that appointment.

The circumstances under which I do this, demand of me some exposition of the actual state of these Indians, and of my own conduct during the time of my sub-agency.

Whether I deserve well or ill of the government, depends upon the solution of these questions:

1. Are the Indians of the Missouri more or less friendly to the United States than at the time of my appointment?

2. Are they altered, better or worse, in their own condition at this time?

1. I received this appointment when war was raging between the United States and Great Britain, and when the activity of British emissaries had armed against the Republic all the tribes of the Upper Mississippi and of the northern lakes. Had the Missouri Indians been overlooked by British agents?

No, your excellency will remember that more than a year before the war broke out, I gave you intelligence that the wampum was carrying by British influence along the banks of the Missouri, and that all the nations of this great river were excited to join the universal confederacy then setting on foot, of which the Prophet was the instrument, and British traders the soul. The Indians of the Missouri are to those of the Upper Mississippi as four is to one. Their weight would be great, if thrown into the scale against us. They did not arm against the Republic; on the contrary, they armed against Great Britain and struck the Iowas, the allies of that power.

When peace was proclaimed more than forty chiefs had intelligence with me; and together, we were to carry an expedition of several thousand warriors against the tribes of the Upper Mississippi, and silence them at once. These things are known to your excellency.

To the end of the war, therefore, the Indians of the Missouri continued friends of the United States. How are they today when I come to lay down my appointment? Still friends, hunting in peace upon their own ground, and we trading with them in security, while the Indians of the Upper Mississippi, silenced but not satisfied, give signs of enmity, and require the presence of a military force. And thus the first question resolves itself to my advantage.

2. Before I ascended the Missouri as sub-agent, your excellency remembers what was accustomed to take place. The Indians of that river killed, robbed and pillaged the traders; these practices are no more. Not to mention the others, my own establishments furnish the example of destruction then, of safety now. I have one at the Mahas

more than six hundred miles up the Missouri, another at
the Sioux, six hundred miles further still. I have from one
to two hundred men in my employment, large quantities
of horses, and horned cattle, of hogs, of domestic fowls;
not one is touched by an Indian; for I count as nothing
some solitary thefts at the instigation of white men, my
enemies; nor as an act of hostility the death of Pedro
Antonio, one of my people, shot this spring, as a man is
sometimes shot among us, without being stripped or mutilated. And thus the morals of these Indians are altered for
the better, and the second question equally results to my
advantage.

But I have had some success as a trader; and this gives
rise to many reports.

"Manuel must cheat the government, and Manuel must
cheat the Indians, otherwise Manuel could not bring down
every summer so many boats loaded with rich furs."

Good. My accounts with the government will show
whether I receive anything out of which to cheat it. A poor
five hundred dollars, as sub-agent salary, does not buy the
tobacco which I annually give to those who call me father.

Cheat the Indians! The respect and friendship which
they have for me, the security of my possessions in the
heart of their country, respond to this charge, and declare
with voices louder than the tongues of men that it cannot
be true.

"But Manuel gets so much rich fur!"

Well, I will explain how I get it. First, I put into my
operations great activity; I go a great distance, while some
are considering whether they will start today or tomorrow.
I impose upon myself great privations; ten months in a
year I am buried in the forest, at a vast distance from my
own house. I appear as the benefactor, and not as the
pillager, of the Indians. I carried among them the seed of
the large pompion, from which I have seen in their possession the fruit weighing 160 pounds. Also the large bean,
the potato, the turnip; and these vegetables now make a
comfortable part of their subsistence, and this year I have
promised to carry the plough. Besides, my blacksmiths

work incessantly for them, charging nothing. I lend them traps, only demanding preference in their trade. My establishments are the refuge of the weak and of the old men no longer able to follow their lodges; and by these means I have acquired the confidence and friendship of these nations, and the consequent choice of their trade.

These things I have done, and I propose to do more. The Aricaras, the Mandans, the Gros-Ventres, and the Assiniboines, find themselves near the establishment of Lord Selkirk upon the Red river. They can communicate with it in two or three days. The evils of such communication will strike the minds of all persons, and it is for those who can handle the pen to dilate upon them. For me I go to form another establishment to counteract the one in question, and shall labor to draw upon us the esteem of these nations, and to prevent their commerce from passing into the hands of foreigners.

I regret to have troubled your excellency with this exposition. It is right for you to hear what is said of a public agent, and also to weigh it, and to consider the source from which it comes. In ceasing to be in the employment of the United States, I shall not be less devoted to its interests. I have suffered enough in person and property, under a different government, to know how to appreciate the one under which I now live.

I have the honor to be, with the greatest respect, your excellency's obedient servant.

MANUEL LISA.

DOCUMENT 40

Fort Rupert, Vancouver Island, 1859

John Keast Lord, Naturalist to the British North American Boundary Commission, visited Fort Rupert, a trading post of the Hudson's Bay Company, in 1859, about fifteen years after its founding. In his book, *The Naturalist in Vancouver Island and British Columbia*, 2 vols.: Vol. I, pp. 162–64 (London: 1866), he describes the post and reports an amusing traditional story which, whether true or not, epitomizes the sophisticated mercantile sense which Europeans quickly discovered in the Kwakiutl Indians of the area.

The trading-post is a square, enclosed by immense trees, one end sunk in the ground; the trees are lashed together. A platform, about the height of an ordinary man from the top of these pickets, is carried along the sides of this square, so as to enable anyone to peep over without being in danger from an arrow or bullet. The entrance is closed by two massive gates, an inner and outer; all the houses— the chief trader's, employés', trading-house, fur-room, and stores—are within the square. The trade-room is cleverly contrived so as to prevent a sudden rush of Indians; the approach, from outside the pickets, is by a long narrow passage, bent at an acute angle near the window of the trade-room, and only of a sufficient width to admit one savage at a time. (This precaution is necessary, inasmuch as, were the passage straight, they would inevitably shoot the trader.)

At the angles nearest the Indian village are two bastions, octagonal in shape, and of a very doubtful style of architecture. Four embrasures in each bastion would lead the uninitiated to believe in the existence of as many formidable cannon, with rammers, sponges, neat piles of round-shot and grape, magazines of powder, and ready hands to load and fire—and, at the slightest symptom of hostility, to work havoc and destruction, on any red-skinned rebels daring to dispute the supremacy of the Hudson's Bay Company. Imagine my surprise, on entering this fortress, to discover all this a pleasant fiction; two small rusty carronades, buried in the accumulated dust and rubbish of years, that no human power could load, were the sole occupants of the mouldy old turrets.

The bell for breakfast recalling me, I jokingly inquired of the trader if he had ever been obliged to use this cannon for defensive purposes. He laughed as he replied, "There is a tradition that, at some remote period, the guns were actually fired, not at the rebellious natives, but over their heads; instead of being terror-stricken at the white man's thunder, away they all scampered in pursuit of the ball, found it, and, marching in triumph back to the fort-gate, offered to trade it, that it might be fired again!"

CHAPTER V

The Missionary Impulse

Conversion of the Indians was stated in most of the early charters as one of the principal aims of English settlement in the New World. The lack of success on the part of the English was soon apparent. Many are the reasons alleged for the failure. The English, particularly the Puritans, insisted upon a high standard of religious understanding. They did not baptize freely as, they charged, the French and Spanish did. They did not have religious orders charged specifically with missionary tasks. The English ministers were, until special provisions were made later in the seventeenth century by newly created missionary organizations, responsible to their own English parishioners, and taught the Indians only as time and interest served. Other reasons may be cited for the great failure, evident in the tone of most missionary writings and seen throughout the following selections, but one of the simplest explanations is that conversion of the Indian —the religious justification for settlement—was not the most compelling motive. Most Englishmen did not really care whether the Indians were converted or not, an attitude that was accentuated when it became evident that the Indians were not going to accommodate their lives to serve the English. The record of the Spanish, French, and Portuguese in the New World is a different one, but the letter of Father Rogel in one of the following selections suggests that conversion was not always as easily accomplished by the Catholic Church as the Protestants believed.

DOCUMENT 41

"The Better to Serve You"

The role played by the clergy as the nexus between the Indians and the Spaniards in the areas conquered by Spain is well portrayed in this chapter from the Franciscan friar Toribio Motolinía's *History of the Indians of New Spain,* written in the middle of the sixteenth century, and translated and edited by Elizabeth Andros Foster, Book III, Chapter IV, pp. 193–96 (Cortes Society, Bancroft Library, Berkeley, Calif.: 1950).

Of the humility of the friars of Saint Francis in their conversion of the Indians, and of their patience in adversities.

So great was the humility and mildness of the Friars Minor in their intercourse and dealings with the Indians that on some occasions when friars of other orders wanted to enter the Indian towns to settle and establish monasteries, the Indians themselves went and besought His Majesty's representative who ruled the land—who was at that time the bishop Don Sebastian Ramírez—asking him not to give them any other friars than those of Saint Francis, because they knew and loved them and were beloved by them. When [Don Sebastian] asked them the reason why they liked these friars better than the others, the Indians answered: "Because these go about poorly dressed and barefooted like us; they eat what we eat, they settle down among us, and their intercourse with us is gentle." On other occasions when the Franciscans wished to leave certain towns so that friars of other orders might go there, the Indians came in tears to say that if the Franciscans went away and left them, they would leave their houses and follow them; and they actually did it and followed the friars. This I saw with my own eyes. Because of this attitude of humility of the friars toward the Indians, all the officials of the royal audiencia treated them with great consideration, although in the beginning they had come from Castile filled with indignation against them and with the intention of reproving and repressing them, because they had been informed that the friars ruled the Indians with a high hand and lorded it over them. After they saw that the opposite was true they became very fond of them and realized that what was said about the friars in Spain was the result of spite.

Some of the friars knew and associated with persons who could have helped them get bishoprics, but they would not allow it; others were actually elected to bishoprics and, when the news of the election came, humbly renounced the honor, saying that they were not worthy or deserving of so high a dignity. There is a difference of opinion as to whether or not they were right in refusing, for in this new land and among these humble people it was very desirable that the bishops should be, as in the primitive church, poor and humble, seeking not for wealth but for souls, and should not need to carry with them anything but their pontifical. It was much better that the Indians should not see luxurious bishops, dressed in delicate shirts, sleeping with sheets and mattresses and wearing soft garments, for those who have the cure of souls should imitate Christ in humility and poverty, bear his cross on their shoulders and wish to die on it. However, as these friars refused the honor simply and for the sake of humility, I believe that in God's judgment they will not be condemned for it.

One of the good things that the friars have in this land is humility, for many of the Spaniards humiliate them with insults and slanders; among the Indians there is nothing to make them vainglorious, for the Indians exceed them in penance and in being scorned of men. And so when there comes fresh from Castile some friar who was there considered to lead a life of great penance and to surpass the others, when he reaches here he is like a river flowing into the sea, for here the whole community lives very poorly and keeps every rule that can be kept. If they look at the Indians, they will see them miserably dressed and barefooted, their beds and dwellings exceedingly poor and their food more meager than that of the strictest penitent, so that these newcomers will find nothing on which to pride themselves. Much less is this so if they are ruled by reason, for everything belongs to God, and he blasphemes who says that any good thing is his own, for he is trying to make himself God. It is therefore madness for man to glory in things that do not belong to him, for one needs patience to await and receive the glory which Christ has promised us, to endure and bear the burden of all tribulations, and to suffer the blows of enemies without injury to the soul. Just as against savage discharges of artillery men set up soft and yielding things on which the shots may wreak their fury, so against the tribulations of the world, the flesh and the devil, one should set up a barrier of patience, for, if not, one's soul will quickly be disturbed and overcome.

In this manner the friars used patience as a shield against the insults of the Spaniards; when the latter very indignantly declared that the friars were destroying the country by favoring the Indians against them, the friars, to mitigate their anger, answered patiently: "If we did not defend the Indians, you would no longer have anyone to serve you; if we favor them, it is for the purpose of preserving them and so that you may have servants, and in defending and teaching them we are serving you and taking the burden from your consciences. When you took charge of them it was with the obligation of teaching them, and you think of nothing but making them serve you and give you all that they have or can get. Since they have little or nothing, if you exhaust them, then who will serve you?" And so, many of the Spaniards—at least the noble and virtuous ones—said, and still say, frequently, that if it were not for the friars of Saint Francis New Spain would be like the Islands, where there is no Indian left to be taught the law of God or to serve the Spaniards.

The latter also complained and spoke ill of the friars because they appeared to love the Indians better than they did the Spaniards and reproved the Spaniards harshly. For this reason many failed to give alms and felt a certain abhorrence of the friars. To this the friars replied that they had always considered the Spaniards as of the family of the Faith and that if any of them ever had any special spiritual or physical need, the friars attended to them rather than to the Indians; but as the Spaniards are very few in comparison to the natives and know better where to seek help—both physical and spiritual—and as the Indians have none to help them except those who have learned the language—the chief and in fact almost all of whom are of the Friars Minor—it is right that the friars should turn to help the Indians who are so numerous and so much in need of help. Even with them the friars cannot do all that they should because the Indians are so numerous. It is very right for the friars to do as they do, for the souls of these Indians did not cost Christ less than those of the Spaniards and Romans, and the law of God obliges one to help and encourage those upon whose lips the milk of the Faith is not yet dry rather than those who have already absorbed it and are accustomed to it.

Because the friars defended the Indians and tried to gain for them some time in which they could be taught the elements of the Faith, and to prevent their being made to work on Sundays and feast days, and because they tried to get them some reduction of the tributes, the Spaniards became so angry with the friars that they were determined to kill some of them, for it seemed to them that because of the friars they were losing the profit that they got out of the poor Indians. The tributes demanded of the Indians were so great that many towns, unable to pay, would sell to the money-lenders among them the lands and the children of the poor, and as the tributes were very frequent and they could not meet them by sell-

ing all that they had, some towns became entirely depopu-
lated and others were losing their population when the
situation was saved by decreasing the tribute. Because of
this friction with the Spaniards the friars were on the point
of leaving this land entirely and returning to Castile, but
God, who helps us in times of the greatest tribulation and
necessity, did not permit it, for when His Catholic Majesty, the Emperor Don Carlos, was informed of the truth
he obtained a license from the Pope for one hundred and
fifty friars to come from Old Spain to this land.

DOCUMENT 42

A Jesuit Missionary in South Carolina, 1569–70

The following is a letter from the Jesuit missionary Father Juan Rogel to Pedro Menéndez de Avilés, Governor of Spanish Florida, written from Havana in 1570 immediately after Father Rogel's return from an unsuccessful attempt at missionizing the Indians of coastal South Carolina. The original letter is in Spanish, the best printed text being in "Monumenta Antiquae Floridae (1566–1572)," edited by Felix Zubillaga, *Monumenta Historica Societatis Iesu* 69, pp. 471–79 (Rome: 1946). The translation given here is by William C. Sturtevant, made directly from the text as published by Zubillaga, assisted by comparison with two previous English translations: a complete one by Daniel G. Brinton ("Rogel's Account of the Florida Mission (1569–70)," *Historical Magazine* [First Series], Vol. V, no. 11, pp. 327–30 [New York: 1861]), and a partial one by Michael Kenny (pp. 250–57 in his *The Romance of the Floridas* [New York: Bruce Publishing Co., 1934]). The footnotes are by Sturtevant, based largely on Zubillaga's notes in the above publication and in his "La Florida: la misión jesuítica (1566–1572) y la colonización española," *Bibliotheca Instituti Historici S.I.*1 (Rome: 1941), and on John R. Swanton's "Early History of the Creek Indians and their Neighbors," *Bureau of American Ethnology Bulletin* 73 (Washington: 1922). Data on the historical context of this mission can be found in Kenny's book, in *The Spanish Missions of Georgia* by John Tate Lanning (Chapel Hill: University of North Carolina Press, 1935), and in Sturtevant's "Spanish-Indian Relations in Southeastern North America," *Ethnohistory*, Vol. IX, pp. 41–94 (1962).

† I H S

Most illustrious Sir. May the grace and love of Jesus
Christ be always in your excellency's soul, amen.

I wish I had far better news to write your excellency
than I do, about the work in which your excellency is so
zealously engaged. But it seems that the Lord in his in-
scrutable judgment permits neither your excellency's desires, labors, and great expense, nor our industry, to come
to fruition. May He always be blessed; I pray His Divine
Majesty that my own great sins be not the impediment. I
will give your excellency an account of what I have been
doing since we left for Santa Elena[1] in June of 1569.

After we had established our house at Santa Elena,
Father Vice-Provincial ordered me to live at Orista,[2]
where I went with much joy from the desire and great
hopes I had that we would begin to produce results. At
first, when I began to deal with the Indians there, those
hopes were greatly increased since I saw that their customs
and manner of living were much better than those of the
Indians of Carlos.[3] I gave praise to God when I saw each
Indian married to only one wife, in charge of his own field,
and maintaining his house and rearing his children with
much care; seeing them not contaminated with the abominable sin, neither incestuous, nor cruel, nor thieves; seeing
how they dealt with each other with much truth, peace,
and simplicity.

It finally seemed to me that we would certainly gain
our prize, and that the delay would be in my learning their
language in order to explain to them the mysteries of our

---

[1] Present Parris Island, South Carolina.

[2] An Indian town or region on an island between Port Royal
and Edisto Island, South Carolina. The inhabitants are included
among the now-extinct Indians called Cusabo by anthropologists
and historians. This account, like other Spanish ones of the
period, often uses the same name for both an Indian town or
region and its chief.

[3] The Calusa Indians near present Fort Myers, Florida, among
whom Father Rogel had undertaken his first mission in Spanish
Florida.

Holy Faith, rather than in their receiving it and becoming Christians. Therefore I and three others I had with me hurried to learn it, with such success that in six months I spoke it with them and preached in it. At the end of these six months I was prepared. I told them those truths of our Holy Faith which can be naturally comprehended, such as the oneness of God, His power and majesty, that He is the cause and creator of all things, and how much He loves good and hates evil; and several truths which faith tells us, such as the rewards and penalties of the next life, the immortality of our souls, and the resurrection of the dead. At first they seemed to listen to me with some attention, and they asked me several questions—although very humble ones, such as whether God has a wife and other similar things. This was the season when they were together, which lasted two and half months. But when the acorn harvest arrived all of them left me alone and went into the woods, each one by himself, and they only gathered together at certain festivals which they had every two months, and this not always in the same spot, but now in one place, now in another. I tried to attend their festivals and gatherings to see whether we could advance our work; but I saw that instead of improving they grew worse, jesting at what I told them. Nevertheless I persevered, thinking I would be able to persuade them that in the spring, which is the time for planting maize, they should plant a great deal so there would be food for the whole year for the subjects of that chief who could then remain in one place. In order to succeed in this, I suggested to them that I would give them iron hoes for digging and as much maize seed as they wanted, and that they should plant a lot at the place where we were, since there was much land which was comparatively good for those provinces, where the soil is very thin. Therefore I brought eight hoes, and five which Esteban de las Alas[4] gave me for this purpose —there were about twenty houses there—and this was reported throughout the country. But the result was that

[4] The Spanish governor in Santa Elena.

after having promised me many times that all would gather there to plant, the inhabitants of those twenty houses divided up into twelve or thirteen farms which were separated from each other by some four, six, ten, or twenty leagues, and only two residents planted at that place. With all this I was not dismayed, but labored to produce what fruit I could at least in those two houses, and preached to them and exhorted them, giving them presents and cherishing them. Then I gave them to understand how they had to believe in one God, Father, Son, and Holy Ghost, and in Jesus Christ, our Lord, and the reason why we Christians venerate the cross. At the end of the eight months I had been among them they showed me great love and friendship, because I protected them as much as I could and they were glad to have us as interpreters. So it seemed to me I had won their good will, and I began to tell them how in order to be children of God it is necessary to be enemies of the devil, because the devil is evil and loves all evil things and God is good and loves everything good. When I began to treat of this, they were so vexed and they conceived such hatred for what I said that never after could they face coming to hear me, and they told the people who were with me that they were very angry and did not believe anything I told them, since I spoke ill of the devil; that the devil was so good that there was nothing better. Then those two households began to move away, and being asked why they left, they replied, because I spoke evil of the devil.[5]

[5] Very likely Father Rogel, preaching in the Indian language, made the mistake of translating the Spanish word for devil (he uses the term *demonio* in his letter) with the local name for some deity whom the Indians believed to be benevolent rather than malevolent. This would be a natural equation, given the outlook of Christian missionaries in the sixteenth century (and many since then). Similarly, in 1587 Governor Menéndez Márques greeted some Franciscans with the statement that the Indians of this general region "take the devil [*demonio*] for a friend and God who created them for an enemy." (Maynard Geiger, *The Franciscan Conquest of Florida* (1573–1618), Catholic Univ. of America, Studies in Hispanic-American History, Vol. 1, p. 55, [Washington: 1937].)

After they left, I went about to other chiefs to offer my services if they wanted to receive me, giving them my word and promise that I would go where they were, to live with them and teach them the law of God if they really desired to become Christians—but if they did not want to be Christians, I had made up my mind to return to Spain. But there was no one who would respond to me. On the Río Dulce[6] where most of the subjects of Orista had gathered, I spoke these same words to them in a meeting. They all began to look sorrowful and to say to me, "But why do you say that you love us greatly, and yet you want to leave us?" So from that I began to think my life was certainly in danger, and seeing how it was, I changed my discourse and coaxed them as one would children, and so was able to return safely to my post where I decided to stay until the Father Vice-Provincial should come and order me to do what he wished. This was already at the end of June.

It happened just at that time that Lt. Juan de la Vandera, your excellency's lieutenant governor in Santa Elena, went to a festival at Escamacu,[7] and, compelled by necessity, ordered three or four chiefs of Escamacu, Orista, and Ahoya[8] to bring to him at Santa Elena a certain number of canoe-loads of maize by a certain date. Also I understood from the same lieutenant that he was forced to send forty soldiers among the Indians for them to maintain until the ship should come, because he did not have enough for them to eat. I knew for certain that if I were among the Indians they would have to appeal to me for protection against that vexation, and on the other hand I saw that I would not be able to remedy the situation because necessity compelled the Christians to do that. Also I saw neither benefit nor hope in this in regard to the conversion, and that my situation there would be useless and vain, and that when I did not protect the Indians they

[6] That is, the "Fresh Water River"—probably the present Edisto River, South Carolina.

[7] A small island near Orista.

[8] Apparently an Indian town on Escamacu Island.

would turn their rage on me—because obviously so many
soldiers going among Indians would treat them as they
customarily do, and the Indians would have to revolt, and
would turn against me because they could very safely do
so. Also I had been ordered by the Father Vice-Provincial
to withdraw to Santa Elena if there should be any appearance of mortal danger. Therefore, after having commended it to God our Lord and having said several Masses
for it, I decided with my heart full of sorrow to tear down
the house and church, eight or ten days before they were
to send the forty soldiers, and to go with my small bundle
to Santa Elena—saying always to the Indians that if they
wished to be Christians they should send for me and I
would return, they could build me another house, and I
would live always among them. Thus I took leave of them
on July 13, this year of 1570.

A few days later the lieutenant sent the soldiers and it
turned out exactly as we have said, for then Escamacu
and Orista and all those Indians revolted, until Capt.
Pedro Menéndez Marqués[9] and Esteban de las Alas arrived and managed to pacify them with gifts and flattery.
When I was about to leave for here I went to visit Orista
and told him I was leaving because they did not want to
be Christians, and if they did want to be, I would abandon
this journey and go with him; but he did not tear my
cassock importuning me to go with him.

Your excellency sees here my reasoning on the method
of proceeding with the Indians, and the scanty returns
and the little disposition I see in them for their conversion, unless God our Lord miraculously provides it. The
main cause of this is that they are so scattered, being
without any fixed abode for nine out of the twelve months
of the year. Even then, if they moved from one place to
another all together, there would be some hope that by
accompanying them one might make some impression by
repetition (like water dripping on a hard stone). But

[9] A naval captain, nephew of Governor Menéndez de Avilés,
and his deputy in Florida.

each one goes his own way, and thus I have experienced the converse of the principle which your excellency has so much at heart, that the faith must spread in this land. What I find is the opposite, that to win any of the blind and wretched souls of these provinces, it is necessary first to give orders that the Indians join together and live in settlements, and cultivate the land to secure sustenance for the whole year. After they are firmly settled, let the preaching be introduced. Because if this is not done, even though the religious go among them for fifty years they will have no more success than we have had these four years that we have gone among them—which is none, not even the hope or semblance of any. To gather them together in this manner, your excellency will understand, will require tremendous labor and a very long time, in order to do it lawfully as God our Lord commands, not forcing them nor with arms. There are two reasons for this: first, because they have been accustomed to live in this way for many thousands of years, and to want them to cease this manner of life seems to them equivalent to death; secondly, even though they should wish to do so, the soil will not permit it, being thin and miserable and quickly worn out. They themselves say it is for this reason that they live so scattered out and wander so much. So I conclude that unless the Lord miraculously provides some means unknown to us (as He could very well do), no human method is apparent to me except that which I have described, and with it there are these difficulties.

Your excellency has already seen what happened at Carlos, it was also clear at Tocobaga,[10] and the same thing happened at Tequesta:[11] in these places, speaking through interpreters, nothing whatever was accomplished. When that door was shut, we all turned to the other which was open, where we began in a different way—going alone among them, learning their language and preaching the mysteries of our Holy Faith in it. Brother Domingo Au-

[10] North of Tampa Bay.
[11] The present Miami, Florida—all three of the places here mentioned being in southern peninsular Florida.

gustín was in Guale more than a year, learned that language so well that he wrote a grammar of it, and then died.[12] Father Sedeño was there fourteen months, the Father Vice-Provincial[13] six, Brother Francisco[14] ten, and Father Alamo[15] four, and all of them have not accomplished anything. They only baptized seven, four of them children and all being about to die. I was there eleven months, and I assure your excellency that God our Lord almost visibly wrought miracles, so that the miserable ones came to me in their travails to petition God to deliver them from their woes; and with all that, they are so obdurate and so averse to what we taught them that they regretted we had learned their language. Thus after I began to disclose to them who the devil was, they seldom or never replied truthfully to what I asked them in order to learn their language, and the Fathers who were in Guale tell me the same.

Now the Father Vice-Provincial has gone to Ajacán[16] with don Luis.[17] Nine have gone, five of the Society and four catechists.[18] I was ordered to come here to live until something else is arranged. Father Sedeño was ordered to come with us as far as the forts,[19] and there to remain to

[12] The Jesuit Brother Domingo Agustín Váez went with Father Antonio Sedeño to Guale (along the present southern Georgia–northern Florida east coast) in early 1569, and died there in late November or early December of the same year. His grammar is not known to have survived.

[13] Father Juan Bautista de Segura.

[14] Brother Francisco Villarreal.

[15] Father Gonzalo de Alamo.

[16] Near present Jamestown, Virginia. Here all but one of the mission were killed by the Indians in early 1571.

[17] An Indian previously carried off from that region, who was baptized with the name Luis de Velasco and played a major part in persuading the Jesuits to return with him to his homeland, where he soon left them and apparently organized the opposition which resulted in their deaths.

[18] Fathers Segura and Luis Quirós, Brothers Ceballos, Gabriel Gómez, and Pedro Linares; the catechists Juan Bautista Menéndez, Gabriel de Solís, Cristóbal Redondo, and Alonso Méndez. Only the last survived.

[19] St. Augustine.

collect the children which the chiefs of Saturiba and Tacatacuru[20] had ordered to be given. But we found such bad conditions at the forts and so many indications that the Indians are hostile, that it did not seem safe to remain there (as Capt. Pedro [Menéndez] Marqués will write at greater length). Hence he came with me to Havana—also because it was necessary to bring with us the sloop needed for the return to Santa Elena.

If the Lord wills that a door be opened in Ajacán, we are ready to do whatever the Father Vice-Provincial commands. I pray to the Divine Majesty to give him such good fortune and show him such a multitude ready for conversion that he will send for us all to go labor there. He directed me to take care to remind these people to send some ship to visit them in the spring.

This, sir, is what I have to make known to your excellency about all that I have done, which amounts to nothing in the end. But your excellency can be consoled, and rest assured that God our Lord will reward all the labor that has been expended here, just as though all Florida had been converted. May He always be with your excellency and favor you with spiritual and temporal fortune, with increase in life and condition, as this His useless servant desires.

From Havana the ninth of December of the year 1570.

> Your excellency's unworthy servant in the Lord,
> † Juan Rogel.

[20] Timucua Indian regions near the coast on either side of the present Georgia–Florida border.

DOCUMENT 43

"How Happy a Thing Had It Been, if You Had Converted Some before You Had Killed Any!"

When the Pilgrims departed for the New World, they left behind, in Leyden, Holland, their spiritual leader, John Robinson. His letter to William Bradford, Governor of the colony, discusses the killing of several Indians in retaliation for Indian attacks engendered by the miscarriages of another group of English under Andrew Weston who had settled at Wessagusset, now Weymouth. Robinson expresses his love for his flock, his respect for Bradford and for Captain Miles Standish, the colony's military chief, while recording his utter inability to understand the need for the severe measures taken against the Indians. The passage is from William Bradford's *Of Plymouth Plantation, 1620–1647*, pp. 374–75, edited by Samuel Eliot Morison (New York: Alfred A. Knopf, 1952).

MY LOVING AND MUCH BELOVED FRIEND, whom God hath hitherto preserved, preserve, and keep you still to His glory, and the good of many; that His blessing may make your godly and wise endeavours answerable to the valuation which they there have, and set upon the same. Of your love to and care for us here, we never doubted; so are we glad to take knowledge of it in that fullness we do. Our love and care to and for you is mutual, though our hopes of coming unto you be small, and weaker than ever. But of this at large in Mr. Brewster's letter, with whom you, and he with you mutually, I know, communicate your letters, as I desire you may do these, etc.

Concerning the killing of those poor Indians, of which

we heard at first by report, and since by more certain relation. Oh, how happy a thing had it been, if you had converted some before you had killed any! Besides, where blood is once begun to be shed, it is seldom staunched of a long time after. You will say they deserved it. I grant it; but upon what provocations and invitements by those heathenish Christians? [Mr. Weston's men] Besides, you being no magistrates over them were to consider not what they deserved but what you were by necessity constrained to inflict. Necessity of this, especially of killing so many (and many more, it seems, they would, if they could) I see not. Methinks one or two principals should have been full enough, according to that approved rule, The punishment to a few, and the fear to many. Upon this occasion let me be bold to exhort you seriously to consider of the disposition of your Captain, whom I love, and am persuaded the Lord in great mercy and for much good hath sent you him, if you use him aright. He is a man humble and meek amongst you, and towards all in ordinary course. But now if this be merely from an humane spirit, there is cause to fear that by occasion, especially of provocation, there may be wanting that tenderness of the life of man (made after God's image) which is meet. It is also a thing more glorious, in men's eyes, than pleasing in God's or convenient for Christians, to be a terrour to poor barbarous people. And indeed I am afraid lest, by these occasions, others should be drawn to affect a kind of ruffling course in the world.

I doubt not but you will take in good part these things which I write, and as there is cause, make use of them. It were to us more comfortable and convenient that we communicated our mutual helps in presence; but seeing that cannot be done, we shall always long after you, and love you, and wait God's appointed time. The Adventurers, it seems, have neither money nor any great mind of us, for the most part. They deny it to be any part of the covenants betwixt us that they should transport us, neither do I look for any further help from them, till means come from you. We here are strangers in effect to the whole course, and so both we and you (save as your own wisdoms and worths have interested you further) of principals intended in this business, are scarce accessories, etc.

My wife, with me, re-salutes you and yours. Unto Him who is the same to His in all places, and near to them which are far from one another, I commend you and all with you, resting,

Yours truly loving,
JOHN ROBINSON

Leyden, December 19, 1623

A Forest Dialogue

The clash of religious beliefs in the American forest is worthy of greater study. The Indian often retained his religious orientation when he had lost or surrendered other aspects of his native culture. In New England, however, where Protestant religious views were ceaselessly and aggressively championed, the Indian view of this world and the next was directly confronted and denounced. A firsthand account of this confrontation appears in Roger Williams' *A Key into the Language of America, or an Help to the Language of the Natives in that Part of America called New-England* (London: 1643), reprinted in the Rhode Island Historical Society, *Collections*, Vol. I, pp. 114–16 (Providence: 1827).

Now because this Book (by Gods good Providence) may come into the hand of many fearing God, who may also have many an opportunity of occasionall discourse with some of these their wild Brethren and Sisters, and may speake a word for their and our glorious Maker, which may also prove some preparatory Mercy to their Soules: I shall propose some proper expressions concerning the Creation of the world, and mans Estate and in particular theirs also, which from myselfe many hundredths of times, great numbers of them have heard with great delight, and great convictions: which who knowes (in Gods holy season) may rise to the exalting of the Lord Jesus Christ in their conversion and salvation?

Nétop Kunnatótemous.	Friend, I will aske you a Question.
Nntótema.	Speake on.
Tocketunnántum?	What thinke you?
Awaun Keesiteoûwin Kéesuck?	Who made the Heavens?
Aûke Wechêkom?	The Earth, the Sea.
Mittauke,	The World

Some will answer Tattá, I cannot tell, some will answer Manittôwock, the Gods.

Tà suóg Manittowock,	How many Gods bee there?
Maunaúog Mishaúnawock	Many, great many.
Netop macháge,	Friend, not so.
Paúsuck naúnt manìt,	There is only one God.
Cuppíssittone,	You are mistaken.
Cowauwaúnemum,	You are out of the way.

A Phrase which much pleaseth them, being proper for their wandring in the Woods, and similitudes greatly please them.

Kukkakótemous, wachitquáshouwe	I will tell you, presently.
Kuttaunchemókous.	I will tell you newes.
Paûsuck naúnt manít kéesittin keesuck, &c.	One onely God made the Heavens &c.
Napannètashèmittan naugecautúmmonabnshque,	Five thousand yeers agoe, and upwards.
Naúgom naúnt wukkesittinnes wâmeteâgun,	He alone made all things.
Wuche mateâg,	Out of nothing.
Quttatashuchuckqunnacauskeesitinneswâme,	In six dayes he made all things.
Nquittaqúnne, Wuckéesitin weqâi,	The first day hee made the Light.
Neesqunne, Wuckéesitin Keésuck,	The second day Hee made the Firmament.

Shúckqunne wuckéesitin Aúkekà wechêkom,	The third day hee made the Earth and sea.
Yóqunne wuckkéesitin Nippaúus kà Nanepaúshat,	The fourth day he made the Sun and the Moon.
Neenash-mamockíuwash wêquanantiganash,	Two great Lights.
Kà wáme anócksuck,	And all the Starres.
Napannetashúckqunne Wuckéesittinpussuck- seesuckwâme,	The fifth day hee made all the fowle.
Keesuckquíuke,	In the Ayre or Heavens
Kawámeaúmúasuck, Wechekommiuke,	And all the Fish in the Sea.
Quttatashúkqunne Wuckkeésittin penashímwock wamè,	The sixth day hee made all the Beasts of the Field.
Wuttàke wuckèwuckeesit- tin pausuck Enìn, or, Eneskéetomp,	Last of all he made one Man.
Wuche mishquòck,	Of red Earth,
Kawesuonckgonnakaûnes Adam, túppautea mishquòck,	And call'd him Adam, or red Earth.
Wuttáke wuchè Câwit mishquòck,	Then afterward, while Adam or red Earth slept.
Wuckaudnúmmenes manit peetaúgonwuche Adam,	God tooke a rib from Adam, or red Earth.
Kà wuchè peteaúgon Wukkeessitínnes pausuck squàw,	And of that rib he made One woman.
Ka pawtouwúnnes Adâmuck	And brought her to Adam.
Nawônt Adam wuttunnawaun nuppeteâgon ewò,	When Adam saw her, he said, this is my bone.
Enadatashúckqunneaquêi	The seventh day hee rested.

Nagaû wvchè   And therefore Englishmen
quttatashúckqune   worke six days
anacaúsuock,
Englishmánnuck,
Enadatashuckqunnóckat-   On the seventh day they
taubataumwock.   praise God.

Obs: At this Relation they are much satisfied, with a
reason why (as they observe) the English and Dutch, &c.
labour six dayes, and rest and worship the seventh.

Besides, they will say, Wee never heard of this before;
and then will relate how they have it from their Fathers,
that *Kautántowwit* made one man and woman of a stone,
which disliking, he broke them in pieces, and made another man and woman of a Tree, which were the Foun-
taines of all mankind.

They apprehending a vast difference of Knowledge betweene the English and themselves, are very observant of
the English lives: I have heard them say to an Englishman
(who being hindred, broke a promise to them) you know
God, will you lie Englishman?

DOCUMENT 45

Church and State

Two representative orders of the General Court of the Colony of the Massachusetts Bay in New England, the governing body of the colony, are given below. They are taken from the *Records of the Governor and Company of the Massachusetts Bay in New England*, edited by Nathaniel B. Shurtleff, Vol. III, pp. 6–7, 98 (Boston: 1854).

10 June 1644

It is ordred, that noe Indian shall come att any towne or howse of the English (without leave) uppon the Lords day, except to attend the publike meeteings; neither shall they come att any English howse uppon any other day in the weeke, but first shall knocke att the dore, and after leave given, to come in, (and not otherwise;) and if any (hereafter) offend contrary to this order, the constable, uppon notice given him, shall bringe him or them Indians, soe offendinge, to a magestrate to bee punisht according to his offence.

Whereas it is the earnest desire of this Courte, that these natives (amongst whome wee live, and whoe have submitted themselves to this governmente) should come to the good knowledge of God, and bee brought on to subject to the scepter of the Lord Jesus, it is therefore ordred, that all such of the Indians as have subjected themselves to our governmente bee henceforward enjoyned (and that they fayle not) to meete att such severall places of appoyntmente as shalbee most convenient on the Lords day, where they may attend such instruction as shalbee given them by those whose harts God shall stirr upp to that worke; and it is hereby further declared (as the desire of this Courte) that those townes that lye most convenient to such places of meetinge of the Indians would make choyce of some of theire brethren (whom God hath best quallified for that worke) to goe to them, (beeinge soe mett,) and instruct them, (by the best interpriter they can gett,) that if possible God may have the glory of the conversion (at least) of some of them in the use of such meanes God gives us to afoard them.

4 November 1646

Albeit faith be not wrought by the sword, but by the word, and therefore such pagan Indians as have submitted themselves to our government, though wee would not neglect any dew helpes to bring them on to grace, and to the meanes of it, yett wee compell them not to the Christian faith, nor to the profession of it, either by force of armes or by poenall lawes, neverthelesse, seing the blaspheming of the true God cannot be excused by any ignorance or infirmity of humane nature, the aetaernall power and Godhead being knowne by the light of nature and the creation of the world, and common reason requireth every state and society of men to be more carefull of preventing the dishonnor and contempt of the Most High God (in whom wee all consist) then of any mortall princes and magistrates, itt is therefore ordered and decreed by this Courte, for the honnour of the aetaernall God, whome only wee worshipp and serve, that no person within this jurisdiction, whether Christian or pagan, shall wittingly and willingly presume to blaspheme his holy name, either by wilfull or obstinate denying the true God, or reproach the holy religion of God, as if it were but a polliticke devise to keepe ignorant men in awe, or deny his creation or government of the world, or shall curse God, or shall utter any other eminent kind of blasphemy of the like nature and degree; if any person or persons whatsoever, within our jurisdiction, shall breake this lawe, they shallbe putt to death.

DOCUMENT 46

The Day-breaking, if Not the Sun-rising of the Gospel

John Eliot, New England's "Apostle to the Indians," labored mightily to convert the Indians in proximity to the Massachusetts Bay settlement. The Puritan method differed from the Catholic in that the ministers were primarily responsible to their own English congregations and could not go far afield, and also in the fact that conversion, to the Puritan, meant a radical alteration in the Indian's way of life, material and spiritual. The Puritans exercised strict control over the towns of "Praying Indians" established in the Bay Colony, as will be evident in the following passage taken from Eliot's anonymously published *The Day-Breaking, If Not the Sun-Rising of the Gospell with the Indians in New-England,* printed in London in 1647 under the supposed authorship of John Wilson, and reprinted in New York for Joseph Sabin in 1865, pp. 27–32.

Wee have cause to be very thankfull to God who hath moved the hearts of the generall court to purchase so much land for them to make their towne in which the *Indians* are much taken with,[1] and it is somewhat observable that while the Court were considering where to lay out their towne, the *Indians* (not knowing of any thing) were about that time consulting about Lawes for themselves,

[1] The towne the Indians did desire to know what name it should have, and it was told them it should bee called Noonatomen, which signifies in English rejoycing, because they hearing the word, and seeking to know God, the English did rejoyce at it, and God did rejoyce at it, which pleased them much, & therefore that is to be the name of their town. [Eliot's note.]

and there company who sit downe with *Waaubon;* there were ten of them, two of them are forgotten.

Their Lawes were these

1. That if any man be idle a weeke, at most a fortnight, hee shall pay five shillings.

2. If any unmarried man shall lie with a young woman unmarried, he shall pay twenty shillings.

3. If any man shall beat his wife, his hands shall bee tied behind him and carried to the place of justice to bee severely punished.

4. Every young man if not anothers servant, and if unmarried, hee shall be compelled to set up a *Wigwam* and plant for himselfe, and not live shifting up and downe to other *Wigwams.*

5. If any woman shall not have her haire tied up but hang loose or be cut as mens haire, she shall pay five shillings.

6. If any woman shall goe with naked breasts they shall pay two shillings sixpence.

7. All those men that weare long locks shall pay five shillings.

8. If any shall kill their lice betweene their teeth, they shall pay five shillings. This Law though ridiculous to English eares yet tends to preserve cleanliness among *Indians.*

Tis wonderfull in our eyes to understand by these two honest *Indians,* what Prayers *Waaubon* and the rest of them use to make, for hee that preacheth to them professeth hee never yet used any of their words in his prayers, from whom otherwise it might bee thought that they had learnt them by rote, one is this.

Amanaomen Jehovah tahassen metagh.
Take away Lord my Stony heart.
Another
Cheehesom Jehovah kekowhogkew,
Wash Lord my soule.
Another
Lord lead me when I die to heaven.
These are but a taste, they have many more, and these

more enlarged then thus expressed, yet what are these but the sprinklings of the spirit and blood of Christ Jesus in their hearts? and 'tis no small matter that such dry barren and long-accursed ground should yeeld such kind of increase in so small a time, I would not readily commend a faire day before night, nor promise much of such kind of beginnings, in all persons, nor yet in all of these, for wee know the profession of very many is but a meere paint, and their best graces nothing but meere flashes and pangs, which are suddainly kindled and as soon go out and are extinct againe, yet God doth not usually send his Plough & Seedsman to a place but there is at least some little peece of good ground, although three to one bee naught: and mee thinkes the Lord Jesus would never have made so fit a key for their locks, unlesse hee had intended to open some of their doores, and so to make way for his comming in. Hee that God hath raised up and enabled to preach unto them, is a man (you know) of a most sweet, humble, loving, gratious and enlarged spirit, whom God hath blest, and surely will still delight in & do good by. I did thinke never to have opened my mouth to any, to desire those in England to further any good worke here, but now I see so many things inviting to speake in this businesse, that it were well if you did lay before those that are prudent and able these considerations.

1 That it is prettie heavy and chargeable to educate and traine up those children which are already offered us, in schooling, cloathing, diet, and attendance, which they must have.

2 That in all probabilities many *Indians* in other places, expecially under our jurisdiction, will bee provoked by this example in these, both to desire preaching, and also to send their children to us, when they see that some of their fellows fare so well among the English, and the civill authoritie here so much favouring and countenancing of these, and if many come in, it will bee more heavy to such as onely are fit to keepe them, and yet have their hands and knees infeebled so many wayes besides.

3 That if any shall doe any thing to encourage this

worke, that it may be given to the Colledge for such an
end and use, that so from the Colledge may arise the
yeerly revenue for their yeerly maintenance. I would not
have it placed in any particular mans hands for feare
cousenage or misplacing or carelesse keeping and improving; but at the Colledge it's under many hands and eyes
the chief and best of the country who have ben & will be
exactly carefull of the right and comely disposing of such
things; and therefore, if any thing bee given, let it be put
in such hands as may immediately direct it to the President of the Colledge, who you know will soone acquaint
the rest with it; and for this end if any in England have
thus given any thing for this end, I would have them
speake to those who have received it to send it this way,
which if it bee withheld I thinke 'tis no lesse than sacri-
lege: but if God moves no hearts to such a work, I doubt
not then but that more weake meanes shall have the
honour of it in the day of Christ.

A fourth meeting with the Indians.

This day being *Decemb*, 9. the children being cate-
chised, and that place of *Ezekiel* touching the dry bones
being opened, and applyed to their condition; the *Indians*
offered all their children to us to bee educated amongst
us, and instructed by us, complaining to us that they were
not able to give any thing to the English for their education: for this reason there are therefore preparations made
towards the schooling of them, and setting up a Schoole
among them or very neare unto them. Sundry questions
also were propounded by them to us, and of us to them;
one of them being askt what is sinne? hee answered a
noughty heart. Another old man complained to us of his
feares, *viz*, that hee was fully purposed to keepe the Sabbath, but still he was in feare whether he should go to hell
or heaven; and thereupon the justification of a sinner by
faith in Christ was opened unto him as the remedy against
all feares of hell. Another complayned of other *Indians*
that did revile them, and call them Rogues and such like

speeches for cutting off their Locks, and for cutting their Haire in a modest manner as the New-English generally doe; for since the word hath begun to worke upon their hearts, they have discerned the vanitie and pride which they placed in their haire, and have therefore of their owne accord (none speaking to them that wee know of) cut it modestly; there were therefore encouraged by some there present of chiefe place and account with us, not to feare the reproaches of wicked *Indians,* nor their witch-craft and *Pawwaws* and poysonings, but let them know that if they did not dissemble but would seeke God un-faignedly, that they would stand by them, and that God also would be with them. They told us also of divers *Indians* who would come and stay with them three or foure dayes, and one Sabbath, and then they would goe from them, but as for themselves, they told us they were fully purposed to keepe the Sabbath, to which wee incouraged them, and night drawing on were forced to leave them, for this time.

DOCUMENT 47

"How Do You Know What Is Done in Heaven?"

Puritan ministers dealing with Indian congregations were often forced to answer questions their English congregations rarely posed. A list of some of these questions, and a dialogue between an orthodox Puritan Indian and English dissenters from the Puritan way in Rhode Island is recounted by John Eliot, the apostle to the Indians, in passages from letters dated December 29, 1649, and October 21, 1650, in Henry Whitfield's *The Light Appearing More and More Towards the Perfect Day, or, A Farther Discovery of the Present State of the Indians in New-England, concerning the Progresse of the Gospel amongst Them*, published in London in 1651, and reprinted in New York for Joseph Sabin in 1865, pp. 25–27, 33–35.

Having some leasure by the Ships delay I will insert a few questions which they have propounded. *viz.*

If a man know Gods Word, but beleeve it not; and he teach others, is that good teaching? and if others beleeve that which he teacheth, is that good beleeving, or faith? upon this question I asked them, how they could tell when a man knoweth Gods Word that he doth not beleeve it? They answered me, *When he doth not do in his practice answerable to that which he knoweth.*

If I teach on the Sabbath that which you have taught us, and forget some, Is that a sin? and some I mistake and teach wrong, Is that a sin?

Do all evill thoughts come from the Devill, and all good ones from God?

What is watchfulnesse?

How shall I finde happinesse?

What should I pray for at night, and what at morning, and what on the Sabbath day?

What is true Repentance, or how shall I know when this is true?

How must I wait on God?

Shall we see Christ at the day of Judgment?

Can we see God?

When I pray for a soft heart, why is it still hard?

Can one be saved by reading the book of the creature? This question was made when I taught them, That God gave us two books, and that in the book of the creature, every creature was a word or sentence, &c.

You said God promised Moses to go with him, how doth he go with us?

When such die as never heard of Christ, whether do they go?

When the wicked die, do they first go to heaven to the judgment seate of Christ to be judged, and then go away to hell?

What is the meaning of the word Hebrews?

Why doth God say, I am the God of the Hebrews?

When Christ arose, whence came his soul? When I answered from heaven; It was replyed, *How then was Christ punished in our stead? Or when did he suffer in our stead, afore death or after?*

When I pray every day, why is my heart so hard still, even as a stone?

How doth God arise, and we worship at his feet, what meaneth it? This was when I preached out of *Psal.* 132.

Why did they eate the Passeover, with loynes girt, and shooes on their feet?

What meaneth, arise O Lord into thy resting place?

What meaneth, hunger and thirst after righteousnesse, and they blessed?

What meaneth, thou shalt not covet any thing that is thy neighbours?

If one purposeth to pray, and yet dieth before that time, whether goeth his soul?

If I teach on the Sabbath something that some other Englishman taught me, the Indians do not like it, if it be not that which you have taught, is this well?

Why must we be like Salt?

If I do not love wicked men, nor good men, am I good?

What meaneth that, love enemies and wicked men?

Doth God know who shall repent, and beleeve, and who not? When I answered in the affirmative, then it was replyed, *Why then did God use so much meanes with* Pharaoh?

What meaneth that his wife shall be like a Vine, and his children like young plants?

What meaneth, that blessed are they that mourn?

When I see a good example, and know that it is right, why do I not do the same?

What meaneth lifting up hands to God?

What anger is good, and what is bad?

Do they dwell in severall houses in heaven, or altogether, and what do they?

How do you know what is done in heaven?

If a child die before he sinne, whether goeth his soul? By this question, it did please the Lord, clearly to convince them of original sin, blessed be his name.

If one that prayes to God, sins like him that prayes not, is not he worse? And while they discoursed of this point, and about hating of wicked persons, one of them shut it up with this, *They must love the man and do him good, but hate his sin.*

Why do Englishmen so eagerly kill all snakes?

May a man have good words and deeds and a bad heart, and another bad words and deeds, and yet a good heart?

What is it to eate Christ his flesh and drink his blood, what meaneth it?

What meaneth a new heaven and a new earth?

. . . .

For the work of the Lord among the Indians, I thank his Majesty he still smileth on it, he favoureth and blesseth it; through his help that strengthneth me, I cease not in

my poor measure to instruct them; and I do see that they
profit and grow in knowledge of the truth, and some of
them in the love of it, which appeareth by a ready obedience to it; and to testifie their growth in knowledge, I will
not (though I could do it if need were) trouble you with
their questions; but I will only relate one story which fell
out about the fifth month of this yeere; Two of my hearers
travelled to *Providence* and *Warwick* where *Gorton* liveth,
and there they spent a Sabbath, and heard them in some
exercises, and had much conference with them; for it
seemeth they perceiving that they had some knowledge in
Religion, and were of my hearers; they endeavour to possesse their minds with their opinions. When they came
home, the next Lecture day, before I began the exercise,
the company being not fully come together, one of them
asked me this question; *What is the reason, that seeing
those English people, where he had been, had the same
Bible that we have, yet do not speake the same things?* I
asked the reason of his question; he said, *because his
brother and he had been at* Providence *and at* Warwick,
*and he perceived by speech with them, that they differ
from us; he said they heard their publike exercise, but did
not understand what they meant,* (though the man under-
standeth the English Language pretty well) But afterwards
said he, *we had much speech*; I asked him in what points;
and so much as his brother and he could call to minde, he
related as followeth.

First, said he, *they said thus they teach you that there
is a Heaven and a Hell, but there is no such matter*; I asked
him what reason they gave; *he answered, that he said there
is no other Heaven then what is in the hearts of good men;
nor no other Hell, then what is in the hearts of bad men*;
Then I asked, and what said you to that; saith he, *I told
them, I did not beleeve them, because Heaven is a place
whether good men go after this life is ended; and Hell is a
place whether bad men go when they die, and cannot be
in the hearts of men*; I approved of this answer. I asked
what else they spake? he answered, *they spake of Baptism*,
and said, *that they teach you that Infants must be baptised,*

but that is a very foolish thing; I asked him what reason they gave? He said, *because Infants neither know God nor Baptisme, nor what they do, and therefore it is a foolish thing to do it;* I asked him what he said to that? He said, *he could not say much, but he thought it was better to baptize them while they be young, and then they are bound and engaged; but if you let them alone till they be grown up, it may be they will flie off, and neither care for God nor for Baptisme;* I approved of this answer also, and asked what else they spake of? He said farther, *they spake of Ministers,* and said, *they teach you that you must have Ministers, but that is a needlesse thing.* I asked what reason they gave? He said, *they gave these reasons,* First, *Ministers know nothing but what they learn out of Gods book, and we have Gods book as well as they and can tell what God saith.* Again, *Ministers cannot change mens hearts, God must do that, and therefore there is no need of Ministers.* I asked him what he said to that? He said, *that he told them, that we must do as God commands us, and if he commands to have Ministers, we must have them.* And farther I told them, I thought it was true, that Ministers cannot change mens hearts; but when we do as God bids us, and hear Ministers preach, then God will change our hearts. I approved this answer also. I asked what else they spake of? He said, *They teach you that you must have magistrates, but that is needlesse, nor ought to be.* I asked what reason they gave? He said, *That they gave this reason, because Magistrates cannot give life, therefore they may not take away life; besides when a man sinneth, he doth not sinne against Magistrates, and therefore why should they punish them? but they sinne against God and therefore we must leave them to God to punish them.* I asked him what he had to say to that, he answered, *I said to that as to the former, we must do as God commands us; If God command us to have Magistrates, and commands them to punish sinners, them we must obey.* I approved this also.

I asked farther what they said; then both of them considered a while, and said, *they could remember no more,* only they said somewhat of the Parliament of *England*, which they did not understand. And by such time as we had done this conference, the company was gathered together, and we went to Prayer, and I did solemnly blesse God who had given them so much understanding in his truth, and some ability to discerne between Truth and Error, and an heart to stand for the Truth, and against Error; and I cannot but take it as a Divine Testimony of Gods blessing upon my poor labours; I afterwards gave him an answer to his first question *viz. Why they having the same Bible with us, yet spake not the same things?* And I answered him by that text, 2 *Thes.* 2. 10, 11. *Because they received not the love of the truth that they might be saved, for this cause God shall send them strong delusions that they should beleeve a lye.* This text I opened unto them; I will adde no more at present to manifest their proficiency in knowledge.

"What Is the Matter That Indians Very Often No Speak True?"

The following dialogue, from Josiah Cotton's *Vocabulary of the Massachusetts (or Natick) Indian Language*, carries us to a level of personal contact between Indian and white in the early eighteenth century (the manuscript was compiled about 1707–08) that is nearly impossible to recapture in any other way. Natick was a town of "Praying Indians" under the control of the Massachusetts Bay authorities, and the cultural dominance implicit in the relationship is evident in the dialogue. The passage is from the edition of the *Vocabulary* published in Cambridge, Massachusetts, in 1829, pp. 94–99.

A Dialogue.

How does your wife, or husband do?	Toh unnuppomântam kummittŭmwus asuh kāsuk.
What is the matter that Indians very often no speak true?	Toh waj unnak Indiansog moochĕke nompe matta sampwe unnoowoōōog.
Have you bin at Squantam lately?	Sun Squantam kuppeyômus pāswe.
Do the souldiers go to Canada? No.	Sun aiyeuehteaenŭog aŭog Canada; matteag.
Then they will do no good, but a great deal of hurt.	Neit nag pish matta toh unné wunnesēog, qut moocheke woskeŭssēog.
Yes they will put the country to a great deal of charge.	Nux, nag pish mishe ōadtehkontamwog wuttohkeōngash.

Is not the fleet come ashore yet?	Sun chuppoonâog asq koppaemŭnnoo.
Do you think they will ever come?	Sun kuttenântam nash pish peyômŏŏash.
It may be not.	Ammiate matteag.
Very likely not.	Ahche ogqueneunkquat matteag.
I believe they are gone to Spain.	Nuttinantam nag monchuk en Spain.
Why do you remove from Natick?	Tohwaj ontootaän wutche Natick.
You will get more money there than at Sandwich.	Woh kummoochke wuttehtīnum teagwas nâut onk Moskeehtŭkqut.
My family is sickly there.	Nutteashinnĭnnēonk wuttit mohchinnonāop.
And were they healthy at Sandwich? Yes.	Kah sun nag wunne pomantamwushanneg ut Moskeehtŭkqut. Nux.
Dont you owe a great deal of money there?	Sunnummatta kummishontukquahwhuttĕoh nâ utt.
Yes, but I hope to clear it quickly.	Nux, qut nuttannôos nuttapoadtehkônat pāswēse.
What if they would put you in prison?	Toh woh unni kuppŭshagkinukquēan.
Then they will hurt themselves and me too.	Neit nag woh woskehheaog wuhhogkāuh kah nen wonk.
It is very cold to day.	Moochĕke tohkoi yeu kesukod.
Almost I freeze my ears and fingers.	Nāhen togquttĭnash nuhtauōgwash kah nuppoohkuhquāuitchēgat.
Why dont you get a thick cap?	Tohwaj matta ahchuehteoŏŏou kohpŏgkag kah onkquontŭpape.
Because I have no money.	Newutche matta nuttohtooo teagwash.

And why dont you work hard?

Kah tohwaj mat menukânâkausēan.

So I would with all my heart, but I am sickly.

Ne woh nuttussen nashpe manŭsse nuttah, qut nummōmohtehŭnam.

But it may be work will cure you, if you would leave off drinking too.

Qut ammiate woh anakausuonk kukketeŏhhuk, tohneit wonk ohksippamwēan.

I think you give good advice, but let me work for you.

Nuttinântam kuttinunūmah wunne kogkahquttüonk koowehquttumauish unnanumeh kutanakausuehtauununat.

How many years old are you?

Noh kutteăshe kodtum wōhkom.

Eighteen; and how old is that boy, or girl.

Piog nishwosuk; kah toh unnukkoohquiyeu noh nonkomp kah nonksq.

Why do boys of that age run about, and do nothing.

Tohwaj nonkompaog ne anoohquiitcheg pumomashaōg, kah matteag usseog.

You had better let me have him, and I will learn him to write, and read.

An wunnegik kuttinninumiin kah pish nunnehtŭhpeh wussukquŏhamŭnat kah ogketamŭnat.

He shall want for nothing, neither meat, drink, cloathing, or drubbing.

Noh matteag pish quenauehhikkoo asuh metsuonk wuttattamoooonk ogkoooonk asuh sasamitahwhuttuonk.

Idleness is the root of much evil.

Nanompanissūonk wutchappehk moocheke machuk.

Do you come, or else send him tomorrow early.

Pasoo asuh nekonchhuash saup nompoāe.

Dont forget your promise.

Wanantōhkon koonoowaonk.

I am glad to see you.

Noowekontam ne kenau-ŭnun.

Where have you been this long time? Hunting. And what did you find?

Tonoh koomūmus yeu qun-nohquompi? Adchânat. Kah teagwas kenamiteoh?

A fox or two.

Wonkqŭssis asuh nees.

I believe so; these drams will ruine Indians and English.

Nuttinantāmun; yeush nuk-quttikkupsash pish pa-pukquanhukqunoōash In-dians kah Châh[quog.]

A great deal of praise that Indian deserves that keeps himself sober.

Moochĕke wowenotuonk noh Indian woh ahto nan-auehhēont wuhhoguh maninniyeuongānit.

I wish such an one would come and set down on my land, I would be kind to him as long as I have any thing.

Nâpehnont neahhenissit peyont kah appit nuttoh-kēit.
Woh nooneunneh tô sâhke ahtou nanwe teag.

Why do you deceive me so often?

Tohwaj wunnompuhkos-sēan ne tohshit.

I am forced to be worse than my word.

Nunnamhit nummatchiteo nukkuttooonk.

I am in debt. To who?

Nuttinohtukquāhwhut. Ut howaneg.

To a great many and they force me to stay and work with them.

Ut monaog kah nag che-kewe nukkogkanunūk-quog anâkausuehtauōnat.

If it be not very much I will pay it.

Tohneit matta wussômē-nook kuttoadtehteanĭ-sish.

I am ashamed to tell you much; it is above 40 pounds.

Nuttohkodch kūmishamau-ununate neatahshik; pa-paumēyeuoo yauinchake poundyeuoo.

O strange! But Indians are not to be trusted any more.

Mohchanitamwe! Qut Indi-ânog mat wonk woh un-nohtŭkquohwhôun ko-oche.

So they say, and I dont care.	Ne unnōōwon kah matta nuttintupantamōōun.
Your house smokes, and so do I smoke, when I can get Tobacco.	Kek pŭkkuttāūo kah nen nuppukkuttohteam uttuh annooh wuttoohpooomweonish.
Will you smoke it now?	Sun woh kootam eyeu.
Yes, and thank you too.	Nux, kah kuttabotômish wonk.
Why dont you ask for what you want?	Tohwaj matta wehquttumōōan uttuh yeu quenauehhikquēan.
Because I am afraid you will be angry.	Newutche noowabis kummosquantamŭnat.
Be very free always when you come to my house.	Moocheke nukkógkittāmwem payoaīnish nekit.
Well, what have you got for dinner?	Neit teagwa kuttohto wutch pohshâquôpōōonk.
Pray give me some drink.	Koowehquttumauish wuttattamwēhe.
Very much I want old coat and stockings.	Nukquenauĕhhik nukkonōgkoo kah muttāsash.
Why dont you come and preach every day?	Tohwaj mat nonche kuhkootumauwēog nishnoh kesukod.
Your father came oftener than you do.	Kooshi moochikit peyāpan onk ken.
Because my father have a great deal more than I.	Newutche nooshi moocheke ahtōai onk nen.
I have five pounds less than others that dont preach so often.	Nunnōgkos ohtom napannatāshe poundyeuash onk onkatogig matta netāhshe kukkootumwehteahitteg.
Pray what is the reason for that?	Koowehquttumauish tohwaj ne ūnnag.
I cant tell.	Mat noowahteooo.
Will you help us husk to night?	Sun woh kuppohkogquttanumiumin yeu nuhkon.

No, I am going to a wedding.

Mat, nuttômwetauwatüongānit.

Who is to be married?

Howan tohqunithittit.

Who married them?

Howan wuttohqunitheūh.

The Indian Justice.

Indiane Nanuunnuaēnin.

Q. How shall I learn Indian?

Uttuh woh nittinne nehtuhtaūan Indianne unnontoowaonk.

A. By talking with Indians, and minding their words, and manner of pronouncing.

Nashpe keketookauāonk Indiansog kah kuhkināsinneat ukkittooonkănnoo kah wuttinnohquatumooonkănnoo.

Q. Is not Indian a very hard language to learn?

Sun mat Indianne unnontoowaonk siogkod nehtuhtauŭnat.

A. Yes, tis very difficult to get their tone.

Nux, ne ahche siogomomŭkquat ohtauŭnat wuttinontoowaonkannoo.

Q. What do you think about me, do you think I shall ever learn?

Toh kuttinantam wutche (papaume) nen, sun kuttinantam pish nunnehtuhtauun.

A. I am afraid not very well.

Nen noowabes mat papaneyeue.

Q. Would it not be better to preach to the Indians in English?

Sun ummat ayn-wanegig kuhkootumauonau Indiansog ut wadtohkōōne 'nontoowaonkanit.

A. Yes, much better than to preach in broken Indian.

Nux, moocheke kooche wunnegen onk neit kuhkootumauonat ut nannohtoohquatumooonkānit.

Q. Can the Indians understand the most that I say?

Sun woh Indiansog wahtamwog uttuh annoowai asuh unnontoowai.

A. Sometimes they can, and sometimes they cant.

Momānĭsh woh watamwog kah momanish woh mat wahtamoowog.

Q. What is the reason for that?

Tohwaj ne ŭnnage.

A. Because you have some of your fathers words, and he learnt Indian at Nope,[1] and because you dont put the tone in the right place.

Newutche kuttahto nawhutche ukkuttooonkash kooshi kah noh nehtuhtoup wuttinontoowaonkannooo Nope Indiansog, kah mat kukkuhkenaŭwe poonummoo wuttinnuhquatumoooonkānoo.

Q. Did your father study Indian at Nope?

Sun kooshi kod wahtamwus Indianne 'nontoowaonk ut Nope.

A. So I hear.

Ne nuttinnehtamunap.

And what is the difference between the language of the Island, and the main.

Kah uttuh unnuppenōōnat wuttinnontoowaonk ne munnohonk neit kohtohkomukoouk.

I cant tell, or dont know, only this I know, that these Indians dont understand every word of them Indians.

Mat woh nummissohhamōōun asuh matta noowahĭteo webe yeu noowahteauun yeug Indiansog mat wahtanooog uag Indiansog ut nishnoh kuttooonganit.

Pray tell me how to pronounce Indian right.

Noowehquttum missŏhhamunat samp-wohquatumunat Indian.

I will do what I can about it.

Uttuh annoohque tapenum nuttissen.

Well, friend, I am sorry you are going away, but I hope it will be for the best.

Netomp nunnooantam asuh kunnouskōsseh nekummoncheonk, qut nuttannôōŭs neanwanegig wutche ken.

[1] The Indian name for the Island of Martha's Vineyard. *Edit.*

I wish you may do and receive good where you are going, and I wish you a good journey.

And I hope you will keep your self soberly and Christianly.

Try to keep your selves from those vices to which Indians are given, and which will bring the wrath of God and men upon you, *viz.* drunkenness, falseness, idleness, and theft, &c.

And God be with you, and bless you. Amen.

Napehnont ussean kah attumunuman uttuh ayoan, napehnont wanegig kuppumwĭshaonk.

Kah nuttannoous pish kummaninnis kah Christiane kenanaueh kuhhog.

Qutchéhtaŭish kenanauehheŏn kuhhog wutche yeush Indiansog womantamwehhitticheh ne woh patonkquĕan ummosquantamooonk God kah wosketompaog kenuhkukkonqŭnat, nahnane, kogkesippamoonk, assookekodteamooonk, nanompanissuonk, kumootooonk.

Kah God wetomŭkquish kah wunnanumŭkquish. Amen.

DOCUMENT 49

Indian Weather Vane

Evidence of the continuing influence of Massachusetts' Indian tradition, as well as a remarkable example of early American decorative arts, is the copper molded Indian weather vane made by Shem Drowne, 1742, which formerly surmounted the cupola of the Province House in Boston. The photograph reproduced in Plate 11, following page 134, is from the Massachusetts Historical Society, Boston.

DOCUMENT 50

Eleazar Wheelock Was a Very Pious Man

Dartmouth College, now located in Hanover, New Hampshire, was founded by Eleazar Wheelock, a minister, whose burning zeal to educate and convert the Indian led him to open an Indian Charity School in Lebanon, Connecticut, for the purpose. A touching picture of the school is evident in the following letter from a Boston merchant, John Smith, to a friend, dated May 18, 1764. Smith's note of the intention of an acquaintance to send his son to "obtain his Education in Mixture with these Indians" is prophetic of what was to come, for Indian attendance declined and white attendance increased as the years went by. One may wonder how well a modern American youth, educated in a cultural context foreign to that of his ancestors, would meet the requirements of eighteenth-century theologically oriented education. The letter, and note on Samson Occum, is taken from James Dow McCallum, ed., *The Letters of Eleazar Wheelock's Indians*, pp. 73–75 (Hanover, N. H.: Dartmouth College Publications, 1932).

John Smith's Letter to a Friend
(HOW THE SCHOOL APPEARED TO A BOSTON MERCHANT)

Boston May 18 1764

SIR

In rideing last week to new London I turned some miles out of my way to see Mr Wheelocks Indian School; nor do I repent my Trouble I had heard in general that it consisted of Twenty or more Indian Boys & Girls of the Mohawks & other Tribes of Indians And that a number of the Ministers of that Province had spoken well of Mr Wheelock & of this undertaking of his, But this I thought was seeing with the Eyes of others & therefore Chose to use my own.

My first observation in travelling through the Towns was the Different acceptation of both Mr Wheelock & his Enterprize there, from what some in Boston had entertained.

Here because of his lively adhering to the Doctrines of Grace he was not accepted by *some*; & when this is the Case you are sensible both Enterprize & Executior of it are too apt to be viewed by an Eye of Surmize & sometimes of Carping: But in Connecticut I found Charity & Candor & every where in passing Mr Wheelock had the Reverence of a Man of God, & his School was had in high Esteem.

I reached his House a little before the Evening Sacrafice & was movingly Touched on giveing out the Psalm to hear an Indian Youth set the Time & the others following him, & singing the Tenor, & Base, with remarkable Gravity & Seirousness, & tho' Mr Wheelock, The Schoolmaster & a minister from our Province (called as I was by Curiosity) joined in Praise; yet they unmoved seemed to have nothing to do but to sing to the Glory of God.

I omit Mr Wheelocks Prayer & pass to the Indians in the morning when on Ringing the School house Bell they Assemble at Mr Wheelocks House about 5 oClock with their Master; who named the Chapter in Course for the Day & called upon the near Indian who read 3 or 4 Verses till the Master said *Proximus*, & then the next Indian read some Verses & so on till all the Indians had read the whole chapter. After this Mr Wheelock Prayes And then they each Indian perse a Verse or two of the Chapter they had read. After this they entered Successively on Prosodia & then on Disputations on some Questions propounded by themselves in some of the Arts & Sciences. And it is really charming to see Indian Youths of Different Tribes & Languages in pure English reading the Word of God & speaking with Exactness & accuracy on points (either chosen by themselves or given out to them) in the Severall arts & Sciences, And especially to see this done with at Least a seeming Mixture of Obedience to God; a fillial Love & Reverence to Mr Wheelock, & yet with great Ambition to Excell each other And indeed in this Morning Exercies I saw a Youth Degraded one lower in the Class who before the Exercises were finished not only recovered his own place but was advanced two Higher.

I learnt hear that my surprize was common to ministers & other persons of Litterature who before me had been to visit this School or rather Colledge for I doubt whither in Colledges in General a better Education is to be expected & in mentioning this to a Gentleman in this Town who had visited this Seminary, He acquainted me that he intended at his own Charge to send his Son to obtain his Education in Mixture with these Indians. There were 4 or 5 of these Indians from 21 to 24 years of age who did not mix with the youth in these Exercies—These I learnt were Perfected in their Literature & stand ready to be sent among the Indians to keep Scools & occasionally to preach as doors open.

On my return Mr Wheelock accompanied me a few Miles & on passing by one House he said here lives one of my Indian Girls who was I hope Converted last week; & calling to the Farmer he unperceiv'd to her brought the Young Girl into our Sight & the pleasure was exquisite to see the Savageness of an Indian moulded into the Sweetness of a follower of the Lamb.

In passing some Days after this through the Mohegan Country I saw an Indian Man on Horseback whom I challenged as Mr *Occum*[1] & found it so. There was something in his mein & Deportment both amiable & venerable & though I had never before seen him I must have been sure

---

[1] Samson Occom, Mohegan (1723–92). He was taught by Wheelock (1743–48) before Moor's Charity School was organized. Occom was the most important non-combatant Indian of the eighteenth century in New England. He became a missionary to the Oneidas, was partner with Nathaniel Whitaker in raising some twelve thousand pounds in England and Scotland for the school, preached as an itinerant in New England, and was a leader in the emigration of the New England Indians to Brothertown, New York.

it was he.—He certainly does Honour to Mr Wheelocks indefatigable, judicious, pious Intentions to send the Gospel among the Indians. I heard Mr Ashpo was then among them but at a Distance & I being hurried & tired Lost the opportunity of seing Mr Wheelock in him & more especially of seeing Christs Image in this Tawney Man but I wont tire you

& am your most
Humble Servant
JOHN SMITH

DOCUMENT 51

Red Jacket and the Missionary

The following dialogue between a Seneca chief and a Boston missionary, in 1805, epitomizes the religious attitudes of both races. Red Jacket's speech, received from "a gentleman who was present when it was delivered, and wrote it sentence by sentence, as translated at the time by the interpreter," was printed by James D. Bemis at Canandaigua, New York, in 1809, in a pamphlet entitled *Indian Speeches; delivered by Farmer's Brother and Red Jacket, Two Seneca Chiefs,* pp. 4–8.

In the summer of 1805, a number of the principal Chiefs and Warriors of the Six Nations, principally Senecas, assembled at Buffalo Creek, in the state of New York, at the particular request of Rev. Mr. Cram, a Missionary from the state of Massachusetts. The Missionary being furnished with an Interpreter, and accompanied by the Agent of the United States for Indian affairs, met the Indians in Council, when the following talk took place:

First, By the Agent:

"*Brothers of the Six Nations*; I rejoice to meet you at this time, and thank the Great Spirit, that he has preserved you in health, and given me another opportunity of taking you by the hand.

"*Brothers*; The person who sits by me, is a friend who has come a great distance to hold a talk with you. He will inform you what his business is, and it is my request that you would listen with attention to his words."

Missionary:

"*My Friends*; I am thankful for the opportunity afforded us of uniting together at this time. I had a great desire to see you, and inquire into your state and welfare; for this purpose I have travelled a great distance, being sent by your old friends, the Boston Missionary Society. You will recollect they formerly sent missionaries among you, to instruct you in religion, and labor for your good. Although they have not heard from you for a long time, yet they have not forgotten their brothers the Six Nations, and are still anxious to do you good.

"*Brothers;* I have not come to get your lands or your money, but to enlighten your minds, and to instruct you how to worship the Great Spirit agreeably to his mind and will, and to preach to you the gospel of his son Jesus Christ. There is but one religion, and but one way to serve God, and if you do not embrace the right way, you cannot be happy hereafter. You have never worshipped the Great Spirit in a manner acceptable to him; but have, all your lives, been in great errors and darkness. To endeavor to remove these errors, and open your eyes, so that you might see clearly, is my business with you.

"*Brothers;* I wish to talk with you as one friend talks with another; and, if you have any objections to receive the religion which I preach, I wish you to state them; and I will endeavor to satisfy your minds, and remove the objections.

"*Brothers;* I want you to speak your minds freely; for I wish to reason with you on the subject, and, if possible, remove all doubts, if there be any on your minds. The subject is an important one, and it is of consequence that you give it an early attention while the offer is made you. Your friends, the Boston Missionary Society, will continue to send you good and faithful ministers, to instruct and strengthen you in religion, if, on your part, you are willing to receive them.

"*Brothers;* Since I have been in this part of the country, I have visited some of your small villages, and talked with your people. They appear willing to receive instructions, but, as they look up to you as their older brothers in council, they want first to know your opinion on the subject.

"You have now heard what I have to propose at present.

I hope you will take it into consideration, and give me an answer before we part."

After about two hours consultation among themselves, the Chief, commonly called by the white people, Red Jacket, (whose Indian name is Sagu-yu-what-hah, which interpreted is *Keeper awake*) rose and spoke as follows:

"*Friend and Brother;* It was the will of the Great Spirit that we should meet together this day. He orders all things, and has given us a fine day for our Council. He has taken his garment from before the sun, and caused it to shine with brightness upon us. Our eyes are opened, that we see clearly; our ears are unstopped, that we have been able to hear distinctly the words you have spoken. For all these favors we thank the Great Spirit; and Him *only*.

"*Brother;* This council fire was kindled by you. It was at your request that we came together at this time. We have listened with attention to what you have said. You requested us to speak our minds freely. This gives us great joy; for we now consider that we stand upright before you, and can speak what we think. All have heard your voice, and all speak to you now as one man. Our minds are agreed.

"*Brother;* You say you want an answer to your talk before you leave this place. It is right you should have one, as you are a great distance from home, and we do not wish to detain you. But we will first look back a little, and tell you what our fathers have told us, and what we have heard from the white people.

"*Brother;* Listen to what we say.

"There was a time when our forefathers owned this great island. Their seats extended from the rising to the setting sun. The Great Spirit had made it for the use of Indians. He had created the buffalo, the deer, and other animals for food. He had made the bear and the beaver. Their skins served us for clothing. He had scattered them over the country, and taught us how to take them. He had caused the earth to produce corn for bread. All this He had done for his red children, because He loved them. If we had some disputes about our hunting ground, they were generally settled without the shedding of much blood. But an evil day came upon us. Your forefathers crossed the great water, and landed on this island. Their numbers were small. They found friends and not enemies. They told us they had fled from their own country for fear of wicked men, and had come here to enjoy their religion. They asked for a small seat. We took pity on them, granted their request; and they sat down amongst us. We gave them corn and meat, they gave us poison (alluding, it is supposed, to ardent spirits) in return.

"The white people had now found our country. Tidings were carried back, and more came amongst us. Yet we did not fear them. We took them to be friends. They called us brothers. We believed them, and gave them a larger seat. At length their numbers had greatly increased. They wanted more land; they wanted our country. Our eyes were opened, and our minds became uneasy. Wars took place. Indians were hired to fight against Indians, and many of our people were destroyed. They also brought strong liquor amongst us. It was strong and powerful, and has slain thousands.

"Brother; Our seats were once large and yours were small. You have now become a great people, and we have scarcely a place left to spread our blankets. You have got our country, but are not satisfied; you want to force your religion upon us.

"Brother; Continue to listen.

"You say that you are sent to instruct us how to worship the Great Spirit agreeably to his mind, and, if we do not take hold of the religion which you white people teach, we shall be unhappy hereafter. You say that you are right and we are lost. How do we know this to be true? We understand that your religion is written in a book. If it was intended for us as well as you, why has not the Great Spirit given to us, and not only to us, but why did he not give to our forefathers, the knowledge of that book, with the means of understanding it rightly? We only know what you tell us about it. How shall we know when to believe, being so often deceived by the white people?

"*Brother*; You say there is but one way to worship and serve the Great Spirit. If there is but one religion; why do you white people differ so much about it? Why not all agreed, as you can all read the book?

"*Brother*; We do not understand these things.

"We are told that your religion was given to your fore-fathers, and has been handed down from father to son. We also have a religion, which was given to our forefathers, and has been handed down to us their children. We worship in that way. It teaches us to be thankful for all the favors we receive; to love each other, and to be united. We never quarrel about religion.

"*Brother*; The Great Spirit has made us all, but he has made a great difference between his white and red children. He has given us different complexions and different customs. To you He has given the arts. To these He has not opened our eyes. We know these things to be true. Since He has made so great a difference between us in other things; why may we not conclude that He has given us a different religion according to our understanding? The Great Spirit does right. He knows what is best for his children; we are satisfied.

"*Brother*; We do not wish to destroy your religion, or take it from you. We only want to enjoy our own.

"*Brother*; We are told that you have been preaching to the white people in this place. These people are our neighbors. We are acquainted with them. We will wait a little while, and see what effect your preaching has upon them. If we find it does them good, makes them honest and less disposed to cheat Indians; we will then consider again of what you have said.

"*Brother*; You have now heard our answer to your talk, and this is all we have to say at present.

"As we are going to part, we will come and take you by the hand, and hope the Great Spirit will protect you on your journey, and return you safe to your friends."

As the Indians began to approach the missionary, he rose hastily from his seat and replied, that he could not take them by the hand; that there was no fellowship between the religion of God and the works of the devil.

This being interpreted to the Indians, they smiled, and retired in a peaceable manner.

It being afterwards suggested to the missionary that his reply to the Indians was rather indiscreet; he observed, that he supposed the ceremony of shaking hands would be received by them as a token that he assented to what they had said. Being otherwise informed, he said he was sorry for the expressions.

DOCUMENT 52

To Know the Right

The problems of the missionary are well summarized in this letter of the Catholic missionary Sévère Joseph Nicolas Dumoulin to his Bishop in Quebec. Dumoulin writes in 1819 from the mission post at Pembina, now in the extreme northeastern corner of North Dakota, at the junction of the Pembina River with the Red River of the North. He is concerned particularly with those traders—*engagés*—who have entered into agreements with merchants in Quebec and elsewhere to trade with the Indians. The economic and spiritual problems which arose within this community of French traders, their Indian wives, and their half-breed offspring, are poignantly portrayed in Father Dumoulin's plea for further instructions. The document, in the Quebec Archiepiscopal Archives, is printed, with the following English translation, in Grace Lee Nute, ed., *Documents Relating to Northwest Missions, 1815–1827*, pp. 168–72 (St. Paul: Minnesota Historical Society, 1942).

Pembina, January 4, 1819.
MY LORD, Permit me to appeal to you for a decision of the following cases, first in order to be more sure, and second, to set my conscience at rest, because it cannot always be satisfied with the decisions of a theologian twenty-five years old with only two and one-half years of theology.

1. What should be exacted of an *engagé* who has traded for his *bourgeois* in the following manner, which is the one generally accepted in this country: upon going to an Indian camp the trader gives the Indians liquor gratis; after making them drunk, he trades with them, dilutes the

rum with water, and ends by getting all they have for very little, so that he has paid even less for the peltries, etc., than the low price agreed upon by the *bourgeois* and the Indians. The *engagé* has done this only to please his *bourgeois*, who has not actually ordered him to add so much water, but who will reproach him for having wasted his goods if he does not trade in this manner; furthermore, the *engagé* knows very well that he has not done right, but he reassures himself by saying that such is the custom, and the profit is not for him.

2. What should be done if this *engagé* has robbed the Indians at the same time, for the same reasons?

3. This *engagé* is the father of a large family whom he supports by hard work.

4. To whom should restitution be made? The Indians mentioned have gone away; they are scattered here and there; perhaps several of them have died.

5. An *engagé* has robbed a company, but this company has refused to pay all his wages; can, and ought, recompense be made?

6. What should be done with *engagés* who buy rum from the *bourgeois* and who then trade it, making too great a profit thereby? Say, for instance, for a gallon of rum they obtained two horses.

7. What is it absolutely necessary to know in order to be baptized and married? N. B. It would, perhaps, be well to be able here to marry Catholics to Protestants in order not to force the people to demand Protestant priests.

8. Is it necessary to teach the wives of Protestants even when it is almost certain that they will not want to be separated when they are told that they must?

9. A *brûlé* was very much given to drinking; he has reformed, but he still drinks occasionally, not being protected by the divine Grace. Is it necessary to wait until he has abandoned it altogether, and how many times must he resist? For it is not possible for him to drink often.

10. All the Indians here would be willing to receive instruction if the means to do so were at hand; further-

more, they realize that once their children are baptized they will be obliged to have them taught, and they are even somewhat afraid to pledge themselves to do so. Can we baptize their small children now four or five years old, who probably will have the means of receiving instruction by the time they are capable of it? One thing which might militate against this course is the fact that should these children fall ill, their infidel fathers would use on them their absurd medicines. These are full of superstition, which, nevertheless, would not keep these poor little ones from going to heaven.

11. Ought one ever to baptize those whose fathers may be bigamists or inveterate drunkards?

12. Would it be right for me to make perhaps 150 people miss hearing Mass on Sundays and feast days in order that I might go to spend some days or weeks among the Indians, to begin to teach them, as well as to learn their language, seeing that it is almost impossible to learn it here? Might I do such a thing even though I knew it would be possible to visit only a very few lodges—for example, ten in two weeks?

13. Some of the Indian women have been taught, and would be ready for baptism and marriage if they were not already married, according to the custom of the land, to drunken Canadians. What shall be done with these women? Must we wait until their husbands are converted or advise them to abandon them? They can do so only at serious cost, such as leaving their children or perhaps returning to the Indians, where it would be impossible for them to receive instruction.

14. Is it better to wait till children over seven are old enough to make their first communion before conferring the sacrament of baptism on them, or would it be better to baptize them as soon as they have been made to understand something of its meaning?

15. Are we allowed, when eating with others, to partake indiscriminately of everything that is offered us, even when we are told that these meats have been received

from the Indians in exchange for rum or otherwise traded
in an illegal manner?

I am, My Lord, etc.,

Sév. Dumoulin, Priest.

His Lordship J. O. Plessis, Bishop of Quebec, Quebec.

CHAPTER VI

War

Our knowledge of Indian-white warfare, as of so many other aspects of Indian-white relations, is obscured by the stereotypes that have developed about such warfare. The earliest forms of Indian-white warfare reflected the overwhelming technical superiority of European weapons, armor, animals, and techniques. The symbol of this relationship is probably the picture of the Indian on San Salvador cutting his hand on the sword of one of Columbus' men, not realizing the nature of the weapon. The early years of Spanish conquest are replete with tales of a handful of Spaniards, armed with swords, muskets, armor, and the awe-inspiring horse, led by resolute leaders, overwhelming untold thousands of naked warriors seeking to restrain their advances. When the result was not sheer slaughterhouse decimation, it was, nevertheless, almost invariably another defeat for the Indians. The psychological consequences of such a doleful history are little charted, but are probably more significant than the changes brought about by trade and other peaceful contacts.

As the Indians acquired European arms, ammunition, animals—as they did despite persistent efforts to deny such advantages to them—the situation altered somewhat. The ability of the Indian to combine his own knowledge of terrain with European weapons made him a formidable opponent. When knowledge of European technique and American terrain was combined with extensive social and political organization, as it was in the case of the Iroquois, the Indian became a foe to be dealt with on an equal basis by the European nations seeking hegemony in the New World.

So successful was the Indian reaction that the Europeans were forced to alter their methods of fighting, both in terms of formations and weapons, and to adopt Indian ways. Pikes and armor were soon discarded as more of a hindrance than a help in fighting a fast-moving "guerrilla"-type war of movement and surprise. Massive formations gave way to self-sufficient individuals, grouped in small units with maximum capabilities in reconnaissance and movement.

In the long run, the burgeoning European population in America swamped the native population. Settlers spread out and reduced the protective cover of the silent forest. Larger white populations produced greater numbers of warriors than could be mustered by the Indian nations, diminished by the force of earlier wars and particularly by the white man's diseases. If one prepares charts showing comparative population statistics for the various colonies, it is possible to see that white success in arms occurred most conspicuously when the white population curve going up crossed that of the Indian going down. This point was reached in the seventeenth century in New England and Virginia, and progressively later in the other colonies and in the later states of the Federal Union. It is well to remember that the U. S. Army was subduing the last vestiges of Indian power late in the nineteenth century only shortly before being called upon to deal with Spain and later Germany.

DOCUMENT 53

The "Black Legend" of Spanish Cruelty

The name of Bartolomé de las Casas creates varied reactions among historians of the Spanish conquest of the New World. He is revered for his efforts to ameliorate the lot of the Indians under the initial impact of Spanish conquest. He is honored for transmitting to us, in more detailed fashion than any other historian, the words and deeds of Columbus. Yet he is denounced by many for blackening the reputation of Spain by allegedly exaggerating the cruelties of the *conquistadores* and the numbers of Indians massacred. In an effort to save the Indian population of the New World which he felt was being decimated, Las Casas published, in Seville, his *Brief Relation of the Destruction of the Indies* in Spanish, in 1552. The present quotation is from the English edition of 1656, translated by John Phillips, and published under the title *The Tears of the Indians: Being An Historical and true Account Of the Cruel Massacres and Slaughters of above Twenty Millions of innocent People*. Publication of this edition was designed to coincide with the English seizure of Jamaica from the Spanish, and was meant, in part, to justify that action, just as an American edition during the Spanish-American War was designed to bolster the American cause. Authorities dispute the numbers of Indians slaughtered by the Spaniards and question details of the Las Casas story, but not its essential basis in fact. The following passage is from pp. 1–10 of the English edition, reproduced from an original in the Henry E. Huntington Museum and Art Gallery, San Marino, California, and published by Academic Reprints, Stanford, California.

Tears of the Indies, or Inquisition for Bloud:
being the Relation of the Spanish Massacre there.

In the year 1492, the *West-Indies* were discovered, in the following year they were inhabited by the *Spaniards*: a great company of the *Spaniards* going about 49 years agoe. The first place they came to, was *Hispaniola*, being a most fertile Island, and for the bignesse of it very famous, it being no less then six hundred miles in compass. Round about it lie an innumerable company of Islands, so throng'd with Inhabitants, that there is not to be found a greater multitude of people in any part of the world. The Continent is distant from this about Two hundred miles, stretching it self out in length upon the sea side for above Ten thousand miles in length. This is already found out, and more is daily discovered. These Countreys are inhabited by such a number of people, as if God had assembled and called together to this place, the greatest part of Mankinde.

This infinite multitude of people was so created by God, as that they were without fraud, without subtilty or malice, to their natural Governours most faithful and obedient. Toward the *Spaniards* whom they serve, patient, meek and peaceful, and who laying all contentious and tumultuous thoughts aside, live without any hatred or desire of revenge; the people are most delicate and tender, enjoying such a feeble constitution of body as does not permit them to endure labour, so that the Children of Princes and great persons here, are not more nice and delicate then the Children of the meanest Countrey-man in that place. The Nation is very poor and indigent, possessing little, and by reason that they gape not after temporal goods, neither proud nor ambitious. Their diet is such that the most holy Hermite cannot feed more sparingly in the wildernesse. They go naked, only hiding the undecencies of nature, and a poor shag mantle about ell or two long is their greatest and their warmest covering. They lie upon mats, only those who have larger fortunes, lye upon a kinde of net which is tied at the four corners, and so fasten'd to the roof, which the *Indians* in their natural language call *Hamecks*. They are a very apprehensive and docible wit, and capable of all good learning, and very apt to receive our Religion, which when they have but once tasted, they are carryed on with a very ardent and zealous desire to make a further progress in it; so that I have heard divers *Spaniards* confesse that they had nothing else to hinder them from enjoying heaven, but their ignorance of the true God.

To these quiet Lambs, endued with such blessed qualities, came the *Spaniards* like most c[r]uel Tygres, Wolves and Lions, enrag'd with a sharp and tedious hunger; for these forty years past, minding nothing else but the slaughter of these unfortunate wretches, whom with divers kinds of torments neither seen nor heard of before, they have so cruelly and inhumanely butchered, that of three millions of people which *Hispaniola* it self did contain, there are left remaining alive scarce three hundred persons. And for the Island of *Cuba,* which contains as much ground in length, as from *Valladolid* to *Rome*; it lies wholly desert, until'd and ruin'd. The Islands of *St. John* and *Jamaica* lie waste and desolate. The *Lucayan* Islands neighbouring toward the North upon *Cuba* and *Hispaniola*, being above Sixty or thereabouts with those Islands that are vulgarly called the Islands of the Gyants, of which that which is least fertile is more fruitful then the King of *Spains* Garden at *Sevil*, being situated in a pure and temperate air, are now totally unpeopled and destroyed; the inhabitants thereof amounting to above 5000000. souls, partly killed, and partly forced away to work in other places: so that there going a ship to visit those parts and to glean the remainder of those distressed wretches, there could be found no more then eleven men. Other Islands there were near the Island of *St. John* more then thirty in number, which were totally made desert. All which Islands, though they amount to such a number containing in length of ground the space of above Two thousand miles, lie now altogether solitary without any people or Inhabitant.

Now to come to the Continent, we are confident, and dare to affirm upon our own knowledge, that there were ten Kingdomes of as large an extent as the Kingdome of *Spain*, joyning to it both *Arragon*, and *Portugal*, containing above a thousand miles every one of them in compass, which the unhumane and abominable villanies of the *Spaniards* have made a wilderness of, being now as it were stript of all their people, and made bare of all their inhabitants, though it were a place formerly possessed by vast and infinite numbers of men; And we dare confidently aver, that for those Forty years, wherin the *Spaniards* exercised their abominable cruelties, and detestable tyrannies in those parts, that there have innocently perish'd above Twelve millions of souls, women and children being numbered in this sad and fatall list; moreover I do verily believe that I should speak within compass, should I say that above Fifty millions were consumed in this Massacre.

As for those that came out of *Spain*, boasting themselves to be Christians, they took two several waies to extirpate this Nation from the face of the Earth, the first whereof was a bloudy, unjust, and cruel war which they made upon them: a second by cutting off all that so much as sought to recover their liberty, as some of the stouter sort did intend. And as for the Women and Children that were left alive, they laid so heavy and grievous a yoke of servitude upon them that the condition of beasts was much more tolerable.

Unto these two heads all the other several torments and inhumanities which they used to the ruine of the these poor Nations may be reduced.

That which led the *Spaniards* to these unsanctified impieties was the desire of Gold, to make themselves suddenly rich, for the obtaining of dignities & honours which were no way fit for them. In a word, their covetousness, their ambition, which could not be more in any people under heaven, the riches of the Countrey, and the patience

of the people gave occasion to this their devillish barbarism. For the *Spaniards* so contemned them (I now
speak what I have seen without the least untruth) that
they used them not like beasts, for that would have been
tolerable, but looked upon them as if they had been but
the dung and filth of the earth, and so little they regarded
the health of their souls, that they suffered this great
multitude to die without the least light or Religion; neither is this lesse true then what I have said before, and
that which those tyrants and hangmen themselves dare
not deny, without speaking a notorious falshood, that the
Indians neevr gave them the least cause to offer them
violence, but received them as Angels sent from heavern,
till their excessive cruelties, the torments and slaughters
of their Countrey-men mov'd them to take Armes against
the *Spaniards*.

Of Hispaniola.

In the Island of *Hispaniola*, to which the *Spaniards*
came first, these slaughters and ruines of mankinde took
their beginning. They took away their women and children
to serve them, though the reward which they gave them
was a sad and fatal one. Their food got with great pain
and dropping sweat, the *Spaniards* still consumed, not
content with what the poor *Indians* gave them gratis out
of their own want; One *Spaniard* consuming in one day as
much as would suffice three families, every one containing
ten persons. Being thus broken with so many evils, afflicted
with so many torments, and handled so ignominiously,
they began at length to believe that the *Spaniards* were not
sent from Heaven. And therefore some of them hid their
Children, others their Wives, others their Victuals in obscure and secret places; Others not being able to endure a
Nation that conversed among them with such a boysterous
impiety sought for shelter in the most abrupt and inaccessible mountains. For the *Spaniards* while they were
among them did not only entertain them with cruel beating them with their fists, and with their staves, but pre-

sumed also to lay violent hands upon the Rulers and
Magistrates of their Cities: and they arriv'd at that height
of impudence and unheard of boldnesse, that a certain
private Captain scrupled not to force the Wife of the most
potent King among them. From which time forward they
began to think what way they might take to expell the
Spaniards out of their Countrey. But good God! what sort
of Armes had they? such as were as available to offend or
defend as bulrushes might be. Which when the *Spaniards*
saw, they came with their Horsemen well armed with
Sword and Launce, making most cruel havocks and slaughters among them. Overrunning Cities and Villages, where
they spared no sex nor age; neither would their cruelty
pity Women with childe, whose bellies they would rip up,
taking out the Infant to hew it in pieces. Thye would
often lay wagers who should with most dexterity either
cleave or cut a man in the middle, or who could at one
blow soonest cut off his head. The children they would
take by the feet and dash their innocent heads against
the rocks, and when they were fallen into the water, with a
strange and cruel derision they would call upon them to
swim. Sometimes they would run both Mother and Infant, being in her belly quite through at one thrust.

They erected certain Gallowses, that were broad but
so low, that the tormented creatures might touch the
ground with their feet, upon every one of which they
would hang thirteen persons, blasphemously affirming that
they did it in honour of our Redeemer and his Apostles,
and then putting fire under them, they burnt the poor
wretches alive. Those whom their pity did think fit to
spare, they would send away with their hands half cut off,
and so hanging by the skin. Thus upbraiding their flight,
*Go carry letters to those who lye hid in the mountains
and are fled from us.*

This Death they found out also for the Lords and
Nobles of the Land; they stuck up forked sticks in the
ground, and then laid certain perches upon them, and so
laying them upon those perches, they put a gentle fire

under, causing the fire to melt them away by degrees, to their unspeakable torment.

One time above the rest I saw four of the Nobles laid upon these perches, and two or three other of these kinde of hurdles furnished after the same manner; the clamours and cries of which persons being troublesome to the Captain, he gave order that they should be hang'd, but the Executioner whose name I know, and whose parents are not obscure, hindered their Calamity from so quick a conclusion, stopping their mouthes, that they should not disturb the Captain, and still laying on more wood, till being roasted according to his pleasure, they yeelded up the ghost. Of these and other things innumerable I have been an eyewitnesse; Now because there were some that shun'd like so many rocks the cruelty of a Nation so inhumane, so void of piety and live to mankinde, and therefore fled from them to the mountains; therefore they hunted them with their Hounds, whom they bred up and taught to pull down and tear the *Indians* like beasts: by these Dogs much humane bloud was shed; and because the *Indians* did now and then kill a *Spaniard*, taking him at an advantage, as justly they might; therefore the *Spaniards* made a Law among themselves, that for one *Spaniard* so slaine, they should kill a hundred *Indians*.

DOCUMENT 54

The Dutch at Manhattan

The problems, personal and international, involved in the settlement of the New World, are carefully brought out in the following passage from the account of David Pieterszoon de Vries of events in the years 1640–42 in the Dutch settlement at Manhattan. Had the colony been governed by De Vries' attitude toward the Indians rather than by Governor William Kieft's, it is possible that it would have been spared some of the effects of the frequent wars that plagued the colony and left it an easy prey to the English in 1664. De Vries' *Short Historical and Journal-Notes of Various Voyages Performed in the Four Quarters of the Globe*, published in Dutch at Alkmaar in 1655, has been reprinted in J. Franklin Jameson, ed., *Narratives of New Netherland, 1609–1664*, Original Narratives of Early American History Series (New York: Charles Scribner's Sons, 1909), from pp. 208–16 of which the following passage is taken.

The 16th July, Cornelis van Thienhoven, secretary of New Netherland,[1] departed with a commission from the head men and council of New Netherland, with a hundred armed men, to the Raritanghe, a nation of savages who live where a little stream runs up about five leagues behind Staten Island, for the purpose of obtaining satisfaction from the Indians for the hostilities committed by them upon Staten Island, in killing my swine and those of the Company, which a negro watched—whom I had been solicited to place there—in robbing the swineherds,

[1] He had been the Company's book-keeper throughout Van Twiller's time, and had become secretary under Kieft.

and in attempting (unsuccessfully) to run off with the
yacht *Peace*, of which Cornelis Pietersz. was master, and
for other acts of insolence. Van Thienhoven having arrived
there with the said troop, demanded satisfaction according to his orders. The troop wished to kill and plunder,
which could not be permitted, as Van Thienhoven said he
had no orders to do so. Finally, on account of the per-
tinacity of the troop, the said Van Thienhoven went away,
protesting against any injury which should happen by
reason of their disobedience and violation of orders; and,
when he had gone about a quarter of a league, the troop
killed several of the savages, and brought the brother of
the chief a prisoner, for whom Van Thienhoven had been
surety before in eighty fathoms of *zeewan*, otherwise he,
too, must have been put to death. Whereupon the Indians,
as will hereafter be related, killed four of my men, burned
my house, and the house of David Pietersz. de Vries,[2]
in revenge. I learned also from Thienhoven that one
Loockmans, standing at the mast, had tortured the chief's
brother in his private parts with a piece of split wood,
and that such acts of tyranny were perpetrated by the
servants of the Company as were far from making friends
with the inhabitants.

The 20th of October, I went with my sloop to Tapaen
in order to trade for maize or Indian corn. I found the
Company's sloop there for the purpose of levying a contribution from the Indian Christians, of a quantity of corn.
The Indians called to me and inquired what I wanted.
I answered that I desired to exchange cloth for corn. They
said they could not help me. I must go somewhat up the
river, and, should the Company's sloop in the mean time
get away, they would then trade with me; that they were
very much surprised that the Sachem, who was now at
the Fort, dare exact it; and he must be a very mean fellow
to come to live in this country without being invited by
them, and now wish to compel them to give him their
corn for nothing; that they had not raised it in great

[2] This is probably a mistake for Frederick de Vries.

abundance, as one chief had generally but two women who planted corn, and that they had calculated only for their own necessities, and to barter some with us for cloth. So this affair began to cause much dissatisfaction among the savages.

The 1st of December. I began to take hold of Vriessendael,[3] as it was a fine place, situated along the river, under a mountain. There is a flat there, an hour and a half's journey in extent, where hay can be raised for two hundred head of cattle, and where there is thirty morgens of corn-land, where I have sown wheat which grew higher than the tallest man in the country. Here were also two fine falls from the mountains, where two good mills could be erected for grinding corn and sawing plank. It was a beautiful and pleasant place for hunting deer, wild turkeys, and pigeons; but the evil of it was that, though I earnestly took hold of the place, I was not seconded by my partner, according to our agreement, who was Frederick de Vries, a director of the Company, and who thought that colonies could be built up without men or means, as his idea was that Godyn, Gilliame[4] van Rensselaer, Bloemaert, and Jan de Laet had established their colonies with the means of the Company, which had brought there all the cattle and the farmers. When the work began to progress, these persons were directors of the Company and commissioners of New Netherland, and helped themselves by the cunning tricks of merchants; and the Company, having about that time come into possession of Pieter Heyn's booty,[5] bestowed not a thought

[3] His plantation. The company had in the previous July issued a new charter of "Privileges and Exemptions," which made provision for patroonships of reduced size, and also for a system of grants of two hundred acres each to lesser colonists. Commercial privileges, under some restrictions, were extended to all free colonists and to all stockholders in the Company. These arrangements, with better provisions for local government, led to a considerable increase of immigration.

[4] Kiliaen.

[5] The chief warlike success of the Dutch West India Company was Admiral Pieter Heyn's capture of the entire Spanish silver-

upon their best trading-post, at Fort Orange, whether people were making farms there or not; but these fellows,
especially Rensselaer, who was accustomed to refine pearls
and diamonds, succeeded in taking it from the other managers—their partners. Then Michael Pauw, discovering
that they had appropriated the land at Fort Orange to
themselves, immediately had the land below, opposite
Fort Amsterdam, where the Indians are compelled to cross
to the fort with their beavers, registered for himself, and
called it Pavonia. The Company seeing afterwards that
they were affected, much contention and jealousy arose
among them, because they who undertook to plant colonies with their own money should have taken the property
of the Company. Thus was the country kept down by
these disputes, so that it was not settled; for at that time
there were friends enough who would have peopled the
country by patroonships, but they were always prevented
by the contention of the managers, who were not willing
to do anything themselves, for they would rather see booty
arrive than to speak of their colonies; but, had the land
been peopled, the fruit thereof would have been long
continued, while their booty has vanished like smoke.
There may be some managers and book-keepers who are
well off by it, but it does no good to the community, like
the cultivation of the soil whereby everyone is well off,
and there is a steady income, which is better than all the
booty which we see consumed in bawdy-houses; for where
is now all the booty of which the Dunkirkers have robbed
us, and also all the booty of Flushing, which was taken
from the Portuguese? It has all gone to smoke, and those
privateers who have taken it have gone to naught. They
have drunk it up to no purpose.

ANNO 1641. The 20th August, the ship *Oak Tree*[6] ar-

___

fleet, in the bay of Matanzas, in December, 1628. The booty
was valued at twelve millions of guilders. The patroonships mentioned in the ensuing sentences were established in 1630.

[6] *Eyckenboom.* Cornelis Melyn, next spoken of, afterward led
the opposition to Kieft, and was persecuted and banished by
Stuyvesant.

rived here, in which came a person named Malyn, who said that Staten Island belonged to him, that it was given by the directors to him and to Heer vander Horst, which I could not believe, as I had sailed in the year thirty-eight to take possession of said island, and had settled my men upon it. I thought better things of the directors than this, as the sixth article of the Privileges mentions that the first occupant shall not be prejudiced in his right of possession.

The 1st of September, my men on Staten Island were killed by the Indians and the Raritans; and they told an Indian, who worked for our people, that we would now come to fight them on account of our men; that we had before come and treated them badly on account of the swine, that there had been laid to their charge what they were not guilty of, and what had been done by the Company's men when they were on their way to the South River, who came ashore on Staten Island to cut wood and haul water, and then at the same time stole the hogs, and charged the act upon the innocent Indians, who, although they are bad enough, will do you no harm if you do them none. Thus I lost the beginning of my colony on Staten Island, through the conduct of Commander Kieft, who wished to charge upon the savages what his own people had done.

The 2d of November, there came a chief of the savages of Tankitekes, named Pacham, who was great with the governor of the fort. He came in great triumph, bringing a dead hand hanging on a stick, and saying that it was the hand of the chief who had killed or shot with arrows our men on Staten Island, and that he had taken revenge for our sake, because he loved the Swannekens (as they call the Dutch), who were his best friends.

The same day Commander Kieft asked me whether I would permit Mallyn to go upon the point of Staten Island, where the maize-land lay, saying that he wished to let him plant it, and that he would place soldiers there, who would make a signal by displaying a flag, to make known at the fort whenever ships were in the bay, to which I consented—but did not wish to be prejudiced thereby—and to let him have twelve to fourteen or fifteen morgens of land, without abridging my right, as he intended only to distil some brandy there and make goat's leather.

ANNO 1642. As I was daily with Commander Kieft, generally dining with him when I went to the fort, he told me that he had now had a fine inn built and of stone, in order to accommodate the English who daily passed with their vessels from New England to Virginia, from whom he suffered great annoyance, and who might now lodge in the tavern. I replied that it happened well for the travellers, but there was great want of a church, and that it was a scandal to us when the English passed there, and saw only a mean barn in which we preached;[7] that the first thing which the English in New England built, after their dwellings, was a fine church, and we ought to do so, too, as the West India Company was deemed to be a principal means of upholding the Reformed Religion against the tyranny of Spain, and had excellent material therefor—namely, fine oak-wood, good mountain stone, and good lime burnt of oyster shells, much better than our lime in Holland. He then inquired who would undertake the work. I answered, the lovers of the Reformed Religion of whom there were enough. He then said that I must be one of them, as I proposed it, and must give an hundred guilders. I told him that I was satisfied, and that he must be the first to give, as he was commander, and then we chose Jochem Pietersz. Kuyter, a devout person of the Reformed Religion, who had good workmen who would quickly provide a good lot of timber, and also chose Damen,[8] because he lived close by the fort. And so we four, as churchwardens, were the ones to undertake the work of building the church. The

[7] The first church, built early in Van Twiller's administration, stood near the East River, where now stands no. 39 Pearl Street.

[8] Jan Jansen Dam or Damen, a prominent colonist. The result was a stone church in the old fort, 72 feet by 50, erected at an expense of 2,500 guilders—equivalent in specie to $1,000.

commander was to give several thousand guilders on behalf of the Company, and we should see whether the rest would be subscribed by the community. The church should be built in the fort, to guard against any surprise by the savages. Thus were the walls of the church speedily begun to be laid up with quarry-stone, and to be covered by the English carpenters with overlapping shingles cleft from oak, which, by exposure to the wind and rain, turn blue, and look as if they were slate.

About the same time a harmless Dutchman, named Claes Rademaker,[9] was murdered by a savage. He lived a short league from the fort by the Densel-bay,[10] where he had built a small house, and had set up the trade of wheelwright. It was on the Wickquasgeck road over which the Indians passed daily. It happened that a savage came to this Claes Rademaker for the purpose of trading beavers with him for duffels cloth, which goods were in a chest. This chest he had locked up, and had stooped down in order to take his goods out, when this murderer, the savage, seeing that the man had his head bent over into the chest, and observing an axe standing behind him, seized the axe, and struck Claes Rademaker on the neck therewith, so that he fell down dead by the chest. The murderer then stole all the goods and ran off. The Commander sent to them and made inquiry in Wickquasgeck why this Dutchman had been so shamefully murdered. The murderer answered that, while the fort was being built, he came with his uncle and another savage to the freshwater, bringing beavers, in order to trade with the Dutchmen, that some Swannekes (as they call the Netherlanders) came there, took away from his uncle his beavers, and then killed him. He was then a small boy, and resolved that, when he should grow up, he would revenge that deed upon the Dutch, and since then he had seen no better chance to do so than with this Claes Rademaker. Thus these savages resemble the Italians, being very re-

[9] Claes Smits, *rademaker, i. e.*, Claes Smits, wheelwright.
[10] A misprint for Deutels Bay, now called Turtle Bay, in the East River.

vengeful. Commander Kieft afterwards tried to attack, sending some soldiers there, of whom Van Dyck, the ensign-bearer, had the command, but in consequence of the darkness of the night the guides missed the way, and arrived there too late in the day, so that the attempt failed, and they returned again without effecting anything.[11] Another expedition against these savages was subsequently sent, which also miscarried. When Commander Kieft saw that these attempts against the savages miscarried, and that trouble would follow, and found that the people began to reproach him with being himself protected in a good fort, out of which he had not slept a single night during all the years he had been there, and with seeking the war in order to make a bad reckoning with the Company, and began to feel that the war would be laid to his charge, he called the people together to choose twelve men to aid him in the direction of the affairs of the country,[12] of which number I was, as a patroon, chosen one. Commander Kieft then submitted the proposition whether or not we should avenge the murder of Claes Rademaker and make war upon the savages. We answered that time and opportunity must be taken, as our cattle were running at pasture in the woods, and we were living far and wide, east, west, south, and north of each other; that it was not expedient to carry on a war with the savages until we had more people, like the English, who make towns and villages. I told Commander Kieft that no profit was to be derived from a war with the savages; that he was the means of my people being murdered at the colony which I had commenced on Staten Island in the year forty; and that I well knew that the directors did not desire a war waged against the savages,

[11] De Vries is in error in placing this episode before the election of the Twelve Men. It happened in March, 1642; the latter, on August 29, 1641.

[12] Stated too broadly. They were only to advise as to the Indian war; their advice may be seen in *Collections of the New York Historical Society*, second series, I. 277, 278. But they proceeded further, demanding many reforms in the provincial system, tending in the direction of popular government.

for when we made our colony in the year 1630, in the South River at Swanendael, otherwise called Hoere-kil, and our people were all murdered through some trifling acts of the commander whom we had stationed there, named Gilles Oset,[13] as I have already mentioned in the beginning of my journal, it was then proposed to the Company to make war upon the savages, but the Company would not permit it, and replied that we must keep at peace with the savages. This I related to Commander Kieft, but he would not listen to it, so it becomes the managers to take care what persons they appoint as Directors, for thereon depends the welfare of the country. Were it the case that the East India Company had gone to work in the East Indies, as the West India Company here, they would soon have to leave there like the West India Company; but in the East Indies they make no person commander of a fort, if he be not well acquainted with the country, and [they] have knowledge of the person's competence. But commanders are sent here whether they be fit or not.

About this time also I walked to Ackingh-sack,[14] taking a gun with me, in order to see how far the colony of Heer vander Horst had advanced, as it was only a short hour's journey behind my house. On approaching Ackinsack, about five or six hundred paces from where the colony was started, a savage met me who was very drunk. He came up to me and stroked my arms, which is a token of friendship among them, and said that I was a good chief; that when they came to my house, I let them have milk and everything for nothing; that he had just come from this house, where they had sold him brandy, into which they had put half water; that he could scoop up the water himself from the river, and had no need of buying it; that they had

[13] Giles Houset.
[14] Hackensack. In the valley of the Hackensack River, which lay southwest from Vriesendael, a small colony had been established in 1641 on a grant of land which had been made to the lord of Nederhorst and Meyndert Meyndertsen van Keren and others.

also stolen his beaver-coat, and he would go home and get his bow and arrows, and would kill some one of the villainous Swannekens who had stolen his goods. I told him he must not do so. I then proceeded on to the house of Heer vander Horst, and I told some soldiers and others who were there, that they must not treat the savages in that manner, as they were a very revengeful people, and resembled the Italians in that particular. I then returned home, and on my way, shot a wild turkey weighing over thirty pounds, and brought it along with me. I was not long home, when there came some chiefs from Ackinsack, and from Reckawanck, which was close by me, and informed me that one of their Indians, who was drunk, had shot a Dutchman dead, who was sitting on a barn thatching it. They asked me what they should do; they said they durst not go to the fort; that they would give one or two hundred fathom of *zeewan* to the widow if thereby they would be at peace. I told them that they must go with me to the fort, and speak to the commander; but they were afraid that, on going to the fort, he would not permit them to return home. I made them of good heart, by telling them that I would deliver them safe home. They went with me, at length, to the fort; and, going to Commander Willem Kieft, told him the misfortune which had happened to them. He answered the chief of the savages that he wanted the savage who had done the act to be brought to him. They said they could not do so, as he had run away a two day's journey to Tanditekes;[15] but if the commander would listen to them, they desired in a friendly way to make the widow contented, and to pay for the man's death with *zeewan*, which is their money; it being a custom with them, if any misfortune befel them, to reconcile the parties with money. They laid the blame upon our people, saying that it was because we sold the young Indians brandy or wine, making them crazy, as they were unaccustomed to drink; that they had even seen our people, who were habituated to strong drink,

15 Near Sing Sing.

frequently intoxicated, and fight with knives. They therefore desired that no liquor should be sold to the Indians, in order to prevent all accident for the future. It
seemed as if they had some fear that the governor would
detain them, so they answered him, that they would do
their best to get the savage, and bring him to the fort.
They then took their departure; but on the way they
told me that they could not deliver up the savage to him,
as he was a *sackemaker's* son—that is to say, as above, a
chief's son. And thus the matter passed off.

DOCUMENT 55

Yamassee War of 1715

The origins of the Yamassee War in South Carolina in 1715 are, like the origins of most of our Indian wars, obscure. The following letter, written on August 10, 1715, by William Tredwell Bull, a missionary of the Society for the Propagation of the Gospel in Carolina, illustrates the complex nature of the causes and effects of such a war. Bull makes several perceptive guesses about the causes of the war. At the same time he shows a calm acceptance of the fact that the complications of the war, both moral and material, are more significant than his own personal losses. The letter is printed in Frank J. Klingberg, "The Mystery of the Lost Yamassee Prince," in the *South Carolina Historical Magazine*, Vol. LXIII, January 1962, pp. 23–26.

The Yamousee nation bordering upon our Southern Settlements began this war on Good Fryday morning the 13th of April last, by the Massacre of our Agent and the Traders that resided among them. Two or three only very miraculously escaping their Cruelty gave warning to the Neighboring Inhabitants to fly, By which good Providence the greater part of them escaped with their Lives, though with the Loss of allmost all their Substance; About an hundred Persons at that time fell into their Hands & were murther'd by them. Some of them after a most inhumane Manner being put to Death with most cruel & lingering Torments.

The Government had three Days before this cruel Massacre receiv'd some slight Intimation of such a design But could not imagine it to be really so, having heard nothing before of any Uneasiness among them. However, the Govemour, desirous of promoting the Peace & Securing the Quiet of the Province undertook himself the trouble of a visit to them to know their Grievances & redress what he found amiss & with a numerous attendance was actually going up to their Towns, when in the Middle of the Journey he receiv'd the fatal news of the Beginning of the war by the cruel Massacre above mention'd.

His Honour the Governour without returning to Charlestown raised all the Forces in Colleton County & with his own attendance, & what other assistance could readily be gotten together march'd directly towards them & the week after Easter encounter'd the Yamousees at the head of a River call'd Combahee & after a very hot Engagement of about three quarters of an Hour put them to the flight. This put a stop to their Incursions at the time & we had great hopes of putting a Speedy end to this Barbarous war, when to our great surprise, we understood that Several other Nations were join'd in the Conspiracy, both the Northern & Southern Indians having kill'd the traders that were among them, so that a Small & very inconsiderable Number of Indians only, that lived interspersed amongst the English, remain'd our Friends, & Even of these some proved to be only Spyes upon our Proceedings & gave intelligence of all that past among us to the Enemy; as we had all the reason imaginable to believe, & particularly from the Death of one Capt. Barker, a brave young Gentleman, who with about an 100 Horse being order'd up to the Congarees, a small Nation of our Northern Indians either to compell them or force them to join us fell into an Ambuscade & himself & near 30 of his Men kill'd. An Indian war Captain, who himself fought for us at the Battle of Combahee & parted from them but the Day before with promise to meet them next day being at the Head of Enemy & fired the first Gun upon Capt. Barker himself.

Not long after this, another Party of Indians under pretence of Peace Surprised a small Garrison of ours of about 20 men, one of them only Escaping to tell the news. This Party however a few days after paid dear for their Treachery. One Captain George Chicken, a brave & bold officer, with a Small party of men came up with them, kill'd Several upon the spot & wounded a great many, took all their ammunition & baggage & a considerable number of their Arms, which through Haste in flight they threw from them. Since this defeat they are fled so far from the Settlement that to the Northwards of the Province they have not been heard of more. To the Southwards a Party of the Enemy of about 500 made an Incursion the Latter end of July into my Parish of St. Paul & burnt & destroyed about 20 Plantations therein, & amongst them the Parsonage House with all the Outhouses, except a small out kitchen, the Greater part of my Household Goods, Provisions & Crop to the value of 200 £, not including the loss of the Buildings. To my church they did no other Damage, Save the breaking a few of the windows & tearing off the Lining from one of the best Pews;—The Books, Pulpit, & Tablecloathe & Communion Plate, I had time to secure, with all my own Books, linnen, & some few of my Household Goods, that were most valuable & easy to be convey'd away.

Mine & my next neighbours house were the last they destroy'd, a Party of our army advancing towards them, they fled with great Expedition out of the Settlement & have not appear'd since.

My Parish is now become the Frontier, the Parishes of Hellens & St. Bartholomew's being entirely deserted, except a very small Garrison in St. Hellens, that is kept more as a spye upon the Yamousees, than for any other Security or advantage to the Country. Brother Osborne being driven out of his Parish with the loss of almost everything he was possess'd of, remain'd in Charlestown till it pleased God to take him out of this troublesome world, He dying the 13th of July last, having left a widowe & two Children now in England.

Brother Guy & my self have resided for the most part of late in Charlestown, there having been no Security in either of our Parishes. His was the first of all in distress & He himself made a very narrow escape. I stay'd at Home till I could not make a Congregation of above 5 persons besides my own Family, the greater part of the men being out in the Army & the women fled for Security to Charlestown. However, as soon as a Garrison or two were Settled in the Parish, tho' I had no convenience of being there, I went up to them on Saturdays & staid till Mondays, officiating the Lord's Day in one of the Garrisons.—And now that we have assistance of Arms Ammunition & men from Virginia, North Carolina, & other Provinces & are in a Condition ('tis to be hoped) to carry the war out of the settlement, I intend God willing in a few Days to return to a Constant Residence in my own Parish at the most convenient place I can find, being in hopes that our Affairs are now fix'd upon so good a Foundation, that Peace & our former Quiet will ere long by the Blessing of God be restored to us.

It may be expected from me perhaps to acquaint you what induced the Indians to begin a War with us. But as I am altogether unacquainted with their Sentiments & reasons of acting, so at most I can only give you my own Private opinion of these matters. The Hand of God to be sure must we in the first place look up to & acknowledge that our Manifold Sins & wickedness have justly drawn down this Judgement from him. I dare not ascribe it to any particular Sin. Nevertheless I cannot but look upon the gross Neglect of the poor slaves amongs us & the little care that is taken by the Generality of the People of having them instructed in the Faith & Principles of Christianity to be one great cause of this severe Visitation.

The Manner also of carrying on the trade among the Indians hath not a little contributed thereunto, The trade being permitted to any Private Person, taking out a licesne from the agent who never deny'd one, & the most profligate & debauch'd generally undertaking that business, such as had hardly any Notions of Justice & common Honesty, & utter Strangers to the Vertues of Temperance & Chastity has undoubtedly occasion'd great Oppressions of several kinds. And yet by all that I can learn from others better acquainted with these affairs, than I can pretend to, the

Indians of late Years have had as little grounds of Complaint, as ever they had since the Settlement of the Province.

Another occasion & yet a very great one of the war, I look upon to be the Poverty of the Indians & the wealth of the English. The European Inhabitants of this Province have by their Industry & prudent Management of late years prodigiously encreased their Estates & this of course has brought up amongst us a more Gentile way of Living, than heretofore, which appears both by Gayety of Dress & handsome furniture of Houses, whilst the Indians, either thro' their Natural Laziness, or more properly I think, the extortion & Knavery of the Traders can hardly procure ordinary Cloathing to cover their Nakedness. This Difference of Circumstances has raised their Envy, & the vast Debts, which I'me inform'd they have contracted, which with all their Diligence 'tis impossible for them to pay in Many Years, have put them upon this war, which at once blotts out all their Debts & furnishes them with plunder Sufficient to gratify their Vanity, & defend them from the Inclemency of the Different seasons here.

There's another Reason also, commonly talk'd of here, whether it be so or no I'm not so well acquainted with the Nature of the Indians as to affirm or deny. They say that the Indians are so naturally addicted to war & Bloodshed & so long Accustom'd to it, that 'tis almost impossible for them to abstain from it. Now 'tis manifest that this Government of late years have endavoured with all their Might to procure the Several Nations about us to be at Peace one with another, which Project in a great Measure had its proposed effect. Now the Indians being hindred from falling out with each other & very much Strengthen'd by being at peace among themselves, were, they thought, a Sufficient Match for us, & therefore resolved to try their Endcavours to cut us all off.

This design Surely of Christians to promote Peace, tho' among Heathen Nations, was very laudable, & had the advancement of God's glory rather than that of Trade & commerce been the great Inducement to so good an undertaking, I'me persuaded, that by the blessing of God, the Consequences thereof would not have been so destructive, nor its Effects so very fatal to us.

This, Sir, is all the Account I can at present give you in relation to the war we are here engaged in, which has so distracted this poor unhappy Country & so dispersed our Parishioners—that I have nothing more to add in relation to the State of my own Parish, than what I communicated to you in my letter of the 20th of January last.

DOCUMENT 56

Plunder and Slaves

The material aspects of the French and Indian War are suggested in this letter from the white trader among the Catawba Indians, Mathew Toole, to Governor James Glen, of South Carolina, of April 9, 1754. The letter also emphasizes the fact that American colonial wars were joint Indian-white affairs, on both sides of the battle line. The following letter is taken from the *Colonial Records of South Carolina*, Series 2, *Documents relating to Indian Affairs, May 21, 1750–August 7, 1754*, edited by William L. McDowell, Jr. (Columbia: South Carolina Archives Department, 1958), p. 488.

Catawba Nation, April the 9th, 1754

May it please Your Excellency, Our Indians all met together Yesterday and held a Council at the King's House, and has agreed to go to meet the Forces that is going against the French and their Indians at the Ohio at the Place of Rendevouse, and wants me very much to go with them, and the white People as lives with me that understands what they say. They are very destitute of Ammuntion and wanted me to let them have it which I would not. If your Excellency thinks proper to give me Orders to go with them and my Hirelings, and to let them have Amunition, we are all willing to go, only wait your Excellency's Answer, and to dispatch the Bearer. We want no Pay, only what we can take and plunder, what Slaves we take to be our own of Indians.

I am your Excellency's very humble and most obedient Servant,

Mathew Toole

The Paxton Boys

The massacre of the peaceful Conestoga Indians by a mob of Pennsylvania settlers in 1763 occasioned the following outburst by Benjamin Franklin, who exerted all his power to save other intended victims of the mob. Readers of D. H. Lawrence on Franklin (see Chapter VIII, Document 108) will be hard put to recognize the author of this narrative. The excerpts are taken from the *Writings* of Benjamin Franklin, edited by A. H. Smyth, 10 vols.; Vol. IV, pp. 289–98, 308–14 (New York: The Macmillan Company, 1905–7).

A Narrative of the Late Massacres, in Lancaster County,
of a Number of Indians, Friends of This Province,
by Persons Unknown.
With Some Observations on the Same.
Printed in the Year MDCCLXIV.

These *Indians* were the Remains of a Tribe of the *Six Nations*, settled at *Conestogoe*, and thence called *Conestogoe Indians*. On the first Arrival of the *English* in *Pennsylvania*, Messengers from this Tribe came to welcome them, with Presents of Venison, Corn, and Skins; and the whole Tribe entered into a Treaty of Friendship with the first Proprietor, William Penn, which was to last "as long as the Sun should shine, or the Waters run in the Rivers."

This Treaty has been since frequently renewed, and the *Chain brightened*, as they express it, from time to time. It has never been violated, on their Part or ours, till now. As their Lands by Degrees were mostly purchased, and the Settlements of the White People began to surround them, the Proprietor assigned them lands on the Manor of *Cones-*

togoe, which they might not part with; there they have
lived many years in Friendship with their White Neighbours, who loved them for their peaceable inoffensive Behaviour.

It has always been observed, that *Indians*, settled in the
Neighbourhood of White People, do not increase, but
diminish continually. This Tribe accordingly went on diminishing, till there remained in their Town on the Manor,
but 20 persons, viz. 7 Men, 5 Women, and 8 Children,
Boys and Girls.

Of these, *Shehaes* was a very old Man, having assisted
at the second Treaty held with them, by Mr. Penn, in
1701, and ever since continued a faithful and affectionate
Friend to the *English*; He is said to have been an exceeding good Man, considering his Education, being naturally
of a most kind, benevolent Temper.

Peggy was *Shehaes's* Daughter; she worked for her aged
Father, continuing to live with him, though married, and
attended him with filial Duty and Tenderness.

John was another good old Man; his Son *Harry* helped
to support him.

George and *Will Soc* were two Brothers, both young
Men.

John Smith, a valuable young Man of the *Cayuga* Nation, who became acquainted with *Peggy*, *Shehaes's*
Daughter, some few Years since, married her, and settled
in that Family. They had one Child, about three Years
old.

Betty, a harmless old Woman; and her son *Peter*, a likely
young Lad.

Sally, whose *Indian* name was *Wyanjoy*, a Woman much
esteemed by all that knew her, for her prudent and good
Behaviour in some very trying situations of Life. She was
a truly good and an amiable Woman, had no Children of
her own, but, a distant Relation dying, she had taken a
Child of that Relation's, to bring up as her own, and performed towards it all the Duties of an affectionate Parent.

The Reader will observe, that many of their Names are
English. It is common with the *Indians* that have an af-

fection for the *English*, to give themselves, and their Children, the Names of such *English* Persons as they particularly esteem.

This little Society continued the Custom they had begun, when more numerous, of addressing every new Governor, and every Descendant of the first Proprietor, welcoming him to the Province, assuring him of their Fidelity, and praying a Continuance of that Favour and Protection they had hitherto experienced. They had accordingly sent up an Address of this Kind to our present Governor, on his Arrival; but the same was scarce delivered, when the unfortunate Catastrophe happened, which we are about to relate.

On *Wednesday*, the 14th of *December*, 1763, Fifty-seven Men, from some of our Frontier Townships, who had projected the Destruction of this little Commonwealth, came, all well mounted, and armed with Firelocks, Hangers and Hatchets, having travelled through the Country in the Night, to *Conestogoe* Manor. There they surrounded the small Village of *Indian* Huts, and just at Break of Day broke into them all at once. Only three Men, two Women, and a young Boy, were found at home, the rest being out among the neighbouring White People, some to sell the Baskets, Brooms and Bowls they manufactured, and others on other Occasions. These poor defenceless Creatures were immediately fired upon, stabbed, and hatcheted to Death! The good *Shehaes*, among the rest, cut to Pieces in his Bed. All of them were scalped and otherwise horribly mangled. Then their Huts were set on Fire, and most of them burnt down. Then the Troop, pleased with their own Conduct and Bravery, but enraged that any of the poor *Indians* had escaped the Massacre, rode off, and in small Parties, by different Roads, went home.

The universal Concern of the neighbouring White People on hearing of this Event, and the Lamentations of the younger *Indians*, when they returned and saw the Desolation, and the butchered half-burnt Bodies of their murdered Parents and other Relations, cannot well be expressed.

The Magistrates of *Lancaster* sent out to collect the remaining *Indians*, brought them into the Town for their better Security against any farther Attempt; and it is said condoled with them on the Misfortune that had happened, took them by the Hand, comforted and *promised them Protection*. They were all put into the Workhouse, a strong Building, as the Place of greatest Safety.

When the shocking News arrived in Town, a Proclamation was issued by the Governor, in the following Terms, viz.

"WHEREAS I have received Information, that on *Wednesday*, the Fourteenth Day of this Month, a Number of People, armed, and mounted on Horseback, unlawfully assembled together, and went to the *Indian* Town in the *Conestogoe* Manor, in *Lancaster County*, and without the least Reason or Provocation, in cool Blood, barbarously killed six of the *Indians* settled there, and burnt and destroyed all their Houses and Effects: And whereas so cruel and inhuman an Act, committed in the Heart of this Province on the said *Indians*, who have lived peaceably and inoffensively among us, during all our late Troubles, and for many Years before, and were justly considered as under the Protection of this Government and its Laws, calls loudly for the vigorous Exertion of the civil Authority, to detect the Offenders, and bring them to condign Punishment; I have therefore, by and with the Advice and Consent of the Council, thought fit to issue this Proclamation, and do hereby strictly charge and enjoin all Judges, Justices, Sheriffs, Constables, Officers Civil and Military, and all other His Majesty's liege Subjects within this Province, to make diligent Search and Enquiry after the Authors and Perpetrators of the said Crime, their Abettors and Accomplices, and to use all possible Means to apprehend and secure them in some of the publick Gaols of this Province, that they may be brought to their Trials, and be proceeded against according to Law.

"And whereas a Number of other *Indians,* who lately lived on or near the Frontiers of this Province, being willing and desirous to preserve and continue the ancient Friendship, which heretofore subsisted between them and the good People of this Province, have, at their own earnest Request, been removed from their Habitations, and brought into the County of *Philadelphia* and seated for the present, for their better Security, on the *Province Island,* and in other places in the Neighbourhood of the City of *Philadelphia,* where Provision is made for them at the public Expence; I do therefore hereby strictly forbid all Persons whatsoever, to molest or injure any of the said *Indians,* as they will answer the contrary at their Peril.

"*Given under my Hand, and the Great Seal of the said Province, at* Philadelphia, *the Twenty-second Day of* December, *Anno Domini One Thousand Seven Hundred and Sixty-three, and in the Fourth Year of His Majesty's Reign.*

"JOHN PENN.

"*By his Honour's Command,*
"JOSEPH SHIPPEN, *Jun., Secretary.*
"God save the King."

Notwithstanding this Proclamation, those cruel Men again assembled themselves, and hearing that the remaining fourteen *Indians* were in the Workhouse at *Lancaster,* they suddenly appeared in that Town, on the 27th of *December.* Fifty of them, armed as before, dismounting, went directly to the Workhouse, and by Violence broke open the Door, and entered with the utmost Fury in their Countenances. When the poor Wretches saw they had *no Protection* nigh, nor could possibly escape, and being without the least Weapon for Defence, they divided into their little Families, the Children clinging to the Parents; they fell on their Knees, protested their Innocence, declared their Love to the *English,* and that, in their whole Lives, they had never done them Injury; and in this Posture they all received the Hatchet! Men, Women and little Children were every one inhumanly murdered!—in cold Blood!

The barbarous Men who committed the atrocious Fact, in defiance of Government, of all Laws human and divine, and to the eternal Disgrace of their Country and Colour, then mounted their Horses, huzza'd in Triumph, as if they had gained a Victory, and rode off—*unmolested!*

The Bodies of the Murdered were then brought out and exposed in the Street, till a Hole could be made in the Earth to receive and cover them.

But the Wickedness cannot be covered, the Guilt will lie on the whole Land, till Justice is done on the Murderers. THE BLOOD OF THE INNOCENT WILL CRY TO HEAVEN FOR VENGEANCE.

It is said that, *Shehaes* being before told, that it was to be feared some *English* might come from the Frontier into the Country, and murder him and his People; he replied, "It is impossible: there are *Indians*, indeed, in the Woods, who would kill me and mine, if they could get at us, for my Friendship to the *English*; but the *English* will wrap me in their Matchcoat, and secure me from all Danger." How unfortunately was he mistaken!

Another Proclamation has been issued, offering a great Reward for apprehending the Murderers, in the following Terms, *viz.*

"WHEREAS on the Twenty-second Day of *December* last, I issued a Proclamation for the apprehending and bringing to Justice, a Number of Persons, who, in Violation of the Public Faith, and in Defiance of all Law, had inhumanly killed six of the *Indians*, who had lived in *Conestogoe* Manor, for the Course of many Years, peaceably and inoffensively, under the Protection of this Government, on Lands assigned to them for their Habitation; notwithstanding which, I have received Information, that on the Twenty-seventh of the same Month, a large Party of armed Men again assembled and met together in a riotous and tumultuous Manner, in the County of *Lancaster*, and proceeded to the Town of *Lancaster*, where they violently broke open the Workhouse, and butchered and put to Death fourteen of the said *Conestogoe Indians*, Men,

Women and Children, who had been taken under the immediate Care and Protection of the Magistrates of the said County, and lodged for their better Security in the said Workhouse, till they should be more effectually provided for by Order of the Government; and whereas common Justice loudly demands, and the Laws of the Land (upon the Preservation of which not only the Liberty and Security of every Individual, but the Being of the Government itself depend) require, that the above Offenders should be brought to condign Punishment; I have therefore, by and with the Advice of the Council, published this Proclamation, and do hereby strictly charge and command all Judges, Justices, Sheriffs, Constables, Officers Civil and Military, and all other His Majesty's faithful and liege Subjects within this Province, to make diligent Search and Enquiry after the Authors and Perpetrators of the said last-mentioned Offence, their Abettors and Accomplices, and that they use all possible Means to apprehend and secure them in some of the public Gaols of this province, to be dealt with according to Law.

"And I do hereby further promise and engage, that any Person or Persons, who shall apprehend and secure, or cause to be apprehended and secured, any Three of the Ringleaders of the said Party, and prosecute them to Conviction, shall have and receive for each, the public Reward of *Two Hundred Pounds*; and any Accomplice, not concerned in the immediate shedding the Blood of the said *Indians*, who shall make Discovery of any or either of the said Ringleaders, and apprehend and prosecute them to Conviction, shall, over and above the said Reward, have all the Weight and Influence of the Government, for obtaining His Majesty's Pardon for his Offence.

"*Given under my Hand, and the Great Seal of the said Province, at* Philadelphia, *the Second Day of January, in the Fourth Year of His Majesty's Reign, and in the Year of our Lord One Thousand Seven Hundred and Sixty-four.*
                                                  "John Penn.

"By his Honour's command,
        "Joseph Shippen, Jun., *Secretary.*
              "God save the King."

These Proclamations have as yet produced no Discovery; the Murderers having given out such Threatenings against those that disapprove their Proceedings, that the whole Country seems to be in Terror, and no one durst speak what he knows; even the Letters from thence are unsigned, in which any Dislike is expressed of the Rioters.

There are some, (I am ashamed to hear it,) who would extenuate the enormous Wickedness of these Actions, by saying, "The Inhabitants of the Frontiers are exasperated with the Murder of their Relations, by the Enemy *Indians*, in the present War." It is possible;—but though this might justify their going out into the Woods, to seek for those Enemies, and avenge upon them those Murders, it can never justify their turning into the Heart of the Country, to murder their Friends.

If an *Indian* injures me, does it follow that I may revenge that Injury on all *Indians*? It is well known, that *Indians* are of different Tribes, Nations and Languages, as well as the White People. In *Europe*, if the *French*, who are White People, should injure the *Dutch*, are they to revenge it on the *English*, because they too are White People? The only Crime of these poor Wretches seems to have been, that they had a reddish-brown Skin, and black Hair; and some People of that Sort, it seems, had murdered some of our Relations. If it be right to kill Men for such a Reason, then, should any Man, with a freckled Face and red Hair, kill a Wife or Child of mine, it would be right for me to revenge it, by killing all the freckled red-haired Men, Women and Children, I could afterwards anywhere meet with.

But it seems these People think they have a better Justification; nothing less than the *Word of God*. With the Scriptures in their Hands and Mouths, they can set at nought that express Command, *Thou shalt do no Murder*; and justify their Wickedness by the Command given *Joshua* to destroy the Heathen. Horrid Perversion of Scripture and of Religion! To father the worst of Crimes on the God of Peace and Love! Even the *Jews*, to whom that particular Commission was directed, spared the *Gibeonites*, on Account of their Faith once given. The Faith of this Government has been frequently given to those *Indians*; but that did not avail them with People who despise Government.

. . . .

I will not dissemble that numberless Stories have been raised and spread abroad, against not only the poor Wretches that are murdered, but also against the Hundred and Forty christianized *Indians*, still threatned to be murdered; all which Stories are well known, by those who know the *Indians* best, to be pure Inventions, contrived by bad People, either to excite each other to join in the Murder, or since it was committed, to justify it; and believed only by the Weak and Credulous. I call thus publickly on the Makers and Venders of these Accusations to produce their Evidence. Let them satisfy the Public that even *Will Soc*, the most obnoxious of all that Tribe, was really guilty of those Offences against us which they lay to his Charge. But if he was, ought he not to have been fairly tried? He lived under our Laws, and was subject to them; he was in our Hands, and might easily have been prosecuted; was it *English Justice* to condemn and execute him unheard? Conscious of his own Innocence, he did not endeavour to hide himself when the Door of the Workhouse, his Sanctuary, was breaking open. "I will meet them," says he, "for they are my Brothers." These Brothers of his shot him down at the Door, while the Word Brothers was between his Teeth.

But if *Will Soc* was a bad Man, what had poor old *Shehaes* done? What could he or the other poor old Men and Women do? What had little Boys and Girls done? What could Children of a Year old, Babes at the Breast, what could they do, that they too must be shot and hatcheted? Horrid to relate! And in their Parents Arms! This is done by no civilized Nation in *Europe*. Do we come to *America* to learn and practise the Manners of *Barbarians*? But this, *Barbarians* as they are, they practise against their Enemies only, not against their Friends.

These poor People have been always our Friends. Their

Fathers received ours, when Strangers here, with Kindness and Hospitality. Behold the Return we have made them! When we grew more numerous and powerful, they put themselves under our *Protection*. See, in the mangled Corpses of the last Remains of the Tribe, how effectually we have afforded it to them!

Unhappy People! to have lived in such Times, and by such Neighbours! We have seen, that they would have been safer among the ancient *Heathens*, with whom the Rites of Hospitality were *sacred*. They would have been considered as *Guests* of the Publick, and the Religion of the Country would have operated in their Favour. But our Frontier People call themselves *Christians!* They would have been safer, if they had submitted to the *Turks*; for ever since *Mahomet's* Reproof to *Khaled*, even the cruel *Turks* never kill Prisoners in cold Blood. These were not even Prisoners. But what is the Example of *Turks* to Scripture *Christians*? They would have been safer, though they had been taken in actual War against the *Saracens*, if they had once drank Water with them. These were not taken in War against us, and have drank with us, and we with them, for Fourscore Years. But shall we compare *Saracens* to *Christians*?

They would have been safer among the *Moors* in *Spain*, though they had been Murderers of Sons; if Faith had once been pledged to them, and a Promise of Protection given. But these have had the Faith of the *English* given to them many Times by the Government, and, in Reliance on that Faith, they lived among us, and gave us the Opportunity of murdering them. However, what was honourable in *Moors*, may not be a Rule to us; for we are *Christians!* They would have been safer it seems among *Popish Spaniards*, even if Enemies, and delivered into their Hands by a Tempest. These were not Enemies; they were born among us, and yet we have killed them all. But shall we imitate *idolatrous Papists*, we that are *enlightened Protestants*? They would have even been safer among the *Negroes* of *Africa*, where at least one manly Soul would have been found, with Sense, Spirit and Humanity enough, to stand in their Defence. But shall *Whitemen* and *Christians* act like a *Pagan Negroe?* In short it appears, that they would have been safe in any Part of the known World, except in the Neighbourhood of the CHRISTIAN WHITE SAVAGES of *Peckstang* and *Donegall!*

O, ye unhappy Perpetrators of this horrid Wickedness! reflect a Moment on the Mischief ye have done, the Disgrace ye have brought on your Country, on your Religion, and your Bible, on your Families and Children! Think on the Destruction of your captivated Country-folks (now among the wild *Indians*) which probably may follow, in Resentment of your Barbarity! Think on the Wrath of the United *Five Nations*, hitherto our Friends, but now provoked by your murdering one of their Tribes, in Danger of becoming our bitter Enemies. Think of the mild and good Government you have so audaciously insulted; the Laws of your King, your Country, and your God, that you have broken; the infamous Death that hangs over your Heads; for Justice, though slow, will come at last. All good People everywhere detest your Actions. You have imbrued your Hands in innocent Blood; how will you make them clean? The dying Shrieks and Groans of the Murdered, will often sound in your Ears: Their Spectres will sometimes attend you, and affright even your innocent Children! Fly where you will, your Consciences will go with you. Talking in your Sleep shall betray you, in the Delirium of a Fever you yourselves shall make your own Wickedness known.

One Hundred and Forty peaceable *Indians* yet remain in this Government. They have, by *Christian* Missionaries, been brought over to a *Liking*, at least, of our Religion; some of them lately left their Nation which is now at War with us, because they did not chuse to join with them in their Depredations; and to shew their Confidence in us, and to give us an equal Confidence in them, they have brought and put into our Hands their Wives and Children. Others have lived long among us in *Northampton* County, and most of their Children have been born there. These are all now trembling for their Lives. They have been hurried from Place to Place for Safety, now concealed in Corners, then sent out of the Province, refused a Passage through a neighbouring Colony, and returned, not unkindly perhaps, but disgracefully, on our Hands. O *Pennsylvania!* Once renowned for Kindness to Strangers, shall the Clamours of a few mean Niggards about the Expence of this *Publick Hospitality*, an Expence that will not cost the noisy Wretches *Sixpence* a Piece, (and what is the Expence of the poor Maintenance we afford them, compared to the Expence they might occasion if in Arms against us) shall so senseless a Clamour, I say, force you to turn out of your Doors these unhappy Guests, who have offended their own Countryfolks by their Affection for you, who, confiding in your Goodness, have put themselves under your Protection? Those whom you have disarmed to satisfy groundless Suspicions, will you leave them exposed to the armed Madmen of your Country? Unmanly Men! who are not ashamed to come with Weapons against the Unarmed, to use the Sword against Women, and the Bayonet against young Children; and who have already given such bloody Proofs of their Inhumanity and Cruelty.

Let us rouze ourselves, for Shame, and redeem the Honour of our Province from the Contempt of its Neighbours; let all good Men join heartily and unanimously in Support of the Laws, and in strengthening the Hands of Government; that JUSTICE may be done, the Wicked punished, and the Innocent protected; otherwise we can, as a People, expect no Blessing from Heaven; there will be no Security for our Persons or Properties; Anarchy and Confusion will prevail over all; and Violence without Judgment, dispose of every Thing.

When I mention the Baseness of the Murderers, in the Use they made of Arms, I cannot, I ought not to forget, the very different Behaviour of *brave Men* and *true Soldiers*, of which this melancholy Occasion has afforded us fresh Instances. The *Royal Highlanders* have, in the Course of this War, suffered as much as any other

Corps, and have frequently had their Ranks thinn'd by an *Indian* Enemy; yet they did not for this retain a brutal undistinguishing Resentment against *all Indians*, Friends as well as Foes. But a Company of them happening to be here, when the 140 poor *Indians* above mentioned were thought in too much Danger to stay longer in the Province, chearfully undertook to protect and escort them to *New York*, which they executed (as far as that Government would permit the *Indians* to come) with Fidelity and Honour; and their captain *Robinson*, is justly applauded and honoured by all sensible and good People, for the Care, Tenderness and Humanity, with which he treated those unhappy Fugitives, during their March in this severe Season.

General *Gage*, too, has approved of his Officer's Conduct, and, as I hear, ordered him to remain with the *Indians* at *Amboy*, and continue his Protection to them, till another Body of the King's Forces could be sent to relieve his Company, and escort their Charge back in Safety to *Philadelphia*, where his Excellency has had the Goodness to direct those Forces to remain for some Time, under the Orders of our Governor, for the Security of the *Indians*; the Troops of this Province being at present necessarily posted on the Frontier. Such just and generous Actions endear the Military to the Civil Power, and impress the Minds of all the Discerning with a still greater Respect for our national Government. I shall conclude with observing, that *Cowards* can handle Arms, can strike where they are sure to meet with no Return, can wound, mangle and murder; but it belongs to *brave* Men to spare and to protect; for, as the Poet says,

"Mercy still sways the Brave."

DOCUMENT 58

The Paxton Boys at Work

Plate 12, following page 134, shows a mid-nineteenth-century depiction of the scene at Lancaster, Pennsylvania, in 1763, when the Paxton Boys massacred the peaceable Conestoga Indians. Reproduced from the copy in The Rare Book Division of the Library of Congress, Washington, D.C., is a lithograph from James Wimer's *Events in Indian History* (Lancaster, Pennsylvania: 1841).

DOCUMENT 59

Joseph Brant

Thayendanegea (Joseph Brant), a Mohawk, was educated at Eleazar Wheelock's Indian Charity School, and became secretary to Guy Johnson, the Indian Superintendent, with whom he is pictured in a portrait by Benjamin West in the National Gallery of Art (not shown), at the beginning of the War for Independence. Brant went to England in the spring of 1776, returned to fight against the rebellious colonists, and went to England a second time in 1786 to collect funds to build a church on the Grand River Indian reservation in Canada. This portrait of Thayendanegea (Plate 13, following page 134), done about 1786 by Gilbert Stuart, is in the collections of the New York State Historical Association, Cooperstown, N.Y.

DOCUMENT 60

Undisciplined Savages?

In 1799 Colonel James Smith, of Bourbon County, Kentucky, wrote *An Account of the Remarkable Occurrences in the Life and Travels of Colonel James Smith, During his Captivity with the Indians, in the Years 1755, '56, '57, '58, & '59,* which was published in Lexington, Kentucky. In it he discussed the Indian mode of warfare and, later, as an old man, at the outbreak of the War of 1812, offered this treatise on warfare in separate form as his contribution to the war effort. Smith's treatise, taken from the Philadelphia, 1831 edition of his *Account,* demonstrates the keen appreciation of the Indian style of warfare which the trans-Appalachian frontiersman of the late eighteenth and early nineteenth century acquired. The passage covers pp. 151–62 of the book.

I have often heard the British officers call the Indians the undisciplined savages, which is a capital mistake—as they have all the essentials of discipline. They are under good command, and punctual in obeying orders: they can act in concert, and when their officers lay a plan and give orders, they will cheerfully unite in putting all their directions into immediate execution; and by each man observing the motion or movement of his right hand companion, they can communicate the motion from right to left, and march abreast in concert, and in scattered order, though the line may be more than a mile long, and continue, if occasion requires, for a considerable distance, without disorder or confusion. They can perform various necessary manœuvres, either slowly, or as fast as they can run: they can form a circle, or semi-circle: the circle they make use of, in order to surround their enemy, and the semicircle, if the enemy has a river on one side of them. They can also form a large hollow square, face out and take trees: this they do, if their enemies are about surrounding them, to prevent being shot from either side of the tree. When they go into battle, they are not loaded or encumbered with many clothes, as they commonly fight naked, save only breech-clout, leggins and moccasins. There is no such thing as corporeal punishment used, in order to bring them under such good discipline: degrading is the only chastisement, and they are so unanimous in this, that it effectually answers the purpose. Their officers plan, order and conduct matters until they are brought into action, and then each man is to fight as though he was to gain the battle himself. General orders are commonly given in time of battle, either to advance or retreat, and is done by a shout or yell, which is well understood, and then they retreat or advance in concert. They are generally well equipped, and exceedingly expert and active in the use of arms. Could it be supposed that undisciplined troops could defeat Generals Braddock, Grant, &c.? It may be said by some, that the French were also engaged in this war: true, they were; yet I know it was the Indians that laid the plan, and with small assistance, put it into execution. The Indians had no aid from the French, or any other power, when they besieged Fort Pitt, in the year 1763, and cut off the communication for a considerable time, between that post and Fort Loudon, and would have defeated General Bouquet's army, (who were on the way to raise the siege,) had it not been for the assistance of the Virginia volunteers. They had no British troops with them when they defeated Colonel Crawford, near the Sandusky, in the time of the American war with Great Britain; or when they defeated Colonel Loughrie, on the Ohio, near the Miami, on his way to meet General Clarke: this was also in the time of the British war. It was the Indians alone that defeated Colonel Todd, in Kentucky, near the Blue Licks, in the year 1782; and Colonel Harmer, betwixt the Ohio and

Lake Erie, in the year 1790, and General St. Clair, in the year 1791; and it is said that there were more of our men killed at this defeat, than there were in any one battle during our contest with Great Britain. They had no aid, when they fought even the Virginia riflemen almost a whole day, at the Great Kenhawa, in the year 1774; and when they found they could not prevail against the Virginians, they made a most artful retreat. Notwithstanding they had the Ohio to cross, some continued firing, whilst others were crossing the river; in this manner they proceeded, until they all got over, before the Virginians knew that they had retreated; and in this retreat, they carried off all their wounded. In the most of the foregoing defeats, they fought with an inferior number, though in this, I believe it was not the case.

Nothing can be more unjustly represented, than the different accounts we have had of their number from time to time, both by their own computations, and that of the British. While I was among them, I saw the account of the number, that they in those parts gave to the French, and kept it by me. When they in their own council-house, were taking an account of their number, with a piece of bark newly stripped, and a small stick, which answered the end of a slate and pencil, I took an account of the different nations and tribes, which I added together, and found there were not half the number, which they had given the French; and though they were then their allies, and lived among them, it was not easy finding out the deception, as they were a wandering set, and some of them almost always in the woods hunting. I asked one of the chiefs what was their reason for making such different returns? He said it was for political reasons, in order to obtain greater presents from the French, by telling them they could not divide such and such quantities of goods among so many.

In the year of General Bouquet's last campaign, 1764, I saw the official return made by the British officers, of the number of Indians that were in arms against us that year, which amounted to thirty thousand. As I was then a lieutenant in the British service, I told them I was of opinion that there was not above one thousand in arms against us, as they were divided by Broadstreet's army, being then at Lake Erie. The British officers hooted at me, and said they could not make England sensible of the difficulties they laboured under in fighting them, as England expected that their troops could fight the undisciplined savages in America, five to one, as they did the East Indians, and therefore my report would not answer their purpose, as they could not give an honourable account of the war, but by augmenting their number. I am of opinion that from Braddock's war, until the present time, there never were more than three thousand Indians, at any time in arms against us, west of Fort Pitt, and frequently not half that number. According to the Indians' own accounts, during the whole of Braddock's war, or from 1755, till 1758, they killed or took fifty of our people, for one that they lost. In the war that commenced in the year 1763, they killed comparatively few of our people, and lost more of theirs, as the frontiers, (especially the Virginians,) had learned something of their method of war: yet, they in this war, according to their own accounts, (which I believe to be true,) killed or took ten of our people, for one they lost.

Let us now take a view of the blood and treasure that was spent in opposing comparatively, a few Indian warriors, with only some assistance from the French, the first four years of the war. Additional to the amazing destruction and slaughter that the frontiers sustained, from James river to Susquehanna, and about thirty miles broad; the following campaigns were also carried on against the Indians:—General Braddock's, in the year 1755; Colonel Armstrong's, against the Cattanyan town, on the Allegheny, 1757; General Forbes's, in 1758; General Stanwick's, in 1759; General Monkton's, in 1760; Colonel Bouquet's, in 1761, and 1763, when he fought the battle of Brushy Run, and lost above one hundred men, but, by the assistance of the Virginia volunteers, drove the Indians; Colonel Armstrong's, up the west branch of Susquehanna, in 1763; General Broadstreet's, up Lake Erie, in 1764; General Bouquet's, against the Indians at Muskingum, 1764; Lord Dunmore's, in 1774; General M'Intosh's, in 1778; Colonel Crawford's, shortly after his; General Clarke's, in 1778–1780; Colonel Bowman's, in 1779; General Clarke's, in 1782–against the Wabash, in 1786; General Logan's, against the Shawanees, in 1786; General Wilkinson's, in ——; Colonel Harmer's, in 1790; and General St. Clair's, in 1791; which, in all, are twenty-two campaigns, besides smaller expeditions—such as the French Creek expedition, Colonels Edwards's, Loughrie's, &c. All these were exclusive of the number of men that were internally employed as scouting parties, and in erecting forts, guarding stations, &c. When we take the foregoing occurrences into consideration, may we not reasonably conclude, that they are the best disciplined troops in the known world? Is it not the best discipline that has the greatest tendency to annoy the enemy and save their own men? I apprehend that the Indian discipline is as well calculated to answer the purpose in the woods of America, as the British discipline in Flanders: and British discipline in the woods, is the way to have men slaughtered, with scarcely any chance of defending themselves.

Let us take a view of the benefits we have received, by what little we have learned of their art of war, which cost us dear, and the loss we have sustained for want of it, and then see if it will not be well worth our while to retain what we have, and also to endeavour to improve in this necessary branch of business. Though we have made considerable proficiency in this line, and in some respects outdo them, viz. as marksmen, and in cutting our rifles, and keeping them in good order; yet, I apprehend, we are far behind in their manœuvres, or in being able to surprise, or prevent a surprise. May we not conclude, that the progress we had made in their art of war, contributed considerably towards our success, in various respects, when contending with Great Britain for liberty? Had the British king attempted to enslave us before Braddock's war, in all probability he might readily have done it, because, except the New Englanders, who had formerly been engaged in war with the Indians, we were unacquainted with any kind of war: but after fighting such a subtle and barbarous enemy as the Indians, we were not terrified at the approach of British red-coats. Was not Burgoyne's defeat accomplished, in some measure, by the Indian mode of fighting? And did not General Morgan's riflemen, and many others, fight with greater success, in consequence of what they had learned of their art of war? Kentucky would not have been settled at the time it was, had the Virginians been altogether ignorant of this method of war.

In Braddock's war the frontiers were laid waste for above three hundred miles long, and generally about thirty broad, excepting some that were living in forts, and many hundreds, or perhaps thousands, killed or made captives, and horses, and all kinds of property carried off: but, in the next Indian war, though we had the same Indians to cope with, the frontiers almost all stood their ground, because they were by this time, in some measure, acquainted with their manœuvres; and the want of this in the first war, was the cause of the loss of many hundreds of our citizens, and much treasure.

Though large volumes have been written on morality, yet it may be all summed up in saying, do as you would wish to be done by: so the Indians sum up the art of war in the following manner:

The business of the private warriors is to be under command, or punctually to obey orders; to learn to march abreast in scattered order, so as to be in readiness to surround the enemy, or to prevent being surrounded; to be good marksmen, and active in the use of arms; to practise running; to learn to endure hunger or hardships with patience and fortitude; to tell the truth at all times to their officers, but more especially when sent out to spy the enemy.

Concerning Officers.—They say that it would be absurd to appoint a man an officer whose skill and courage had

never been tried—that all officers should be advanced
only according to merit; that no one man should have the
absolute command of an army; that a council of officers
are to determine when, and how an attack is to be made;
that it is the business of the officers to lay plans to take
every advantage of the enemy; to ambush and surprise
them, and to prevent being ambushed and surprised themselves. It is the duty of officers to prepare and deliver
speeches to the men, in order to animate and encourage
them; and on the march, to prevent the men, at any
time, from getting into a huddle, because if the enemy
should surround them in this position, they would be exposed to the enemy's fire. It is likewise their business at
all times to endeavour to annoy their enemy, and save
their own men, and therefore ought never to bring on an
attack without considerable advantage, or without what
appeared to them the sure prospect of victory, and that
with the loss of few men; and if at any time they should
be mistaken in this, and are like to lose many men by
gaining the victory, it is their duty to retreat, and wait
for a better opportunity of defeating their enemy, without the danger of losing so many men. Their conduct
proves that they act upon these principles, therefore it is,
that from Braddock's war to the present time, they have
seldom ever made an unsuccessful attack. The battle at
the mouth of the Great Kenhawa is the greatest instance
of this; and even then, though the Indians killed about
three for one they lost, yet they retreated. The loss of the
Virginians in this action was seventy killed, and the same
number wounded: the Indians lost twenty killed on the
field, and eight, who died afterwards of their wounds.
This was the greatest loss of men that I ever knew the
Indians to sustain in any one battle. They will commonly
retreat if their men are falling fast; they will not stand
cutting like the Highlanders or other British troops; but
this proceeds from a compliance with their rules of war
rather than cowardice. If they are surrounded they will
fight while there is a man of them alive, rather than
surrender. When Colonel John Armstrong surrounded the

Cattanyan town, on the Allegheny river, Captain Jacobs, a Delaware chief, with some warriors, took possession of a house, defended themselves for some time, and killed a number of our men. As Jacobs could speak English, our people called on him to surrender. He said, that he and his men were warriors, and they would all fight while life remained. He was again told that they should be well used if they would only surrender; and if not, the house should be burned down over their heads. Jacobs replied, he could eat fire; and when the house was in a flame, he, and they that were with him, came out in a fighting position, and were all killed. As they are a sharp, active kind of people, and war is their principal study, in this they have arrived at considerable perfection. We may learn of the Indians what is useful and laudable, and at the same time lay aside their barbarous proceedings. It is much to be lamented, that some of our frontier riflemen are too prone to imitate them in their inhumanity. During the British war, a considerable number of men from below Fort Pitt, crossed the Ohio, and marched into a town of friendly Indians, chiefly Delawares, who professed the Moravian religion. As the Indians apprehended no danger, they neither lifted arms nor fled. After these riflemen were some time in the town, and the Indians altogether in their power, in cool blood they massacred the whole town, without distinction of age or sex. This was an act of barbarity beyond any thing I ever knew to be committed by the savages themselves.

Why have we not made greater proficiency in the Indian art of war? Is it because we are too proud to imitate them, even though it should be a means of preserving the lives of many of our citizens? No! We are not above borrowing language from them, such as homony, pone, tomahawk, &c. which is of little or no use to us. I apprehend, that the reasons why we have not improved more in this respect are as follow: no important acquisition is to be obtained but by attention and diligence; and as it is easier to learn to move and act in concert, in close order, in the open plain, than to act in concert in scattered order in the woods, so it is easier to learn our discipline than the Indian manœuvres. They train up their boys in the art of war from the time they are twelve or fourteen years of age; whereas, the principal chance our people had of learning was, by observing their manœuvres when in action against us. I have been long astonished that no one has written upon this important subject, as their art of war would not only be of use to us in case of another rupture with them; but were only part of our men taught this art, accompanied with our continental discipline, I think no European power, after trial, would venture to show its head in the American woods.

If what I have written should meet the approbation of my countrymen, perhaps I may publish more upon this subject in a future edition.

DOCUMENT 61

Indian Warfare

In 1824 the Reverend Dr. Joseph Doddridge of Wellsburgh, Virginia, published in that town his *Notes on the Settlement and Indian Wars, of the Western Parts of Virginia & Pennsylvania, from the year 1763 until the year 1783 inclusive. Together with a view, of the state of society and manners of the first settlers of the Western Country.* In his Chapter 24 on "Indian Warfare," pp. 207–13, he summarizes his view of this aspect of Indian-white relations.

Preliminary observations on the character of the Indian mode of warfare and its adoption by the white people.

This is a subject, which presents human nature in its most revolting features, as subject to a vindictive spirit of revenge, and a thirst of human blood, leading to an indiscriminate slaughter of all ranks, ages and sexes, by the weapons of war, or by torture.

The history of man, is for the most part, one continued detail of bloodshed, battles and devastations. War has been, from the earliest periods of history, the almost constant employment of individuals, clans, tribes and nations. Fame, one of the most potent objects of human ambition, has at all times, been the delusive; but costly reward of military achievements. The triumph of conquest, the epithet of greatness, the throne and the sceptre, have uniformly been purchased, by the conflict of battle, and garments rolled in blood.

If the modern European laws of warfare, have softened in some degree the horrid features of national conflicts, by respecting the rights of private property, and extending humanity to the sick, wounded and prisoners; we ought to reflect that this amelioration is the effect of civilization only. The natural state of war, knows no such mixture of mercy with cruelty. In his primitive state, man knows no object in his wars, but that of the extermination of his enemies, either by death or captivity.

The wars of the Jews were exterminatory in their object. The destruction of a whole nation was often the result of a single campaign. Even the beasts themselves were sometimes included in the general massacre.

The present war between the Greeks and Turks, is a war upon the ancient model: a war of utter extermination.

It is to be sure, much to be regreted, that our people so often followed the cruel examples of the Indians, in the slaughter of prisoners, and sometimes women and children; yet let them receive a candid hearing at the bar of reason and justice, before they are condemned, as barbarians, equally with the indians themselves.

History, scarcely presents an example of a civilized nation, carrying on a war with barbarians, without adopting the mode of warfare of the barbarous nation. The ferocious Suwarrow, when at war with the Turks was as much of a savage as the Turks themselves. His slaughters were as indiscriminate as theirs; but during his wars against the French, in Italy, he faithfully observed the laws of civilized warfare.

Were the Greeks now at war with a civilized nation, we should hear nothing of the barbarities which they have committed on the Turks; but being at war with barbarians, the principle of self defence compels them to retaliate on the Turks, the barbarities which they commit on them.

In the last rebellion, in Ireland, that of united Irishmen, the government party, were not much behind the rebels, in acts of lawless cruelty. It was not by the hands of the executioner alone they perished. Summary justice, as it was called, was sometimes inflicted. How many perished under the torturing scourge of the drummer, for the purpose of extorting confessions. These extra-judicial executions were attempted to be justified, on the ground of the necessity of the case.

Our revolutionary war has a double aspect: on the one hand we carried on a war with the English, in which we observed the maxims of civilized warfare, with the utmost strictness; but the brave, the potent, the magnanimous nation of our forefathers had associated with themselves, as auxilaries, the murderous tomahawk and scalping knife of the indian nations around our defenceless frontiers, leaving those barbarous sons of the forest to their own savage mode of warfare, to the full indulgence of all their native thirst for human blood.

On them then, be the blame of all the horrid features of this war between civilized and savage men, in which the former were compelled, by every principle of self defence, to adopt the indian mode of warfare, in all its revolting and destructive features.

Were those who were engaged in the war against the Indians, less humane than those who carried on the war against their English allies? No. They were not. Both parties carried on the war on the same principle of reciprocity of advantages and disadvantages. For example, the English and Americans take each one thousand prisoners.—They are exchanged: Neither army is weakened by this arrangement. A sacrafice is indeed made to humanity, in the expense of taking care of the sick, wounded and prisoners; but this expense is mutual. No disadvantages result from all the clemency of modern warfare, excepting an augmentation of the expenses of war. In this mode of warfare, those of the nation, not in arms, are safe from death by the hands of soldiers. No civilized warrior dishonors his sword with the blood of helpless infancy, old age, or that of the fair sex. He aims his blows only at those whom he finds in arms against him. The indian kills indiscriminately. His object is the total extermination of his enemies. Children are victims of his vengeance, because, if males, they may hereafter become warriors, or if females, they may become mothers. Even the foetal state is criminal in his view. It is not enough that the foetus should perish with the murdered mother, it is torn from her pregnant womb and elevated on a stick or pole, as a trophy of victory and an object of horror, to the survivors of the slain.

If the indian takes prisoners, mercy has but little concern in the transaction; he spares the lives of those who fall into his hands, for the purpose of feasting the feelings of ferocious vengeance of himself and his comrades, by the torture of his captive, or to increase the strength of his nation by his adoption into an indian family, or for the purpose of gain, by selling him for an higher price, than his scalp would fetch, to his christian allies of Canada; for be it known that those allies were in the constant practice of making presents for scalps, and prisoners, as well as furnishing the means for carrying on the indian war, which for so many years desolated our defenceless frontiers. No lustration can ever wash out this national stain. The foul blot must remain, as long as the page of history shall convey the record of the foul transaction, to future generations.

The author would not open wounds which have, alas! already bled so long; but for the purpose of doing justice to the memory of his forefathers and relatives, many of whom perished in the defence of their country, by the hands of the merciless indians.

How is a war of extermination, and accompanied with such acts of attrocious cruelty to be met by those on whom it is inflicted? Must it be met by the lenient maxims of civilized warfare? Must the Indian captive be spared his life?—What advantage would be gained by this course? The young white prisoners, adopted into indian families often become complete indians, but in how few instances did ever an indian become civilized. Send a cartel for an exchange of prisoners; the indians knew nothing of this measure of clemency in war; the bearer of the white flag for the purpose of effecting the exchange, would have exerted his humanity, at the forfeit of his life.

Should my countrymen be still charged with barbarism,

in the prosecution of the indian war, let him who harbours this unfavourable impression concerning them, portray in immagination the horrid scenes of slaughter, which
frequently met their view in the course of the indian war.
Let him, if he can bear the reflection, look at helpless
infancy, virgin beauty, and hoary age, dishonoured by the
ghastly wounds of the tomahawk and scalping knife of
the savage. Let him hear the shrieks of the victims of the
indian torture by fire, and smell the surrounding air,
rendered sickening by the effluvia of their burning flesh
and blood.—Let him hear the yells, and view the hellish
features of the surrounding circle of savage warriors, riot-
ing in all the luxuriance of vengeance, while applying the
flaming torches to the parched limbs of the sufferers, and
then suppose those murdered infants, matrons, virgins
and victims of torture, were his friends and relations, the
wife, sister, child, or brother; what would be his feelings!
—After a short season of grief, he would say "I will now
think only of revenge."

Philosophy shudders at the destructive aspect of war in
any shape, Christianity, by teaching the religion of the
good Samaritan altogether forbids it; but the original
settlers of the western regions, like the greater part of the
world, were neither philosophers, nor saints. They were
"Men of like passions with others." And therefore adopted
the indian mode of warfare from necessity, and a motive
of revenge; with the exception of burning their captives
alive, which they never did; if the bodies of savage enemies were sometimes burned, it was not until after they
were dead.

Let the voice of nature, and the law of nations plead
in favour of the veteran pioneers of the desert regions of
the west. War has hitherto been prominent trait in the
moral system of human nature, and will continue such,
until a radical change shall be effected in favour of science,
morals and piety, on a general scale.

In the conflicts of nations, as well as those of individuals, no advantages are to be conceded: If mercy may
be associated with the carnage and devastations of war,

that mercy must be reciprocal but a war of utter extermination, must be met by a war of the same character; or
by an overwhelming force which may put an end to it,
without a sacrafice of the helpless and unoffending part
of hostile nation; such a force was not at the command
of the first inhabitants of this country. The sequel of the
indian war goes to show that in a war with savages, the
choice lies between extermination and subjugation. Our
government has wisely and humanely pursued the latter
course.

The author begs to be understood, that the foregoing
observations, are not intended as a justification, of the
whole of the transactions of our people with regard to
the indians during the course of the war. Some instances
of acts of wanton barbarity occurred on our side, which
have received, and must continue to receive the unequivo-
cal reprobation of all the civilized world. In the course
of this history, it will appear that more deeds of wanton
barbarity took place on our side than the world is now
acquainted with.

DOCUMENTS 62, 63

Captured by Indians

Indian captivity narratives, read voraciously throughout the seventeenth, eighteenth, and nineteenth centuries, served various purposes and satisfied various needs. They were considerably more than the adventure stories featured in "men's magazines" of today. They served to classify an entire segment of American society—the Indian—and to provide good reason why he should be treated the way he was treated by that society. The facts were sometimes lost in the process, but a martyrology was created that helped sustain the ire of those exposed to the "cutting edge" of the frontier as well as gain the support of those who were not. The crude but powerful woodcuts shown in Plates 14 and 15, following page 134, tell the story without the need for words. The image of the noble savage was largely erased by such impressions, while at the same time the concept of the noble frontiersman was enhanced. The illustrations are from the *Narrative of the Capture and Providential Escape of Misses Frances and Almira Hall* ([New York] 1835), in the Rare Book Division, Library of Congress, Washington, D.C.

DOCUMENT 64

The Beau Ideal

What was it like for a nineteenth-century American to gaze upon the countenance of a dead Indian foe? The following passage gives an excellent insight into the thoughts of an officer in a regiment of South Carolina volunteers in the Second Seminole War, 1835–42, as he gazed at the dishonored corpse of a captured enemy. Before the Indian's skull was placed in the Doctor's cabinet and subjected to the prying fingers of the amateur phrenologists, his fleshy carnal remains served to inspire ideals and ideas common to nineteenth-century America. The following quotation is from the anonymous *Sketch of the Seminole War, and Sketches during a Campaign:* By a Lieutenant, of the Left Wing, pp. 246–50 (Charleston: 1836).

It was impossible to ascertain exactly the execution done by our fire in the skirmish. A man on board the Steamboat, observed a few Indians get as he thought into the river to cross, some hundred yards above, but he could not see distinctly. The next morning, the body of an Indian was discovered, laid among the bushes at the side of the river, about where the individual had made the observation, and marks were seen where, apparently two or three others had been dragged; some clothing likewise was picked up; if there were any more killed, they must have been sunk in the river. From the blood which their trail showed, they must have suffered not a little.

The Indian found dead, was said, by the guide, and a gentleman who knew him, and supposed to be a chief, Uchee Billy (or Billy Hicks, as his real name was, son of old Hicks) who headed a band of Uchees, that had a settlement at Spring Garden, and made Volusia and the vicinity, the scene of their hostilities—they may have consisted of between 50 and 100 warriors, but it is difficult to say, as they imperfectly disclosed themselves in the woods, and an Indian trail furnishes but equivocal evidence of their number, but from the shots fired, there must have been at least 50. If the body was that of a chief, it had been stripped of any distinguishing marks.

When it is considered that savages are looked upon by some, as little better than wild beasts, that the feelings of our men were excited at the recent loss and injury we had sustained, and that for this and the previous slaughter at McCrea's, we had no revenge, the triumph which some indulged in over this slain Indian (the first victim that the fortune of treacherous war had made an oblation to our arms) which humanity and the sentiment of civilization, that teach us to respect the dead, would on another and a cooler occasion, have arisen in their bosoms to condemn; may be excused perhaps. He was scalped, his body stretched naked upon a pole, and brought into camp for the curious to look at.

I felt myself entrained along with the crowd—nature, philosophy remonstrated—why should I indulge in the vulgar curiosity, to steal a look at the forbidding corrupt clay, to gaze upon the sad remains of a human being?—was it not a petty weakness? was there any thing commendable in my acknowledging a feeling of triumph over this solitary slain foe? was there not something shocking and criminal in acknowledging it *thus* over a mutilated, and dishonored corpse? I scouted the idea, but my sterner feelings got the better, and with a real curiosity, which was not objectless and idle, I conquered my reluctance.

A fine specimen he was of the goodly handy work of nature—his limbs were cast in an almost perfect mould, but an evident difference was observed in the upper and lower part of the shoulders and arms, and of the rest of the body from the waist down to the toe. The former were small, and by no means remarkable for power; but strength, agility, and grace distinguished the latter; the bone straight like an arrow: the compact thews of thigh and calf; the elastic sinews of knee and ancle, and the rounded symmetry that ended in the remarkable high instep, and firm, straight, handsome foot and heel; it was a study for the sculptor.

But the face of that stern warrior, whose red brow so lately frowned with battle's terror; whose parted lip bespoke the bloody thought, and the demoniac cruelty of his race, now paled from its natural hue—livid with death —and quelled, scarcely softened into the silent, mute, and petrified expression—here indeed was a model for the artist. I lingered, in spite of my repugnance to the unpleasantness of the scene, to gaze on the beautiful specimen of savage inflexibility before me; I had seen Indians before, and attempted fac-similies, and ideals which endeavored to portray the fierce lineaments of the legitimate savage, but not in any living originals, nor in any attempts of art, have I recognized so perfect a *beau ideal* of that savageness, which we are accustomed to consider as an inherent quality in the unhumanized son of the forest; an element in his nature, single, and whole, of which the Tiger furnishes the aptest type, and which is not incompatible with beauty of phisiognomy, as I realized in the countenance of this Uchee. There was a calmness, and a curl, as of scorn, on the divided lip; the muscles were relaxed with a subdued expression, of fierce glee, as though the war yell had been suddenly cut short by the death stroke; and this feature, the compressed brow, and the haughty nose, evinced dauntless daring, resolution, and contempt of death.

It was undoubtedly a noble countenance; the features were regular and handsome, and I wished that I could have seen him when they were animated by the small, black, piercing eye, and heightened and set off by the long raven hair and plume of the warrior.

He was apparently about 50 years of age, as his scalp was sprinkled with grey hairs, and his teeth shewed some signs of decay, but with these exceptions his limbs and countenance appeared to have all the freshness and vigour of youthful prime. His head was preserved in the Dr's. cabinet, and afforded a fine subject for the speculations of the phrenologists, of whom there were not a few in Camp, and if in other instances the followers of the science agreed as happily in their results as they did in this, Phrenology would not have to contend against so many opponents. The sconce of the unconscious and condemned Uchee was thumbed and kneaded into one leavened mass of destructiveness, and the basilar region of his brain was so spacious that every other bad quality appertaining thereto found an equal room in it, and merged all difficulties about *Bumps*; while the moral and intellectual organs were supposed too insignificant to merit attention— his forehead, however, though retreating, was strongly marked by the perceptive organs.

I have been rather particular in describing this Indian, as he was one of a tribe, noted as being the most savage and ill disposed of our Southern Indians. Of the origin and native customs of the Uchees, little is known. They are one of the broken tribes, which the Muscogees associated with them, to give their confederacy strength. They still speak a language radically different from that of the Creeks. It is supposed to be the Shawanese, or a dialect of that tongue. They are called Uchees, probably from their town having been formerly situated opposite the Chatta-Uchee River. They have a lighter complexion than the Creeks.

DOCUMENT 65

General Mitchell and the Big Mandan

While other units gained glory against the Confederates, the 7th Iowa Cavalry, in 1864, found itself fighting Sioux and Cheyennes in the Dakotas, Colorado, Wyoming, Kansas, and Nebraska. Captain Ware, of Company "F," put together his recollections of the period after the war, on the basis of a daily journal he had kept and with the aid of long letters written to his mother, which the latter had saved. His account of a grand council with the Indians at Cottonwood Springs, in April of 1864, is remarkable for its acute observation both of the whites, under General Robert B. Mitchell, and of the Indians, represented by such leaders as the Big Mandan, "six feet four, and about a yard across." The passage is from *The Indian War of 1864* by Captain Eugene F. Ware, pp. 146–63. (Topeka, Kansas: Crane & Co., 1911). A recent edition, edited by Clyde C. Walton, has been published by St. Martin's Press (New York: 1960).

In the Meantime the Indians were coming in, and camping together near the river outside of the two miles limit. We had all of our men fully armed, and everything ready to prevent a surprise of our post. The Indians were ordered not come within two miles of the post, except that they might send a delegation in of one hundred, to accompany their speakers to the place of rendezvous. Our sutler, Ben Gallager, had started in to build a large sutler store, twenty-five feet square. Holes for the doors and windows had been sawed from the logs, and most of the roof was on. But it had no floor nor any furnishing. It had a large doorhole in the north and one in the south; the

opening on the south side faced our camp. With great
pomp the Indians to the number of about one hundred,
all fully armed and finely mounted, came down towards
our camp about nine o'clock. Then seventeen chiefs threw
off their weapons, leaving them behind with their escort,
and came forward to the new sutler-house with great pomp
and ceremony. Then all of the officers of the post, coming
up to within about fifty feet of the building, took off their
sabres and revolvers and left them in a pile with a guard.
We had three interpreters, the principal one of whom was
named Watts. He had been with the Indians and traded
with them for many years. His usual name was "Snell,"
which was an abbreviation of his Indian name, which was
Wah-see-cha-es-snel-la (The "lonesome white man").
There were two other interpreters besides Watts. Among
the Indians there was an Indian who, it was said, readily
understood English. The Indians formed a semicircle, in
the building, sitting down on the ground, and we formed
one, sitting on cracker-boxes opposite them, except that
General Mitchell sat in a large camp-chair. He looked like
a king. He was an exceedingly handsome man, with a full,
dark-brown curly beard and mustache. Major George M.
O'Brien sat on his right, also a fine-looking man, standing
six feet one inch. . . . He afterwards practiced law in
Omaha, and on his death was buried there.

On the Left of the General sat Captain O'Brien, six feet
high. I was six feet, and we tapered off at both sides, making a pretty good showing, in full uniforms, with our red
silk sashes on, which hadn't seen the light for several
months. Back of the General was a man whom the General had brought along with him, and from whom he appeared to take advice as to preliminaries and procedure.
I didn't find who he was. To the left front of the General,
and immediately in front of Captain O'Brien, on a cracker-
box, sat the interpreter, Watts. The Indians all through
this matter seemed to be unusually important, and punc-
tilious. They all had their blankets on, and although they
had ostensibly left their arms behind, every one had probably a sharp butcher-knife in the folds of his blanket. At

least, Watts said so. As a sort of stand-off, we, who had left our arms behind us, each had a pistol in his hip pocket so as not to be taken unawares. Nothing was said for several minutes, and we all sat in silence. Every once in a while an Indian made a sort of sign or signal, and it would go around like penitents crossing. It was some kind of a slight significant sign made instantly and simply, which would be taken up and gone through with as if it were a signal of some kind, or an invocation of some kind. Directly opposite General Mitchell was Shan-tag-a-lisk, which is translated as "Spotted Tail." He was the greatest warrior in the Sioux nation, said to be the greatest either past or present. He was said to be able to count twenty-six "cooz." He belonged to the Brulé Sioux. On his right was my friend, "Bad Wound." On the left were "Two Strike," and "Two Crows," and the "Big Mandan." On the opposite side were "Prickly Pear," and "Eagle Twice." These are all the names I have preserved. "Two Strike" was said to have killed two Pawnees with one bullet. These Indians represented the four tribes of the Sioux that were nearest to us. Those south of the river were the "Ogallallah," of whom "Bad Wound" was chief. Northwest were the "Brulés," of whom "Shan-tag-a-lisk" was chief. North of us and east of the Brulés were what were called the "Minne-kaw'-zhouz." The latter word signified shallow water. The "shallow water" Sioux lived upon the streams which through a great scope of country were all shallow. "Two Strike" was said to be their chief. East of them on the Missouri river were a lot of Indians represented by the Big Mandan. The word Brulé, which is a French word, means "sun-burnt"; it was derived from the Indian name which in the Indian tongue meant "burnt-thighs." Their thighs exposed to the sun were sunburned in their constant riding on horseback. The words meant more than at first appeared; for, Indians who walked on the ground did not get their thighs burned more than other parts, especially as the Indians went practically naked when the sun was hot. Hence the words "burnt-thighs" meant that the Brulé Indians were riders; that they belonged to the

cavalry, that is, the Chivalry; in other words, they were of
the equestrian class. The words constituted a boast that
they were better than others and were the Rough-Riders
of the plains. Such was the tradition of the name. Peace
or war upon the plains, as to us, depended largely upon
our satisfying all these Indians.

Strange as it May Appear, all of the Indians had extremely feminine faces, except the Big Mandan. Spotted
Tail looked exactly like a woman; and in short, as I had
already observed, and often afterwards observed, the Indian men seemed to have a feminine look and the women
to have a rather masculine look, which increased as they
grew older. An old Indian woman had a much more dan-
gerous-looking face than an old Indian man. So much has
been written about the noble looks and appearance of the
red man, and his fine physique, and all that kind of stuff,
that it seems strange to contradict it; but, as a matter of
fact, the Indian warriors as a whole looked more like
women than like men, and their extermination, I believe,
is due to the fact that they did not have the surviving
power nor the sufficient fibre. In addition to this, these
Indians had revolting and beastly habits and vices, just as
bad as could be, and their names, many of them, were
such that no interpretation in the English would be print-
able.

The word "Ogallallah" meant "the split-off band," because in former years the band had split off from the main
Sioux tribe, and gone down into what was said to have
been Pawnee territory. But concerning those facts I could
never get anything but contradictory stories. The "split-off"
must have been a long while before. They called themselves Lah-ko-tahs. The interpreter told me that the separation had been so long, and so distant, that one part of the
Sioux tribe had lost the consonant "d" and the other the
use of the consonant "l," and one called themselves "Lah-
ko-tahs," and the other "Dah-ko-tahs." Once I talked with
two Irish travelers in regard to the Indians. One of them
asked me what the word "Ogallallah" meant, and I told
him that it meant "the split-off band," and he spoke up

and said, "That is a pure Irish word, and in the old Irish
language means, 'secessionist.'" I may say here that it was
not unusual for persons in referring to the language of the
northern Sioux to say that there were words in use among
them that were distinctly Irish and Welsh. I took no note
of them at the time, considering them to be merely acci-
dental coincidences, and now I remember only the word
"Ogallallah."

It was Very Interesting, the silent way in which we sat
on both sides and gazed at each other. When it came to
muscle and physique, our men, man for man, could have
thrown them all outdoors and walked on them, except perhaps as to the "Big Mandan." We were all larger than the
Indians except him, and he was about six feet four, and
about a yard across, about forty years of age, and very
light-colored for an Indian. It would have been a close
tussle between him and Major O'Brien. Finally, one Indian
got out a pipe from under his blanket. It had a stem about
two and a half feet long. It was made of red pipestone,
and had a good-sized bowl, but the orifice was scant for
the tobacco. It was filled with great pomp and solemnity
by the man who took it, and he did it little by little, as if
it was a great function. He felt the weight and importance
of the ceremony. Then he passed the pipe down to the
end of the line, and there an Indian with a flint-and-steel
and a piece of punk started the pipe. Then it went from
mouth to mouth, the parties each taking three whiffs.
When it had gone along the entire Indian line, it struck
the end of our line. We were all trying to look solemn.
The Indians were dreadfully solemn. They acted as if they
thought they were doing the greatest deed in their lives;
we did not wish to hurt their feelings by impairing the
solemnity of the occasion, so we just looked as wise as we
could. But when the pipe struck the end of our line,
where Lieutenant Williams was, before he put the pipe
into his mouth he drew it under his sleeve, saying as he
did so, "I don't believe I want to swap saliva with that
crowd." This being said in a ponderous and thoughtful
way, perhaps impressed the crowd on the other side as

being a mental benediction on receiving the utensil. We all kept looking solemn, however, although it was hard work. When the pipe got to the General he pulled out his silk handkerchief and polished off the mouthpiece, took three profound whiffs, and passed it on. After it had gone through with our line it went across to where it had started from.

Finally Spotted Tail said something which, being interpreted, was: "The white brother has sent for us. What does the white brother want?" Then General Mitchell, with much assumed and natural dignity, combined, began to tell the Indians how the whites and Indians had lived side by side in peace for so many years, and how the Indians were prosperous through contact with the whites, and were getting guns, and killing game more easily, and having a better time of it generally; and how persons had conspired to bring about a want of amity and friendship; and how it was his desire to meet the red brother, and tell him what the Great Father in Washington wanted. It was a long preamble which General Mitchell had evidently conned over in his mind, because he wound up with a statement that the white man wanted peace, *and wanted the Sioux to keep out of the Platte Valley*.

Thereupon the Big Mandan rose up, throwing off his blanket, and standing out with nothing on but breechclout and moccasins. He commenced a speech which started out slow and low, beginning to rise in volume and increase in rapidity, until he was spouting away like a man running for office before a county convention. No report that I know of was ever made of what took place at this powwow, and my notes concerning it are meager. But the "Big Mandan" told about how in former days they had fought the Chippewas clear up to the Lakes in the east, and now they were being crowded away from the Missouri River; that they owned the land, and they owned the buffalo, and the antelope, and the deer, and the wild ducks, and the geese; and how the white man was pushing them all the time, and killing their cattle, and their birds, and catching their fish, and making it harder all the time

for them to get a living. It was the old, old story. During
his speech the Indians all sat and looked mutely at the
ground. All at once at a passage of the speech they brightened up, and grunted an applause. I said to the interpreter,
"What is that sentence?" He said, "The Indian coined a
new word." It appears that it is one of the characteristics
of the Indian language to run words together; to take a
vowel from one and a consonant from another, forming a
combination of thought, and boiling it down into a word.
And it was the part of an orator to make new words which
his hearers could immediately comprehend the meaning
of, and it was on this occasion that the Big Mandan had
met the dramatic situation by the coining of a new word
for the Sioux vocabulary.

General Mitchell Made a Speech, a brief reply, sitting
in his chair, intending to assuage the sentiment that the
Big Mandan had raised. Major O'Brien wanted to make
a talk, but General Mitchell would not allow anybody to
talk but himself, fearing the matter might break up into
something which would resemble a town row. Then another
of the Indians got up and went over the story again; how
they were a hungry people; how the white brother had
everything, and they had nothing; how the white brother
had flour and bacon and sugar and everything else in vast
quantities more than they wanted, while the Indian had a
continual struggle with poverty, and had nothing to eat
but dried pumpkin, and buffalo-berries, and jerked meat.
General Mitchell replied to this speech by saying that the
Government gave them blankets enough and clothing
enough, to clothe them for all seasons of the year; that the
Government gave them flour, bacon and supplies, which if
prudently used would always enable them to have plenty
to eat; that the Government desired them to live in houses,
and had offered them carpenters and blacksmiths, and to
teach them how to build houses; and how to become
civilized and live like the whites, but they would not do it,
and that their troubles arose from their perversity and
want of thought.

Then another of the Indian orators got up, and began to

talk about the white people sending whisky into their villages, and cheating them out of their beaver-skins, and the mink and otter and muskrats, and buffalo-robes, and how the Indians were getting fewer and poorer all the time from the "drunk-water" which the white man sent out. To this General Mitchell replied that there were bad white men as well as bad Indians; that the white man put chains on those who sold whisky to Indians, and kept them in confinement, when they could be caught; that such white men were bad white men; that the Indians ought to kill them on sight when they brought whisky into their village; that the difficulty with the Indians was they wanted the white man to bring the whisky in, and would not punish him; that they wanted the whisky, and therefore they were complaining of themselves, and not of the white men.

And So it Went, Speech after Speech, General Mitchell always replying to every speech. He had thought it all up, and I must say he beat the Indians in their controversy. He told the Indians that they had no right to claim all of the land. He told them that the good Manitou, who put us all on earth, intended that each one should have his share of the earth, and the Indians had no right to take ten times as much land per head as they allowed the white people. And he pointed out that the white people had to live all penned up and in discomfort, so that the Indian could have ten times the amount of land that he ought to have, and kill the buffalo which belonged to everybody on the earth alike, but which the Indians claimed the entire ownership of. And that the Indian had kept the white man back, and the latter was so crowded that if the lands which the white man had were divided, each white man would have only a small piece, so small that an Indian could shoot an arrow across it, while the Indian had land he could not see over.

The Manner of Discussion was that the Indian would speak a sentence, and then the interpreter would interpret it. Then the Indian would speak another sentence, and that would be interpreted. When the General spoke, his speech was put into the Sioux language, and the man behind the General was there as overseer to see that "Snell" translated it correctly, and several times the overseer interfered to have the translation explained, the great object being to have the true idea which each one brought forth, presented to the other. The debate ran on, and the pipe was relit and passed around several times during the silences which ensued. Silences of five to ten minutes ensued after each of General Mitchell's speeches. Then the pipe would go around with the same formality. Spotted Tail, sitting quietly, said: "Why are we here? Why has the white brother asked us to come?" Then General Mitchell said: "The object of this meeting is to have an understanding, and make a treaty, so each will know what he ought to do. We want you Sioux to stay off from the Platte Valley. You can come down to the hills on the edge of the valley while you are hunting, but you must not come down into the valley, for it scares our women and children traveling, going up and down, and it scares the women and children that are living in the houses in the valley. If you wish to cross the road, and go north or south of the river, you must send in word during the daytime to one of the posts, and then you will be escorted across the valley from the hills on one side to the hills on the other, and then you can go where you will. But you mustn't come down in the valley or allow spies, beggars, or bad Indians to come down into the valley. You must restrain your bad men; we will hold you responsible; this is an ultimatum. This we insist upon your doing. If it takes more to feed you, if it takes more bacon or blankets and corn, we will give you more, but you must stay out of the Platte Valley."

This Speech of General Mitchell's seemed to nettle them all. Shan-tag-a-lisk was their greatest warrior, but he was not much of a talker. Their principal orator was the Big Mandan, but Shan-tag-a-lisk got up with his blanket on, and his arms folded across his breast, and began talking in a low, hesitating tone. He said: "The Sioux nation is a great people, and we do not wish to be dictated to by the whites or anybody else. We do not care particularly

about the Platte valley, because there is no game in it.
Your young men and your freighters have driven all the
game out, or killed it, so we find nothing in the Platte
valley. But we want to come and trade in the Platte valley
wherever we please. We want places where we can sell our
beaver-skins and our buffalo-robes. The Platte valley is
ours, and we do not intend to give it away. We have let
the white man have it so that he could pass, but he has
gone over it so often now that he claims it and thinks he
owns it. But it is still ours, and always has been ours. It
belonged to our forefathers, and their graves are along the
hills overlooking the valley from the Missouri river to the
mountains, and we do not expect to give it up. We are not
afraid of the white man, nor are we afraid to fight him.
We have not had in late years any very serious difficulties
with the white men. Trouble has been brought about by
'drunk-water.' Bad whites have given it to bad Indians, and
they have got both of us into trouble. The donations
which the white men have been giving us are not sufficient; they are not adequate for the concessions which we
have made. The goods that were brought us at Woc-co-
pom'-any agency were neither as good as had been promised us, nor were they in amount as had been promised us.
The Great Father through his army officers makes us great
promises, but the agents, who are not army officers, cheat
us, and do not carry out the treaty obligations. Last fall
at the Woc-co-pom'-any agency, when the agent asked us
to sign for our goods, we would not sign, because they were
not what they should be in value or amount, and one of
the army officers who was there told us not to sign, and he
swore at the agent, and told him he was a thief, and was
cheating us. The army officers treat us well enough, but
those who are not officers cheat us when they can, and we
do not want to deal with any but the army officers. Besides
this, we will not give up the Platte valley to you until we
have a regular treaty, and until we have all agreed to it,
and have been paid for it. It will soon be that you will
want other roads to the west. If we give you this you will
want another, and if we give you that you will want a

third. Before we will agree to anything you must stop the surveyors that are going west at this very time on the river Niobrara. All of these things must be considered before we will make a treaty."

Then General Mitchell Asked if anyone present knew about the Niobrara, and some one of the party spoke and said that a surveying party was going west up the Niobrara with an escort. The Niobrara river was a river running west from the Missouri river parallel with the Platte, and about a hundred miles north of where we then were. Spotted Tail said that the Niobrara river went through their good country, and that they would resist the white man putting a road through, and that unless the work was stopped they were going to drive off or kill the expedition. And he also said that he wanted the road out on the Smoky Hill closed up, because it went through their best buffalo country. And he further said that they would not for the present carry out the wishes of General Mitchell until their demands were agreed to. The speech of Shan-tag-a-lisk wound up with a regular bluff, and it made General Mitchell a little angry; he got up, and told the Indians that he was not there to coax them, but was there to tell them what to do. That he would stop the survey up on the Niobrara river until there was another conference; that the Smoky Hill route was a route much used, and was necessary for the white man, and it would not be closed. And he wound up by saying that if the Sioux did not keep away from the Platte river he would station a soldier to every blade of grass from the Missouri River to the Rocky Mountains. This counter "bluff" on the part of General Mitchell brought Spotted Tail immediately to his feet. He got up and said that the Sioux nation was not afraid of the white people; that there were more Sioux Indians than there were white people; that the Sioux nation had twenty-six thousand Ar-ke'-che-tas* (organized warriors), and could put more soldiers into the Platte valley than the white people

* NOTE.—The Arkecheta was the Sioux regular army soldier, as apart from the hunter or lay-Indian. It was a sort of military guild among the Sioux.

could; that they knew all about the white people, and the
white people were not smart enough to fool them; that the
white people were all the while trying to fool the Indians
and deceive them as to numbers so as to scare them. That
the whites were parading before the Indians all the time
so as to show off their numbers; that the same people that
came up the Platte valley went back by the way of Smoky
Hill. "We have seen them, and recognize them time and
again. Some of them come back by way of Platte river, but
that is only to fool us. The white men are marching around
in a ring so that we may see them and be led to believe
that there is a great number of them. They cannot fool us.
We recognize the same people, and they are too few; we
are not afraid of them—we outnumber them."

It Had Got Well Along into the afternoon; no headway
had been made, but General Mitchell seemed to think
that the ground had been broken for a future conference.
It was finally decided that the conference should adjourn,
and meet again at the same place in fifty days. Nothing
whatever had been gained. Both parties had been bluffing,
and neither side was afraid of the other. But General
Mitchell promised to stop the Niobrara expedition, and to
get permission from the Great Father at Washington to
make a new treaty, that would cede the Platte valley; that
every one present should think the matter over; and come
back in fifty days; and that the Indians should bring other
chiefs with them if they wished. Then General Mitchell
with great formality took Spotted Tail by the hand and
said, "How cola?" and had the interpreter tell him that
they would all be fed before they left the post. Thereupon
the Indians were all taken to the cookhouse, where everything had been kept in readiness, and they were given all
they could eat, which was an enormous amount. The boiled
beef and coffee and hard-bread (which the boys called
"Lincoln shingles") were spread out with panfuls of molasses, and things went along all right. A lot of supplies
had been sent to the Indian camps during the day. The
Indians invited our officers to go over to their camp and
have a dog feast. It was not considered advisable for more

than three to go, together with some civilians who were there. Captain O'Brien was one of the officers, and he requested me to be on guard until he came back, and have the horses all saddled and the men ready to mount on a moment's notice. He wanted to go to the Indian camp, and did not know what might happen, but he never seemed to fear any danger. One of the Indians asked the visitors to bring some coffee; so one of them, on his horse, took a little bag of roasted coffee, perhaps ten pounds. Captain O'Brien's story is that they were entertained by the principal chiefs; that they had dog to eat, and that the dog wasn't so bad after all. That the Indians put coffee into a big camp-kettle, and commenced boiling and kept filling the camp-kettle and boiling coffee until he came away about ten o'clock at night. He said the Indians drank coffee hot by the gallon, and didn't seem to be able to get enough of it. He said they appeared to be all right, and friendly; he didn't believe there would be any Indian trouble.

The next morning there was not an Indian in sight, and current matters at our post went along in the same usual way. General Mitchell left as soon as the Indians did. I will speak more of him further on, but will say here that his honored grave may be seen on one of the sunlit slopes of the Arlington National Cemetery near Washington.

Shan-tag-a-lisk was over forty years old, but claimed to be about thirty. Pioneers said the Indians would not tell the truth about their ages, because they thought it might give the white men some occult advantage over them.

DOCUMENT 66

The Battle of the Little Big Horn

Too much has been written about General George A. Custer's gallant last stand at the Battle of the Little Big Horn, June 26, 1876, during the Second Sioux War. Generations of Americans have gazed over foaming beers at the various reproductions of the scene that used to be a fixture in countless bars thanks to the generosity and public relations skill of American brewers and barkeepers. In addition to the details of practical mayhem evident in every nook and cranny of the canvas, there is also a sense of elevation achieved in the depiction of Custer, dramatically occupying the central position, usually bathed in a shaft of light with sword upraised for a final blow. Clearly we have a picture here which, in a gentler age, might have been titled "The Apotheosis of Custer." The version reproduced in Plate 16, following page 134, is derived from a lithograph published in San Francisco in 1878, now in the Prints and Photographs Division of the Library of Congress, Washington, D.C.

DOCUMENTS 67, 68

Geronimo

Geronimo (1834–1909), a Chiricahua Apache, was one of the last of the Indian "chiefs" who disputed white occupancy of the continent. Because his feats are recent and took place in what has become the most photogenic territory of the Republic, he has won a special place in the consciousness of the American people. The two photographs reproduced in Plates 17 and 18, following page 334, show him first in 1886, already fifty-two but with fire in his eye, in a photograph by A. Frank Randall, and secondly, nearly twenty years later, in 1905, old and tired, in a photograph by DeLancey Gill. Both photographs are from the Bureau of American Ethnology, Smithsonian Institution, Washington, D.C.

DOCUMENT 69

The Ute "War" of 1915

Few people will believe that the United States fought an Indian "War" in 1915 that excited the attention of the American public and caused grave concern in Washington. Yet the so-called Ute "War" was "fought," and a bloody war it was, in the eyes of some Western editors. The following pamphlet by M. K. Sniffen, Secretary of the Indian Rights Association, dated November 15, 1915, gives a brief account of the war. A recent treatment of the episode is Forbes Parkhill, *The Last of the Indian Wars* (New York: Collier Books, 1962).

THE MEANING OF THE UTE "WAR."
BY M. K. SNIFFEN,
Secretary Indian Rights Association.

History has repeated itself many times in Indian Affairs, and the recent trouble with the non-reservation Utes, in Utah, is merely one of those incidents that were so common in the early days of this country.

In order that we might learn what really was behind that incident, and what actually happened in that inaccessible region, while visiting some Indian reservations I took a horseback trip, last September, from Cortez, Colorado, to Bluff and vicinity in the State of Utah.

I found that there were two distinct elements among these Utes: two small groups, under the leadership of Polk and Posey (both of whom are reputed, generally, to be lawless and defiant), with no settled homes, but usually camping near Bluff, and a much larger number of industrious Indians living on the public domain in Allen Can-

yon and on the Montezuma Creek. In the trouble that
was developed, however, there was no discrimination between the good and the bad—all were regarded in the
same light, as a nuisance (or a hindrance) to the white
man.

The principal character in this affair was the son of
Polk, Tse-Ne-Gat (or Everett Hatch, as he is usually
called), a Ute Indian accused of murdering a Mexican
sheepherder. This matter was fully exploited in the news-
papers last spring, when it was made to appear that all
the Utes in that section were on the war-path, "armed
to the teeth," and prepared to resist any effort of the
authorities to arrest Hatch. In view of this "dangerous"
state of affairs, and the alleged inability of the United
States marshal to get Hatch, a posse was organized in
Colorado and sent to Bluff, Utah, near where the Indian
wanted was supposed to be. According to the best information I could obtain from people in position to know about
two-thirds of this posse was composed of the "rough-neck"
and "tin-horn" class, to whom shooting an Indian would
be real sport! Probably twenty-five of these eminent citizens, fully armed with everything but a warrant, attacked
those Utes who were camped near Bluff one morning
about daybreak.

That the Indians were not spoiling for a fight, or even
prepared for it, is evident from the fact that they did
not take the precaution to guard their camp, and they
were therefore easily surprised. Indeed, I was informed
that some of them were unarmed, their guns being in
pawn. The posse took positions on both sides of the hills
overlooking the Indians' camp, in the wash near Bluff,
and fired a volley into the tents. Naturally, the Indians
were aroused, and thinking they were going to be killed,
they tried to escape. Polk and his son, with several other
Indians, sought a sheltered spot and returned the fire.
Meanwhile, Posey, hearing the shooting, came up from
his camp, a mile or so below, as his son was visiting the
Bluff contingent. In the brief battle an Indian child was
shot through the legs, one Indian who was seeking shelter

was killed, and a member of the posse was also killed. And the attempt to arrest Hatch ingloriously failed.

Later, Mancos Jim, at the urgent request of the whites at Bluff, visited the camp of the Indians and induced the men to surrender. As they were coming towards the town Polk and Posey and a few of their followers escaped. Several of the Indians were made prisoners and confined in a second-story room over the Zion Co-operative Store at Bluff. They were shackled hand and foot and armed guards placed in charge of them. After the posseman was killed his friends were eager to "shoot anything that looked like an Indian"; and it was not strange to learn that one of the prisoners who "attempted to escape" by jumping from the second-story window was shot to death. The prisoners were securely ironed and incapable of doing serious harm to the armed guards, who were fully prepared for any emergency. It is claimed by one of the prisoners, after his release, that the guards indulged in the "gentle" pastime of holding guns to their heads and against their bodies, at the same time threatening to shoot. In view of these circumstances, it would seem that the killing of the prisoner was a deliberate act of vengeance, and wholly unnecessary, since he could readily have been restrained by physical force.

The rest of the "dangerous" Indians were driven from the vicinity of Bluff, and started up the San Juan river for the Navajo reservation. Bluff was strongly guarded by the posse, but no protection was arranged for the traders and the Government farmer, with their families, on whom these Indians were turned loose. A warning was not even sent them. What happened? Those so-called dangerous Indians stopped at the traders' stores, bought some supplies, and camped among or near the Navajos, and no one was disturbed!

After the bungling attempt to arrest Hatch, the posse camped at Bluff and merely "marked time." General Hugh L. Scott, of the United States Army, was sent by the Government to handle the situation. Incidentally, the first thing he did was to disband the posse. Then he went out to the few belligerent Indians and had no trouble in inducing them to surrender, in spite of the fact that one of the Mormons at Bluff said he "would have been willing to bet a thousand dollars that Scott could not bring those Indians in."

Subsequently, Hatch was tried in the Federal Court at Denver on the charge of murder. The case of the Government was so weak, and the argument of the defense so convincing, that it took the jury less than five minutes to return a verdict of "not guilty." The evidence against Hatch was insufficient, in the first place, and had there been no other motive behind this effort, opportunities were not lacking when he could have been arrested in Bluff. But the case against Hatch was only a pretext for something else. One of the Mormons declared that "when they get Hatch, they will take all the other Indians away from this part of Utah."

For many years, one hundred or more Indians made their homes in Allen Canyon and on the Montezuma Creek (on the public domain) in San Juan County, Utah. They were industrious, peaceable and self-supporting, and a number of them had built permanent homes, had fenced fields, and were making good progress. That part of Allen Canyon where Mancos Jim and his band lived is now included in a National Forest Reserve. He has a certificate stating that "the Forest Service has set aside the allotment for the said Mancos Jim and his little band of Indians, and all trespassers will be dealt with according to law."

As soon as the posse arrived in Bluff the cattlemen rode among these industrious Indians in Allen Canyon and along Montezuma Creek, and by threats and intimidating methods so frightened them that they fled for their lives, as they believed.

As has been stated, there was also a lawless element of the Utes, several small bands of them, without permanent homes, who "drifted" up and down along the San Juan River, and undoubtedly caused trouble among the Indians and whites. Had they been taken in hand, it would

have been well for all concerned. Even now steps should
be taken by the authorities to bring that element under
law and discipline.

The principal industry in San Juan County, Utah, in
which Bluff is situated, is the stock business. The herds
and flocks of the white men had been steadily increasing,
and the question of range was bothering them. Consequently, they wanted to get the Indians off the public
domain and have undisputed possession of the range. The
Hatch incident afforded just the opportunity they were
looking for. It was then discovered how "dangerous" the
Utes were; they must be "returned" to their reservation.
While they are registered on the Ute Mountain reservation, in Colorado, as a matter of fact, most of the Indians concerned were born and raised in the sections where
they had been living.

It should also be noted that a law was enacted by Congress in 1884 to encourage Indians to leave the reservation and settle on the public domain; and that under the
fourth section of the Severalty Act of 1887, they could be
protected in their holdings. These Indians had done the
very thing that Congress had sought to encourage, namely,
to maintain themselves off the reservation, and their rights
should be protected in every possible way. In the face of
these facts, it is extraordinary that an official of the Indian Service, located in Utah, took the ground that these
Indians ought to be put on the reservation and forced to
stay there if it took troops to accomplish that result!

The Ute Mountain reservation, to which these Indians
nominally belong, is a tract of 480,000 acres (in south-
western Colorado), but not more than 10,000 acres of it
is capable of irrigation, *if* water could be secured. At the
present time there is no more water than is needed for
the Indians who are permanently located on the reservation, and if any additional number were put there it would
work a great hardship on all of them. These non-reservation Utes were "making good," and they certainly should
not be forced to go on a reservation unless they could be
given something at least as good as that which they are

asked to give up. To forcibly remove them now would mean to sweep away all the progress they have made in industry, self-support, and self-respect, to say nothing of the discouragement incident to making another start under adverse circumstances. In fact, they could not make a living on the reservation under present conditions; they would have to be put on a ration basis; reduced from a progressive, independent element to an absolutely dependent class—certainly a distinct backward step.

At the present time these industrious Utes are camped on or near the extension of the Navajo reservation, in southeastern Utah. Many of them, in their hurried leaving, had to abandon their stock and other possessions. One of them told me how he had developed his home on Montezuma Creek; the way he was ordered away by armed cowboys, the loss of his stock, etc., and his desire to go back to it. He said, "Washington no savvy; no talk. If Washington talk, 'You go back,' I say 'all right; give me paper; I go back.' Me have good ranch; nice place. Now, no home, no land, no water. Navaho Springs no good." He is only one of a number. This progressive element is now at a standstill, waiting to see what the Government intends to do on their behalf. They contend that the Navaho Springs reservation is "no good, no wood, no water." And they are right; I visited the reservation. At present they have nothing to do but draw rations twice a month. If some steps are not soon taken to change their status trouble is likely to develop. It is not a good plan to have a hundred or more Indians "sit down, every day all same Sunday." Furthermore, it is not just to the Navajos; their range is limited, and bringing on additional stock will not improve conditions.

In line with the effort to drive out all the Utes from San Juan County, at the time of my visit the cattlemen were riding around among a number of Navajo families living on the public domain, along the San Juan River, ordering them to "get out." These Navajos also have been located there for generations; they are industrious and self-supporting, and their rights also should be respected.

It is interesting to note that seven years ago Mr. Levi Chubbuck, then an inspector of the Interior Department, was sent to investigate "complaints made by the whites against the Indians in San Juan County, Utah." His report, submitted under date of August 22, 1908, contained recommendations which, had they been properly acted upon, might have afforded protection for these non-reservation Utes. But nothing was done.

In Mr. Chubbuck's report the opinion is expressed that "the trouble between the whites and the Indians arose largely from a desire on the part of the whites to acquire more grazing land as their flocks and herds increased."

According to this report, among those who made complaints against the Indians were "the three white men most vitally interested in the grazing privilege of the district in dispute."

Mr. Chubbuck further states: "The white complaints were surprised to learn that under the land laws of the United States of the Indian Homestead Act of July 4, 1884, the Indians had a right to go on the public domain and take up land, and that it was the policy of the Indian Office to encourage them to do this; that the whole tendency of modern administration of Indian Affairs is in the direction of breaking up rather than consolidating the reservation system."

In spite of this information that was given to those cattlemen, seven years ago, as to the legal rights of the Indians to be on the public domain, they would not let the Utes alone. It would seem that there is a class of white men in San Juan County, Utah, that ought to be taught to respect the law. Let the United States authorities deal not only with them, but also the lawless element among the Utes that has caused trouble for both whites and Indians.

Rev. Sherman Coolidge, President of the Society of American Indians, when in San Francisco during the past summer, met a Ute boy who was playing in a band. He said to him, "What you Utes need is a white man's chance." The boy replied, "No! Give us half a chance and we will take care of the other half."

The progressive Utes herein referred to are now patiently waiting to see if the United States Government intends to give them "a white man's chance." Surely they have proved their right to it.

CHAPTER VII

Governmental Relations

The official relationship between the American Indians and the alien governments that came more and more to encroach upon their independence has not been a smooth or happy one for either side. The relationship has been handicapped by a persistent misunderstanding and distrust on both sides. Few opportunities for reconciliation or understanding have existed in the official dealings between white man and red, as in the case of personal relationships between individual members of the two groups. Some would consider the administration of the Indian Bureau during the commissionership of John Collier under the Indian Reorganization Act of 1934 an exception, but the reversal of the Collier policy and the continuing debate about the place of the Indian in American society indicates that neither reconciliation between the two elements of our society nor agreement among individual members within each group on the proper relationship between the white man and the red has been reached.

DOCUMENT 70

The Spanish Requirement

Spanish legalism was responsible for the formal "Requirement," detailing Spain's rights in the Indies, which was read to the uncomprehending Indians before each Spanish attack. The fact that the Indians could not understand the language of the document, with its demand for recognition of the Spanish claim to dominion over their lands, did not invalidate its legal significance. Indeed, it was often read from shipboard out of earshot of its intended audience. Formulated by a learned Spanish jurist, Dr. Palacios Rubios, the *Requerimiento* has moved historians to tears and laughter. The following translation (with interspersed comments) is from Arthur Helps, *The Spanish Conquest in America*, 4 vols.; Vol. I, pp. 358–61 (New York: Harper & Brothers, 1856–57). Additional information concerning the *Requerimiento* is available in Lewis Hanke's *The Spanish Struggle for Justice in the Conquest of America*, pp. 31–36 (Philadelphia: University of Pennsylvania Press, 1949).

"On the part of the king, Don Fernando, and of Doña Juana, his daughter, queen of Castile and Leon, subduers of the barbarous nations, we their servants notify and make known to you, as best we can, that the Lord our God, living and eternal, created the heaven and the earth, and one man and one woman, of whom you and we, and all the men of the world, were and are descendants, and all those who come after us. But, on account of the multitude which has sprung from this man and woman in the five thousand years since the world was created, it was necessary that some men should go one way and some another, and that they should be divided into many kingdoms and provinces, for in one alone they could not be sustained.

"Of all these nations God our Lord gave charge to one man, called St. Peter, that he should be lord and superior of all the men in the world, that all should obey him, and that he should be the head of the whole human race, wherever men should live, and under whatever law, sect, or belief they should be; and he gave him the world for his kingdom and jurisdiction.

"And he commanded him to place his seat in Rome, as the spot most fitting to rule the world from; but also he permitted him to have his seat in any other part of the world, and to judge and govern all Christians, Moors, Jews, Gentiles, and all other sects. This man was called Pope, as if to say Admirable Great Father and Governor of men. The men who lived in that time obeyed that St. Peter, and took him for lord, king, and superior of the universe" (imagine what Tiberius or Nero would have said to this assertion!); "so also they have regarded the others who after him have been elected to the pontificate, and so has it been continued even till now, and will continue till the end of the world.

"One of these pontiffs, who succeeded that St. Peter as lord of the world in the dignity and seat which I have before mentioned, made donation of these isles and Terra-firma to the aforesaid king and queen and to their successors, our lords, with all that there are in these territories, as is contained in certain writings which passed upon the subject as aforesaid, which you can see if you wish.

"So their highnesses are kings and lords of these islands and land of Terra-firma by virtue of this donation; and some islands, and indeed almost all those to whom this has been notified, have received and served their highnesses, as lords and kings, in the way that subjects ought to do, with good will, without any resistance, immediately, without delay, when they were informed of the aforesaid facts. And also they received and obeyed the priests whom their highnesses sent to preach to them and to teach them our Holy faith; and all these, of their own free will, without any reward or condition, have become Christians, and are so, and their highnesses have joyfully and benignantly received them, and also have commanded them to be treated as their subjects and vassals; and you too are held and obliged to do the same. Wherefore, as best we can, we ask and require you that you consider what we have said to you, and that you take the time that shall be necessary to understand and deliberate upon it, and that you acknowledge the Church as the ruler and superior of the whole world (*por Señora y Superiora del universo mundo*), and the high priest called Pope, and in his name the king and queen Doña Juana our lords, in his place, as superiors, and lords, and kings of these islands and this Terra-firma by virtue of the said donation, and that you consent and give place that these religious fathers should declare and preach to you the aforesaid.

"If you do so you will do well, and that which you are obliged to do to their highnesses, and we in their name shall receive you in all love and charity, and shall leave you your wives, and your children, and your lands free without servitude, that you may do with them and with yourselves freely that which you like and think best, and they shall not compel you to turn Christians, unless you yourselves, when informed of the truth, should wish to be converted to our holy Catholic faith, as almost all the inhabitants of the rest of the islands have done; and, besides this, their highnesses award you many privileges and exemptions" (hard words in a new world!), "and will grant you many benefits.

"But if you do not do this, and maliciously make delay in it, I certify to you that, with the help of God, we shall powerfully enter into your country, and shall make war against you in all ways and manners that we can, and shall subject you to the yoke and obedience of the Church and of their highnesses; we shall take you, and your wives, and your children, and shall make slaves of them, and as such shall sell and dispose of them as their highnesses may command; and we shall take away your goods, and shall do you all the mischief and damage that we can, as to vassals who do not obey, and refuse to receive their lord, and resist and contradict him; and we protest that the deaths and losses which shall accrue from this are your fault, and not that of their highnesses, or ours, nor of these cavaliers who come with us. And that we have said this to you, and made this Requisition, we request the notary here present to give us his testimony in writing, and we ask the rest who are present that they should be witnesses of this Requisition."

If ever there was a document which it was worth while to give in full in such a narrative as the present, it is this Requisition, drawn up by the learned Doctor Palacios Rubios. The folly that spreads through it, when contrasted with the sagacity which pervades the instructions and the private letters of the king and the council, is an illustration of how long foolish conceits linger in the halls of learning and among professions, even when they are beginning to be banished from the world at large. I must confess that the comicality of the document has often cheered me in the midst of tedious research or endless details of small battles. The logic, the history, even the grammatical construction, are all, as it seems to me, alike in error.

DOCUMENT 71

Equal Justice

The history of Indian-white relations is replete with
violence, of which murder is not the least known. A
typical altercation is described by Governor William
Bradford of Plymouth Plantation in his discussion of
events of the year 1638. What is unusual about the
case is that the English guilty of murdering an Indian
were sentenced to death and executed, a punishment of
great rarity in the eighteenth and nineteenth centuries.
The intervention of Roger Williams of Rhode Island,
who served as a useful link between Indians and English, helped the course of justice in this instance. The
passage is from Bradford's *Of Plymouth Plantation,
1620–1647,* pp. 299–301, edited by Samuel Eliot
Morison (New York: Alfred A. Knopf, 1952).

This year Mr. Thomas Prence was chosen Governor.

Amongst other enormities that fell out amongst them;
this year three men were after due trial executed for robbery and murder which they had committed. Their names
were these: Arthur Peach, Thomas Jackson and Richard
Stinnings. There was a fourth, Daniel Cross, who was also
guilty, but he escaped away and could not be found.

This Arthur Peach was the chief of them, and the ring-
leader of all the rest. He was a lusty and a desperate young
man, and had been one of the soldiers in the Pequot War
and had done as good service as the most there, and one of
the forwardest in any attempt. And being now out of
means and loath to work, and falling to idle courses and
company, he intended to go to the Dutch plantation; and
had allured these three, being other men's servants and apprentices, to go with him. But another cause there was

also of his secret going away in this manner. He was not only run into debt, but he had got a maid with child (which was not known till after his death), a man's servant in the town, and fear of punishment made him get away. The other three complotting with him ran away from their masters in the night, and could not be heard of; for they went not the ordinary way, but shaped such a course as they thought to avoid the pursuit of any. But falling into the way that lieth between the Bay of Massachusetts and the Narragansetts, and being disposed to rest themselves, struck fire and took tobacco, a little out of the way by the wayside.

At length there came a Narragansett Indian by, who had been in the Bay a-trading, and had both cloth and beads about him—they had met him the day before, and he was now returning. Peach called him to drink tobacco with them, and he came and sat down with them. Peach told the other he would kill him and take what he had from him, but they were something afraid. But he said, "Hang him, rogue, he had killed many of them." So they let him alone to do as he would. And when he saw his time, he took a rapier and ran him through the body once or twice and took from him five fathom of wampum and three coats of cloth and went their way, leaving him for dead. But he scrambled away when they were gone, and made shift to get home, but died within a few days after. By which means they were discovered. And by subtlety the Indians took them; for they, desiring a canoe to set them over a water, not thinking their fact had been known, by the sachem's command they were carried to Aquidneck Island and there accused of the murder, and were examined and committed upon it by the English there.

The Indians sent for Mr. Williams and made a grievous complaint; his friends and kindred were ready to rise in arms and provoke the rest thereunto, some conceiving they should now find the Pequots' words true, that the English would fall upon them. But Mr. Williams pacified them and told them they should see justice done upon the offenders, and went to the man and took Mr. James, a

physician, with him. The man told him who did it, and
in what manner it was done; but the physician found his
wounds mortal and that he could not live, as he after
testified upon oath before the jury in open court. And so
he died shortly after, as both Mr. Williams, Mr. James
and some Indians testified in court.

The Government in the Bay were acquainted with it but
referred it hither because it was done in this jurisdiction;[1]
but pressed by all means that justice might be done in it,
or else the country must rise and see justice done; otherwise it would raise a war. Yet some of the rude and ignorant sort murmured that any English should be put to
death for the Indians. So at last they of the Island[2] brought
them hither, and being often examined and the evidence
produced, they all in the end freely confessed in effect all
that the Indian accused them of, and that they had done it
in the manner aforesaid. And so, upon the forementioned
evidence, were cast by the jury and condemned, and executed for the same, September 4. And some of the Narragansett Indians and of the party's friends were present
when it was done, which gave them and all the country
good satisfaction. But it was a matter of much sadness to
them here, and was the second execution which they had
since they came; being both for wilful murder, as hath
been before related. Thus much of this matter.

[1] And yet afterwards they laid claim to those parts in the
controversy about Seekonk (Bradford.)
[2] Rhode Island. This is believed to have been the first case of
Englishmen being tried, found guilty and executed for the murder
of an Indian. The reaction of the "rude and ignorant" is as significant as the action of the jury. More on this case in *Plymouth
Colony Records* I 96, and 1912 ed. Bradford II 265–8. Crose
or Cross, the murderer who escaped, was given sanctuary at the
plantation he belonged to, Piscataqua, where (says Governor
Winthrop) "all such lewd persons as fled from us" were given
"countenance."

DOCUMENT 72

Honi Soit Qui Mal y Pense

Following the turmoil of Bacon's Rebellion and its attendant Indian war in Virginia in 1676–77, King Charles II attempted to restore order and harmony by the introduction of British troops and by the dispensing of justice to English and Indians alike. One of the first orders of business was to reassure the Indian allies of the English, who had been wantonly attacked by Bacon's rebels, that they could count on the King's protection and good faith. As a visible token of this faith, Charles caused to be made in England a silver badge or "frontlet" which was presented to the loyal Queen of Pamunkey in 1677. A photograph of the frontlet is reproduced in Plate 19, following page 334, courtesy of the Association for the Preservation of Virginia Antiquities, Richmond, Virginia. For a full account of Bacon's Rebellion and the Indian relations of the period, see Wilcomb E. Washburn, *The Governor and the Rebel: A History of Bacon's Rebellion in Virginia* (Chapel Hill: University of North Carolina Press, 1958).

Documents 73, 74

Penn's Treaty

Plates 20 and 21, following page 334, show how the honesty of William Penn's dealings with the Indians of Pennsylvania, in carefully purchasing Indian title to the lands prepared for his colonists in the early 1680's, affected craftsmen and artists of later times. In one of his many paintings illustrating the theme of the "Peaceable Kingdom," Edward Hicks, in the period 1830–35, recalled the time

> When the great PENN his famous treaty made,
> With indian chiefs beneath the elm-trees shade.

The painting is in the collection of the New York State Historical Association, Cooperstown, New York.

At about the same time that Hicks was painting his interpretation of the treaty, someone constructed a mahogany-framed couch covered in a blue linen with the quotation—usually attributed to Voltaire—"The Only Treaty Never Ratified by an Oath and Never Broken," and with scenes at either end showing William Penn in conversation with an Indian chief, and a Quaker with the American flag at his feet. The couch is in the collection of William Young, Antique Dealer, Aberdeen, Scotland.

DOCUMENT 75

"How to Crowd, and Still Be Kind"

Samuel Sewall was one of the earliest Americans to be concerned with the plight of the Indian and the Negro in his association with the white man. The following letter, of May 3, 1700, to Sir William Ashhurst, concerning his work with the Society for Propagating the Gospel among the Indians, reflects his sensitive and practical thinking on the subject of Indian boundaries or "reservations," provision for recruiting missionaries from converted Indians, and the like. It is taken from the *Letter-Book of Samuel Sewall*, published in the Massachusetts Historical Society, *Collections*, 6th series, Vol. I, pp. 231–33 (Boston: 1886).

May 3, 1700.

HONORABLE SIR,—The last Fall, I had notice of my being entrusted with a share in managing the Indian Affairs, And presently upon it, the Commissoners were pleasd to appoint me their Secretary. As I account it an honor to be thus employed; so according to my mean ability, I shall endeavour faithfully to serve the Corporation and Commissioners, as I shall receive Instructions from them. I have met with an Observation of some grave Divines, that ordinarily when God intends Good to a Nation, He is pleasd to make use of some of themselves, to be instrumental in conveying of that Good unto them. Now God has furnished several of the Indians with considerable abilities for the Work of the Ministry, and Teaching School, And therefore I am apt to believe, that if the Indians so qualified, were more taken notice of in suitable Rewards, it would conduce very much to the propagation of the Gospel among them. Besides the Content they might have in a provision of necessary Food and Raiment, the Respect and honor of it, would quicken their Industry, and allure others to take pains in fitting themselves for a fruitfull discharge of those Offices. One thing more, I would crave leave to suggest, We have had a very long and grievous War with the Eastern Indians, and it is of great Concernment to His Majesty's Interests here that a peace be concluded with them upon firm and sure foundations. Which in my poor opinion cannot well be, while our Articles of Accord with them remain so very General as they doe. I should think it requisite that convenient Tracts of Land should be set out to them; and that by plain and natural Boundaries, as much as may be; as Lakes, Rivers, Mountains, Rocks, Upon which for any English man to encroach, should be accounted a Crime. Except this be done, I fear their own Jealousies, and the French Friers will persuade them, that the English, as they encrease, and think they want more room, will never leave till they have crouded them quite out of all their Lands. And it will be a vain attempt for us to offer Heaven to them, if they take up prejudices against us, as if we did grudge them a Living upon their own Earth. The Savoy-Confession of Faith, Engl. on one side and Indian on the other, has been lately printed here; as also several Sermons of the Presidents [of Harvard, Increase Mather] have been Transcribed into Indian, and printed, Which I hope in God's Time will have a very good Effect. To see it and be employed in giving your Honor an Account of it would be a very desirable piece of Service to him who is

your Honors

most humble Servant

SAM. SEWALL.

DOCUMENT 76

Queen Anne's American Kings

The photograph reproduced in Plate 22, following page 334, depicts murals in the Warner House, Portsmouth, New Hampshire, dating from about 1716, showing two of the Indian chiefs who visited London in 1710. The unknown artist who executed the murals probably worked from the mezzotints struck off by John Simon in 1710 from the portraits by John Verelst. For further information about the visit see Richmond P. Bond, *Queen Anne's American Kings* (New York: Oxford University Press, 1952).

Ugh!

It is significant that the treaty talks that were held between whites and Indians generally followed the rules of Indian protocol. These rules governed the time and manner of meeting, the form of gifts and hospitality, and the order and even imagery of the speeches. They not only provided the eighteenth century with a literature whose appeal was recognized by Benjamin Franklin, who printed the treaty talk given below, but furnish the twentieth-century anthropologist with significant insights into the culture of the Indians. It is of particular interest to the historian of material culture to note the relationship between idea and object in the Indian frame of reference. The following treaty talk is taken from the text of *A Treaty of Friendship held with the Chiefs of the Six Nations at Philadelphia, in September and October, 1736*, printed by Benjamin Franklin in Philadelphia in 1737, and reprinted in Julian P. Boyd, ed., *Indian Treaties Printed by Benjamin Franklin, 1736–1762*, pp. 5–12 (Philadelphia: Historical Society of Pennsylvania, 1938).

At a Council held in the *Great Meeting-House*
at *Philadelphia,*
the 2d Day of *October* 1736.
PRESENT,
The Honourable THOMAS PENN, Esq; Proprietary,
JAMES LOGAN, Esq; President.

Samuel Preston,	Ralph Assheton,	
Anthony Palmer,	Thomas Griffitts,	Esqrs;
Clement Plumsted,	Charles Read.	
Thomas Lawrence,		

Present also

The *MAYOR* and *Recorder* of the City,

With divers Gentlemen, and a very large Audience
that filled the House and its Galleries.

The *Indian* Chiefs being come and seated,

The President, before proceeding to hear them, thought proper to inform the Audience, that in *August* 1732, a great Treaty having been held in this Place with several Chiefs of the Six Nations, they had made report thereof on their Return to their Great Council, where the several Propositions that had been made to them on the Part of this Government, had been fully considered; and that these Chiefs now present, of whom there never at any time before had been so great a Number met in this Province, were now come to return their Answer.

The *Indians* being made acquainted with what the President had said, were told, that we were ready to hear them.

Whereupon *Kanickhungo* their Speaker, addressing himself to their Brother *ONAS* (which signifies *PENN*) to their Brother *JAMES LOGAN*, and the Gentlemen of the Council, spoke as follows by *Conrad Wyser* the Interpreter;

BRETHREN,

"We are now come down from the Towns of our several Nations to give our Answer to the great Treaty, which we and you held together, at this Place, about four Years since: This Answer has been agreed and concluded upon by our great Council, who have carefully considered all that passed between you and us, and expressed their great Satisfaction in the friendly and good Dispositions of you our Brethren, towards all the *Indians* of the *Six Nations;* and as you received us kindly, and at that Treaty undertook to provide and keep for us a Fire in this great City, we are now come to warm ourselves thereat, and we desire and hope it will ever continue bright and burning to the End of the World."

Hereupon he laid down a large Belt of white Wampum
of eleven Rows, with four black St. George's *Crosses in
it; and proceeding, said*

BRETHREN,

"Soon after our Brother ONAS, who is now here, came into this Country, he and we treated together; he opened and cleared the Road between this Place and our Nations, which was very much to our good Liking, and it gave us great Pleasure. We now desire that this Road, for the mutual Accommodation and Conveniency of you and us who Travel therein to see each other, may be kept clear and open, free from all Stops or Incumbrances; and if, since the time that we last cleared it with you, any Tree has fallen across it, or if it is any way stopt up, of which however we know nothing, we are now willing to open and clear the same from every Interruption; and it is our hearty Desire that it may so continue, while the Earth endureth."

Hereupon he presented a Bundle of Skins in the Hair, and went on;

BRETHREN,

"One of the chief Articles of our late Treaty together, was the brightning of the Chain of Friendship between us, and the preserving it free from all Rust and Spots; and that this Chain was not only between this Government and us, but between all the *English* Governments and all the *Indians.* We now assure you our Brethren, that it is our earnest Desire this Chain should continue, and be strengthned between all the *English* and all our Nations, and likewise the *Delawares, Canays,* and the *Indians* living on *Sasquehannah,* and all the other *Indians* who now are in League and Friendship with the *Six Nations*; in Behalf of all whom, and as a lasting Confirmation of this great Article, to endure until this Earth passeth away and is no more seen, we now deliver you this Beaver Coat."

Here he laid down a large Beaver Coat.

The Proprietor gave them Thanks in Behalf of this Government for what they had spoke touching these three important Articles of the Fire, Road and Chain of Friendship, and told them their Discourse thereon was very satisfactory.

The Speaker proceeded and said;

BRETHREN,

"To conclude all that we have now said, it is our Desire that we and you should be as of one Heart, one Mind, and one Body, thus becoming one People, entertaining a mutual Love and Regard for each other, to be preserved firm and entire, not only between you and us, but between your Children, and our Children, to all succeeding Generations.

"We who are now here, are old Men, who have the Direction of Affairs in our own Nations; and as we are old, it may be thought that the Memory of these things may be lost with us, who have not, like you, the Art of preserving it by committing all Transactions to Writing: We nevertheless have Methods of transmitting from Father to Son, an Account of all these Things, whereby you will find the Remembrance of them is faithfully preserved, and our succeeding Generations are made acquainted with what has passed, that it may not be forgot as long as the Earth remains."

They were told, *That it was very agreeable to us to know that they took such effectual Care in this Point.*
Then proceeding he said;

BRETHREN,

"We desire that this brightning of the Chain, and establishing a strong and firm League of Friendship, may be understood by you, as we understand it to be, not only between the Chiefs of our Nations, and the Chiefs or Principal Men of this Government, but likewise between all our People, and all your People, and between you and all our *Warriours* who go abroad and sometimes pass near this Government, to all of whom we have given the strictest Charge to behave themselves agreeable to the Friendship which is established between you and us, that so we all may continue to be one People for ever.

"At the last Treaty you advised us to strengthen ourselves by entring into firm Leagues of Friendship and Alliance with several other Nations of *Indians* around us; this Advice was truly good, and we thank our Brethren for it; we have accordingly treated with these Six following

Nations, *to wit*, the *Onichkaryagoes, Sissaghees, Tiou-mitihagas, Attawantenis, Twechtwese,* and *Oachtamughs,* and have engaged them so heartily in our Interest, that they acknowledge us for their Elder Brethren, and have promised to join with us as one People, and to act altogether in Concert with us.

"You likewise then advised us to call home all those of our Nations who are at *Canada,* or live amongst the *French,* lest if any Occasion of Difference should arise, they might then be prevented from returning. We esteem this likewise as sound good Advice, and we thank our Brethren for it; the *French* were formerly our cruel Enemies, and we are taking such Measures as we hope will be effectual to bring back our People, if any new Breach should happen."

The Speaker said,

"To confirm all that we have now said, we would be glad if we had a large Present of Skins to deliver, in Return to the considerable one in Goods which we had of you; but we must own to you that we are at present but very ill provided and poor, and have only a very small Quantity of Skins, which nevertheless we hope our Brethren will accept."

Here he laid down two small Bundles of Skins.

"We have now nothing more to say in Publick; but having other Matters to treat on with the Proprietor, we will enter upon them at another time."

They were told, *That the Proprietor, President and Council thank'd them very kindly in Behalf of this Government, for all they had now said; that they had returned full and distinct Answers to all the Chief Articles or Propositions made at the last great Treaty in 1732, they had spoke to each of them like honest Men and true Brethren; and as they had consulted together before they delivered their Answer, so now the Council would meet and consider together of all that had passed at present.*

Which being interpreted to them, they expressed their Satisfaction by a Sound peculiar to them, in which they all joined, and then withdrew.

At a Council held at *Philadelphia, October* 4. 1736.
PRESENT,
The Honourable JAMES LOGAN, Esq; President.

Anthony Palmer,	Ralph Assheton,	
Clement Plumsted,	Thomas Griffitts,	Esqrs;
Thomas Lawrence,	Charles Read.	

The President representing to the Board the Necessity of dispatching the *Indians* of the *Six* Nations, who being very numerous remain here at a great Charge, proposed that the Consideration of the Value of the Present to be given them, should be now proceeded upon; and accordingly the Board entering upon the same, and observing that for these many Years there has not been so great an Appearance here of Chiefs of these Nations as at this time, and that they have returned very full and distinct Answers to every Article of the Treaty with them in 1732, are of Opinion, that proper Goods for them to the Value of about *Two Hundred Pounds,* should be provided and given them; and that to *Conrad Weyser,* the Interpreter, who is extremly useful on all such Occasions, and on the present one has been very serviceable, there be given *Twenty Pounds.*

At a Council held at *Philadelphia, October* 12. 1736.
PRESENT,
The Honourable JAMES LOGAN, Esq; President.

Samuel Preston,	Samuel Hasell,	
Clement Plumsted,	Thomas Griffitts,	Esqrs;
Thomas Lawrence,	Charles Read.	

The President informed the Board, that agreeable to the Minute of the 4th, Care had been taken to provide Goods for the Indians: But next Day, after Council, consulting with *Conrad Weyser,* the Interpreter, he had advised that the Delivery of the Present should be delayed till the *Indians* had finished with the Proprietary, with whom they were then to treat about the Purchase of Lands; that most of last Week being spent therein, the *Indians* had Yester-

day ended with the Proprietary, having signed Releases to
him for all the Lands lying between the Mouth of *Sasquehannah*, and *Kekachtaninius* Hills, and that it now remained to conclude on the Quantity and Quality of the
several Goods to be given them, and on the Substance of
what should be proper to be spoke to them; The Board
are of Opinion, that considering the large Quantity of
Goods which they have had from the Proprietor on the
Purchase, it may not at this time be necessary to give
them, in Behalf of this Government, so great a Present as
the Value ordered by the aforesaid Minute; but that it
may very well be considerably reduced; and accordingly,
it is *Ordered*, that it be reduced to between *Sixty* and
Seventy Pounds.

The President likewise acquainting the Board, that the
Indians, at a Meeting with the Proprietor and him, had
taken Notice that *Conrad Weyser*, and *Shekallamy*, were
by the Treaty of 1732, appointed as fit and proper Persons
to go between the *Six Nations*, and this Government, and
to be employed in all Transactions with one another,
whose Bodies the *Indians* said were to be equally divided
between them and us, we to have one half, and they the
other; that they had found *Conrad* faithful and honest,
that he is a true good Man, and had spoke their Words,
and our Words, and not his own; and the *Indians* having
presented him with a drest Skin to make him Shoes, and
two Deer Skins, to keep him warm, they said, as they had
thus taken Care of our Friend, they must recommend
their's (*Shekallamy*) to our Notice; and the Board judging
it necessary that a particular Notice should be taken of
him, acccordingly, it is, *Ordered*, That *Six Pounds* be laid
out for him in such things as he may most want.

It was then recommended to the President, and he
undertook, to prepare a Draught of what might be proper
to be said to these *Indians* at giving the Present from this
Government, and to lay the same before the Board to
morrow Morning, at Ten a Clock, to which time the Council adjourned.

At a Council held at *Philadelphia, October 13th,* 1736.
PRESENT,
The Honourable THOMAS PENN, Esq; Proprietary,
JAMES LOGAN, Esq; President.

Samuel Preston,   Ralph Assheton, ⎫
Clement Plumsted,   Samuel Hasell,   ⎬ Esqrs;
Thomas Lawrence,   Thomas Griffitts. ⎭

The President laid before the Board a draught of a concluding Speech to the Indians, which being read and approved, they were sent for, who being come and seated,
the said Speech was delivered to them by the Interpreter
as follows.

OUR BRETHREN,
"Four Years since at a great Treaty held here with your
Chiefs, we confirmed all our former Treaties with you,
we brightned the Chain, kindled our Fire to be kept always burning here for you, opened and cleared the Path
between your Country and Ours, and made ourselves and
you one Body and one People.

"The Chiefs of all your Nations, being met at your great
Fire or Council in the Country of the *Onondagoes,* having
heard of and considered that Treaty, were so well pleased
with it, that it was agreed, as you have told us, that you,
who are the principal of all your Chiefs, should come down
and visit us, and more fully and absolutely confirm that
Treaty, which you accordingly did a few Days since at our
great House in Town, in the presence and hearing of some
Thousands of our People, and it was done not only in Behalf of us ourselves and yourselves, but for our Children
and Children's Children, to all Generations, as long as the
Sun, Moon, and Earth, endure.

"Thus this Treaty, by which we are to become as one
People, and one Body, is in the strongest Terms con-
firmed, never to be changed, but to be kept in everlasting
Remembrance.

"But, besides what we have already concluded, we shall
now for the further brightning the same Chain, and that

no Spot or Blemish may be fixt on it, speak to some Particulars for your more full Satisfaction.

"It has been agreed between us, that we should suffer no Injury to be done to one of your People more than to our own, nor without punishing the Offender in the same manner as if it had been done to one of our People; and you also engaged on your parts that you would give us the like Satisfaction for every Injury done by your People to any of ours, and whatever should happen of this kind, it should make no other Difference, than as if the Injury were done by one *English* or White Man to another, and so in the Case of an *Indian*. Now since you came hither, we have heard that a White Man one of our People, and one of yours, being both in Liquor, quarrelled at *Allegheny*, that the *Indian* struck at the White Man with a Knife, and the white Man gave the *Indian* some Blows on the Head, of which he died in four or five Days after; that the White Man got out of the way, and hid, and when he heard the Man was dead, he ran away to the *Southward* of *Virginia*: Who was first in the Fault in this matter we know not, but we have now issued a Proclamation for apprehending the White Man, and proposed a Reward of *Ten Pounds*, to any one who will seize and deliver him to some Magistrate or Officer, that he may be put in Prison and tried for his Life; if then it appears that he willfully kill'd the Man, he will be hanged by our Law; if it was in Defence of his own Life, he is not to die for it, but after he is tried we shall acquaint you how the matter appeared. The first Account we had of it was in a Letter, which the Interpreter shall read and acquaint you with it; but that Story being told only on one side, we do not depend on it for the Truth; and thus we shall act in all such Cases, as Brethren always ought whenever they unfortunately happen.

"We are very sensible Rum is the principal occasion of these Disorders, and we heartily wish any means could be possibly found to prevent the Abuse of it: You have desired us in your Discourse with the Proprietor to recall all our Traders from *Ohio* or *Allegheny* and the Branches of

Sasquehannah; We desired at our Treaty four Years ago that all our Indians, the *Delawares, Shawanese,* and others, should be recalled from *Ohio,* for we knew not then but there might be War with the *French,* and you know the Strength of a People consists in their being drawn close together as into one Body, and not to be scattered; but we know not what you mean by recalling our Traders; for you are sensible the *Indians* cannot live without being supplied with our Goods: They must have Powder and Lead to hunt, and Cloaths to keep them warm; and if our People do not carry them, others will, from *Maryland, Virginia, Jerseys,* or other Places; and we are sure you do not desire that *Indians* should trade with those People rather than with ours. The Traders of all Nations find the *Indians* are so universally fond of Rum, that they will not deal without it: We have made many Laws against carrying it; we have ordered the *Indians* to stave the Caggs of all that is brought amongst them; but the Woods have not Streets like *Philadelphia,* the Paths in them are endless, and they cannot be stopt, so that it will be carried either from one Country or another; and on the other hand the *Indians* are so very fond of the Liquor, even the best of them, that instead of taking it from those who bring it, and staving it, they take and drink it, which is both unjust in it self, and does more Mischief; for the Traders, if they kept it, would hand it out by stealth in small Quantities, but the *Indians* when they take it, drink it off by great Quantities; so that no Method we can find will prevent the *Indians* having it, till they are so wise as to refrain it of themselves; and, Why are they not so wise? they shew very good strong Sense in other things, and why cannot they act like us? All of us here, and all you see of any Credit in the Place, can every Day have as much Rum of their own to drink as they please, and yet scarce one of us will take a Dram, at least not one Man will on any Account be drunk, no not if he were hired to it with great Sums of Money.

"And now to bind and confirm all these our Words, we have provided for you the following Goods, which will be

delivered to you to morrow at the President's Lodgings,
to wit.

One Hundred Pounds of Powder,	Twenty five Hatchets,
	One Hundred Knives,
One Hundred & Fifty Pounds of Lead,	Thirty one Yards and ¼ of half Thicks,
Twelve Strowd Matchcoats,	Two Hundred Flints,
Twelve Kettles,	One dozen Looking-Glasses,
Twelve Blankets,	Three dozen Scissars.
Twelve Duffels,	

With some Tobacco, Pipes, Rum, and Sugar.

The Council rising, and the President with the Proprietor staying, the *Indians* entered into further Discourse,
and said, *They had received a Message with some* Wampum *from the Governor of* Maryland, *informing them, he
had received a Letter from the King of* England, *ordering
him to see that they should not be wronged of their Lands;
that he had understood this Government had wronged
them, and if they would send some of their People to
him, he would take care they should be righted, he would
write to the great King, who would give such Orders as
that they should have Justice done them. Being asked how
they received that Message, they said, the Man who brought
it was here now with them, they had the* Wampum *and
would shew it to us; and they earnestly pressed that we
would write to the Governors of* Maryland *and* Virginia
*to make them Satisfaction for the Lands belonging to them
(the* Indians*) which the People of those Governments
were possessed of, that had never been purchased of them;
that all the Lands on* Sasquehannah *and at* Chanandowa
*were theirs, and they must be satisfied for them; that they
had agreed with us for the Lands they now released to us,
but they had never received any thing from the other
Governments to the Southward, for theirs.*

They were told, That on their receiving the Present to
morrow, they should be answered on these Heads; and
after being entertained by the Proprietor, they withdrew.

DOCUMENT 78

Treaty Talk

The following exchange between Indians and English at a treaty talk in Philadelphia on July 7, 1742, illustrates some of the differing conceptions and values, particularly those concerning land, of the two groups. The passage is taken from Cadwallader Colden's *The History of the Five Indian Nations of Canada*, published in London, 1747, and reprinted (New York: New Amsterdam Book Company, 1902), Vol. II, pp. 84–91; it is also printed in Julian P. Boyd, ed., *Indian Treaties Printed by Benjamin Franklin, 1736–1762*, pp. 26–29 (Philadelphia: Historical Society of Pennsylvania, 1938).

At a Council held in the Meeting-House,
July 7, 1742.
PRESENT,
The Honourable GEORGE THOMAS, Esq;
Lieutenant-Governor.

James Logan,	Samuel Preston,	
Thomas Lawrence,	Samuel Hasell,	Esqrs;
Abraham Taylor,	Robert Strettell,	

CANASSATEEGO's Speech on Behalf of
the Six Nations.

"BRETHREN, *the Governor and Council, and all present,*

"According to our Promise we now propose to return you an Answer to the several Things mentioned to us Yesterday, and shall beg Leave to speak to publick Affairs first, tho' they were what you spoke to last. On this Head you Yesterday put us in Mind, first, "Of William Penn's early and constant Care to cultivate Friendship with all the Indians; of the Treaty we held with one of his Sons, about ten Years ago; and of the Necessity there is at this Time of keeping the Roads between us clear and free from all Obstructions. We are all very sensible of the kind Regard that good Man William Penn had for all the Indians, and cannot but be pleased to find that his Children have the same. We well remember the Treaty you mention held with his Son on his Arrival here, by which we confirmed our League of Friendship, that is to last as long as the Sun and Moon endure: In Consequence of this, we, on our Part, shall preserve the Road free from all Incumbrances; in Confirmation whereof we lay down this String of Wampum.

"You in the next Place said you would enlarge the Fire and make it burn brighter, which we are pleased to hear you mention; and assure you, we shall do the same, by adding to it more Fewel, that it may still flame out more strongly than ever: In the last Place, you were pleased to say that we are bound by the strictest Leagues, to watch for each others Preservation; that we should hear with our Ears for you, and you hear with your Ears for us: This is equally agreeable to us; and we shall not fail to give you early Intelligence, whenever any Thing of Consequence comes to our Knowledge: And to encourage you to do the same, and to nourish in your Hearts what you have spoke to us with your Tongues, about the Renewal of our Amity and the Brightening of the Chain of Friendship; we confirm what we have said with another Belt of Wampum."

"BRETHREN,

"We received from the Proprietors Yesterday, some Goods in Consideration of our Release of the Lands on the West-side of Sasquehannah. It is true, we have the full Quantity according to Agreement; but if the Proprietor had been here himself, we think, in Regard of our Numbers and Poverty, he would have made an Addition to them.—If the Goods were only to be divided amongst the Indians present, a single Person would have but a small

Portion; but if you consider what Numbers are left behind, equally entitled with us to a Share, there will be extremely little. We therefore desire, if you have the Keys of the Proprietor's Chest, you will open it, and take out a little more for us.

"We know our Lands are now become more valuable: The white People think we do not know their Value; but we are sensible that the Land is everlasting, and the few Goods we receive for it are soon worn out and gone. For the future, we will sell no Lands but when Brother Onas is in the Country; and we will know beforehand, the Quantity of the Goods we are to receive. Besides, we are not well used with respect to the Lands still unsold by us. Your People daily settle on these Lands, and spoil our Hunting.—We must insist on your removing them, as you know they have no Right to settle to the Northward of Kittochtinny-Hills.—In particular, we renew our Complaints against some People who are settled at Juniata, a Branch of Sasquahannah, and all along the Banks of that River, as far as Mahaniay; and desire they may be forthwith made to go off the Land, for they do great Damage to our Cousins the Delawares.

"We have further to observe, with respect to the Lands lying on the West-side of Sasquahannah, that though Brother Onas (meaning the Proprietor) has paid us for what his People possess, yet some Parts of that Country have been taken up by Persons, whose Place of Residence is to the South of this Province, from whom we have never received any Consideration. This Affair was recommended to you by our Chiefs at our last Treaty; and you then, at our earnest Desire, promised to write a Letter to that Person who has the Authority over those People, and to procure us his Answer: As we have never heard from you on this Head, we want to know what you have done in it. If you have not done any Thing, we now renew our Request, and desire you will inform the Person whose People are seated on our Lands, that that Country belongs to us, in Right of Conquest; we having bought it with our Blood, and taken it from our Enemies in fair War; and we expect, as Owners of that Land, to receive such a Consideration for it as the Land is worth. We desire you will press him to send a positive Answer: Let him say Yes or No: If he says Yes, we will treat with him; if No, we are able to do ourselves Justice; and we will do it, by going to take Payment ourselves.

"It is customary with us to make a Present of Skins, whenever we renew our Treaties. We are ashamed to offer our Brethren so few, but your Horses and Cows have eat the Grass our Deer used to feed on. This has made them scarce, and will, we hope, plead in Excuse for our not bringing a larger Quantity. If we could have spared more, we would have given more; but we are really poor; and desire you'll not consider the Quantity, but few as they are, accept them in Testimony of our Regard."

Here they gave the Governor a Bundle of Skins.

The Governor immediately replied.

"BRETHREN,

"We thank you for the many Declarations of Respect you have given us, in this solemn Renewal of our Treaties: We receive, and shall keep your String and Belts of Wampum, as Pledges of your Sincerity, and desire those we gave you may be carefully preserved, as Testimonies of ours.

"In answer to what you say about the Proprietaries. —They are all absent, and have taken the Keys of their Chest with them; so that we cannot, on their Behalf, enlarge the Quantity of Goods: Were they here, they might perhaps, be more generous; but we cannot be liberal for them.—The Government will, however, take your Request into Consideration; and in Regard to your Poverty, may perhaps make you a Present. I but just mention this now, intending to refer this Part of your Speech to be answered at our next Meeting.

"The Number of Guns, as well as every Thing else, answers exactly with the Particulars specified in your Deed of Conveyance, which is more than was agreed to be given you. It was your own Sentiments, that the Lands on the West-side of Sasquahannah, were not so valuable as those on the East; and an Abatement was to be made, proportionable to the Difference in Value: But the Proprietor overlooked this, and ordered the full Quantity to be delivered, which you will look on as a Favour.

"It is very true, that Lands are of late become more valuable; but what raises their Value? Is it not entirely owing to the Industry and Labour used by the white People, in their Cultivation and Improvement? Had not they come amongst you, these Lands would have been of no Use to you, any further than to maintain you. And is there not, now you have sold so much, enough left for all the Purposes of Living?—What you say of the Goods, that they are soon worn out, is applicable to every Thing; but you know very well, that they cost a great deal of Money; and the Value of Land is no more, than it is worth in Money.

"On your former Complaints against People's settling the Lands on Juniata, and from thence all along on the River Sasquahannah as far as Mahaniahy, some Magistrates were sent expressly to remove them, and we thought no Persons would presume to stay after that."

Here they interrupted the Governor, and said:—

"These Persons who were sent did not do their Duty: So far from removing the People, they made Surveys for themselves, and they are in League with the Trespassers. We desire more effectual Methods may be used, and honester Persons employed."

Which the Governor promised, and then proceeded:

"BRETHREN,

"According to the Promise made at our last Treaty with you, Mr. Logan, who was at that Time President, did write to the Governor of Maryland, that he might make you Satisfaction for such of your Lands as his People had taken up, but did not receive one Word from him upon that Head. I will write to him again, and endeavour to procure you a satisfactory Answer. We do not doubt but he will do you Justice: But we exhort you to be careful not to exercise any Acts of Violence towards his People, as they likewise are our Brethren, and Subjects of the same great King; and therefore Violence towards them, must be productive of very evil Consequences.

"I shall conclude what I have to say at this Time, with Acknowledgments for your Present; which is very agreeable to us, from the Expressions of Regard used by you in Presenting it: Gifts of this Nature receiving their Value from the Affection of the Giver, and not from the Quantity or Price of the Thing given."

PLATE 17. *Geronimo (1834–1909)*, from a photograph by A. Frank Randall, 1886. Courtesy of the Smithsonian Institution, Bureau of American Ethnology, Washington, D.C.

PLATE 18. *Geronimo*, from a photograph by DeLancey Gill, 1905. Courtesy of the Smithsonian Institution, Bureau of American Ethnology, Washington, D.C.

PLATE 19. *Honi Soit Qui Mal y Pense.* Courtesy of the Association for the Preservation of Virginia Antiquities, Richmond, Virginia. Photograph by Thomas L. Williams.

The lion with the fatling on did move.
A little child was leading them in love.

The leopard with the harmless kid laid down.
And not one savage beast was seen to frown.

When the great PENN his famous treaty made,
With indian chiefs beneath the elm-trees shade.

The wolf did with the lambkin dwell in peace.
His grim carnivorous nature there did cease.

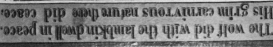

PLATE 20. *Penn's Treaty: "Peaceable Kingdom"* by Edward Hicks. Courtesy of the New York State Historical Association, Cooperstown, New York. Photograph by LeBel's Studio.

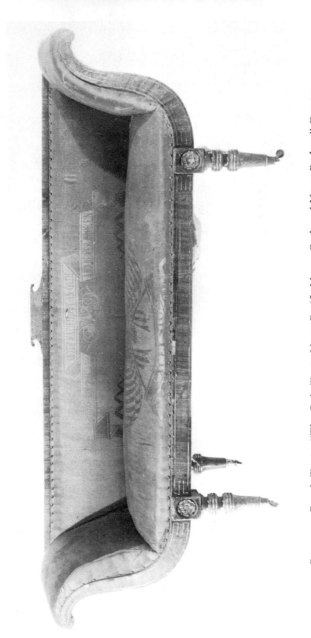

PLATE 21. *Penn's Treaty:* "The Only Treaty Never Ratified by an Oath and Never Broken." Courtesy of William Young, Antique Dealer, Aberdeen, Scotland.

PLATE 22. *Queen Anne's American Kings*. Courtesy of the Warner House Association, Portsmouth, New Hampshire. Photograph by Douglas Armsden, Kittery Point, Maine.

GEORGE WASHINGTON
PRESIDENT.
1792.

PLATE 23. *Red Jacket's Medal.* Courtesy of the Buffalo and Erie County Historical Society, Buffalo, New York.

PLATE 24. *Pipe of Peace.* Courtesy of the Smithsonian Institution, Washington, D.C.

PLATE 25. "Young Omawhaw, War Eagle, Little Missouri, and Pawnees. Painted at Washington City, 1821," by Charles Bird King. Courtesy of the Smithsonian Institution, Washington, D.C.

PLATE 26. *Two views of Wi-jun-hon (an Assiniboin Chief), "going to and returning from Washington," painted by George Catlin. Courtesy of the Smithsonian Institution, Washington, D.C.*

PLATE 27. *Sequoyah*. Courtesy of the Library of Congress.

PLATE 28. *Bureaucracy and the Indian: Supplicant Indian*, a contemporary carving by D. Williams. Courtesy of the Museum of Anthropology, The University of British Columbia, Vancouver, Canada.

PLATE 29. *Bureaucracy and the Indian: Indian Agent*, a contemporary carving by D. Williams. Courtesy of the Musuem of Anthropology, The University of British Columbia, Vancouver, Canada.

PLATE 30. *Rescue Group*, by Horatio Greenough. Courtesy of the Architect of the Capitol, Washington, D.C.

PLATE 31. *The Progress of Civilization*, by Thomas Crawford. Courtesy of the Architect of the Capitol, Washington, D.C.

PLATE 32. *Aztec Sculpture.* Courtesy of the Chicago Natural History Museum.

DOCUMENT 79

Smiths instead of Jesuits

The following letter, written on March 20, 1751, to James Parker, reflects the practical spirit of its author, Benjamin Franklin, and the age he so brilliantly epitomizes. His comments range from Indian trade to Indian political organization to Indian methods of warfare, and all are cited as examples which the white colonials can employ to their benefit. The text, without editorial footnotes, is taken from Leonard W. Labaree, et al., eds., *The Papers of Benjamin Franklin*, Vol. IV, pp. 117–21 (New Haven: Yale University Press, 1961).

Dear Mr. Parker,   Philadelphia, March 20, 1750/1

I have, as you desire, read the Manuscript you sent me; and am of Opinion, with the publick-spirited Author, that securing the Friendship of the Indians is of the greatest Consequence to these Colonies; and that the surest Means of doing it, are, to regulate the Indian Trade, so as to convince them, by Experience, that they may have the best and cheapest Goods, and the fairest Dealing from the English; and to unite the several Governments, so as to form a Strength that the Indians may depend on for Protection, in Case of a Rupture with the French; or apprehend great Danger from, if they should break with us.

This Union of the Colonies, however necessary, I apprehend is not to be brought about by the Means that have hitherto been used for that Purpose. A Governor of one Colony, who happens from some Circumstances in his own Government, to see the Necessity of such an Union, writes his Sentiments of the Matter to the other Governors, and desires them to recommend it to their respective

Assemblies. They accordingly lay the Letters before those
Assemblies, and perhaps recommend the Proposal in general Words. But Governors are often on ill Terms with
their Assemblies, and seldom are the Men that have the
most Influence among them. And perhaps some Governors, tho' they openly recommend the Scheme, may pri-
vately throw cold Water on it, as thinking additional
publick Charges will make their People less able, or less
willing to give to them. Or perhaps they do not clearly see
the Necessity of it, and therefore do not very earnestly
press the Consideration of it: And no one being present
that has the Affair at Heart, to back it, to answer and remove Objections, &c. 'tis easily dropt, and nothing is done.
Such an Union is certainly necessary to us all, but more immediately so to your Government. Now, if you were to pick
out half a Dozen Men of good Understanding and Address,
and furnish them with a reasonable Scheme and proper
Instructions, and send them in the Nature of Ambassadors to the other Colonies, where they might apply
particularly to all the leading Men, and by proper Management get them to engage in promoting the Scheme;
where, by being present, they would have the Opportunity
of pressing the Affair both in publick and private, obviat-
ing Difficulties as they arise, answering Objections as soon
as they are made, before they spread and gather Strength
in the Minds of the People, &c. &c. I imagine such an
Union might thereby be made and established: For reasonable sensible Men, can always make a reasonable
Scheme appear such to other reasonable Men, if they take
Pains, and have Time and Opportunity for it; unless from
some Circumstances their Honesty and good Intentions
are suspected. A voluntary Union entered into by the
Colonies themselves, I think, would be preferable to one
impos'd by Parliament; for it would be perhaps not much
more difficult to procure, and more easy to alter and improve, as Circumstances should require, and Experience
direct. It would be a very strange Thing, if six Nations of
ignorant Savages should be capable of forming a Scheme
for such an Union, and be able to execute it in such a Man-

ner, as that it has subsisted Ages, and appears indissoluble; and yet that a like Union should be impracticable for ten or a Dozen English Colonies, to whom it is more necessary, and must be more advantageous; and who cannot be supposed to want an equal Understanding of their Interests.

Were there a general Council form'd by all the Colonies, and a general Governor appointed by the Crown to preside in that Council, or in some Manner to concur with and confirm their Acts, and take Care of the Execution; every Thing relating to Indian Affairs and the Defence of the Colonies, might be properly put under their Management. Each Colony should be represented by as many Members as it pays Sums of   Hundred Pounds into the common Treasury for the common Expence; which Treasury would perhaps be best and most equitably supply'd, by an equal Excise on strong Liquors in all the Colonies, the Produce never to be apply'd to the private Use of any Colony, but to the general Service. Perhaps if the Council were to meet successively at the Capitals of the several Colonies, they might thereby become better acquainted with the Circumstances, Interests, Strength or Weakness, &c. of all, and thence be able to judge better of Measures propos'd from time to time: At least it might be more satisfactory to the Colonies, if this were propos'd as a Part of the Scheme; for a Preference might create Jealousy and Dislike.

I believe the Place mention'd is a very suitable one to build a Fort on. In Times of Peace, Parties of the Garrisons of all Frontier Forts might be allowed to go out on Hunting Expeditions, with or without Indians, and have the Profit to themselves of the Skins they get: By this Means a Number of Wood-Runners would be form'd, well acquainted with the Country, and of great Use in War Time, as Guides of Parties and Scouts, &c. Every Indian is a Hunter; and as their Manner of making War, viz. by Skulking, Surprizing and Killing particular Persons and Families, is just the same as their Manner of Hunting, only changing the Object, Every Indian is a disciplin'd

Soldier. Soldiers of this Kind are always wanted in the Colonies in an Indian War; for the European Military Discipline is of little Use in these Woods.

Publick Trading Houses would certainly have a good Effect towards regulating the private Trade; and preventing the Impositions of the private Traders; and therefore such should be established in suitable Places all along the Frontiers; and the Superintendant of the Trade, propos'd by the Author, would, I think, be a useful Officer.

The Observation concerning the Importation of Germans in too great Numbers into Pennsylvania, is, I believe, a very just one. This will in a few Years become a German Colony: Instead of their Learning our Language, we must learn their's, or live as in a foreign Country. Already the English begin to quit particular Neighbourhoods surrounded by Dutch, being made uneasy by the Disagreeableness of disonant Manners; and in Time, Numbers will probably quit the Province for the same Reason. Besides, the Dutch under-live, and are thereby enabled to under-work and under-sell the English; who are thereby extreamly incommoded, and consequently disgusted, so that there can be no cordial Affection or Unity between the two Nations. How good Subjects they may make, and how faithful to the British Interest, is a Question worth considering. And in my Opinion, equal Numbers might have been spared from the British Islands without being miss'd there, and on proper Encouragement would have come over: I say without being miss'd, perhaps I might say without lessening the Number of People at Home. I question indeed, whether there be a Man the less in Britain for the Establishment of the Colonies. An Island can support but a certain Number of People: When all Employments are full, Multitudes refrain Marriage, 'till they can see how to maintain a Family. The Number of Englishmen in England, cannot by their present common Increase be doubled in a Thousand Years; but if half of them were taken away and planted in America, where there is Room for them to encrease, and sufficient Employment and Subsistance; the Number of Englishmen would be doubled in 100 Years: For those left at home, would multiply in that Time so as to fill up the Vacancy, and those here would at least keep Pace with them.

Every one must approve the Proposal of encouraging a Number of sober discreet Smiths to reside among the Indians. They would doubtless be of great Service. The whole Subsistance of Indians, depends on keeping their Guns in order; and if they are obliged to make a Journey of two or three hundred Miles to an English Settlement to get a Lock mended; it may, besides the Trouble, occasion the Loss of their Hunting Season. They are People that think much of their temporal, but little of their spiritual Interests; and therefore, as he would be a most useful and necessary Man to them, a Smith is more likely to influence them than a Jesuit; provided he has a good common Understanding, and is from time to time well instructed.

I wish I could offer any Thing for the Improvement of the Author's Piece, but I have little Knowledge, and less Experience in these Matters. I think it ought to be printed; and should be glad there were a more general Communication of the Sentiments of judicious Men, on Subjects so generally interesting; it would certainly produce good Effects. Please to present my Respects to the Gentleman, and thank him for the Perusal of his Manuscript. I am, Yours affectionately.

Document 80

"Indian Title"

In the great debate preceding the American Revolution, the historical basis of the colonies' relationship to the mother country was examined critically by both sides. Did the English kings have the right or power initially to give away the American lands to their subjects, or were these lands properly the possession of the Indians? Did the King conquer the American wilderness or did the colonists? Under what conditions did the settlers come? Richard Bland, of Virginia, in his *Inquiry into the Rights of the British Colonies,* published in Williamsburg in 1766, took the view frequently taken by the colonists against the officials of the mother country: that local rights based on purchase from, or conquest of, the Indians, could not be summarily dismissed or ignored by the King or by Parliament. The following passage is taken from the edition of the *Inquiry* edited by Earl Gregg Swem, and reprinted by the Appeals Press, Inc., for the William Parks Club (Richmond: 1922, pp. 20–21).

America was no Part of the Kingdom of *England;* it was possessed by a savage People, scattered through the Country, who were not subject to the *English* Dominion, nor owed Obedience to its Laws. This independent Country was settled by *Englishmen* at their own Expense, under particular Stipulations with the Crown: These Stipulations then must be the sacred Band of Union between *England* and her Colonies, and cannot be infringed without Injustice. But you Object that 'no Power can abridge the Authority of Parliament, which has never exempted any from the Submission they owe to it; and no other Power can grant such an Exemption.'

I will not dispute the Authority of the Parliament, which is without Doubt supreme within the Body of the Kingdom, and cannot be abridged by any other Power; but may not the King have Prerogatives which he has a Right to exercise without the Consent of Parliament? If he has, perhaps that of granting License to his Subjects to remove into a *new* Country, and to settle therein upon particular Conditions, may be one. If he has no such Prerogative, I cannot discover how the Royal Engagements can be made good, that 'the Freedom and other Benefits of the *British* Constitution' shall be secured to those People who shall settle in a new Country under such Engagements; the Freedom, and other Benefits of the *British* Constitution, cannot be secured to a People without they are exempted from being taxed by any Authority but that of their Representatives, chosen by themselves. This is an essential Part of *British* Freedom; but if the King cannot grant such an Exemption, in Right of his Prerogative, the Royal Promises cannot be fulfilled; and all Charters which have been granted by our former Kings, for this Purpose, must be Deceptions upon the Subjects who accepted them, which to say would be a high Reflection upon the Honour of the Crown.

DOCUMENT 81

"Red Jacket Medals"

Plate 23, following page 334, portrays a medal given
by President George Washington to the Seneca chief
Red Jacket during an Indian conference held in Philadelphia in March 1792. Similar medals, which became
known as "Red Jacket medals," were later given to other
Indian leaders. The historian Samuel G. Drake tells of
an incident occurring about 1794 when an officer presented a Western chief with a medal, on one side of
which President Washington was pictured as armed
with a sword, and on the other, an Indian was seen in
the act of burying the hatchet. The chief was sensible
at once of the discrepancy and asked "Why does not the
President bury his sword, too?" For further information
about such medals, see Bauman L. Belden, *Indian Peace
Medals Issued in the United States* (New York: American Numismatic Society, 1927).

DOCUMENT 82

Fallen Timbers

Indian policy in the immediate post-Revolutionary period is frequently overlooked by later historians in their enthusiasm for the separation from Great Britain and for the later exploits of the vigorous new nation. Nevertheless, Indian power continued, as in the colonial period, to limit and to condition the development of the United States. Early defeats of American forces by the Indians delayed the settlement of the Western territories now available to the federal and state governments. Eventually, the victory of General Anthony Wayne at Fallen Timbers in Northwest Ohio on August 20, 1794, and the subsequent Treaty of Greenville, signed August 3, 1795, laid the basis for the rapid expansion that was to follow. The prototype of the medal prepared for the Indian leaders attending the Greenville Treaty talks is illustrated in the previous document. The following letter, of April 8, 1795, from the Secretary of War to General Wayne, casts light on the Indian problems of the period. It is taken from Richard C. Knopf, ed., *Anthony Wayne: A Name in Arms . . . The Wayne-Knox-Pickering-McHenry Correspondence*, pp. 393–403 (Pittsburgh: University of Pittsburgh Press, 1959).

War Office April 8. 1795.

Sir,

The overtures for peace which have been made by the Indians North West of the Ohio bear the appearance of sincerity, and viewed in connection with the events of the last year, it is hardly to be doubted that their overtures have been made in good faith. Taking this for granted, it becomes necessary to communicate to you the ideas of the

President of the United States relative to the terms on which peace is now to be negociated. To gratify the usual expectation of Indians assembling for the purposes of treaty and thereby facilitate the negociation, it is thought best to provide and forward a quantity of Goods. These will amount to at least twenty five thousand dollars, but are to be delivered only in case of a successful treaty: except such small portions of them as humanity may call for pending the negociation. The residue are to be delivered to them as one of the conditions for their final relinquishment of the lands which the treaty shall comprehend.

Besides the goods, you will stipulate to pay them a sum not exceeding Ten thousand dollars annually, as a further and full consideration for all the lands they relinquish.

You will consider how the goods for the treaty should be distributed. Perhaps Indians of several Nations will attend, who have no sort of Claim to any of the lands we shall retain: yet being present they will expect to participate; and they must participate. In what degree, can be adjusted with the Chiefs of the tribes who were the true Owners of the land. These alone (the true Owners) if they can be ascertained, or agreed on, are to enjoy the annuity: the share of each Nation to be fixed if possible; and it is presumed they will agree on the principles by which your calculation will be governed. They will doubtless, as formerly, manifest their wishes to recover a large part of their best hunting Ground, as necessary to their subsistence: but the annuity is intended to compensate them for the loss of the Game: while its amount granted under the present circumstances, will evince the liberality of the United States.

With respect to the *general* boundary line, that described in the treaty made at Fort Harmar the 9. January 1789, will still be satisfactory to the United States; and you will urge it accordingly.

The reservations of divers pieces of land for trading posts, as in the tenth article of the treaty of Fort Harmar, and the strip six Miles wide from the River Rosine to Lake St. Clair in the 11th Article, as a convenient appendage to Detroit, to give room for settlements, it is desirable to have retained for those uses. Some of the military posts which are already established, or which you may judge necessary to have established, to preserve, or complete, a chain of communication from the Ohio to the Miami of the lake; and from the Miami Villages to the head of the Wabash, and down the same to the Ohio and from the Miami villages down to the mouth of the Miami River at Lake Erie, it will also be desirable to secure: but *all* these Cessions are not to be insisted on; for *peace* and not *increase* of *territory* has been the object of this expensive War. Yet, the success of the last campaign authorizes a demand of some indemnification for the blood and treasure expended, Such a boundary line therefore as would formerly have been acquiesced in, for the sake of peace, will not now be proposed.

The treaty of Fort Harmar, as you have announced to the Chiefs, is to be the basis of the new treaty. The old boundary line from the mouth of Cayahoga to the forks of Muskingum, at the crossing place above fort Lawrance [Laurens], and thence westerly straight to the portage between a branch of the Miami of the Ohio and the river St. Marys (which is a Branch of the Miami of the Lake) is still to be adhered to: but from this portage the line may run down the aforementioned branch of the Miami of the Ohio to the main river and thence down the same to the Ohio: making the line now described, from the mouth of Cayahoga to the mouth of the Miami of the Ohio, the general boundary of the lands of the United States over the Ohio.

All the lands North and West of this general boundary line, to which, by virtue of former treaties with the Western Indians, the United States have claims, may be relinquished excepting,

1. The lands which being occupied by the British troops and subjects, and the Indian title to the same being extinguished, were ceded by Great Britain in full right to the United States by the treaty of 1783.

2d. Those detached pieces of land on which you have

established or shall think proper to establish military
posts to form, or complete a chain of communication between the Miami of the Ohio and the Miami of Lake
Erie, and by the latter from the Lake to Fort Wayne and
thence to the Wabash and down the same to the Ohio.

3. The One hundred and fifty thousand Acres granted
to General Clarke for himself and his warriors near the
rapids of the Ohio—

4. The lands in possession of the French people and
other white settlers among them, who hold their lands by
the Consent of the United states.

5th. The military posts now occupied by the Troops of
the United States on the Wabash and the Ohio.

The object of these reservations may be explained to
the Indians: That they are not destined for their annoyance, or to impose the smallest restraint on their enjoyment of their lands; but to connect the settlements of the
people of the United States by rendering a passage from
one to the other more practicable and convenient. These
posts will also prove convenient to the Indians themselves,
as Traders may reside at some or all of them to supply
them with goods. For these reasons some land about each
of these posts, not less than two square miles—should also
be reserved, together with a right of passage from one to
another.

If the Indians are sincere, and desire to have our friendship, they cannot object to these means of useful intercourse, which will cement that friendship while they will
afford a very necessary and important accommodation to
the people of the United States; and in the way of trade
to the Indians themselves.

The reservations to the United States of the lands occupied by the British troops, will of course comprehend the
post of Michilimackinac; but without any definite boundary. The present post there is on an island: but a very
barren one. If the former post on the main is situated in a
better soil, and it can be ascertained that the Indian title
to any quantity of land there was extinguished, it will be
ours of course: but if the Indian title was not extinguished,

an attempt may be made to obtain it: but if objected to there need be no difficulty in renouncing it.—

The treaties heretofore made with the Western Indians, have comprized a number of nations; and if there be any truth in their pretensions of late years, their interests are blended together. Hence may result the necessity, of continuing their former mode of treating. And their uniting in one instrument will save much time and trouble, and prevent tedious, and perhaps inconvenient altercations among themselves, about their boundaries, which are often extremely vague. For instance, the Chiefs of the Six Nations, last Autumn, declared that their title to the lands between the Allegany and French Creek on the East, and the Muskingum and Cayahoga on the West, was acknowledged by *all* the Western Indians: but when I pressed them on this point, to cede that tract to the United States; they confessed that the four most hostile tribes denied their right to it: and I am well satisfied, that whatever claim the Six Nations might formerly have to the lands Westward of the Allegany, they long ago relinquished the same to the Delawares, and others of the present Western Indians. The relinquishment of the Country, therefore to the United States by the Six nations I consider as affording us but the shadow of a title to it.

The principal reasons given by the Western Indians for not adhering to the treaties of Fort McIntosh, Miami and Fort Harmar have been these

1. That the Chiefs who treated were not an adequate representation of the Nations to whom the lands belonged.

2d. That they were *compelled* by *threats* to subscribe some of the treaties.

3d. That the claim of the United States to the full property of the Indians lands, under colour of the treaty of 1783, with Great Britain, was unfounded and unjust.

To prevent a repetition of such complaints you will use every practicable means to obtain a full representation of all the nations claiming property in the lands in question. And to obviate future doubts it may be expedient to get lists of all the principal and other Chiefs of each nation, to ascertain who are absent, and whether those present may be fairly considered as an adequate representation of their nation. The explanations and declarations of the Chiefs on this point may be noted, and subscribed by them upon each list.

As they will be collected within your power at Greenville, it will highly concern the honor and justice of the United States, that strong and decided proofs be given them that they are not under even the shadow of duress: Let them feel that they are at perfect liberty to speak their sentiments, and to sign or refuse to sign such a treaty as you are now authorized to negociate.

The unfortunate construction put by the first Commissioners on our treaty of peace with Great Britain and thence continued by General St. Clair in 1789, has since been repeatedly renounced. The Commissioners who went to Canada in 1793, were explicit on this head, in their messages to the Western Indians—copies whereof you will receive. As this construction grasped the whole Indian Country Southward of the great lakes, and Eastward of the Mississippi, as the *full* and *absolute* property of the United States, a construction as unfounded in itself as it was unintelligible and mysterious to the Indians—a construction which, with the use made of it by the British Advisers of those Indians, has probably been the main spring of the distressing war on our frontiers, it cannot be too explicitly renounced. At the same time you will carefully explain and maintain the pre-emption right of the United States. Some delicacy however will be required to state even this claim, without exciting their displeasure. If the land is theirs (and this we acknowledge) they will say "Why shall we not sell it to whom we please? Perhaps in some such way as the following it may be rendered inoffensive.

The white Nations, in their treaties with one another, agree on certain boundaries, beyond which neither is to advance a step. In America, where these boundaries agreed on by the white people, pass along the Countries of the Indians, the meaning of the treaties is this—That one white nation shall not purchase or take possession of any Indian land beyond their own boundary so agreed on; even altho' the Indians should offer to sell or give it to them. The individuals indeed have often attempted to purchase and possess such lands, but being bound by the treaty of their nation, their purchases and possessions have no strength, and the other nation has a right to dispossess and drive them off.

So likewise the *Individuals* of a white nation have no right to purchase and possess Indian lands within the boundaries of their own Nations, unless the nation consents. For each white Nation makes certain rules about Indian lands, which every one of the people is obliged to follow. The most important of these rules is that which forbids Individuals taking hold of Indian lands without the consent of the nation. When individuals do such things; it is because they wish to cheat not only the Indians but their own nation; which therefore has a right to punish them and to take away the lands so unlawfully obtained. The United States have made such a rule, the design of which is to protect the Indian lands against such bad Men.

With respect to our Citizens who are prisoners among the Indians, the most diligent and strenuous endeavours are to be used to recover them. Their restoration must be made an essential condition of the peace. The witholding any of them will be deemed a breech of the treaty. Perhaps the most effectual method will be, what has been often practised, the taking of hostages. It has been by former instructions, and still is left to your judgment to stipulate or not a ransom for our prisoners. On one hand it would introduce a precedent that would not seem the most honorable: on the other hand the expectation of reward might save the lives of prisoners in future wars; and perhaps of some of those now in captivity, whom their possessors may sacrifice rather than surrender without a compensation—

It has been thought necessary to appoint Agents to reside among the Creeks and Cherokees, to gain their good will to counteract the influence of Agents from another quarter, to protect them from abuse by our own people, and to receive and represent their Complaints. But the Northwestern hostile tribes are separately so small, it will probably be unnecessary to adopt the like measure with them: especially if trading posts, on public account, should be established. This, by the way of experiment, will be attempted this year with the Southern Indians: and there is a disposition to extend the provision, if it can be guarded from abuses. The plan proposed has been to sell the Goods to the Indians and receive their skins and furs in exchange, at such rates as would merely balance the expenses of the establishment. Whatever shall be said to the Western Indians on this subject, must be to represent the measure as *probable* only and not *certain* for it depends on the future decision of the *legislature*. But if *public* traffic should not be carried on, *private* trade will be regulated with a view to prevent abuses: and the regulations it is hoped will be effectual, as soon as the United States are in the possession of the posts which can controul the traders.

The instructions on the subject of a treaty with the Western Indians, given at the War Office on the fourth day of April 1794, are still to be attended to, and to aid and influence your negociations in all matters not varied by the present instructions, the chief of which have resulted from a change in our relative situation to the hostile Indians and to the European powers, especially the British.

One great principle ought to govern all public negociations—*a rigid adherence to truth*—a principle that is essential in negociations with *Indians,* if we would gain their permanent confidence and a useful influence over them. Jealousy is strongest in minds uninformed: so that the utmost purity and candor will hardly escape suspicion: Suspicions occasion delays, and issue in discontents, and these in depredations and War.

April 14th. Since the foregoing instructions were draughted, it has been thought that they might be rendered more useful by expressing the ideas contained in them in the form of a treaty. Such a form is now inclosed, of which some explanations may be proper.

Article II. It is supposed that we have but very few Indian prisoners; and if the hostile nations agree to leave hostages for the delivery of our Citizens remaining in their hands at the close of the treaty, that our security will be better than if we only return the prisoners. But it will merit consideration whether hostages shall be taken: it will depend on the conduct of the Indians, on the number of prisoners they bring with them to be exchanged at the treaty; and on all those circumstances, which will enable you to judge whether their Solemn stipulations by treaty, for the delivery of the remainder, may or may not be relied on. Strong evidences exhibited of their placing entire confidence in the United States, would seem to require a reciprocation of our confidence in them. Unfounded suspicion may produce realities. Greeneville and Fort Defiance presented themselves as eligible places for the surrender of the remaining prisoners but if any others are more proper you will substitute them.

Article III. The fork of that branch of the Miami where Loramies store is marked in the map drawn by Lieutenant Demler is supposed to be the Southern end of the portage on the Great Miami, intended in the Treaty of Fort Harmar, to which the boundary line was to run straight from the forks of the Muskingum. See the fifteenth article of that treaty—It is that old line, or one not materially variant, which is to be insisted on. The final cession and relinquishment by the Indians of the entire body of land lying Eastward and Southward of the general boundary here described, from the mouth of Cayahoga to the mouth of the Great Miami of the Ohio, *are to be an indispensable condition of peace*. To so much, at least, we are entitled, by way of indemnity for our losses and expenses, and as a consideration for the goods which will be presented, and the annuity which will be granted to them.

From a view of the Country at this distance, the first eight detached tracts enumerated in this article have been designated as worth obtaining your knowledge of the Country will enable you to decide whether to retain, to reject, or to substitute others, and to add such as you may deem very eligible on the Wabash. These it is desirable to have ceded to the United States as trading posts and posts of Communication between the settlements of the United States. I refer particularly to the time when we shall be possessed of Detroit and Michilimackinac. Among these eight posts the one in Sandusky bay, as the future harbour to our vessels navigating Lake Erie is considered as peculiarly important on account of the scarcity of harbours on that lake. The one towards the mouth of the Miami of the Lake is also deemed important; and as the British have last year erected a fort there with the consent of the Indians, the latter ought not to object to our succeeding the possession of it, when the British Garrison shall be withdrawn. We shall make at least as good a use of it as their former friends.

But however desirable it may be to obtain a cession of these detached tracts which will be military stations as well as posts for trade and communication; and altho in a military view they may operate usefully by deterring the Indians from recommencing hostilities: yet they are by no means to be made the criterion of peace or war. When weighed in the balance against peace they are light as air.

In [John] Mitchells map it appears that the French formerly built a fort and made a settlement on the mainland Northward of the Island of Michilimackinac; but that the same had been abandoned. Then it was, probably, that the post on the Island was taken. This former establishment on the main has suggested the idea that it may be worth while to resume it: from your information you will decide: but as already observed, if objected to by the Indians, it may be renounced.

Article IV. Invoices of the goods to be delivered in case of a successful treaty will be forwarded. They will show only the prime cost with the charges of purchasing and packing without the transportation. To these, if attainable, will be added the expences of transportation to the place of delivery, in order to ascertain the real value of the goods delivered. But so far as the charges on the goods shall not be *ascertained* the nature of the expence of transportation may be explained to the Indians to give them a due sense of the value of the Goods.

With respect to the annuity proposed to be stipulated, I am satisfied it will be best to set its amount at the prime cost of the goods in the City or place in the United States, in which they shall here after be procured; and it may be so much less as the average expence if the transportation may amount to. The mode heretofore proposed of fixing a tariff at the treaty to include the prime cost and charges, if not impracticable, will be embarrassing—whereas the prime cost will be certain; satisfactory evidence thereof may be produced; and disputes and uneasiness thereby prevented. The highest price you are authorized to stipulate—ten thousand dollars for the annuity, includes the real charges of transportation with the prime cost. If the transportation may be fairly set at One thousand fifteen hundred or two thousand dollars, so much should be deducted. But your calculations in this case need not be very nice. The great object is to effect a *peace* and such a peace as shall let the Indians go away *with their minds at ease*; otherwise it may be but the era of renewed hostilities.

I will end these remarks with one observation: That the enclosed form of a treaty is such as a view of our affairs, in relation to the Western Indians, at this distance, has suggested. The disposition of the Indians and various circumstances not now known, may require many alterations, which you will accordingly make.

A provision for their delivering up murderers *to be punished by our laws* is purposely omitted: because experience has too long shown, that regardless of our stipulations *we cannot punish our own*. It is a maxim with the frontier people not to hang a White Man who murders an Indian. We ought to make no engagement that we have not a moral certainty of fulfilling.

Your authority to negociate a treaty with the Western

Indians I find has hitherto been grounded solely on your instructions. These it will be improper to produce. I have therefore made out a certificate under the seal of this Office which you will exhibit and have interpreted to the Indians. It is similar to the Certificate which I received to evidence my authority to negociate the treaty with the six Nations. A Commission in the usual form was not given: it being doubted whether it would be proper, seeing my appointment was made by the President alone the Senate not [torn]

The proceedings at former treaties with the Western Indians, Copies of divers Indian treaties and other documents enumerated in the list enclosed, some of which might be necessary and *others* useful in your negociations are now forwarded—

I am sir with great respect Your obedient servant

TIMOTHY PICKERING
Secy. of War

Major General Wayne.

DOCUMENT 83

Tippecanoe and Tyler Too!

The battle of Tippecanoe, November 7–8, 1811, was a landmark both nationally, for the young country striding westward, and personally, for the Governor of the Indiana Territory, William Henry Harrison, whose attack on the Indians became the substance for a legend which later sent him to the White House in 1841. The background of the battle is subtly recounted by Henry Adams, in the following chapter (footnotes omitted) from his *History of the United States of America during the First Administration of James Madison,* II (New York: Charles Scribner's Sons, 1890), 67–89.

Although no one doubted that the year 1812 was to witness a new convulsion of society, if signs of panic occurred they were less marked in crowded countries where vast interests were at stake, than in remote regions which might have been thought as safe from Napoleon's wars as from those of Genghis Khan. As in the year 1754 a petty fight between two French and English scouting parties on the banks of the Youghiogheny River, far in the American wilderness, began a war that changed the balance of the world, so in 1811 an encounter in the Indian country, on the banks of the Wabash, began a fresh convulsion which ended only with the fall of Napoleon. The battle of Tippecanoe was a premature outbreak of the great wars of 1812.

Governor William Henry Harrison, of the Indiana Territory, often said he could tell by the conduct of his Indians, as by a thermometer, the chances of war and peace for the United States as estimated in the Cabinet at London. The remark was curious, but not surprising. Uneasiness would naturally be greatest where least control and most irritation existed. Such a region was the Northwestern Territory. Even the spot where violence would break out might be predicted as somewhere on the waterline of the Maumee and the Wabash, between Detroit at one extremity and Vincennes at the other. If a guess had been ventured that the most probable point would be found on that line, about half way between Lake Erie and the Ohio River, the map would have shown that Tippecanoe Creek, where it flowed into the Wabash, corresponded with the rough suggestion.

The Indiana Territory was created in 1800; and the former delegate of the whole Northwestern Territory, William Henry Harrison, was then appointed governor of the new division. Until the year 1809, Illinois formed part of the Indiana Territory; but its single settlement at Kaskaskia was remote. The Indiana settlement consisted mainly of two tracts,—one on the Ohio, opposite Louisville in Kentucky, at the falls, consisting of about one hundred and fifty thousand acres, called Clark's Grant; the other, at Vincennes on the Wabash, where the French had held a post, without a definite grant of lands, under an old Indian treaty, and where the Americans took whatever rights the French enjoyed. One hundred miles of wilderness separated these two tracts. In 1800, their population numbered about twenty-five hundred persons; in 1810, nearly twenty-five thousand.

Northward and westward, from the bounds of these districts the Indian country stretched to the Lakes and the Mississippi, unbroken except by military posts at Fort Wayne and Fort Dearborn, or Chicago, and a considerable settlement of white people in the neighborhood of the fortress at Detroit. Some five thousand Indian warriors held this vast region, and were abundantly able to expel every white man from Indiana if their organization had been as strong as their numbers. The whites were equally eager to expel the Indians, and showed the wish openly.

Governor Harrison was the highest authority on matters connected with the northwestern Indians. During eight years of Harrison's government Jefferson guided the Indian policy; and as long as Jefferson insisted on the philanthropic principles which were his pride, Harrison, whose genius lay in ready adaptation, took his tone from the President, and wrote in a different spirit from that which he would have taken had he represented an aggressive chief. His account of Indian affairs offered an illustration of the law accepted by all historians in theory, but adopted by none in practice; which former ages called "fate," and metaphysicians called "necessity," but which modern science has refined into the "survival of the fittest." No acid ever worked more mechanically on a vegetable fibre than the white man acted on the Indian. As the line of American settlements approached, the nearest Indian tribes withered away.

Harrison reported conscientiously the incurable evils which attended the contact of the two hostile forms of society. The first, but not the most serious, was that the white man, though not allowed to settle beyond the Indian border, could not be prevented from trespassing far and wide on Indian territory in search of game. The practice of hunting on Indian lands, in violation of law and existing treaties, had grown into a monstrous abuse. The Kentucky settlers crossed the Ohio River every autumn to kill deer, bear, and buffalo for their skins, which they had no more right to take than they had to cross the Alleghanies, and shoot or trap the cows and sheep in the farm-yards of Bucks County. Many parts of the Northwestern Territory which as late as 1795 abounded in game, ten years afterward contained not game enough to support the small Indian parties passing through them, and had become worthless for Indian purposes except as a barrier to further encroachment.

The tribes that owned these lands were forced either to remove elsewhere, or to sell their old hunting-grounds to the government for supplies or for an annuity. The tribes that sold, remaining near the settlements to enjoy their annuity, were more to be pitied than those that removed, which were destined to destruction by war. Harrison reported that contact with white settlements never failed to ruin them. "I can tell at once," he wrote in 1801, "upon looking at an Indian whom I may chance to meet, whether he belongs to a neighboring or to a more distant tribe. The latter is generally well-clothed, healthy, and vigorous; the former half-naked, filthy, and enfeebled by intoxication, and many of them without arms excepting a knife, which they carry for the most villanous purposes." Harrison estimated the number of Indian warriors then in the whole valley of the Wabash as not exceeding six hundred; the sale of whiskey was unlawful, yet they were supposed to consume six thousand gallons of whiskey a year, and their drunkenness so often ended in murder that among three of the tribes scarcely a chief survived.

"I have had much difficulty," wrote Harrison in the same letter from Vincennes, "with the small tribes in this immediate neighborhood; namely the Piankeshaws, the Weas, and the Eel River Miamis. These three tribes form a body of the most depraved wretches on earth. They are daily in this town in considerable numbers, and are frequently intoxicated to the number of thirty or forty at once, when they commit the greatest disorders, drawing their knives and stabbing every one they meet with; breaking open the houses of the citizens, killing their cattle and hogs, and breaking down their fences. But in all their frolics they generally suffer the most themselves. They kill each other without mercy. Some years ago as many as four were found dead in a morning; and although those murders were actually committed in the streets of the town, yet no attempt to punish them has ever been made."

The Piankeshaws were reduced to twenty-five or thirty warriors; the Weas and Eel River Indians were mere remnants. The more powerful tribes at a distance saw with growing alarm the steady destruction of the border warriors; and the intelligent Indians everywhere forbade the introduction of whiskey, and tried to create a central authority to control the degraded tribes.

A third evil was much noticed by Harrison. By treaty, if an Indian killed a white man the tribe was bound to surrender the murderer for trial by American law; while if a white man killed an Indian, the murderer was also to be tried by a white jury. The Indians surrendered their murderers, and white juries at Vincennes hung them without scruple; but no jury in the territory ever convicted a white man of murdering an Indian. Harrison complained to the President of the wanton and atrocious murders committed by white men on Indians, and the impossibility of punishing them in a society where witnesses would not appear, criminals broke jail, and juries refused to convict. Throughout the territory the people avowed the opinion that a white man ought not in justice to suffer for killing an Indian; and many of them, like the uncle of Abraham Lincoln, thought it a virtuous act to shoot an Indian at sight. Harrison could combat this code of popular law only by proclamations offering rewards for the arrest of murderers, who were never punished when arrested. In 1801 the Delawares alone complained of six unatoned murders committed on their tribe since the Treaty of Greenville, and every year increased the score.

"All these injuries," reported Harrison in 1801, "the Indians have hitherto borne with astonishing patience; but though they discover no disposition to make war on the United States at present, I am confident that most of the tribes would eagerly seize any favorable opportunity for that purpose; and should the United States be at war with any of the European nations who are known to the Indians, there would probably be a combination of more than nine tenths of the Northern tribes against us, unless some means are used to conciliate them."

So warmly were the French remembered by the Indians, that if Napoleon had carried out his Louisiana scheme of 1802 he could have counted on the active support of nearly every Indian tribe on the Mississippi and the Lakes; from Pensacola to Detroit his orders would have been obeyed. Toward England the Indians felt no such sentimental attachment; but interest took the place of sentiment. Their natural line of trade was with the Lakes, and their relations with the British trading-post at Malden, opposite Detroit, became more and more close with every new quarrel between Washington and London.

President Jefferson earnestly urged the Indians to become industrious cultivators of the soil; but even for that reform one condition was indispensable. The Indians must be protected from contact with the whites; and during the change in their mode of life, they must not be drugged, murdered, or defrauded. Trespasses on Indian land and purchases of tribal territory must for a time cease, until the Indian tribes should all be induced to adopt a new system. Even then the reform would be difficult, for Indian warriors thought death less irksome than daily labor; and men who did not fear death were not easily driven to toil.

There President Jefferson's philanthropy stopped. His greed for land equalled that of any settler on the border, and his humanity to the Indian suffered the suspicion of having among its motives the purpose of gaining the Indian lands for the whites. Jefferson's policy in practice offered a reward for Indian extinction, since he not only claimed the territory of every extinct tribe on the doctrine of paramount sovereignty, but deliberately ordered his Indian agents to tempt the tribal chiefs into debt in order to oblige them to sell the tribal lands, which did not belong to them, but to their tribes:—

"To promote this disposition to exchange lands which they have to spare and we want, for necessaries which we have to spare and they want, we shall push our trading-houses, and be glad to see the good and influential individuals among them in debt; because we observe that when these debts get beyond what the individuals can pay, they become willing to lop them off by a cession of lands."

No one would have felt more astonishment than Jefferson had some friend told him that this policy, which he believed to be virtuous, was a conspiracy to induce trustees to betray their trusts; and that in morals it was as improper as though it were not virtuously intended. Shocked as he would have been at such a method of obtaining the neighboring estate of any Virginia family, he not only suggested but vigorously carried out the system toward the Indians.

In 1804 and 1805, Governor Harrison made treaties with the Miamis, Eel Rivers, Weas, Piankeshaws, and Delawares,—chiefly the tribes he called "a body of the most depraved wretches upon earth,"—by which he obtained the strip of country, fifty miles wide, between the Ohio and the White rivers, thus carrying the boundary back toward the Wabash. The treaty excited deep feeling among the better Indians throughout the territory, who held long debates on their means of preventing its execution.

Among the settlers in Indiana, an internal dispute mingled with the dangers of Indian relations. For this misfortune Harrison himself was partially to blame. A Virginian by birth, naturally inclined toward Southern influences, he shared the feelings of the Kentucky and Virginia slave-owners who wanted the right of bringing their slaves with them into the Territory, contrary to the Ordinance of 1787. The men who stood nearest the governor were earnest and active in the effort to repeal or evade the prohibition of slavery, and they received from Harrison all the support he could give them. With his approval, successive appeals were made to Congress. Perhaps the weightiest act of John Randolph's career as leader of the Republican majority in the House was to report, March 2, 1803, that the extension of slavery into Indiana was "highly dangerous and inexpedient," and that the people of Indiana "would at no distant day find ample remuneration for a temporary privation of labor and immigration" in the beneficence of a free society. Cæsar Rodney, of Delaware, in March, 1804, made a report to a contrary effect, recommending a suspension for ten years of the anti-slavery clause in the Ordinance; but the House did not act upon it.

The advocates of a slave system, with Harrison's cooperation, then decided that the Territory should pass into the second grade, which under the Ordinance of 1787 could be done when the population should number five thousand male whites of full age. The change was effected in the winter of 1804–1805, by means open to grave objection. Thenceforward Harrison shared his power with a Legislative Council and a House of Representatives; while the legislature chose a territorial delegate to Congress. The first territorial legislature, in 1805, which was wholly under Harrison's influence, passed an Act, subsequently revised and approved Sept. 17, 1807, permitting owners of slaves to bring them into the Territory and keep them there for a number of days, during which time the slave might be emancipated on condition of binding himself to service for a term of years to which the law set no limit.

The overpowering influence and energy of the governor and his Southern friends gave them during these years undisputed control. Yet the anti-slavery sentiment was so strong as to make the governor uncomfortable, and almost to endanger his personal safety; until at last, in 1808, the issue was fairly brought before the people in the elections. Both in that and in the following year the opponents of slavery outvoted and defeated the governor's party. Feelings became exceedingly bitter, and the Territory was distracted by feuds which had no small influence on matters of administration, and on the Indian troubles most of all. Between the difficulties of introducing negroes and expelling Indians, Harrison found that his popularity had been lessened, if not lost. He could not fail to see that a military exploit was perhaps his only hope of recovering it; and for such an exploit he had excuses enough.

The treaties of 1804–1805, which threatened the Indians with immediate loss of their hunting-grounds in the Wabash valley, caused a fermentation peculiarly alarming because altogether new. Early in 1806 Harrison learned that a Shawanee Indian, claiming to be a prophet, had gathered a number of warriors about him at Greenville, in Ohio, and was preaching doctrines that threatened trouble. Harrison attributed the mischief to the Prophet; but he learned in time that the Prophet's brother Tecumseh —or more properly Tecumthe—gave the movement its chief strength.

Indians and whites soon recognized Tecumthe as a phenomenon. His father was a Shawanee warrior, in no way distinguished; his mother, a Creek or Cherokee Indian, captured and adopted by the Shawanee,—and of these parents three children at one birth were born about the year 1780, a few miles from Springfield, Ohio. The third brother lived and died obscure; Tecumthe and the Prophet became famous, although they were not chiefs of their tribe, and had no authority of office or birth. Such of the chiefs as were in the pay or under the power of the United States government were jealous of their influence, and had every reason for wishing to suppress the leaders of a movement avowedly designed to overthrow the system of tribal independence. From the first, Tecumthe aimed at limiting the authority of the tribes and their chiefs in order to build up an Indian confederacy, embracing not the chiefs but the warriors of all the tribes, who should act as an Indian Congress and assume joint ownership of Indian lands.

This scheme was hostile to the plans though not to the professions of President Jefferson. Its object was to prevent the piecemeal sale of Indian lands by petty tribal chiefs, under pressure of government agents. No one could honestly deny that the object was lawful and even regular; for in the Treaty of Greenville in 1795, which was the only decisive authority or precedent, the United States had admitted and acted on the principle for which Tecumthe contended,—of accepting its cessions of land, not from single tribes, but from the whole body of northwestern Indians, without entering on the subject of local ownership. Governor Harrison and President Jefferson were of course aware of the precedent, and decided to disregard it in order to act on the rule better suited to their purposes; but their decision was in no way binding

on Tecumthe or the tribes who were parties to the treaty
of Greenville.

During the year 1807 Tecumthe's influence was increased by the "Chesapeake" excitement, which caused
the Governor-general of Canada to intrigue among the
Indians for aid in case of war. Probably their increase of
influence led the Prophet and his brother, in May or
June, 1808, to establish themselves on Tippecanoe Creek,
the central point of Indian strategy and politics. Vincennes
lay one hundred and fifty miles below, barely four-and-
twenty hours down the stream of the Wabash; Fort Dearborn, or Chicago, was a hundred miles to the northwest;
Fort Wayne the same distance to the northeast; and excepting a short portage, the Tippecanoe Indians could
paddle their canoes to Malden and Detroit in one direction, or to any part of the waters of the Ohio and Mississippi in the other. At the mouth of Tippecanoe Creek
the reformers laid out a village that realized Jefferson's
wish, for the Indians there drank no whiskey, and avowed
themselves to be tillers of the soil. Their professions
seemed honest. In August, 1808, the Prophet came to
Vincennes and passed two weeks with Governor Harrison,
who was surprised to find that no temptation could overcome the temperance of the Prophet's followers. The
speech then made in the public talk with the governor
remains the only record of the Prophet's words, and of
the character he wished to pretend, if not to adopt.

"I told all the redskins," he said to Harrison, "that the
way they were in was not good, and that they ought to
abandon it; that we ought to consider ourselves as one
man, but we ought to live agreeable to our several customs,
—the red people after their mode, and the white people
after theirs; particularly that they should not drink whiskey; that it was not made for them, but the white people,
who alone know how to use it; and that it is the cause of
all the mischiefs which the Indians suffer. . . . Determine to listen to nothing that is bad; do not take up the
tomahawk, should it be offered by the British or by the

Long-knives; do not meddle with anything that does not
belong to you, but mind your own business, and cultivate
the ground, that your women and your children may have
enough to live on. I now inform you that it is our intention to live in peace with our father and his children
forever."

Whatever want of confidence Harrison felt in these professions of peace, he recorded his great surprise at finding
the temperance to be real; and every one who visited the
settlement at Tippecanoe bore witness to the tillage,
which seemed to guarantee a peaceful intent; for if war
had been in Tecumthe's mind, he would not have placed
town, crops, and stock within easy reach of destruction.

Nothing could be more embarrassing to Jefferson than
to see the Indians follow his advice; for however well-
disposed he might be, he could not want the Indians to
become civilized, educated, or competent to protect themselves,—yet he was powerless to protect them. The Prophet
asked that the sale of liquor should be stopped; but the
President could no more prevent white settlers from selling liquor to the Indians than he could prevent the Wabash from flowing. The tribes asked that white men who
murdered Indians should be punished; but the President
could no more execute such malefactors than he could
execute the smugglers who defied his embargo. The Indians had rights recognized by law, by treaty, and by custom, on which their existence depended; but these rights
required force to maintain them, and on the Wabash President Jefferson had less police power than the Prophet
himself controlled.

Wide separation could alone protect the Indians from
the whites, and Tecumthe's scheme depended for its only
chance of success on holding the white settlements at a
distance. The Prophet said nothing to Harrison on that
point, but his silence covered no secret. So notorious was
the Indian hostility to land-cessions, that when Governor
Hull of Michigan Territory, in November, 1807, negoti-
ated another such cession at Detroit, the Indian agent at

Fort Wayne not only doubted its policy, but insinuated that it might have been dictated by the British in order to irritate the Indians; and he reported that the Northern Indians talked of punishing with death the chiefs who signed it.

Aware of the danger, Harrison decided to challenge it. The people of his Territory wanted the lands of the Wabash, even at the risk of war. The settlement at Tippecanoe was supposed to contain no more than eighty or a hundred warriors, with four or five times that number within a radius of fifty miles. No immediate outbreak was to be feared; and Harrison, "conceiving that a favorable opportunity then offered" for carrying the boundary from the White River to the Wabash, asked authority to make a new purchase. Secretary Eustis, July 15, 1809, wrote him a cautious letter, giving the required permission, but insisting that, "to prevent any future dissatisfaction, the chiefs of all the nations who had or pretended right to these lands" were to be present as consenting parties to the treaty. On this authority Harrison once more summoned together "the most depraved wretches upon earth," —Miamis, Eel Rivers, Delawares, Pottawatomies, and Kickapoos,—and obtained from them, Sept. 30, 1809, several enormous cessions of territory which cut into the heart of the Indian country for nearly a hundred miles up both banks of the Wabash valley. These transfers included about three million acres.

Harrison knew that this transaction would carry despair to the heart of every Indian in his Territory. The Wabash valley alone still contained game. Deprived of their last resource, these Indians must fall back to perish in the country of the Chippewas and Sioux, their enemies. Already impoverished by the decrees of Napoleon, the Orders in Council, and the embargo, which combined to render their peltry valueless, so that they could scarcely buy the powder and shot to kill their game, the Indians had thenceforward no choice but to depend on British assistance. Harrison's treaty immediately strengthened the influence of Tecumthe and the Prophet. The Wyandots, or Hurons, regarded by all the Indian tribes in the Territory as first in dignity and influence, joined Tecumthe's league, and united in a declaration that the late cessions were void, and would not be recognized by the tribes. The winter of 1809–1810 passed quietly; but toward May, 1810, alarming reports reached Vincennes of gatherings at the Prophet's town, and of violence to be expected. When the salt, which was part of the usual annuity, reached Tippecanoe, Tecumthe refused to accept it, and drove the boatmen away. He charged the American government with deceiving the Indians; and he insisted, as the foundation of future peace, that the cessions of 1809 should be annulled, and no future cession should be good unless made by all the tribes.

Harrison knew that his treaties of 1809 opened an aggressive policy, which must naturally end in an Indian war. Some of the best citizens in the Territory thought that the blame for the consequences ought not to rest on the Indians. Since the election of Madison to the Presidency in November, 1808, war with England had been so imminent, and its effect on the Indians so marked, that Harrison could not help seeing the opportunity of a military career, and he had given much study to military matters. His plans, if they accorded with his acts, included an Indian war, in which he should take the initiative. His treaties of 1809 left him no choice, for after making such a war inevitable, his only safety lay in crushing the Indians before the British could openly aid them. Unfortunately, neither Madison nor Eustis understood his purpose, or would have liked it. They approved his land-purchases, which no Administration and no citizen would have dared reject; but they were very unwilling to be drawn into an Indian war, however natural might be such a consequence of the purchases.

So it happened that as early as the summer of 1810 war was imminent in the Wabash and Maumee valleys, and perhaps only British influence delayed it. British interests imperatively required that Tecumthe's confederacy should be made strong, and should not be wrecked pre-

maturely in an unequal war. From Malden, opposite Detroit, the British traders loaded the American Indians with
gifts and weapons; urged Tecumthe to widen his confederacy, to unite all the tribes, but not to begin war till
he received the signal from Canada. All this was duly reported at Washington. On the other hand, Harrison sent
for Tecumthe; and August 12, 1810, the Indian chief
came for a conference to Vincennes. Indians and whites,
in considerable numbers, armed and alert, fearing treachery on both sides, witnessed the interview.

Tecumthe took, as his right, the position he felt himself to occupy as the most powerful American then living,
—who, a warrior himself, with five thousand warriors behind him, held in one hand an alliance with Great Britain,
in the other an alliance with the Indians of the southwest.
Representatives of the Wyandots, Kickapoos, Pottawatomies, Ottawas, and Winnebagoes announced the adhesion
of their tribes to the Shawanee Confederacy and the election of Tecumthe as their chief. In this character he
avowed to Harrison, in the broadest and boldest language,
the scope of his policy:—

"Brother, since the peace was made in 1795 you have
killed some of the Shawanee, Winnebagoes, Delawares,
and Miamis, and you have taken our land from us; and
I do not see how we can remain at peace with you if you
continue to do so. . . . You try to force the red people
to do some injury; it is you that are pushing them on to
do mischief. You endeavor to make distinctions; you wish
to prevent the Indians from doing as we wish them,—
from uniting and considering their land as the common
property of the whole. You take tribes aside and advise
them not to come into this measure. . . . The reason, I
tell you, is this: You want, by your distinctions of Indian
tribes, in allotting to each a particular tract of land, to
make them to war with each other. You never see an Indian come and endeavor to make the white people do so.
You are continually driving the red people; and at last

you will drive them into the great lake, where they cannot either stand or work.

"Since my residence at Tippecanoe we have endeavored to level all distinctions, to destroy village chiefs by whom all mischief is done: it is they who sell our lands to the Americans. Our object is to let all our affairs be transacted by warriors. This land that was sold, and the goods that were given for it, was only done by a few. The treaty was afterward brought here, and the Weas were induced to give their consent because of their small numbers. . . . In future we are prepared to punish those chiefs who may come forward to propose to sell their land. If you continue to purchase of them, it will produce war among the different tribes, and at last I do not know what will be the consequence to the white people."

Earnestly denying the intention of making war, Tecumthe still declared that any attempt on Harrison's part to enter into possession of the land lately ceded would be resisted by force. In the vehemence of discussion he used language in regard to the United States which caused great excitement, and broke up the meeting for that day; but he lost no time in correcting the mistake. After the conference closed, he had a private interview with Harrison, and repeated his official ultimatum. He should only with great reluctance make war on the United States, against whom he had no other complaint than their land-purchases; he was extremely anxious to be their friend, and if the governor would prevail upon the President to give up the lands lately purchased, and agree never to make another treaty without the consent of all the tribes, Tecumthe pledged himself to be a faithful ally to the United States, and to assist them in all their wars with the English; otherwise he would be obliged to enter into an English alliance.

Harrison told him that no such condition had the least chance of finding favor with the Government. "Well," rejoined Tecumthe, as though he had expected the answer, "as the great chief is to decide the matter, I hope the

Great Spirit will put sense enough into his head to induce him to direct you to give up this land. It is true, he is so far off he will not be injured by the war; he may sit still in his town and drink his wine, while you and I will have to fight it out."

Therewith Tecumthe and Harrison parted, each to carry on his preparations for the conflict. The Secretary of War wrote to Harrison in November instructing him to defer the military occupation of the new purchase on the Wabash, but giving no orders as to the policy intended to be taken by the Government. Wanting peace, he threw on Harrison the responsibility for war.

"It has indeed occurred to me," wrote the secretary, "that the surest means of securing good behavior from this conspicuous personage [Tecumthe] and his brother, would be to make them prisoners; but at this time more particularly, it is desirable that peace with all the Indian tribes should be preserved; and I am instructed by the President to express to your Excellency his expectation and confidence that in all your arrangements this may be considered (as I am confident it ever has been) a primary object with you."

DOCUMENT 84

Pipe of Peace

Plate 24, following page 334, depicts a silver pipe of peace made by an unknown American silversmith and presented to the Delaware Tribe of Indians by Major General William Henry Harrison on July 8, 1814. The pipe, which is in the Smithsonian Institution, Washington, D.C., is described by G. Carroll Lindsay, "The Treaty Pipe of the Delawares," *Antiques,* Vol. LXXIV, pp. 44–45 (July 1958).

DOCUMENTS 85, 86

Calling on the "Great White Father"

Following the Revolution the supreme power of the English in America—who could now be properly called Americans—lay where the Federal Government established itself. From 1800 on, that place was Washington, D.C., and Indian leaders, instead of traveling to London as they had occasionally done in the eighteenth century when they were not dealing with regional or colonial representatives, now journeyed to the banks of the Potomac. There, it is recorded, their presence could ruffle diplomatic feelings as occurred, for example, when President Jefferson ignored the British Ambassador at a reception to fuss over the rarer types of human beings from beyond the Mississippi. As American power grew stronger and the Indians became progressively more remote and dependent upon the "Great White Father" in Washington, the visits took on interest more for their form than for their substance. Characteristic of the interest engendered by these exotic visitors is the painting by Charles Bird King, labeled by him "Young Omawhaw, War Eagle, Little Missouri, and Pawnees. Painted at Washington City, 1821" (Plate 25, following page 334), and the two views of Wi-jun-hon, an Assiniboin Chief, "going to and returning from Washington," painted by George Catlin in 1832 (Plate 26, following page 334). Both are in the Smithsonian Institution, Washington, D.C. King's Indians glow with strength, simplicity, and honesty. Who is to say that King did not see these noble features in 1821? Catlin, eleven years later, catalogues a sorrier scene. As described by Catlin, Wi-jun-hon was taken to Washington in 1832, in a beautiful Indian dress, by Major Sanford, the Indian agent, and returned to his country the next spring in a Colonel's uniform. He lectured awhile to his people on the customs of the whites, when he was denounced by them for telling lies, which he had learned of the whites, and was, by his own people, put to death at the mouth of the Yellowstone River.

DOCUMENT 87

Security of Property

The following Memorial to Congress by various inhabitants of the Florida Territory in 1832 illustrates an attitude common to white frontiersmen whose interests were hampered by the presence of neighboring Indian groups. In the early nineteenth century, this attitude expressed itself most frequently in demands for the removal of the Indians to other areas. The existence of a sanctuary to which escaped Negro slaves could flee was intolerable to the white neighbors of the Seminoles, and they demanded an end to it. They succeeded, in large measure, in accomplishing their objective. The passage is from Clarence Edwin Carter, ed., *The Territorial Papers of the United States;* Vol. XXIV, *The Territory of Florida, 1828–1834,* pp. 678–79 (Washington, D.C.: Government Printing Office, 1959).

MEMORIAL TO CONGRESS BY INHABITANTS
OF THE TERRITORY
[Referred *March* 26, 1832]
To the Hon. the Senate & House of Representatives of the United States In Congress Assembled
The Memorial of the undersigned humbly shewith; that your memorialists Inhabitants Florida, are and have been for a long time greatly annoyed by the Semenole or Florida Indians; who are constantly wandering from their own Country and trespassing upon the property of the Whites: Their depredations upon our stock; are so frequent and extensive, that we cannot for a moment, feel any thing like Security, in relation to this description of our property & unless some measures are adopted by the Government to give us protection, we see no alternative left, but to

abandon the settlements we have made at much expence & toil & retire to situation affording greater safety & less troublesome neighbours. We apprehend that unless the Indians are entirely removed from our Territory to some distant position, the evil in view, can not be effectfully remedied. The wildness & unsettled character of the frontier, (being in extent more than three hundred miles) between the whites and Indians, afford much ample facility for them to indulge their national disposition to wander, that it will be next to impossible to confine them within their own Territorial limits:—But were it possible to restrain & keep them at home, there is still to be found a most weighty objection to their continuing to occupy, (as they now do) a tract of Country, within the geographical boundaries, of of our Territory: in the fact, that absconding Slaves, find ready security among the Indians & such aid as is amply sufficient, to enable them successfully to alude the best efforts of their masters to recover them. It is believed that their are at this time, fifty or more runaway negroes in the Indian nation, who have taken refuge their since the treaty of 1823; to whom the Indians give protection, (in the way of secrecy at least) notwithstanding they are in that treaty obligated by a solemn pledge to apprehend & surrender all Slaves who may seek shelter in their Country. So long as a state of things thus dangerous to the interests of the inhabitants of Florida continues she cannot hope for prosperity or improvement: It cannot be expected that people of property will settle in a Country where their is so little security in relation to their property. We humbly pray therefore that your honourable body will take the matter into consideration and award to us such relief as is in your opinion necessary & proper.—

And in duty bound Your Memorialists will ever pray

DOCUMENT 88

Sequoyah

No Indian "tribe" (as nineteenth-century Americans came to denominate the Indian ethnic groups whom they had normally called "nations" in the earlier centuries) adopted white ways and modes so quickly as the Cherokees. The well-kept and productive Cherokee farmsteads, healthy cattle, and the like, were the ostensible goal which the Americans wished to see the Indians attain in their march toward "civilization." However, the Cherokees may have gone too far. Their written constitution offended the State of Georgia, and their very success in imitating American industriousness and frugality seemed to contradict the notion that the Indian problem would just "fade away." Suggestive of the sophistication of the Cherokee way before its head-on collision with the State of Georgia is this portrait of 1838 of Sequoyah, the Cherokee, pointing to the alphabet he devised for his people (Plate 27, following page 334). The lithograph was published in Thomas L. McKenney and James Hall, *History of the Indian Tribes of North America,* 3 vols. (Philadelphia: 1836–44), and is reproduced from the copy in the Prints and Photographs Division of the Library of Congress, Washington, D.C.

DOCUMENT 89

From Warpath to Reservation

One of the most perceptive observers of the Western scene was John Wesley Powell, leader of a Smithsonian Institution exploration mission down the Colorado River in 1869, founder of the Bureau of American Ethnology of the Smithsonian Institution in 1879, and first chief of the U. S. Geological Survey. Powell's analysis of the state of the scattered Indians of the Rocky Mountain area, published in the *Report of Special Commissioners J. W. Powell and G. W. Ingalls on the Condition of the Ute Indians of Utah; the Pai-Utes of Utah, Northern Arizona, Southern Nevada, and Southeastern California; the Go-si Utes of Utah and Nevada; the Northwestern Shoshones of Idaho and Utah; and the Western Shoshones of Nevada* (Washington: Government Printing Office, 1874), pointed out the futility of dealing with the Indians in this area by traditional Army methods, and the need to group them on reservations which "should be a school of industry and a home for these unfortunate people." Powell's analysis of the genesis of the "wars" between whites and Indians in the mountains is revealing. The following passage is taken from pages 23–26 of his report.

GENERAL REMARKS.

All of the Indians who have been visited by the commission fully appreciate the hopelessness of contending against the Government of the United States and the tide of civilization.

They are broken into many small tribes, and their homes so interspersed among the settlements of white men, that their power is entirely broken and no fear should be entertained of a general war with them. The time has passed when it was necessary to buy peace. It only remains to decide what should be done with them for the relief of the white people from their petty depredations, and from the demoralizing influences accompanying the presence of savages in civilized communities, and also for the best interests of the Indians themselves. To give them a partial supply of clothing and a small amount of food annually, while they yet remain among the settlements, is to encourage them in idleness, and directly tends to establish them as a class of wandering beggars. If they are not to be collected on reservations they should no longer receive aid from the General Government, for every dollar given them in their present condition is an injury. This must be understood in the light that it is no longer necessary to buy peace. Perhaps the Utes of the Uintah Valley should be excepted from this statement, as they might thus be induced to join the Utes of Western Colorado who are yet unsubdued.

Again, they cannot be collected on reservations and kept there without provision being made for their maintenance. To have them nominally on a reservation and actually, the greater part of the year, wandering among the settlements, is of no advantage, but rather an injury, as the people, believing that they should remain on their reservations, and considering that they are violating their agreements with the Government in wandering away, refuse to employ them and treat them with many indignities. And this consolidation of a number of tribes of Indians in one body makes them stronger, more independent, and more defiant than they would be if scattered about the country as small tribes. If, then, they are to be collected on reservations and held there by furnishing them with an adequate support, it is evident wisdom that they should be provided with the necessary means and taught to work, that they may become self-supporting at the earliest possible day; and it is urgently recommended that steps be taken to secure this end, or that they be given over to their own resources and left to fight the battle of life for themselves. It is not pleasant to contemplate the effect and final result of this last-mentioned course. The Indian in his relations with the white man rarely associates with the better class, but finds his companions in the lowest and vilest of society—men whose object is to corrupt or plunder. He thus learns from the superior race everything that is bad, nothing that is good. His presence in the settlement is a source of irritation and a cause of fear, especially among the better class of people.

Such persons will not employ him, for they do not desire the presence of a half-naked, vicious savage in their families.

Nor are the people of these communities willing to assume the trouble or expense of controlling the Indians by the ordinary agencies of local government, but are always ready to punish either real or supposed crimes by resort to arms.

Such a course, together with the effects of crime and loathsome disease, must finally result in the annihilation of the race.

By the other alternative, putting them on reservations and teaching them to labor, they must for a number of years be a heavy expense to the General Government, but it is believed that the burden would not be as great as that on the local governments if the Indians were left to themselves. It is very probable, also, that in the sequel it will be found cheaper for the General Government to collect them on reservations, for there is always serious danger of petty conflicts arising between the Indians and white men which will demand the interference of the General Government and entail some expense. The commission does not consider that a reservation should be looked upon in the light of a pen where a horde of savages are to be fed with flour and beef, to be supplied with blankets from the Government bounty, and to be furnished with paint and gew-gaws by the greed of traders, but that a reservation should be a school of industry and a home for these unfortunate people. In council with the Indians great care was taken not to implant in their minds the idea that the Government was willing to pay them for yielding lands which white men needed, and that as a recompense for such lands they would be furnished with clothing and food, and thus enabled to live in idleness. The question was presented to the Indian something in this light: The white men take these lands and use them, and from the earth secure to themselves food, clothing, and many other desirable things. Why should not the Indian do the same? The Government of the United States is anxious for you to try. If you will unite and agree to become farmers, it will secure to you permanent titles to such lands as you need, and will give you the necessary assistance to begin such a life, expecting that you will soon be able to take care of yourselves, as do white men and civilized Indians.

All the tribes mentioned in this census table, and many others, have been visited by the commission, and frequent consultations held with them concerning the importance of their removing to reservations, and they have discussed it among themselves very fully.

Care has been taken to secure common consultation among those tribes which should be united as represented in the plans above, and we doubt not that these questions will form the subject of many a night's council during the present winter; and if the suggestions made by the commission should be acted upon, it is to be hoped that next summer will find the great majority of these Indians prepared to move.

SUGGESTIONS IN REGARD TO
THE MANAGEMENT OF THESE RESERVATIONS.

With a view of ultimately civilizing these Indians, the commission beg leave to make some suggestions concerning the management of reservations.

First. All bounties given to the Indians should, so far as possible, be used to induce them to work. No able-bodied Indian should be either fed or clothed except in payment for labor, even though such labor is expended in providing for his own future wants. Of course these remarks apply only to those who form the subject of our report—those with whom it is no longer necessary to deal as public enemies, and with the understanding that they must be conciliated to prevent war. It has already been stated that such a course is unnecessary with these Indians.

Second. They should not be provided with ready-made clothing. Substantial fabrics should be given them from which they can manufacture their own garments. Such a course was taken during the past year with the Pi-Utes, under the direction of the commission, and the result was very satisfactory. For illustration, on the Pi-Ute reservation four hundred Indians received uncut cloth sufficient to make each man, woman, and child a suit of clothes. With these fabrics thread, needles, buttons, &c., were issued. The services of an intelligent, painstaking woman were secured to teach the woman how to cut and make garments for themselves and their families. Three weeks after the issue of this material the commission revisited the reservation and found these Indians well clothed in garments of their own make. At first they complained bitterly that ready-made clothing was not furnished to them as it had been previously, but when we returned to the reservation it was found that they fully appreciated that the same money had been much more advantageously spent than on previous occasions.

Where the Indians have received ready-made clothing for a number of years, the change should not be made too violently, but a wise and firm agent could soon have all his Indians making their own clothing.

Third. The Indians should not be furnished with tents; as long as they have tents they move about with great facility, and are thus encouraged to continue their nomadic life. As fast as possible houses should be built for them. Some of the Indians are already prepared for such a change, and greatly desire to live in houses. A few, especially the older people, are prejudiced against such a course, and perhaps at first could not be induced to live in them; but such a change could be made gradually to the great advantage of the Indian, both for his health and comfort and for its civilizing influence.

Fourth. Each Indian family should be supplied with a cow, to enable them to start in the accumulation of property. The Indians now understand the value of domestic cattle, and are anxious to acquire this class of property, and a few of them have already made a beginning in this direction. Some have ten, twenty, thirty, and even fifty head, though these are exceptional cases, and it is interesting to notice that, as soon as an Indian acquires property, he more thoroughly appreciates the rights of property, and becomes an advocate of law and order.

Fifth. In all this country the soil cannot be cultivated without artificial irrigation, and under these conditions agricultural operations are too complicated for the Indian without careful superintendence. It will be impossible also to find a sufficient body of land in any one place for the necessary farms; they must be scattered many miles apart. There will, therefore, be needed on each reservation a number of farmers to give general direction to all such labor.

Sixth. On each reservation there should be a blacksmith, carpenter, and a saddle and harness maker, and each of these mechanics should employ several Indian apprentices, and should consider that the most important part of his duty was to instruct such apprentices, and from time to time a shoemaker and other mechanics should be added to this number.

Seventh. An efficient medical department should be organized on each reservation. A great number of the diseases with which the Indian is plagued yield readily to medical treatment, and by such a course many lives can be saved and much suffering prevented. But there is another very important reason for the establishment of a medical department. The magician or "medicine-man" wields much influence, and such influence is always bad; but in the presence of an intelligent physician it is soon lost.

Eighth. It is unnecessary to mention the power which schools would have over the rising generation of Indians. Next to teaching them to work, the most important thing is to teach them the English language. Into their own language there is woven so much mythology and sorcery that a new one is needed in order to aid them in advancing beyond their baneful superstitions; and the ideas and thoughts of civilized life cannot be communicated to them in their own tongues.

THE RELATION OF THE ARMY TO THESE INDIANS.

Your commission cannot refrain from expressing its opinion concerning the effect of the presence of soldiers among these Indians where they are no longer needed to keep them under subjection. They regard the presence of a soldier as a standing menace, and to them the very name of soldier is synonymous with all that is offensive and evil. To the soldier they attribute their social demoralization and the unmentionable diseases with which they are infested. Everywhere, as we traveled among these Indians, the question would be asked us, "If we go to a reservation will the Government place soldiers there?" And to such a removal two objections were invariably urged; the first was, "We do not wish to desert the graves of our fathers," and the second, "We do not wish to give our women to the embrace of the soldiers."

If the troops are not absolutely necessary in the country for the purpose of overawing these Indians, or protecting them in their rights against the encroachments of white men, it will be conceded that they should be removed.

We have already expressed the opinion that they are not needed to prevent a general war, and we believe that they are not useful in securing justice between white men and Indians and between Indians and Indians. In war we deal with people as organized into nationalities, not as individuals. Some hungry Indian steals a beef, some tired Indian steals a horse, a vicious Indian commits a depredation, and flies to the mountains. No effort is made to punish the real offender, but the first Indian met is shot at sight. Then, perhaps, the Indians retaliate, and the news is spread through the country that war has broken out with the Indians. Troops are sent to the district and wander around among the mountains and return. Perhaps a few Indians are killed, and perhaps a few white men. Usually in all such cases the white man is the chief sufferer, for he has property which can be spoiled, and the Indian has none that he cannot easily hide in the rocks. His methods of warfare are such that we cannot cope with him without resorting to means which are repugnant to civilized people; and, after spending thousands, or even millions of dollars, on an affair which, at its inception, was but a petty larceny, we make a peace with the Indians, and enter into an agreement to secure him lands, which we cannot fulfill, and to give him annuities, the expense of which are a burden on the public Treasury.

This treatment of the Indians as nations or tribes is in every way bad. Now, the most vicious Indian in any tribe has it in his power, at any moment that he may desire, to practically declare war between his own tribe, and perhaps a dozen surrounding tribes, and the Government of the United States.

What now is needed with all these subdued Indians is, some method by which individual criminals can be arrested and brought to justice. This cannot be done by the methods of war. As long as the Indians are scattered among the settlements the facts show that this cannot be done. The Indian has no knowledge of legal methods, and avenges his own wrongs by ways which are traditional with him, while the prejudices against savages which has grown through centuries of treacherous and bloody warfare, and the prejudices of race, which are always greatly exaggerated among the lower class of people, with whom the Indian is most liable to associate, are such that the Indian cannot secure justice through the intervention of the local authorities.

There is now no great uninhabited and unknown region to which the Indian can be sent. He is among us, and we must either protect him or destroy him. The only course left by which these Indians can be saved is to gather them on reservations, which shall be schools of industry and civilization, and the superintendents of which shall be the proper officers to secure justice between the two races, and between individuals of the Indian race. For this purpose on each reservation there should be a number of wise, firm men, who, as judges and police officers, would be able in all ordinary cases to secure substantial justice. In extraordinary cases no hasty steps should be taken. Surprises and massacres need no longer be feared, and if a larger force is needed than that wielded by the employés on the reservations, it would be easy to increase it by civil methods.

For this purpose laws should be enacted clearly defining the rights of the Indians and white men in their mutual relations, and the power of the officers of the Indian Department, and the methods of procedure to secure justice. It might possibly be unwise to withdraw all the troops at once. It might be better to remove them *pari passu* with the establishment of the Indians on reservations.

Permit the remark just here, that the expense of the military and civil methods stand in very glaring contrast. Within the territory which has heretofore been described it is probable that about two million dollars will be expended in the support of troops during the present fiscal year, and much less than two hundred thousand dollars through the Indian Department for feeding, clothing, and civilizing the Indians.

We beg leave again to mention that these remarks apply only to conquered tribes.

There are some Indians in other portions of the United States, whom it is necessary to manage by other methods, who yet have the pride and insolence and treachery of savages. But by far the greater part of the Indians scattered throughout the territory from the Rocky Mountains to the Pacific coast are in a condition substantially the same as those who form the subject of this report.

DOCUMENT 90

Land in Severalty

Reformers trying to do good for the Indian as well as those attempting to exploit him tended to agree on the necessity of breaking up the Indian reservations and allotting the land communally held by the tribes among the several individuals thereof (hence the term "severalty"). It was felt by almost all whites that the Indian must adopt white conceptions of land ownership and use before he could be "civilized." The wishes of the Indian were not considered. The following quotation comprises the text of a pamphlet issued by the Indian Rights Association, of Philadelphia, in 1884 advocating passage of the Coke Bill, an "Act to provide for the allotment of lands in severalty to Indians on the various reservations, and to extend the protection of the laws of the States and Territories over the Indians, and for other purposes," introduced in the Forty-eighth Congress, First Session. Though the Coke Bill failed to be enacted into law, its purpose was achieved in the Dawes Severalty Act of 1887, which governed U. S. policy toward the Indians until the administration of Franklin D. Roosevelt. The results of the severalty policy are summarized in the report of John Collier, Commissioner of Indian Affairs under Roosevelt, in Document 91. The pamphlet quoted below is entitled "Indian Land in Severalty, as provided for by the Coke Bill," pp. 3–7 (Philadelphia: Indian Rights Association, 1884).

For many years past those who have given earnest thought to the best method of placing the Indian on a right footing among us, and patient effort to accomplish this result, have united in the belief that the allotment of land to individual Indians by a secure title would prove one of the most powerful agencies in the advancement of the race.

It has been often pointed out that we have by our policy taken from the Indian the ordinary and essential stimulus to labor. While under our system of pauperizing Indians by the issuing of rations we deprive them of the ordinary necessity for self-support, by our refusal to protect them in the possession of their land and by our incessant removals we take away the common motives for cultivating it. The great mass of men work from the imperative necessity for self-support, and from the knowledge that the law will protect them in the possession of their rightful earnings. We have so alienated the Indian from all natural and general conditions, we have placed him in such an artificial and unjust position, that he has neither the necessity for self-support nor any proper protection in the result of his labor. It is a matter of surprise to all who fairly consider all the elements in the case, not that the result is no better, but that it is not far worse.

To give the Indian, then, a secure title to land, so that he may have the assurance of reaping what he has sown, is the plainest justice and good policy.

The thought and labor of those who have long worked for this end has taken shape in a most carefully and skillfully prepared bill for the allotment to Indians in severalty of land on the reservations. This bill is the outcome of long and intimate experience in the condition of the various Indian tribes; the result of a rare combination of practical knowledge and legal training. Its passage will greatly affect for the better the lives of nearly three hundred thousand human beings, besides the incalculable and yet wider influence in the life of a race and in the settlement of a question of national importance. The bill passed the Senate at the last session of the present Congress, and only its passage by the House of Representatives this coming winter is required to make it a law.

By the first section the President is authorized to issue patents for Indian reservations, set apart by treaty or act of Congress, in favor of the several tribes occupying them.

Under these patents the United States is to hold the patented land in trust for the several tribes for twenty-five years, and at the end of that time to convey it by patent to the different tribes clear of encumbrance. The President is also given authority to delay in any case the issuing of the final patent if he consider it best for the Indians to do so. These patents are to be recorded and open to inspection.

This first section simply secures the tribe *as such* in the possession of its reservation. It places the strong restraint of the law upon the unjust occupation of Indian lands in the incessant push of Western settlement.

The second section authorizes the President, whenever he thinks it for the best interests of the Indians on a reservation, to have it surveyed or resurveyed, and to allot it to the Indians in severalty—to the heads of families one-quarter, to single persons over eighteen one-eighth, and to orphan children under eighteen one-eighth of a section; to other persons under eighteen one-sixteenth of a section. If there is not sufficient land on a reservation to make such allotment, the land is to be allotted pro rata.

Treaty stipulations setting apart a reservation and providing for the allotment of land in larger quantities are to be fulfilled. The taking of land for grazing purposes by two or more Indians in common is provided for.

In section third provision is made for the manner in which the allotments are to be selected by the Indians, with the proviso that if such selection is not made within five years from the direction to take allotments the agent shall be directed to select for Indians failing to do so. The allotments are to be made under such rules as the Secretary of the Interior may prescribe by agents specially appointed by the President.

Any Indian not residing upon a reservation or belonging to a tribe for which no reservation has been provided is entitled to settle upon unappropriated land of the United States, and on applying to the local land office can have the land allotted to him and to his children in the same manner as Indians residing on a reservation take allotments under the act. The fees of the local land office are to be paid out of the United States Treasury.

The sixth section provides that patents shall be issued to individual allottees, declaring that the United States will hold the land in trust for the allottee or his heirs for twenty-five years, and then convey it to him or them absolutely and clear of all encumbrance. The land cannot be conveyed or charged during the time it is so held in trust, and the patents to individual allottees shall override the patent issued to the tribe. After the issue of patents the land shall descend according to the law of the State or Territory in which a reservation is situated. After all the lands on a reservation have been allotted, *or sooner, if the President deem it for the best interests of the Indians,* the Secretary of the Interior may negotiate with a tribe for the purchase of any unallotted portion of its reservation. This purchase is not complete until ratified by Congress. The principal of the purchase-money shall be held by the United States for twenty-five years to the credit of the tribe, and the interest at five per cent., paid annually to the Secretary of the Interior, to be applied to the education and support of the tribe. After twenty-five years, by express authority of Congress, the principal shall be payable to the tribe. Proper provision is made for religious bodies now occupying land on the reservations.

Section Seventh extends over a tribe, upon the completion of the allotments, the laws, both civil and criminal, of the State or Territory in which they reside, and prohibits the passage by the local government of any law denying Indians the equal protection of the law.

Section Eighth, in view of the important fact that the value of land in the West often depends largely upon its proper irrigation, authorizes the Secretary of the Interior to prescribe such rules as he may deem necessary to secure a just distribution of water among the Indians.

Section Ninth excepts the five civilized tribes of Indian Territory and the Seneca Indians of New York from the provisions of the act.

Section Tenth appropriates one hundred thousand dollars for the survey or resurvey of reservations necessary under the act, and provides that the sum expended be repaid out of the proceeds from the sale of reservation lands.

Section Eleventh provides that, except as to the issuing of the tribal patents, the provisions of the act shall not extend to any tribe *as such* until the consent of two-thirds adult male members shall have been obtained, but that, notwithstanding this, the President may make allotments to *individual Indians* in the manner provided irrespective of the consent of the two-thirds.

Section Twelfth provides that the act shall not affect the right of Congress to grant a right of way for railroads, highways, or telegraph lines for the public use through any lands granted to an Indian or to a tribe upon just compensation being made.

The provisions of this act have been thus stated somewhat in detail because an exact understanding of it is considered most desirable, and because only a close examination reveals the wisdom and care with which many contingencies and possible difficulties have been provided for.

The Main Points of the Bill.

The broad and general advantages of the bill may be summed up in a few words. It secures the tribes in possession of their reservations, and ends the notorious wrong of taking the Indian's land by fraud or force without his consent. The United States is to hold the reservations in trust for the tribes, but not as a permanent arrangement. The bill contemplates the breaking up of the entire reservation system; it contemplates the protection of Indian land from the grasp of unscrupulous whites only until the Indian has been given the proper training and preparation to enable him to take care of his own. In the meanwhile, the bill provides an important part of this training. On the consent of two-thirds of the adult males, allotments are to be made to a whole tribe in severalty. The reservations are divided into separate farms, the members of the tribe are given time to firmly plant and settle themselves before, by the extinguishment of the trust in which the reservation is held for the tribe, they are left to take care of themselves. Should the consent of the two-thirds not be obtained, the individual Indians can at once take allotments under the act. There is neither a compulsion of the majority nor the slightest disregard of the wants of the minority. The law of the white man is to be extended when, by the completion of the allotments, the Indians have shown themselves reasonably fit for it. Nor does the act overlook the undoubted fact that it is neither wise nor right to let these great, solid blocks of reservations stand in the way of traffic and settlement. Right of way through Indian land can be granted at any time to railroads, highways, and telegraph companies, and *at any time* unallotted land can be purchased, proper compensation being given. Such is the wise admixture in this bill of what is best in the views of those who regard this question from a radical or a conservative standpoint; land in severalty is to be given at once to all who desire it; the Indian is protected against the greed of the whites; a process of tribal disintegration is at once started, and the blotting out of the reservations as fast as it can be safely done, is the ultimate object of the bill.

In the light of the lasting importance of this measure to so many who are unrepresented among the legislators we have selected to do our will, you are asked to fairly and honestly consider it, and if it seems to you desirable and right, you are most earnestly and respectfully reminded that there rests on you a personal responsibility to give your influence, your time and thought, to secure its passage.

HENRY S. PANCOAST,
Chairman of the Committee on Laws.
October 9th, 1884.

DOCUMENT 91

A New Deal for the Red Men

The passage of the Indian Reorganization Act of 1934 marked an about-face in American Indian policy. No longer was the aim to break up the tribal and communal aspects of Indian life, to make each individual Indian abandon his group culture and live according to the value patterns of his conqueror. Instead, the New Deal of Franklin D. Roosevelt was applied in the Indian field as in other areas. Indian culture was accorded a measure of respect and encouragement. A sympathetic Commissioner of Indian Affairs, John Collier, was appointed. The Indian land base, so much of which had been lost under previous policies, was built up. Tribal governments, which previous administrations had tried to destroy, were encouraged. The following passage is from Collier's *Report* of the Commissioner of Indian Affairs, 1938, reprinted from the *Annual Report of the Secretary of the Interior, 1938*, pp. 209–11 (Washington: Government Printing Office, 1938).

In all our colorful American life there is no group around which there so steadfastly persists an aura compounded of glamour, suspicion and romance, as the Indian. For generations, the Indian has been, and is today, the center of an amazing series of wonderings, fears, legends, hopes.

Yet those who have worked with Indians know that they are neither the cruel, warlike, irreligious savages imagined by some, nor are they the "fortunate children of nature's bounty" described by tourists who see them for an hour at some glowing ceremonial. We find the Indians, in all the basic forces and forms of life, human beings like ourselves. The majority of them are very poor people living under severely simple conditions. We know them to be deeply religious. We know them to be possessed of all the powers, intelligence, and genius within the range of human endowment. Just as we yearn to live out our own lives in our own ways, so, too, do the Indians, in their ways.

For nearly 300 years white Americans, in our zeal to carve out a nation made to order, have dealt with the Indians on the erroneous, yet tragic, assumption that the Indians were a dying race—to be liquidated. We took away their best lands; broke treaties, promises; tossed them the most nearly worthless scraps of a continent that had once been wholly theirs. But we did not liquidate their spirit. The vital spark which kept them alive was hardy. So hardy, indeed, that we now face an astounding, heartening fact.

The Indians Are No Longer a Dying Race

Actually, the Indians, on the evidence of Federal census rolls of the past 8 years, are increasing at almost twice the rate of the population as a whole.

With this fact before us, our whole attitude toward the Indians has necessarily undergone a profound change. Dead is the centuries-old notion that the sooner we eliminated this doomed race, preferably humanely, the better. No longer can we, with even the most generous intentions, pour millions of dollars and vast reservoirs of energy, sympathy, and effort into any unproductive attempts at some single, artificial permanent solution of the Indian problem. No longer can we naively talk of or think of the "Indian problem." Our task is to help Indians meet the myriad of complex, interrelated, mutually dependent situations which develop among them, according to the very best light we can get on those happenings—much as we deal with our own perplexities and opportunities.

We, therefore, define our Indian policy somewhat as follows: So productively to use the moneys appropriated by the Congress for Indians, as to enable them, on good, adequate lands of their own, to earn decent livelihoods and lead self-respecting, organized lives in harmony with their own aims and ideals, as an integral part of American life. Under such a policy, the ideal end result will be the ultimate disappearance of any need for Government aid or supervision. This will not happen tomorrow; perhaps not in our lifetime; but with the revitalization of Indian hope due to the actions and attitudes of this Government during the last few years, that aim is a probability, and a real one.

Such being the policy, expressed necessarily in general terms, let us see, concretely and specifically, how, and to what extent, this policy has been approached during the fiscal year ending June 30, 1938.

In looking at the Indian picture as a social whole, we will consider certain broad phases—land use and industrial enterprises, health and education, roads and rehabilitation, political organization—which touch Indian life everywhere, including the 30,000 natives of Alaska for whose health, education, and social and economic advancement the Indian Service is responsible.

Lastly, this report will tell wherein the Indian Service, or the Government's effort as a whole for the Indians, still falls short.

Indian Lands

So intimately is all of Indian life tied up with the land and its utilization that to think of Indians is to think of land. The two are inseparable. Upon the land and its intelligent use depends the main future of the American Indian.

The Indian feels toward his land not a mere ownership sense but a devotion and veneration befitting what is not only a home but a refuge. At least 9 out of 10 Indians remain on or near the land. When times are good, a certain number drift away to town or city to work for wages. When times become bad, home to the reservation the Indian comes, and to the comparative security which he knows is lands held in trust for the Indians by the Government had been increased to approximately 51,540,307 acres— approximately 67 percent tribally owned, and 33 percent in allotments held in trust for the benefit of individuals.

waiting for him. The Indian still has much to learn
adjusting himself to the strains of competition amid
acquisitive society; but he long ago learned how to co
tend with the stresses of nature. Not only does the Indian
major source of livelihood derive from the land, but his
social and political organizations are rooted in the soil.

A major aim, then, of the Indian Service is to help the
Indians to keep and consolidate what lands they now have
and to provide more and better lands upon which they
may effectively carry on their lives. Just as important is
the task of helping the Indian make such use of his land
as will conserve the land, insure Indian self support, and
safeguard or build up the Indian's social life. Many subsequent chapters of this report deal with this latter task.

In 1887, the General Allotment Act was passed, providing that after a certain trust period, fee simple title
to parcels of land should be given to individual Indians.
Individual proprietorship meant loss—a paradox in view
of the Indian's love for the land, yet an inevitable result,
when it is understood that the Indian by tradition was
not concerned with possession, did not worry about titles
or recordings, but regarded the land as a fisherman might
regard the sea, as a gift of nature, to be loved and feared,
to be fought and revered, and to be drawn on by all as
an inexhaustible source of life and strength.

The Indian let the ownership of his allotted lands slip
from him. The job of taking the Indian's lands away
begun by the white man through military expeditions an
treaty commissions, was completed by cash purchase—
ways of course, of the best lands which the Indian h
left. In 1887, the Indian had remaining 130,000,000 ac
In 1933, the Indian had left only 49,000,000 acres, m
of it waste and desert.

Since 1933, the Indian Service has made a cond
effort—an effort which is as yet but a mere beginni
help the Indian to build back his land holdings to a
where they will provide an adequate basis for
sustaining economy, a self-satisfying social orga

By the close of the fiscal year 1938, the are

DOCUMENT 92

Termination

Government policy with regard to Indian affairs since 1953 reflects the impact of House Concurrent Resolution 108, 83d Congress, 1st Session, passed August 1, 1953 and quoted below, which looks to the "termination" of federal supervision and control over many of the Indian groups. Praised and assailed by Indians and whites, the policy underlies termination acts for specific Indian groups that have been introduced since its passage.

Whereas it is the policy of Congress, as rapidly as possible, to make the Indians within the territorial limits of the United States subject to the same laws and entitled to the same privileges and responsibilities as are applicable to other citizens of the United States, to end their status as wards of the United States, and to grant them all of the rights and prerogatives pertaining to American citizenship; and

Whereas the Indians within the territorial limits of the United States should assume their full responsibilities as American citizens: Now, therefore, be it

Resolved by the House of Representatives (the Senate concurring), That it is declared to be the sense of Congress that, at the earliest possible time, all of the Indian tribes and the individual members thereof located within the States of California, Florida, New York, and Texas, and all of the following named Indian tribes and individual members thereof, should be freed from Federal supervision and control and from all disabilities and limitations specially applicable to Indians: The Flathead Tribe of Montana, the Klamath Tribe of Oregon, the Menominee Tribe of Wisconsin, the Potowatamie Tribe of Kansas and Nebraska, and those members of the Chippewa Tribe who are on the Turtle Mountain Reservation, North Dakota. It is further declared to be the sense of Congress that, upon the release of such tribes and individual members thereof from such disabilities and limitations, all offices of the Bureau of Indian Affairs in the States of California, Florida, New York, and Texas and all other offices of the Bureau of Indian Affairs whose primary purpose was to serve any Indian tribe or individual Indian freed from Federal supervision should be abolished. It is further declared to be the sense of Congress that the Secretary of the Interior should examine all existing legislation dealing with such Indians, and treaties between the Government of the United States and each such tribe, and report to Congress at the earliest practicable date, but not later than January 1, 1954, his recommendations for such legislation as, in his judgment, may be necessary to accomplish the purposes of this resolution.

Attest: LYLE O. SNADER,
                Clerk of the House of Representatives.

Attest: J. MARK TRICE,
                    Secretary of the Senate.

DOCUMENTS 93, 94

Bureaucracy and the Indian

Plates 28 and 29, following page 334, depict two contemporary carvings, of an Indian and an Indian agent, in the Museum of Anthropology of the University of British Columbia, Vancouver, Canada. As described by the carver, D. Williams, a Salish Indian of the North Shore Reserve, Vancouver, the Indian is destitute, even starving, and goes to the agent for economic relief. The agent is very glum, and gives him a long lecture on how he should have saved his money, etc., and reluctantly gives him paper script with which to buy some flour and potatoes. The figures are noted in "The Artist in tribal society: the Northwest Coast," by Harry B. Hawthorn, in *The Artist and Tribal Society*, ed. Marian W. Smith (London: Routledge & Kegan Paul, 1961), p. 61.

The Indian Speaks

The growing sympathy between anthropologists who study the Indians and the Indians themselves led, during the week of June 13–20, 1961, to the American Indian Chicago Conference, a gathering of 460 Indians of ninety tribes under the encouragement of Dr. Sol Tax, Professor of Anthropology at the University of Chicago, and Dr. Nancy Lurie of the University of Michigan. A "Declaration of Indian Purpose" was issued by the Indians attending the meeting, recommending a course of action for American Indian policy in the coming years. The following quotation, from the section discussing "Law and Jurisdiction," and from the "Concluding Statement," is from pp. 13–16 and 19–20 of the report.

LAW AND JURISDICTION

In view of the termination policy and particularly Public Law 280, many Indian people have been vitally concerned and fearful that their law and order systems will be supplanted, without their consent, by state law enforcement agencies which, perhaps, might be hostile toward them. In *U.S. v. Kagama* (1885) 118 U.S. 375, 383, the Court, speaking of Indians, said:

"They are communities dependent on the United States; . . .; dependent for their political rights. They owe no allegiance to the States, and receive from them no protection. Because of the local ill feeling of the people, states where they are found are often their deadliest enemies. From their very weakness and helplessness, so largely due to the course of dealing of the Federal Government with them and treaties in which it has been promised, there arises a duty of protection, and with it the power."

That statement by the Supreme Court is considered to be as true today as when written.

The repeated breaking of solemn treaties by the United States has also been a concern which is disheartening to the tribes and it is felt that there is no apparent concern by the Government about breaking treaties.

RECOMMENDATIONS

1. Return of Indian Lands: We urge the Congress to direct by appropriate legislation the return in trust of that part of the Public Domain formerly owned by an Indian tribe or nation which the Secretary of Interior shall determine to be excess and non-essential to the purpose for which such land was originally taken or which was covered by a reversionary clause in the treaty or cession or other lands declared to be surplus to the government's needs. Restore all Indian lands that were consumed by termination policy.

2. Indian Claims Commission: We urge that Congress ascertain the reasons for the inordinate delay of the Indian Claims Commission in finishing its important assignment. The Congress should request the views of the attorneys for the tribes on this in order to balance the views already expressed to Congress by the attorneys for the United States.

The woeful lack of sufficient personnel to handle the case load in the Justice Department, we believe, is the *sole cause* for the delay, so damaging to the tribes, in expediting the Commission's work.

The law clearly directs that each tribe be represented by counsel and there would seem to exist no possible reason why the Justice Department should not be required to increase its personnel in the Indian Claims Section of the Lands Division to remove this just criticism. Simple justice suggests that this be speedily done or else irreparable damage to the tribes will result. We believe the

Congress will want to correct this situation as promptly as possible.

3. Title to Reservations: The Secretary of the Interior, if he has the authority, or the Congress should act to determine the legal beneficiaries of reservations created under the Indian Reorganization Act or other authority for "Landless and Homeless Indians," also reservations established by executive order or prior act of Congress, where the naming of the beneficial users has been left indefinite or ambiguous. As Indians improve such lands, or as mineral wealth or other assets of value are discovered, ownership is in jeopardy unless clearly defined.

4. Submarginal Lands: Submarginal and other surplus lands adjoining or within the exterior boundaries of Indian reservations and purchased for the benefit of the Indians, should be transferred to the tribes under trust.

5. Land Purchase Funds: The land purchase funds authorized by the Indian Reorganization Act should again be appropriated on an annual basis, to permit tribes to add to their inadequate land base, to purchase heirship lands and allotments on which restrictions are removed, and otherwise improve their economy.

6. Voting on the Indian Reorganization Act: Amend the Indian Reorganization Act to permit tribes to vote on its acceptance at any time.

7. Protect Indian Water Rights: Adopt legislation to protect all Indian water rights of Indian reservations against appropriators who, because the government may be negligent in providing for Indian development, are able to establish a record of prior use.

9. Heirship Lands: Adopt a manageable and equitable heirship lands bill.

10. Amend P.L. 280: Amend P.L. 280 (83rd Congress) to require Indian consent to past and future transfers of jurisdiction over civil and criminal cases to the state in which a reservation is located, and to permit such transfers to take place, with Indian consent, on a progressive or item by item basis.

11. Reservation Boundaries: In order that Indian tribes

may be properly protected in their reservation and may proceed with the orderly development of their resources, it is recommended that authority, if required, and funds be appropriated for the immediate survey and establishment of reservation boundaries.

TAXATION

Grave concern has arisen as a result of the recent rulings of the Bureau of Internal Revenue which in substance directly violate the solemn treaty obligations made with the American Indian.

In fact, within the past few years, there has been a steady trend by both the federal and state taxing departments to encroach upon the rights of the Indian in the taxing of Indian property.

Recently, the Bureau of Internal Revenue has boldly claimed that it has the right to levy upon and collect income taxes upon income received by Indians which is derived from the sale of livestock grazed upon restricted Indian lands. Already the Internal Revenue Service has levied upon, assessed and collected income taxes upon income received from restricted Indian production.

The taxing department of the federal government has arbitrarily made these rulings which are wholly contrary to the solemn provisions of the treaties made with the American Indian. These rulings have been made and are being enforced notwithstanding the fact that it was never intended that the Indian was to be taxed in any manner upon his restricted Indian lands, or upon the income derived from the same.

In fact the greater amount of Indian lands located in the western part of the nation are dry and arid lands and suitable for grazing purposes only. In other words, the Indian is by nature restricted as to the use of his lands since the same can only be used for grazing purposes.

Therefore, in order to further prevent the establishment of such arbitrary rules of the Bureau of Internal Revenue, and to correct the rules already existing, we deem it necessary that legislation be enacted which will clearly spell out the intent and purposes of the existing treaties and agreements made with Indian tribes. Specifically, a clear statement must be made by law that income received by an enrolled member of an Indian tribe, which is derived from tribal, allotted and restricted Indian lands, whether by original allotment, by inheritance, by exchange or purchase, or as a leasee thereof, while such lands are held in trust by the United States in trust, is exempt from Federal and State income taxes.

TREATY RIGHTS

It is a universal desire among all Indians that their treaties and trust-protected lands remain intact and beyond the reach of predatory men.

This is not special pleading, though Indians have been told often enough by members of Congress and the courts that the United States has the plenary power to wipe out our treaties at will. Governments, when powerful enough, can act in this arbitrary and immoral manner.

Still we insist that we are not pleading for special treatment at the hands of the American people. When we ask that our treaties be respected, we are mindful of the opinion of Chief Justice John Marshall on the nature of the treaty obligations between the United States and the Indian tribes.

Marshall said that a treaty ". . . is a compact between two nations or communities, having the right of self-government. Is it essential that each party shall possess the same attributes of sovereignty to give force to the treaty? This will not be pretended, for on this ground, very few valid treaties could be formed. The only requisite is, that each of the contracting parties shall possess the right of self-government, and the power to perform the stipulations of the treaty."

And he said, "We have made treaties with (the Indians); and are those treaties to be disregarded on our part, because they were entered into with an uncivilized people? Does this lessen the obligation of such treaties? By entering into them have we not admitted the power of this people to bind themselves, and to impose obligations on us?"

The right of self-government, a right which the Indians possessed before the coming of the white man, has never been extinguished; indeed, it has been repeatedly sustained by the courts of the United States. Our leaders made binding agreements—ceding lands as requested by the United States; keeping the peace; harboring no enemies of the nation. And the people stood with the leaders in accepting these obligations.

A treaty, in the minds of our people, is an eternal word. Events often make it seem expedient to depart from the pledged word, but we are conscious that the first departure creates a logic for the second departure, until there is nothing left of the word.

We recognize that our view of these matters differs at times from the prevailing legal view regarding due process.

When our lands are taken for a declared public purpose, scattering our people and threatening our continued existence, it grieves us to be told that a money payment is the equivalent of all the things we surrender. Our forefathers could be generous when all the continent was theirs. They could cast away whole empires for a handful of trinkets for their children. But in our day, each remaining acre is a promise that we will still be here tomorrow. Were we paid a thousand times the market value of our lost holdings, still the payment would not suffice. Money never mothered the Indian people, as the land has mothered them, nor have any people become more closely attached to the land, religiously and traditionally.

We insist again that this is not special pleading. We ask only that the United States be true to its own traditions and set an example to the world in fair dealing.

CONCLUDING STATEMENT

To complete our Declaration, we point out that in the beginning the people of the New World, called Indians by accident of geography, were possessed of a continent and a way of life. In the course of many lifetimes, our people had adjusted to every climate and condition from the Arctic to the torrid zones. In their livelihood and family relationships, their ceremonial observances, they reflected the diversity of the physical world they occupied.

The conditions in which Indians live today reflect a world in which every basic aspect of life has been transformed. Even the physical world is no longer the controlling factor in determining where and under what conditions men may live. In region after region, Indian groups found their means of existence either totally destroyed or materially modified. Newly introduced diseases swept away or reduced regional populations. These changes were followed by major shifts in the internal life of tribe and family.

The time came when the Indian people were no longer the masters of their situation. Their life ways survived subject to the will of a dominant sovereign power. This is said, not in a spirit of complaint; we understand that in the lives of all nations of people, there are times of plenty and times of famine. But we do speak out in a plea for understanding.

When we go before the American people, as we do in this Declaration, and ask for material assistance in developing our resources and developing our opportunities, we pose a moral problem which cannot be left unanswered. For the problem we raise affects the standing which our nation sustains before world opinion.

Our situation cannot be relieved by appropriated funds alone, though it is equally obvious that without capital investment and funded services, solutions will be delayed. Nor will the passage of time lessen the complexities which beset a people moving toward new meaning and purpose.

The answers we seek are not commodities to be purchased, neither are they evolved automatically through the passing of time.

The effort to place social adjustment on a money-time interval scale which has characterized Indian administration, has resulted in unwanted pressure and frustration.

When Indians speak of the continent they yielded, they are not referring only to the loss of some millions of acres in real estate. They have in mind that the land supported a universe of things they knew, valued, and loved.

With that continent gone, except for the few poor parcels they still retain, the basis of life is precariously held, but they mean to hold the scraps and parcels as earnestly as any small nation or ethnic group was ever determined to hold to identity and survival.

What we ask of America is not charity, not paternalism, even when benevolent. We ask only that the nature of our situation be recognized and made the basis of policy and action.

In short, the Indians ask for assistance, technical and financial, for the time needed, however long that may be, to regain in the America of the space age some measure of the adjustment they enjoyed as the original possessors of their native land.

Chapter VIII

Literature and the Arts

The Indian struck imaginative men differently from the way he impressed practical men. Using a pen, brush, or sculptor's tool rather than a sword, the writer and artist tried to understand rather than to conquer. The writer normally had to see the Indian though the eyes of the explorer; hence his picture was sometimes distorted, though often he was able to "see" things from his distant vantage point that the explorer on the spot, reporting the "facts," could not himself "see." The artist, more often than not, accepted the prevailing view of the meaning of the relationship and dramatized it, often with results that were as potent in their influence as they were misguided in their truth. The following documents suggest the impact of the Indian upon the artist and the writer. Perhaps, in losing a physical battle, the Indian gained an intellectual victory.

"Base and Mechanical Victories!"

Michel de Montaigne, the great French essayist, wrote some of his most incisive comments about European deeds in the New World in his essay "Of coaches," composed in the period 1585–88. The following passage from the essay is taken from *The Complete Works of Montaigne: Essays, Travel Journal, Letters*, translated by Donald M. Frame (Stanford, California: Stanford University Press, 1957), Book III, Chap. 6, pp. 693–95.

Our world has just discovered another world (and who will guarantee us that it is the last of its brothers, since the daemons, the sibyls, and we ourselves have up to now been ignorant of this one?) no less great, full, and well-limbed than itself, yet so new and so infantile that it is still being taught its A B C; not fifty years ago it knew neither letters, nor weights and measures, nor clothes, nor wheat, nor vines. It was still quite naked at the breast, and lived only on what its nursing mother provided. If we are right to infer the end of our world, and that poet is right about the youth of his own age, this other world will only be coming into the light when ours is leaving it. The universe will fall into paralysis; one member will be crippled, the other in full vigor.

I am much afraid that we shall have very greatly hastened the decline and ruin of this new world by our contagion, and that we will have sold it our opinions and our arts very dear. It was an infant world; yet we have not whipped it and subjected it to our discipline by the advantage of our natural valor and strength, nor won it over by our justice and goodness, nor subjugated it by our magnanimity. Most of the responses of these people and most of our dealings with them show that they were not at all behind us in natural brightness of mind and pertinence.

The awesome magnificence of the cities of Cuzco and Mexico (and, among many similar things, the garden of that king in which all the trees, the fruits, and all the herbs were excellently fashioned in gold, and of such size and so arranged as they might be in an ordinary garden; and in his curio room were gold replicas of all the living creatures native to his country and its waters), and the beauty of their workmanship in jewelry, feathers, cotton, and painting, show that they were not behind us in industry either. But as for devoutness, observance of the laws, goodness, liberality, loyalty, and frankness, it served us well not to have as much as they: by their advantage in this they lost, sold, and betrayed themselves.

As for boldness and courage, as for firmness, constancy, resoluteness against pains and hunger and death, I would not fear to oppose the examples I could find among them to the most famous ancient examples that we have in the memories of our world on this side of the ocean. For as regards the men who subjugated them, take away the ruses and tricks that they used to deceive them, and the people's natural astonishment at seeing the unexpected arrival of bearded men, different in language, religion, shape, and countenance, from a part of the world so remote, where they had never imagined there was any sort of human habitation, mounted on great unknown monsters, opposed to men who had never seen not only a horse, but any sort of animal trained to carry and endure a man or any other burden; men equipped with a hard and shiny skin and a sharp and glittering weapon, against men who, for the miracle of a mirror or a knife, would exchange a great treasure in gold and pearls, and who had neither the knowledge nor the material by which, even in full leisure, they would pierce our steel; add to this the lightning and thunder of our cannon and harquebuses—capable of disturbing Caesar himself, if he had been surprised by them

with as little experience and in his time—against people
who were naked (except in some regions where the invention of some cotton fabric had reached them), without other arms at the most than bows, stones, sticks, and
wooden bucklers; people taken by surprise, under color of
friendship and good faith, by curiosity to see strange and
unknown things: eliminate this disparity, I say, and you
take from the conquerors the whole basis of so many
victories.

When I consider that indomitable ardor with which so
many thousands of men, women, and children came forth
and hurled themselves so many times into inevitable dangers for the defense of their gods and of their liberty,
and that noble, stubborn readiness to suffer all extremi-
ties and hardships, even death, rather than submit to the
domination of those by whom they had been so shamefully deceived (for some of them when captured chose
rather to let themselves perish of hunger and fasting than
to accept food from the hands of such basely victorious
enemies), I conclude that if anyone had attacked them
on equal terms, with equal arms, experience, and numbers,
it would have been just as dangerous for him as in any
other war we know of, and more so.

Why did not such a noble conquest fall to Alexander
or to those ancient Greeks and Romans? Why did not
such a great change and alteration of so many empires
and peoples fall into hands that would have gently polished and cleared away whatever was barbarous in them,
and would have strengthened and fostered the good seeds
that nature had produced in them, not only adding
to the cultivation of the earth and the adornment of cities
the arts of our side of the ocean, in so far as they would
have been necessary, but also adding the Greek and
Roman virtues to those originally in that region? What an
improvement that would have been, and what an amelioration for the entire globe, if the first examples of our conduct that were offered over there had called those peoples
to the admiration and imitation of virtue and had set up
between them and us a brotherly fellowship and under-

standing! How easy it would have been to make good use of souls so fresh, so famished to learn, and having, for the most part, such fine natural beginnings! On the contrary, we took advantage of their ignorance and inexperience to incline them the more easily toward treachery, lewdness, avarice, and every sort of inhumanity and cruelty, after the example and pattern of our ways. Who ever set the utility of commerce and trading at such a price? So many cities razed, so many nations exterminated, so many millions of people put to the sword, and the richest and most beautiful part of the world turned upside down, for the traffic in pearls and pepper! Base and mechanical victories! Never did ambition, never did public enmities, drive men against one another to such horrible hostilities and such miserable calamities.

Coasting the sea in quest of their mines, certain Spaniards landed in a fertile, pleasant, well-populated country, and made their usual declarations to its people: that they were peaceable men, coming from distant voyages, sent on behalf of the king of Castile, the greatest prince of the habitable world, to whom the Pope, representing God on earth, had given the principality of all the Indies; that if these people would be tributaries to him, they would be very kindly treated. They demanded of them food to eat and gold to be used in a certain medicine, and expounded to them the belief in one single God and the truth of our religion, which they advised them to accept, adding a few threats.

The answer was this: As for being peaceable, they did not look like it, if they were. As for their king, since he was begging, he must be indigent and needy; and he who had awarded their country to him must be a man fond of dissension, to go and give another person something that was not his and thus set him at strife with its ancient possessors. As for food, they would supply them. Gold they had little of, and it was a thing they held in no esteem, since it was useless to the service of their life, their sole concern being with passing life happily and pleasantly; however, they might boldly take any they could find, except what was employed in the service of their gods. As for one single God, the account had pleased them, but they did not want to change their religion, having followed it so advantageously for so long, and they were not accustomed to take counsel except of their friends and acquaintances. As for the threats, it was a sign of lack of judgment to threaten people whose nature and means were unknown to them. Thus they should promptly hurry up and vacate their land, for they were not accustomed to take in good part the civilities and declarations of armed strangers; otherwise they would do to them as they had done to these others—showing them the heads of some executed men around their city.

Rousseau and the "Noble Savage"

The impact of the new discoveries and the "natural man" revealed by the European explorers is evident in the writings of literary and philosophical figures of Europe. Not least in importance is Jean Jacques Rousseau, a portion of whose *Discourse upon the Origin and Foundation of the Inequality among Mankind*, first published in 1755, is reprinted below from the English translation published in London in 1761, pp. 114–18 and note, pp. 252–56. It has become fashionable for twentieth-century critics to ridicule the "noble savage" presumably "created" by such writers, but it is evident that the assumptions of twentieth-century writers about seventeenth- or eighteenth-century Indians must be examined as critically as the assumptions of the earlier writers. It is well to remember that the "noble savage" was created first of all by the explorers and missionaries whose accounts were utilized by such men as Rousseau. For a discussion of some of the problems involved in the matter, see Wilcomb E. Washburn, "A Moral History of Indian-White Relations: Needs and Opportunities for Study," *Ethnohistory*, Vol. IV, pp. 47–61 (Winter 1957).

Men no sooner began to set a Value upon each other, and know what Esteem was, than each laid claim to it, and it was no longer safe for any Man to refuse it to another. Hence the first Duties of Civility and Politeness, even among Savages; and hence every voluntary Injury became an Affront, as besides the Mischief, which resulted from it as an Injury, the Party offended was sure to find in it a Contempt for his Person more intolerable than the Mischief itself. It is thus that every Man,

punishing the Contempt expressed for him by others in
proportion to the value he set upon himself, the Effects
of Revenge became terrible, and Men learned to be
sanguinary and cruel. Such precisely was the Degree attained by most of the savage Nations with whom we are
acquainted. And it is for want of sufficiently distinguishing
Ideas, and observing at how great a Distance these People
were from the first state of Nature, that so many Authors
have hastily concluded that Man is naturally cruel, and
requires a regular System of Police to be reclaimed;
whereas nothing can be more gentle than him in his primitive State, when placed by Nature at an equal Distance
from the Stupidity of Brutes, and the pernicious good
Sense of civilized Man; and equally confined by Instinct
and Reason to the Care of providing against the Mischief which threatens him, he is withheld by natural Compassion from doing any Injury to others, so far from being
ever so little prone even to return that which he has received. For according to the Axiom of the wise Locke,
Where there is no Property, there can be no Injury.

But we must take notice, that the Society now formed
and the Relations now established among Men required
in them Qualities different from those, which they derived
from their primitive Constitution; that as a Sense of Morality began to insinuate itself into human Actions, and every
Man, before the enacting of Laws, was the only Judge and
Avenger of the Injuries he had received, that Goodness of
Heart suitable to the pure State of Nature by no Means
suited infant Society; that it was necessary Punishments
should become severer in the same Proportion that the
Opportunities of offending became more frequent, and
the Dread of Vengeance add Strength to the too weak
curb of the Law. Thus, tho' Men were become less patient,
and natural Compassion had already suffered some Alteration, this Period of the Development of the human Faculties, holding a just Mean between the Indolence of the
primitive State, and the petulant Activity of Self-love,
must have been the happiest and most durable Epocha.

The more we reflect on this State, the more convinced we shall be, that it was the least subject of any to Revolutions, the best for Man,[1] and that nothing could have drawn

[1] It is very remarkable, that for so many Years past that the *Europeans* have been toiling to make the Savages of different Parts of the World conform to their Manner of living, they have not as yet been able to prevail upon one of them, not even with the Assistance of the Christian Religion; for though our Missionaries sometimes make Christians, they never make civilized Men of them. There is no getting the better of their invincible Reluctance to adopt our Manners and Customs. If these poor Savages are as unhappy as some People would have them, by what inconceivable Depravation of Judgment is it that they so constantly refuse to be governed as we are, or to live happy among us; whereas we read in a thousand Places that *Frenchmen* and other *Europeans* have voluntarily taken Refuge, nay, spent their whole Lives among them, without ever being able to quit so strange a kind of Life; and that even very sensible Missionaries have been known to regret with Tears the calm and innocent Days they had spent among those Men we so much despise. Should [it] be observed that they are not knowing enough to judge soundly of their Condition and ours, I must answer, that the Valuation of Happiness is not so much the Business of the Understanding as of the Will. Besides, this Objection may still more forcibly be retorted upon ourselves; for our Ideas are more remote from that Disposition of Mind requisite for us to conceive the Relish, which the Savages find in their Way of Living, than the Ideas of the Savages from those by which they may conceive the Relish we find in ours. In fact, very few Observations [are necessary] to shew them that all our Labours are confined to two Objects, namely the Conveniencies of Life and the Esteem of others. But how shall we be able to form to ourselves any Notion of that kind of Pleasure, which a Savage takes in spending his Days alone in the Heart of a Forest, or in Fishing, or in blowing into a wretched Flute without ever being able to fetch a single Note from it, or ever giving himself any Trouble to learn how to make a better Use of it.

Savages have been often brought to *Paris*, to *London*, and to other Places; and no Pains omitted to fill them with high Ideas of our Luxury, our Riches, and all our most useful and curious Arts; yet they were never seen to express more than a stupid Admiration at such Things, without the least Appearance of coveting them. Among other Stories I remember one concerning the Chief of some *North-America* Indians brought about thirty Years ago to the Court of *London*. A thousand Things were laid before him, in order to find out what Present would him out of it but some fatal Accident, which, for the public good, should never have happened. The Example of the Savages, most of whom have been found in this Condition, seems to confirm that Mankind was formed ever to remain in it, that this Condition is the real Youth of the World, and that all ulterior Improvements have been so many Steps, in Appearance towards the Perfection of Individuals, but in Fact towards the Decrepitness of the Species.

---

be acceptable to him, without hitting upon any one thing that he seemed to like. Our Arms appeared heavy and inconvenient to him; our Shoes pinched his Feet; our Cloaths incumbered his Body; he would accept of nothing; at length, he was observed to take up a Blanket, and seemed to take great Pleasure in wrapping himself up in it. You must allow, said the *Europeans* about him, that this, at least, is an useful Piece of Furniture? Yes, answered the *Indian*, I think it almost as good as the Skin of a Beast. And even this he would not have allowed, had he wore both under a Shower.

Perhaps I may be told that it is Habit, which, making every Man like best his own Way of Life, hinders the Savages from perceiving what is good in ours. But upon this Footing it must appear at least very extraordinary, that Habit should have more Power to maintain in Savages a Relish for their Misery, than in *Europeans* for their Happiness. But to make to this last Objection an Answer which will not admit the least Reply, without speaking of all the young Savages whom no Pains have been able to civilize; particularly the *Greenlanders* and *Icelanders*, whom Attempts have been made to rear and educate in *Denmark*, and who either pined away with Grief ashore, or perished at Sea in attempting to swim back to their own Country; . . .

DOCUMENT 98

Cannibalism

The existence, extent, and meaning of cannibalism in the New World is a subject concerning which there is much dispute, much confusion, and many theories. The Spanish frequently utilized the charge to justify hostilities against the Indians. The revulsion felt by Europe at the practice is brought out in the following passage from Edward Bancroft's *Essay on the Natural History of Guiana, in South America,* pp. 258–63 (London: 1769). Bancroft's *Essay,* which relates principally to the Dutch territories in Guiana on the northern coast of South America, notes the controversy in Europe over the existence of the habit, and contributes a moral critique of the practice and analogous European practices. The reader interested in considering the anthropological evidence concerning the nature and extent of the practice can profitably start with E. M. Loeb, *The Blood Sacrifice Complex,* Memoirs of the American Anthropological Association, No. 30 (1923).

The *Carribbee Indians* are at perpetual variance with the *Spaniards,* and frequently commit hostilities on their settlements at the River *Oronoque.* They retain a tradition of an *English* Chief, who many years since landed amongst them, and encouraged them to persevere in enmity to the *Spaniards,* promising to return and settle amongst them, and afford them assistance; and it is said that they still preserve an *English* Jack, which he left them, that they might distinguish his countrymen. This was undoubtedly Sir *Walter Raleigh,* who, in the year 1595, made a descent on the Coast of *Guiana,* in search of the fabulous Golden City of *Manoa del Dorado,* and conquered Fort *Joseph,* on the River *Oronoque.*

At the late insurrection of the Slaves in the Colony of *Berbice*, these *Indians* were engaged, by the Governor of *Essequebo*, to fight against the Rebel Negroes, many of whom they killed, as appeared by the number of hands which they brought away, and for which they received a considerable reward. But an adherence to truth obliges me to inform you of a circumstance relative to this expedition, which I am persuaded you will read with disgust; this is, that they ate the bodies of those Negroes whom they killed on this occasion: an action, which is considered by *European* nations as so horrid and unnatural, that the very existence of Cannibals has been lately denied by several modern Compilers of History, notwithstanding the repeated attestations of Travellers to the contrary. For persons, however, who have never quitted their native country, to determine concerning the manners of distant unknown nations, and, on the strength of plausible appearances, to impeach the veracity of Travellers, and positively deny those things which, at most, they are but permitted to doubt, is a culpable temerity, which well deserves reprehension. I must, however, do these *Indians* the justice to declare, that they never eat any of the human species, except their enemies killed in battle, to which they think they have as good a right as those animals by whom they would otherwise be eaten. But you will doubtless think it unnatural for any animal to devour those of its species, even when necessarily killed in self-defence; and in this I am of your opinion; tho' I am sensible that we have been educated in a state of civilization, so different from that of Nature, that we are but ill able to determine what is, or what is not natural. It is certainly more unnatural to kill each other by unnecessary wars, than to eat the bodies of those we have killed: the crime consists in killing, not in eating, as the worm and vultur testify, that human flesh is by no means sacred. But tho' civilized nations abhor eating, they are familiarized to the custom of killing each other, which they practise with less remorse than the Savages. But custom is able to reconcile the mind to the most unnatural objects. What but habitude and custom could enable us to survey, without an involuntary horror, the mangled carcases of inoffensive animals, exposed in a *London* market, who have been killed to gratify our appetites, and whose care and sollicitude for the preservation of life, demonstrates that they enjoyed a degree of happiness therein, of which at least it is cruelty to deprive them. Man's right over the lives of subordinate animals I will not dispute; the apparent difference in the mechanism of the masticatory and digestive organs of carnivorous and granivorous animals, evidently demonstrates, that Nature designed some for the prey of others: But mankind have a natural capacity for subsisting indiscriminately, either on animal or vegetable food; and numerous instances testify, that the latter is most conducive to health and longevity; and therefore not only humanity, but self-interest, conspire to engage us at least to abridge the quantity of animal food, which at present we devour with so much avidity.

Document 99

On the Nature of Man in America

The question of the nature of man in America and the effects of the environment on him fascinated the philosophers of the eighteenth-century enlightenment of Europe. Many wrote without the benefit of direct knowledge of the scene. Thomas Jefferson's letter of June 7, 1785, to the Marquis de Chastellux, discusses some of these theories and gives his opinion on the nature of the Indian in America. The letter is taken from *The Papers of Thomas Jefferson*, edited by Julian P. Boyd, Vol. VIII, pp. 184–86 (Princeton: Princeton University Press, 1953).

DEAR SIR   Paris June 7, 1785

I have been honoured with the receipt of your letter of the 2d. instant, and am to thank you, as I do sincerely for the partiality with which you receive the copy of the Notes on my country. As I can answer for the facts therein reported on my own observation, and have admitted none on the report of others which were not supported by evidence sufficient to command my own assent, I am not afraid that you should make any extracts you please for the Journal de physique which come within their plan of publication. The strictures on slavery and on the constitution of Virginia are not of that kind, and they are the parts which I do not wish to have made public, at least till I know whether their publication would do most harm or good. It is possible that in my own country these strictures might produce an irritation which would indispose the people towards the two great objects I have in view, that is the emancipation of their slaves, and the settlement of their constitution on a firmer and more permanent basis.

If I learn from thence, that they will not produce that effect, I have printed and reserved just copies enough to be able to give one to every young man at the College. It is to them I look, to the rising generation, and not to the one now in power for these great reformations. The other copy delivered at your hotel was for Monsr. de Buffon. I meant to ask the favour of you to have it sent to him, as I was ignorant how to do it. I have one also for Monsr. Daubenton: but being utterly unknown to him I cannot take the liberty of presenting it till I can do it through some common acquaintance.

I will beg leave to say here a few words on the general question of the degeneracy of animals in America. 1. As to the degeneracy of the man of Europe transplanted to America, it is no part of Monsr. de Buffon's system. He goes indeed within one step of it, but he stops there. The Abbé Raynal alone has taken that step. Your knowledge of America enables you to judge this question, to say whether the lower class of people in America, are less informed and less susceptible of information than the lower class in Europe: and whether those in America who have received such an education as that country can give, are less improved by it than Europeans of the same degree of education. 2. As to the Aboriginal man of America, I know of no respectable evidence on which the opinion of his inferiority of genius has been founded but that of Don Ulloa. As to Robertson, he never was in America, he relates nothing on his own knowledge, he is a compiler only of the relations of others, and a mere translator of the opinions of Monsr. de Buffon. I should as soon therefore add the translators of Robertson to the witnesses of this fact, as himself. Paw, the beginner of this charge, was a compiler from the works of others; and of the most unlucky description; for he seems to have read the writings of travellers only to collect and republish their lies. It is really remarkeable that in three volumes 12mo. of small print it is scarcely possible to find one truth, and yet that the author should be able to produce authority for every fact he states, as he says he can. Don Ulloa's testimony is of the

most respectable. He wrote of what he saw. But he saw
the Indian of South America only, and that after he had
passed through ten generations of slavery. It is very unfair,
from this sample, to judge of the natural genius of this
race of men: and after supposing that Don Ulloa had not
sufficiently calculated the allowance which should be made
for this circumstance, we do him no injury in considering
the picture he draws of the present Indians of S. America
as no picture of what their ancestors were 300 years ago.
It is in N. America we are to seek their original character:
and I am safe in affirming that the proofs of genius given
by the Indians of N. America, place them on a level with
Whites in the same uncultivated state. The North of Europe furnishes subjects enough for comparison with them,
and for a proof of their equality. I have seen some thousands myself, and conversed much with them, and have
found in them a male, sound understanding. I have had
much information from men who had lived among them,
and whose veracity and good sense were so far known to
me as to establish a reliance on their information. They
have all agreed in bearing witness in favour of the genius
of this people. As to their bodily strength, their manners
rendering it disgraceful to labour, those muscles employed
in labour will be weaker with them than with the European labourer: but those which are exerted in the chase
and those faculties which are employed in the tracing an
enemy or a wild beast, in contriving ambuscades for him,
and in carrying them through their execution, are much
stronger than with us, because they are more exercised. I
beleive the Indian then to be in body and mind equal to
the whiteman. I have supposed the blackman, in his present state, might not be so. But it would be hazardous to
affirm that, equally cultivated for a few generations, he
would not become so. 3. As to the inferiority of the other
animals of America, without more facts I can add nothing
to what I have said in my Notes. As to the theory of Monsr.
de Buffon that heat is friendly and moisture adverse to
the production of large animals, I am lately furnished with
a fact by Doctr. Franklin which proves the air of London

and of Paris to be more humid than that of Philadelphia, and so creates a suspicion that the opinion of the superior humidity of America may perhaps have been too hastily adopted. And supposing that fact admitted, I think the physical reasonings urged to shew that in a moist country animals must be small, and that in a hot one they must be large, are not built on the basis of experiment. These questions however cannot be decided ultimately at this day. More facts must be collected, and more time flow off, before the world will be ripe for decision. In the mean time doubt is wisdom.

I have been fully sensible of the anxieties of your situation, and that your attentions were wholly consecrated, where alone they were wholly due, to the succour of friendship and worth. However much I prize your society I wait with patience the moment when I can have it without taking what is due to another. In the mean time I am solaced with the hope of possessing your friendship, and that it is not ungrateful to you to receive assurances of that with which I have the honour to be Dear Sir Your most obedient and most humble servt., TH: JEFFERSON

Indian Oratory

American schoolboys no longer find Logan's speech in their readers, as did their predecessors in the nineteenth century. Nevertheless, Indian eloquence in general, and Logan's speech in particular, continue to attract the interest of historian and the general reader. Thomas Jefferson was one of many to comment on this aspect of Indian character. In his *Notes on the State of Virginia*, first published in London in 1787, he discussed Logan's speech, and its background, at length. The following passage is taken from William Peden's edition of Jefferson's *Notes on the State of Virginia*, pp. 62–63 (Chapel Hill: University of North Carolina Press, 1955). Appendix No. 4, pp. 226–258, contains documents relative to the murder of Logan's family. The historical accuracy of Logan's famous speech of 1774 and its great influence in later American literature, politics, and education is discussed in Edward D. Seeber's "Critical Views on Logan's Speech," *Journal of American Folklore*, Vol. 60, pp. 130–46 (1947).

The principles of their society forbidding all compulsion, they are to be led to duty and to enterprize by personal influence and persuasion. Hence eloquence in council, bravery and address in war, become the foundations of all consequence with them. To these acquirements all their faculties are directed. Of their bravery and address in war we have multiplied proofs, because we have been the subjects on which they were exercised. Of their eminence in oratory we have fewer examples, because it is displayed chiefly in their own councils. Some, however, we have of very superior lustre. I may challenge the whole orations of

Demosthenes and Cicero, and of any more eminent orator, if Europe has furnished more eminent, to produce a single passage, superior to the speech of Logan, a Mingo chief, to Lord Dunmore, when governor of this state. And, as a testimony of their talents in this line, I beg leave to introduce it, first stating the incidents necessary for understanding it. In the spring of the year 1774, a robbery was committed by some Indians on certain land-adventurers on the river Ohio. The whites in that quarter, according to their custom, undertook to punish this outrage in a summary way. Captain Michael Cresap, and a certain Daniel Great-house, leading on these parties, surprized, at different times, travelling and hunting parties of the Indians, having their women and children with them, and murdered many. Among these were unfortunately the family of Logan, a chief celebrated in peace and war, and long distinguished as the friend of the whites. This unworthy return provoked his vengeance. He accordingly signalized himself in the war which ensued. In the autumn of the same year a decisive battle was fought at the mouth of the Great Kanhaway, between the collected forces of the Shawanese, Mingoes, and Delawares, and a detachment of the Virginia militia. The Indians were defeated, and sued for peace. Logan however disdained to be seen among the suppliants. But, lest the sincerity of a treaty should be distrusted, from which so distinguished a chief absented himself, he sent by a messenger the following speech to be delivered to Lord Dunmore.

"I appeal to any white man to say, if ever he entered Logan's cabin hungry, and he gave him not meat; if ever he came cold and naked, and he clothed him not. During the course of the last long and bloody war, Logan remained idle in his cabin, an advocate for peace. Such was my love for the whites, that my countrymen pointed as they passed, and said, 'Logan is the friend of white men.' I had even thought to have lived with you, but for the injuries of one man. Col. Cresap, the last spring, in cold blood, and unprovoked, murdered all the relations of Logan, not sparing even my women and children. There runs not a drop of my blood in the veins of any living creature. This called on me for revenge. I have sought it: I have killed many: I have fully glutted my vengeance. For my country, I rejoice at the beams of peace. But do not harbour a thought that mine is the joy of fear. Logan never felt fear. He will not turn on his heel to save his life. Who is there to mourn for Logan?—Not one."

DOCUMENT 101

An Early New York Orator

The League of the Iroquois, often known as the Five (later Six) Nations, or the Iroquois Confederation, has fascinated generations of white men. Among the admired characteristics have been the effectiveness of the League in dealing with Corlear or Corlaer (the Iroquois name first for the Dutch and later for the English authorities of New York and Albany) and with Yonnondio or Onontio (the Iroquois name for the French authority in Canada). De Witt Clinton was not only a successful American politician of the early nineteenth century, but a student of the Iroquois, and the following passage, concerning his view of Iroquois eloquence, and an example of it, are taken from William W. Campbell, *The Life and Writings of De Witt Clinton,* pp. 237–39, and Appendix, pp. 365–69 (New York: 1849). A more stilted translation of the speeches is contained in Reuben Gold Thwaites' edition of Baron de Lahontan's *New Voyages to North-America,* 2 vols.; Vol. I, pp. 77–84 (Chicago: A. C. McClurg & Co., 1905), reprinted from the English edition of 1703.

The Confederates were as celebrated for their eloquence, as for their military skill and political wisdom. Popular, or free governments have, in all ages, been the congenial soil of oratory. And it is, indeed, all important in institutions merely advisory; where persuasion must supply the place of coercion; where there is no magistrate to execute, no military to compel; and where the only sanction of law is the controlling power of public opinion. Eloquence being, therefore, considered so essential, must always be a great standard of personal merit, a certain road to popular favor, and an universal passport to public honors. These combined inducements operated with powerful force on the mind of the Indian; and there is little doubt but that oratory was studied with as much care and application among the Confederates, as it was in the stormy democracies of the eastern hemisphere. I do not pretend to assert that there were, as at Athens and Rome, established schools and professional teachers for the purpose; but I say that it was an attainment to which they devoted themselves, and to which they bent the whole force of their faculties. Their models of eloquence were to be found, not in books, but in the living orators of their local and national assemblies; their children, at an early period of life, attended their councils fires, in order to observe the passing scenes, and to receive the lessons of wisdom. Their rich and vivid imagery was drawn from the sublime scenery of nature, and their ideas were derived from the laborious operations of their own minds, and from the experience and wisdom of their ancient sages.

The most remarkable difference existed between the Confederates and the other Indian nations with respect to eloquence. You may search in vain in the records and writings of the past, or in events of the present times, for a single model of eloquence among the Algonkins, the Abenaquis, the Delawares, the Shawanese, or any other nation of Indians, except the Iroquois. The few scintillations of intellectual light—the faint glimmerings of genius which are sometimes to be found in their speeches, are evidently derivative, and borrowed from the Confederates.

Considering the interpreters who have undertaken to give the meaning of Indian speeches, it is not a little surprising that some of them should approach so near to perfection. The major part of the interpreters were illiterate persons, sent among them to conciliate their favor, by making useful or ornamental implements; or they were prisoners who learnt the Indian language during their captivity. The Reverend Mr. Kirkland, a missionary among the Oneidas, and sometimes a public interpreter, was indeed a man of liberal education; but those who have seen him officiate at public treaties must recollect how incompetent he was to infuse the fire of Indian oratory into his expressions; how he labored for words and how feeble and inelegant his language. Oral is more difficult than written interpretation or translation. In the latter case, there is no pressure of time, and we have ample opportunity to weigh the most suitable words, to select the most elegant expressions, and to fathom the sense of the author; but in the former case, we are called upon to act immediately; no time for deliberation is allowed; and the first ideas that occur must be pressed into the service of the interpreter. At an ancient treaty, a female captive officiated in that capacity; and at a treaty held in 1722, at Albany, the speeches of the Indians were first rendered into Dutch, and then translated into English. I except from these remarks, the speech of the Onondaga chief, Garangula, to M. Delabarre, delivered on the occasion which I have before mentioned. This was interpreted by Monsieur Le Maine, a French Jesuit, and recorded on the spot by Baron La Hontan—men of enlightened and cultivated minds, from whom it has been borrowed by Colden, Smith, Herriot, Trumbull, and Williams. I believe it to be impossible to find, in all the effusions of ancient or modern oratory, a speech more appropriate and more convincing. Under the veil of respectful profession it conveys the most biting irony; and while it abounds with rich and splendid imagery, it contains the most solid reasoning. I place it in the same rank with the celebrated speech of Logan; and I cannot but express astonishment at the conduct of two respectable writers, who have represented this interesting interview, and this sublime display of intellectual power, as "a scold between the French generals and an old Indian."

. . . .

Monsieur De La Barre's Speech, addressed to Garangula, an Onondaga Chief, the Indians and French officers at the same time forming a circle round about him.

"The king, my master, being informed that the Five Nations have often infringed the peace, has ordered me to come hither with a guard, and to send Ohguesse to the Onondagas, to bring the chief sachems to my camp. The intention of the great king is, that you and I may smoke the calumet of peace together; but on this condition, that you promise me, in the name of the Senecas, Cayugas, Onondagas, and Mohawks, to give entire satisfaction and reparation to his subjects, and for the future never to molest them.

"The Senecas, Cayugas, Onondagas, Oneidas, and Mohawks, have robbed and abused all the traders that were passing to the Illinois and Miamies, and other Indian nations, the children of my king; they have acted, on these occasions, contrary to the treaty of peace with my predecessor. I am ordered, therefore, to demand satisfaction; and to tell them, that in case of refusal, or their plundering us any more, that I have express orders to declare war. This belt confirms my words. The warriors of the Five Nations have conducted the English into the lakes, which belong to the king, my master, and brought the English among the nations that are his children to destroy the trade of his subjects, and to withdraw these nations from him. They have carried the English thither, notwithstanding the prohibition of the late Governor of New York, who foresaw the risk that both they and you would run. I am willing to forget those things; but if ever the like should happen for the future, I have express orders to declare war against you. This belt confirms my words. Your warriors have made several barbarous incursions on the Illinois and Miamies. They have massacred men, women, and children; they have made many of these nations prisoners, who thought themselves safe in their villages in time of peace. These people, who are my king's children, must not be your slaves: you must give them their liberty, and send them back into their own country. If the Five Nations shall refuse to do this, I have express orders to declare war against them. This belt confirms my words.

"This is what I have to say to Garangula, that he may

carry to the Senecas, Onondagas, Oneidas, Cayugas, and Mohawks, the declaration which the king, my master, has commanded me to make. He doth not wish them to force him to send a great army to Cadarackui Fort, to begin a war, which must be fatal to them. He would be sorry that this fort, that was the work of peace, should become the prison of your warriors. We must endeavor on both sides to prevent such misfortunes. The French, who are the brethren and friends of the Five Nations, will never trouble their repose, provided that the satisfaction which I demand be given; and that the treaties of peace be hereafter observed. I shall be extremely grieved if my words do not produce the effect which I expect from them; for then I shall be obliged to join with the Governor of New York, who is commanded by his master to assist me, and burn the castles of the Five Nations, and destroy you. This belt confirms my words."

Garangula, after walking five or six times round the circle, answered the French Governor, who sat in an elbow chair, in the following strain:

"YONNONDIO,

"I honor you, and the warriors that are with me likewise honor you. Your interpreter has finished your speech: I now begin mine. My words make haste to reach your ears; hearken to them.

"Yonnondio, you must have believed, when you left Quebec, that the sun had burnt up all the forests which render our country inaccessible to the French, or that the lakes had so far overflown the banks that they had surrounded our castles, and that it was impossible for us to get out of them. Yes, Yonnondio, surely you must have dreamt so; and the curiosity of seeing so great a wonder has brought you so far. Now you are undeceived, since that I and the warriors here present, are come to assure you that the Senecas, Cayugas, Onondagas, Oneidas, and Mohawks, are yet alive. I thank you in their name for bringing back into their country the calumet which your predecessor received from their hands. It was happy for you that you left under ground that murdering hatchet which has been so often dyed in the blood of the French. Hear, Yonnondio: I do not sleep; I have my eyes open, and the sun which enlightens me, discovers to me a great captain at the head of a company of soldiers, who speaks as if he were dreaming. He says that he only came to the lake to smoke on the great calumet with the Onondagas; but Garangula says that he sees the contrary; that it was to knock them on the head if sickness had not weakened the arms of the French.

"I see Yonnondio raving in a camp of sick men, whose lives the Great Spirit has saved by inflicting this sickness on them. Hear, Yonnondio: our women had taken their clubs, our children and old men had carried their bows and arrows into the heart of your camp, if our warriors had not disarmed them, and kept them back, when your messenger Ohguesse came to our castles. It is done, and I have said it. Hear, Yonnondio: we plundered none of the French but those that carried guns, powder, and ball to the Twightwies and Chictaghicks, because those arms might have cost us our lives. Herein we follow the example of the Jesuits, who stove all the kegs of rum brought to our castles, lest the drunken Indians should knock them on the head. Our warriors have not beaver enough to pay for all these arms that they have taken; and our old men are not afraid of the war. This belt preserves my words.

"We carried the English into our lakes to trade there with the Utawawas and Quatoghies as the Andirondacks brought the French to our castles to carry on a trade, which the English say is theirs. We are born free. We neither depend on Yonnondio nor Corlear.

"We may go where we please, and carry with us whom we please. If your allies be your slaves, use them as such. Command them to receive no other but your people. This belt preserves my words.

"We knocked the Twightwies and Chictaghicks on the head because they had cut down the trees of peace which were the limits of our country. They had hunted beavers on our land. They had acted contrary to the customs of all Indians; for they left none of the beavers alive: they killed both male and female. They brought the Satanas into the country to take part with them, after they had concerted ill designs against us. We have done less than either the English or French, that have usurped the lands of so many Indian nations, and chased them from their own country. This belt preserves my words.

"Hear, Yonnondio; what I say is the voice of all the Five Nations: hear what they answer. Open your ears to what they speak. The Senecas, Cayugas, Onondagas, Oneidas, and the Mohawks say, that when they buried the hatchet at Cadarackui (in the presence of your predecessor) in the middle of the fort, they planted the tree of peace in the same place, to be there carefully preserved, that in place of a retreat for soldiers, that fort might be a rendezvous for merchants; that in place of arms and ammunition of war, beavers and merchandize should only enter there.

"Hear, Yonnondio: take care for the future, that so great a number of soldiers as appear there, do not choke the tree of peace planted in so small a fort. It will be a great loss if after it had so easily taken root you should stop its growth, and prevent its covering your country and ours with its branches. I assure you, in the name of the Five Nations, that our warriors shall dance to the calumet of peace under its leaves, and shall remain quiet on their mats, and shall never dig up the hatchet till their brother Yonnondio, or Corlear, shall, either jointly or separately, endeavor to attack the country which the Great Spirit has given to our ancestors. This belt preserves my words; and this other, the authority which the Five Nations have given me."

Then Garangula, addressing himself to Monsieur La Main, said: "Take courage, Ohguesse; you have spirit, speak—explain my words; forget nothing; tell all that your brethren and friends say to Yonnondio, your governor, by the mouth of Garangula, who loves you, and desires you to accept of this present of beaver, and take part with me in my feast, to which I invite you. This present of beaver is sent to Yonnondio on the part of the Five Nations.

Melville on Parkman's Indians

The literary image of the American Indian is varied and contradictory. "Noble savage"? "Dirty savage"? Reality? Imagination? Writers rarely doubted their ability to judge the Indian. The reality was concealed amidst the lost historical facts of the past, the unborn theories of modern anthropological knowledge, and the psychological problem of how one knows what he thinks he knows. Herman Melville, best known for his *Moby-Dick*, but also author of two romances of the South Seas, *Typee* and *Omoo*, based on his personal knowledge of the Pacific natives—an acquaintance more intimate than Francis Parkman's knowledge of the Western Indians—wrote the following anonymous review of Parkman's *The California and Oregon Trail* in *The Literary World*, Vol. IV, p. 291, (March 31, 1849).

In a brief and appropriate preface Mr. Parkman adverts to the representations of the Indian character given by poets and novelists, which he asserts are for the most part mere creations of fancy. He adds that "the Indian is certainly entitled to a high rank among savages, but his good qualities are not those of an Uncas or Outalissa." Now, this is not to be gainsaid. But when in the body of the book we are informed that it is difficult for any white man, after a domestication among the Indians, to hold them much better than brutes; when we are told, too, that to such a person, the slaughter of an Indian is indifferent as the slaughter of a buffalo; with all deference, we beg leave to dissent.

It is too often the case, that civilized beings sojourning among savages soon come to regard them with disdain and contempt. But though in many cases this feeling is almost natural, it is not defensible; and it is wholly wrong. Why should we contemn them? Because we are better than they? Assuredly not; for herein we are rebuked by the story of the Publican and the Pharisee. Because, then, that in many things we are happier? But this should be ground for commiseration, not disdain. Xavier and Elliot despised not the savages; and had Newton or Milton dwelt among them they would not have done so. When we affect to contemn savages, we should remember that by so doing we asperse our own progenitors; for they were savages also. Who can swear, that among the naked British barbarians sent to Rome to be stared at more than 1500 years ago, the ancestor of Bacon might not have been found? Why, among the very Thugs of India, or the bloody Dyaks of Borneo, exists the germ of all that is intellectually elevated and grand. We are all of us—Anglo-Saxons, Dyaks, and Indians—sprung from one head, and made in one image. And if we regret this brotherhood now, we shall be forced to join hands hereafter. A misfortune is not a fault; and good luck is not meritorious. The savage is born a savage; and the civilized being but inherits his civilization, nothing more.

Let us not disdain, then, but pity. And wherever we recognise the image of God, let us reverence it, though it hung from the gallows.

Parkman on Cooper's Indians

The fastidious Bostonian Francis Parkman set out consciously to write the history of the American forest, and he found himself more attracted to the forest than to its aboriginal inhabitants. His histories dealt with the great struggle for the North American continent in the seventeenth and eighteenth centuries, in the eastern part of the continent, but his acquaintance with Indians was principally with nineteenth-century Plains Indians already affected by white civilization. Nevertheless, Parkman spoke with customary assuredness in all matters, and, in an anonymous review of the novels of James Fenimore Cooper, let the public know how far Cooper's Indians failed to measure up to his standard. The following quotation is from the *North American Review*, Vol. LXXIV, pp. 150–52 (January 1852).

The merit of a novelist is usually measured less by his mere power of description than by his skill in delineating character. The permanency of Cooper's reputation must, as it seems to us, rest upon three or four finely conceived and admirably executed portraits. We do not allude to his Indian characters, which it must be granted, are for the most part either superficially or falsely drawn; while the long conversations which he puts into their mouths, are as truthless as they are tiresome. Such as they are, however, they have been eagerly copied by a legion of the smaller poets and novel writers; so that, jointly with Thomas Campbell, Cooper is responsible for the fathering of those aboriginal heroes, lovers, and sages, who have long formed a petty nuisance in our literature. The portraits of which we have spoken are all those of white men, from humble ranks of society, yet not of a mean or vulgar stamp. Conspicuous before them all stands the well known figure of Leatherstocking. The life and character of this personage are contained in a series of five independent novels, entitled, in honor of him, The Leatherstocking Tales. Cooper has been censured, and even ridiculed, for this frequent reproduction of his favorite hero, which, it is affirmed, argues poverty of invention; and yet there is not one of the tales in question with which we would willingly part. To have drawn such a character is in itself sufficient honor; and had Cooper achieved nothing else, this alone must have insured him a wide and merited renown. There is something admirably felicitous in the conception of this hybrid offspring of civilization and barbarism, in whom uprightness, kindliness, innate philosophy, and the truest moral perceptions are joined with the wandering instincts and hatred of restraint which stamp the Indian or the Bedouin. Nor is the character in the least unnatural. The white denizens of the forest and the prairie are often among the worst, though never among the meanest, of mankind; but it is equally true, that where the moral instincts are originally strong, they may find nutriment and growth among the rude scenes and grand associations of the wilderness. Men as true, generous, and kindly as Leatherstocking may still be found among the perilous solitudes of the West. The quiet, unostentatious courage of Cooper's hero had its counterpart in the character of Daniel Boone; and the latter had the same unaffected love of nature which forms so pleasing a feature in the mind of Leatherstocking.

Civilization has a destroying as well as a creating power. It is exterminating the buffalo and the Indian, over whose fate too many lamentations, real or affected, have been sounded for us to renew them here. It must, moreover, eventually sweep from before it a class of men, its own precursors and pioneers, so remarkable both in their virtues and their faults, that few will see their extinction without regret. Of these men Leatherstocking is the representative; and though in him the traits of the individual are quite as prominent as those of the class, yet his character is not on this account less interesting, or less worthy of permanent remembrance. His life conveys in some sort an epitome of American history, during one of its most busy and decisive periods. At first, we find him a lonely young hunter in what was then the wilderness of New York. Ten or twelve years later, he is playing his part manfully in the Old French War. After the close of the Revolution, we meet him again on the same spot where he was first introduced to us; but now every thing is changed. The solitary margin of the Otsego lake is transformed into the seat of a growing settlement, and the hunter, oppressed by the restraints of society, turns his aged footsteps westward in search of his congenial solitudes. At length, we discover him for the last time, an octogenarian trapper, far out on the prairies of the West. It is clear that the successive stages of his retreat from society could not well be presented in a single story, and that the repetition which has been charged against Cooper as a fault was indispensable to the development of his design.

DOCUMENT 104

Greenough's Rescue Group

Probably no image of Indian-white relations has maintained itself in the historical consciousness of the American people better than that captured in Horatio Greenough's "Rescue Group" that formerly graced the steps of the East Front of the Capitol (Plate 30, following page 334). Contracted for in 1838 and finished in 1851 in Florence, Italy, the sculpture shows an Indian stayed in his attempt to scalp a helpless white family. The dramatic group served as a model for numerous illustrations, such as the lithograph (not reproduced) entitled "Daniel Boone Protects his Family" (New York: 1874), and, more importantly, summarized and symbolized, in shorthand form, the prevailing white view of the Indian-white relationship: the Indian male representing the strange and savage threat to the white mother and child, rescued at the last moment by the white male.

During the renovation of the Capitol in 1959 the figures were temporarily removed from the East Front. They have not been put back. Some friends of the Indian have urged that they not be returned to public view. These critics have been joined by others who feel that the symbolism is no longer pertinent if, indeed, it ever was.

King Philip and the English: One View

The difficulty of learning the truth about Indian-white relations is illustrated in the following two selections, both dealing with the impact of the war of King Philip, a Wampanoag, with the New England colonies in 1675–76. The first selection is from John Gorham Palfrey's *History of New England during the Stuart Dynasty*, 3 vols.; Vol. III, pp. 216–19, 222–23 (Boston: Little, Brown & Co., 1858–64). Palfrey's footnotes have been omitted.

That in such circumstances [those brought on by King Philip's War] the Colonists should have become intensely exasperated, may well be supposed. A sense of enormous ingratitude on the part of their assailants deepened their resentment. If, in single instances, injustice or unkindness had been done to Indians, it had been done contrary to law, by vagabonds such as infest every community, and whom no community is able absolutely to control. They who had the management of affairs knew that, as far as they and the government which they represented were concerned, there was no act of theirs, whether of commission or of omission, of which the natives could rightfully complain. The government had not disturbed their homes; it had bought their lands as often as it had desired to buy and they were disposed to sell, and, when they did not wish to sell, it had let them alone. With the best exertion of its power, it had restrained its subjects from cheating or otherwise maletreating them. In tenderness to their rights, it had refused to sanction contracts made with them by individuals for their lands, on account of their exposure to be circumvented in such dealings. With a solicitous

care, it had devised remedies for them against all wrongs
to which they were liable. It had regulated, with a humane
regard for their advantage, that commerce in articles of
their production, which would give them an opportunity
to rise from the scarcely human life, which hitherto they
had led, to the decencies and comforts of civilization. It
had freely offered to them the benefits of instruction in
various departments of that knowledge by which man advances in dignity and happiness. It had been at great trouble and expense to impart to them what in the estimation
of the giver was the most precious of all gifts,—the saving
knowledge of Christianity; and in this disinterested labor
it had been flattered with the hope of much success. Looking for better things hereafter, it had borne with their
frequent contumacy; and while, for the sake of both parties, it had maintained a firm authority, it had aimed to
carry restraint no further than was demanded for security.

And now, without provocation and without warning,
they had given full sway to the inhuman passions of their
savage nature. They had broken out into a wild riot of
pillage, arson, and massacre. By night they had crept up,
with murderous intent, to the doors of dwellings familiar
to them by the experience of old hospitality. They had
torn away wives and mothers from ministrations to dying
men, and children from their mothers' arms, for death in
cruel forms. They had tortured their prisoners with
atrocious ingenuity. Repeatedly, after they rose in arms,
overtures of friendship had been made to them. But
whether they disregarded such proposals or professed to
close with them, it was all the same. The work of massacre
and ravage still went on. The ferocious creature had tasted
blood, and could not restrain himself till he should be
surfeited. There was not a settlement in New England
free from a distressing sense of instant danger. Brook-
field, Springfield, Lancaster, bore signal witness how little
reliance was to be placed on habits of friendly intercourse
long kept up, or on professions of conversion to the Christian faith. The heart of English life in New England was
all but reached by the assassins; at one time they were at

Weymouth, within twelve miles of the capital; and if only the interior towns had been wholly devastated, the result could scarcely have been other than the total abandonment of New England by the portion of its civilized people that should be left alive.

It must be allowed that the sense of obligations imposed by a common humanity was not in all respects so operative in those times as it is now. Before their departure from their native country the emigrants had known no men of other blood than their own. Controlled by a habit of mind which an insular position and other circumstances have formed in Englishmen, they were capable of only a very imperfect sympathy even with men of Italy or France. How much more feeble would the tie of fraternity be felt to be between themselves and a race which, even as to outward aspect, would seem to them to have little of humanity beyond the likeness of a human shape, and which, as to reason, conscience, and affections, corresponded to no idea of humanity to which they had been used. That even the bond of human fellow-feeling is by white men apt to be recognized in its full strength only within the limits of their own division of the human family, is a fact illustrated by the condition of the African race wherever they are found in large numbers in communities of different complexion. And to what an intensity of vindictiveness English blood is apt to be stirred when savages, of whatever color, indulge their savage nature in revolting cruelties to English men and women, every reader knows who is acquainted with the recent history of the revolt in Hindostan.

. . . .

The careful reader of the contemporaneous narratives of transactions of this period finds reason to distrust conceptions which have prevailed of both the policy and the character of Philip. Partly by one of those caprices to which history is liable, and partly perhaps because he was both an old acquaintance of the English, and the scene of his maraudings was nearer to the vitals of their Commonwealth, he has been widely distinguished from other red men who were engaged in inflicting the misery of this terrible war, and who, so far as we may now judge from their recorded conduct, possessed capacity and character at least equal to his,—from Canonchet, for instance, the stubborn Narragansett Sachem, and from the Etetchemin chiefs Squando, Madockawando, and Mugg, who directed the devastation of the Eastern settlements. To a lively imagination it has appeared that, with considerate foresight, Philip took alarm at the prospect of the extirpation of his race and the occupation of their land by strangers; that, with a strenuous purpose, a capacity for political combination, and an aptness for influencing the action of men, such as belong to minds of a high class, he slowly matured a conspiracy to rid the country of the English interloper by a united movement, and restore it to its ancient owners; that, though unlucky circumstances caused the rising to occur prematurely, this misadventure did not prevent him from carrying out the contest to its disastrous end with vigor and determination; and that his life and death deserve the eulogies which are fit to be bestowed on a brave and sagacious patriot. And the title of *King*, which it has been customary to attach to his name, disguises and transfigures to the view the form of a squalid savage, whose palace was a sty; whose royal robe was a bearskin or a coarse blanket, alive with vermin; who hardly knew the luxury of an ablution; who was often glad to appease appetite with food such as men who are not starving loathe; and whose nature possessed just the capacity for reflection and the degree of refinement, which might be expected to be developed from the mental constitution of his race by such a condition and such habits of life. To royalty belong associations of dignity and magnificence, which it is not worth while to attempt to dissect. Civilization, philosophy, humanity, are not yet mature enough to be competent to that analysis. But, at all events, the Indian *King Philip* is a mythical character.

DOCUMENT 106

King Philip and the English: Another View

Writing about the same time as Palfrey, Peter Oliver's
account of *The Puritan Commonwealth: An Historical
Review of the Puritan Government in Massachusetts in
its Civil and Ecclesiastical Relations from its Rise to the
Abrogation of the First Charter* (Boston: Little, Brown
& Co., 1856), took a diametrically opposed position on
the subject of the justice of English relations with the
Indians and the character of King Philip. The following
passage, concerning the preliminaries of King Philip's
War, 1675–76, is taken from pp. 135–37 of Oliver's
book. Oliver's footnotes have been omitted. For an explanation of Oliver's reference to John Robinson, see
elsewhere in this volume, pp. 176–78.

Allusion has already been made to Philip, sachem of
the Wampanoags, who, perhaps, stands out in bold relief
from all the other native chiefs. It was not in power that
he excelled Canonchet [a Narragansett chief], for the
warriors of his own tribe were not nearly so numerous as
those of the Narragansett chief; it was not in their more
warlike character that he had the advantage of Sassacus,
for the Pequods were the terror of all the Indians in their
vicinity. His superiority is to be attributed alone to his
stern resolution. His bold and active character soon made
him an object of dislike to his neighbors of Plymouth; and
he was charged with ambition, in aspiring to the sovereignty of a country which was his heritage; with perfidy,
for breaking promises which were extorted from him in
duress; with impiety, for contemptuously declining to receive the gospel at the hands of the despoilers of his people. But Philip was neither ambitious, perfidious, nor

wicked. He had the good sense to distinguish between fair, *bonâ fide* contracts, and those made by means of fraud and deception; and he, without hesitation, repudiated the latter, as an oppression of the weak by the strong.

The injuries inflicted by the Plymouth Colony upon Massasoit and his people are not attributable to Massachusetts; and it is beyond our purpose to detail the various treaties of submission and tribute, which, for a long series of years, were juggled by the disciples of Robinson from the sachems of Pokanoket. Though "even like lions" to the rest of their neighbors, yet to the starving, feeble band of Independents, who intruded upon their shores, the Wampanoags had been "*like lambs, so kind, so submissive and trusty, as a man may truly say many Christians are not so kind or so sincere.*" But how were they requited? Suffice it that Massasoit, though called an "enemy to Christianity," continued a firm friend of the Plymouth settlers until his death; that his eldest son and successor, Wamsutta, renewed the league of amity, which existed between his father and Plymouth; and, as if to seal the friendly compact, accepted from the governor of that colony the name of Alexander, which he retained during his brief career; that, a few years after, Alexander died of a broken heart, on account of his ignominious treatment by that colony, which, without cause, suspected his fidelity; that his brother, Metacom, who also had accepted the name of Philip, pardoning this outrage, ratified a compact, which was fast ruining the wild glory of his race; and that these leagues or treaties were entirely of an *ex parte* nature, enuring favorably to the English, and being of no manner of benefit to the Indians. For, in what position did Philip find his people, when called upon to direct their affairs? Their lands, formerly extending from the easterly boundary of the Narragansetts to the westerly limits of what is now the county of Plymouth, in Massachusetts, and comprehending generally the present county of Bristol, were, for the most part, in the hands of the English, and the native proprietors were confined to a few tongues of land, jutting out into the sea, the chief of which is now known as Bristol, in Rhode Island. These necks of land were alone, of all their possessions, rendered by the Plymouth laws inalienable by the Indians; partly, it was said, *because they were "more suitable and convenient" for them, and partly because the English were of a "covetous disposition," and the natives, when in need, were "easily prevailed upon to part with their lands."* Here, then, Philip found his people huddled together, by the insidious policy of the Plymouth Colony, surrounded on three sides by the ocean, and, on the fourth, hemmed in by the ever-advancing tide of civilization. And this was all that forty years of friendship with "the Pilgrims" had benefited the Wampanoags.

DOCUMENT 107

Crawford's Progress of Civilization

Plate 31, following page 334, portrays the pediment of the United States Senate building, showing the sculptured figures, entitled "The Progress of Civilization," executed by Thomas Crawford. The theme of the group is the advancement of the white race and the decline of the Indian. Authorized in 1853, the figures were installed in 1863. In the center stands America, a majestic goddess, extending her left hand toward the pioneer, for whom she asks the protection of the Almighty. With her right hand she holds laurel and oak wreaths, rewards of civil and military merit, toward a soldier, merchant, youth, schoolmaster, pupil, and mechanic. Beyond the pioneer, who is represented as felling a tree, the decline of the Indian is symbolized by figures of a hunter, Indian brave, Indian mother and child, and Indian grave. The grave serves to balance the anchor and sheaf of wheat, symbolic of hope and fertility, in the other corner of the pediment. In an experiment to test the qualities of native marble in comparison with Italian marble, marble from quarries in Lee, Massachusetts, was used and has proved outstandingly successful in withstanding the effects of Washington weather.

Devil in the Flesh

In 1923 D. H. Lawrence published his *Studies in Classic American Literature*. The following passage is from the chapter entitled "Fenimore Cooper's White Novels," pp. 43–46 of the convenient 1953 Doubleday Anchor Book edition. Lawrence does violence to Benjamin Franklin's true beliefs, of course. But his psychological probe into the Indian-white relationship strikes a sensitive spot in all of us.

Benjamin Franklin had a specious little equation in providential mathematics:

$$Rum + Savage = 0$$

Awfully nice! You might add up the universe to nought, if you kept on.

Rum plus Savage may equal a dead savage. But is a dead savage nought? Can you make a land virgin by killing off its aborigines?

The Aztec is gone, and the Incas. The Red Indian, the Esquimo, the Patagonian are reduced to negligible numbers.

Où sont les neiges d'antan?

My dear, wherever they are, they will come down again next winter, sure as houses.

Not that the Red Indian will ever possess the broad lands of America. At least I presume not. But his ghost will.

The Red Man died hating the white man. What remnant of him lives, lives hating the white man. Go near the Indians, and you just feel it. As far as we are concerned, the Red Man is subtly and unremittingly diabolic. Even when he doesn't know it. He is dispossessed in life, and unforgiving. He doesn't believe in us and our civilization, and so is our mystic enemy, for we push him off the face of the earth.

Belief is a mysterious thing. It is the only healer of the soul's wounds. There is no belief in the world.

The Red Man is dead, disbelieving in us. He is dead and unappeased. Do not imagine him happy in his Happy Hunting Ground. No. Only those that die in belief die happy. Those that are pushed out of life in chagrin come back unappeased, for revenge.

A curious thing about the Spirit of Place is the fact that no place exerts its full influence upon a newcomer until the old inhabitant is dead or absorbed. So America. While the Red Indian existed in fairly large numbers the new colonials were in a great measure immune from the daimon, or demon of America. The moment the last nuclei of Red life break up in America, then the white men will have to reckon with the full force of the demon of the continent. At present the demon of the place and the unappeased ghosts of the dead Indians act within the unconscious or under-conscious soul of the white American, causing the great American grouch, the Orestes-like frenzy of restlessness in the Yankee soul, the inner malaise which amounts almost to madness, sometimes. The Mexican is macabre and disintegrated in his own way. Up till now, the unexpressed spirit of America has worked covertly in the American, the white American soul. But within the present generation the surviving Red Indians are due to merge in the great white swamp. Then the Daimon of America will work overtly, and we shall see real changes.

There has been all the time, in the white American soul, a dual feeling about the Indian. First was Franklin's feeling, that a wise Providence no doubt intended the extirpation of these savages. Then came Crèvecoeur's contradictory feeling about the noble Red Man and the innocent life of the wigwam. Now we hate to subscribe to Benjamin's belief in a Providence that wisely extirpates the Indian to make room for "cultivators of the soil." In

Crèvecoeur we meet a sentimental desire for the glorification of the savages. Absolutely sentimental. Hector pops over to Paris to enthuse about the wigwam.

The desire to extirpate the Indian. And the contradictory desire to glorify him. Both are rampant still, to-day.

The bulk of the white people who live in contact with the Indian to-day would like to see this Red brother exterminated; not only for the sake of grabbing his land, but because of the silent, invisible, but deadly hostility between the spirit of the two races. The minority of whites intellectualize the Red Man and laud him to the skies. But this minority of whites is mostly a high-brow minority with a big grouch against its own whiteness. So there you are.

I doubt if there is possible any real reconciliation, in the flesh, between the white and the red. For instance, a Red Indian girl who is servant in the white man's home, if she is treated with natural consideration will probably serve well, even happily. She is happy with the new power over the white woman's kitchen. The white world makes her feel prouder, so long as she is free to go back to her own people at the given times. But she is happy because she is playing at being a white woman. There are other Indian women who would never serve the white people, and who would rather die than have a white man for a lover.

In either case, there is no reconciliation. There is no mystic conjunction between the spirit of the two races. The Indian girl who happily serves white people leaves out her own race-consideration, for the time being.

Supposing a white man goes out hunting in the mountains with an Indian. The two will probably get on like brothers. But let the same white man go alone with two Indians, and there will start a most subtle persecution of the unsuspecting white. If they, the Indians, discover that he has a natural fear of steep places, then over every precipice in the country will the trail lead. And so on. Malice! That is the basic feeling in the Indian heart, towards the white. It may even be purely unconscious.

Supposing an Indian loves a white woman, and lives with

her. He will probably be very proud of it, for he will be a big man among his own people, especially if the white mistress has money. He will never get over the feeling of pride at dining in a white dining-room and smoking in a white drawing-room. But at the same time he will subtly jeer at his white mistress, try to destroy her white pride. He will submit to her, if he is forced to, with a kind of false, unwilling childishness, and even love her with the same childlike gentleness, sometimes beautiful. But at the bottom of his heart he is gibing, gibing, gibing at her. Not only is it the sex resistance, but the race resistance as well.

There seems to be no reconciliation in the flesh.

That leaves us only expiation, and then reconciliation in the soul. Some strange atonement: expiation and oneing.

"Killed off by an Infamous Band of Robbers"

Morality and history are inseparably intertwined in any account of the conquest of America. A violently anti-Spanish account is Egon Friedell's *A Cultural History of the Modern Age*, published in three volumes in Munich, 1927–32. The following passage is from Vol. I, *Renaissance and Reformation: from the Black Death to the Thirty Years' War*, translated by Charles Francis Atkinson, pp. 217–23 (London: Alfred A. Knopf, 1930). A New York edition was published by Knopf in 1953.

At about the same time Central America, and about ten years later the western coast of South America, were opened up to Europeans. Let us pause a little over these two achievements, the conquest of Mexico and Peru, for they are among the most shocking and senseless performances in the whole of history.

On his landing in Mexico in 1519 Hernando Cortez found there a highly developed and, indeed, over-developed culture, far superior to that of Europe; but, a white man and a Catholic, blinded by the double conceit of his religion and his race, he could not rise to the idea that beings of a different colour and a different world-view could be even his equals. It is tragic and grotesque to see with what arrogance the Spaniards, members of the most brutal, superstitious, and uncultured nation of their continent, looked down upon this culture, of the bases of which they had not the smallest inkling. Nevertheless, we cannot deny all greatness to the figure of Cortez; he may have been a *conquistador* like the rest of them, coarse, cunning, avaricious, untroubled by higher moral restraints, but he was not wanting in fertile courage, political shrewdness, and a sort of elementary decency. Nor did he ever act through mere love of bloodshed—he had, indeed, a sort of horror of it, and his abolition of the blood-sacrifice of the Aztecs was perhaps the only action that was worthy of civilized man in the whole course of the Spanish Conquista. His followers—with some few exceptions, notably among the clergy—were fellows of the lowest sort, rowdies and criminals ejected by their native land, down-and-out Spaniards, the scum of the scum of contemporary Europe. The sole motive for the expedition was a vulgar lust of gold: as Cortez remarked with a certain superior irony to the governor sent by Montezuma to meet him, "the Spaniards suffer from a heart-disease for which gold is a peculiarly suitable remedy."

The culture of Mexico is to be imagined as being more or less in the same stage as that of the Empire in Rome. It is evident that it had already reached the phase which Spengler calls "Civilization" and which is characterized by a life of huge cities, of refined comforts, of autocratic forms of government and expansionist imperialism, of massiveness in architecture and extravagance in ornament, of ethical fatalism and barbarized religion. The capital, Tenochtitlan, built on platforms in a wondrous lake, displayed huge temples and obelisks, extensive arsenals, hospitals, barracks, zoölogical and botanical gardens, barbers' shops, vapour-baths, and fountains, tapestries and paintings of gorgeous feather-mosaic, costly goldsmith's work and finely tooled plates of tortoise-shell, splendid woollen cloaks and leather gear, ceilings of fragrant carved wood, hot-plates, scent-sprayers, and hot-water systems. In the weekly markets, attended by hundreds of thousands, wares of every conceivable kind were exposed for sale. A wonderfully organized postal service, of fast couriers, plying on the network of well-built highways and ramps which traversed the land, carried every item of news with amazing speed and precision; police and fiscal arrangements worked with the greatest accuracy and reliability. The kitchens of the wealthy were fragrant with the most select foods and drinks, game, fish, waffles, preserves, delicate soups, spiced dishes; and withal a number of things unknown to the Old World, turkey, *chocolatl*—the favourite dish of the Mexicans, to them no drink, but a fine *crême*, eaten cold with vanilla and other spices—*pulque*, an intoxicating drink made from aloes (which also yielded a tasty artichoke-like vegetable and first-class sugar), and *yetl*, tobacco, smoked either mixed with liquid ambar in gilded wooden pipes, or like a cigar in fine silver holders. The streets were so clean, a Spanish text tells us, that in passing along them one soiled one's feet no more than one's hands. The population was as honest as it was clean: all houses were left open, and when a dwelling was unoccupied, its owner merely set up a reed on the door-mat to indicate his absence, without fear of theft; in fact, the courts were almost never called upon to deal with cases of violating property. Writing was by means of a very elaborate picture-writing, and there were also lightning painters who could fix all occurrences with amazing rapidity in almost speaking designs. The mathematical sense of the Aztecs must have been highly developed, for their arithmetical system was built up on the difficult principle of raising to a power, the basic number being 20, the next 20^2 or 400, the next 20^3 or 8000, and so on; further, the Maya are supposed to have invented, independently of the Indians, the idea of zero, a fertile and complicated notion which only made its way into Europe slowly, viâ the Arabs.

The American cultures were probably part of that great girdle of cultures which embraced the whole inhabited earth in what are for us prehistoric times: extending from Egypt and Nearer Asia over India and China to Central America and presumably including the two pre-Classical European worlds of Etruria and the Aegean. Under the name of Pan-Babylonism the theory of this belt of cultures has evoked much opposition and found much support, and as a matter of fact the Aztecs do show considerable similarity to the Babylonians in their chronology, their picture-writing, and their star-worship, and moreover there is a whole series of things which remind us vividly of Egypt, such as the type of government, a mixture of God-kingship and priestly despotism, the bureaucracy whose chief administrative task was a pedantic guardianship of the masses, the carefully systematized and ceremonious etiquette of intercourse, the monstrosity and animal forms of their gods, the great gift for naturalistic portraiture, combined with a strong tendency towards stylization of the higher forms, the extravagant luxury and exuberant massiveness of their buildings.

Most remarkable of all, however, are the parallels between the Mexican and Christian religions. The crown of the emperor, who was at the same time high priest, was of almost identical form with the papal tiara. The mythology knew the stories of Eve and the serpent, the Flood and the tower of Babel. In somewhat altered form they knew the sacraments of baptism, confession, and communion, and they had monks who spent their time in vigil, fasting, and scourging. The cross was a holy symbol and they had even a dim idea of the Trinity and the Incarnation. Their ethical commands sometimes show an almost verbal identity with the Bible. One of their doctrines ran: "Keep peace with all men, endure insults with patience, for God, who sees all, will avenge thee"; and another: "Whoso looks with too great intentness at a married woman commits adultery with his eyes."

This religion, like the contemporary Christianity, was stained by the institution of human sacrifice, in which captives played the rôle of heretics. They were led on fixed days to the temple, when a priest, specially appointed for the service, cut open the breast with a sharp knife of bone and tore out the still beating and smoking heart, to be cast upon the altar of the god. Quite naturally, this custom has revolted later generations and given rise to the idea that the Mexicans were after all only a race of savages, but there is much that may be said in their excuse. In the first place, the custom was restricted to the Aztecs—the Toltecs did not know the practice—and even among them it seemed that it was disappearing, for at least in Cholula, the second city of Mexico, there was a temple of the god Quetzalcoatl, in whose worship human sacrifice was replaced by a vegetable sacrifice. Moreover, there was no lust for blood or cruelty for its own sake, this being, even if a barbaric, yet a religious ceremony, through which the believer sought to win the favour of his god, and so little dishonouring that occasionally the pious offered themselves as willing victims. It was merely fear and superstition and was certainly not on a lower moral level than the Spanish *autos-da-fé*, of which the motive was fanaticism and vengeance, and undoubtedly higher than the gladiatorial games at Rome, where captives were killed as an enjoyment.

One of the most striking elements of the Mexican religion was the belief in the second coming of the god Quetzalcoatl, of whom it was believed that he had in ancient days ruled his people and taught them every useful art and instituted all existing social arrangements, and that he had finally sailed away in his magic boat with the promise to return some day. It happened that just at this time the priests had declared the moment of the god's return to be near; he was expected from the east and it was said that he would be distinguished from the Aztecs by his white skin, blue eyes, and fair beard. All these prophecies were to be fulfilled, and it was this touching faith, exploited in the most shameless way by the Spaniards, that largely enabled a runagate band of illiterate bandits not merely to subdue this world, but to trample it to pieces. There were other reasons: the deficient physical energy of the natives, whose existence seems to have become somewhat vegetative or plantlike through the enervating tropical climate and centuries of peace and luxury; the equipment of the Europeans with fire-arms, artillery, steel armour, and horses, all of them wholly unknown to the Mexicans and producing on them, in addition to the physical effects, an amazing moral impression; the higher level of Spanish tactics, which bore somewhat the same relation to the Aztec as the Macedonian had to the Persian;

the inner disunion of the kingdom and the desertion of powerful tribes. The chief reason, however, may well have been that the Mexican culture had reached the period of its agony and was doomed, in some way or other, to collapse. We can follow the spectacle, throughout the whole of history, of older cultures giving place to the younger: the Sumerian to the Babylonian, the Babylonian to the Assyrian, Assyrian to Persian, Persian to Greek, Greek to Roman, and Roman to Germanic. But we observe, in all these cases, that the lower assimilates the higher; for instance, the Babylonians took over Sumerian cuneiform, Persians the Chaldean astrology, Rome Greek art and philosophy, the Germans the Roman Church. But in America nothing of the sort, for the Indian culture vanished without leaving a trace behind. This instance, unique in the whole of history, is, however, explicable by the also unique fact of a whole people being, not brought into subjection by another people (barbaric or otherwise), but ruined and killed off by an infamous band of robbers, and thus it came to pass that while long-vanished cultures like the Egyptian and Mesopotamian, not to mention the Greek or Roman, still exercise their fructifying influence, the shameful crime of the Conquista robbed humanity of a noble and unique world-view and made it, so to say, poorer by a sense.

The kindred culture of Peru stood perhaps still higher than the Aztec—though they seem to have known nothing of each other, there is great resemblance between the two peoples. The whole land was covered with miracles of engineering. Countless canals, aqueducts, and terraceworks brought it to the extreme of fertility, and the utmost care was spent in cultivating it, vertically no less than horizontally. Even above the clouds there were orchards. Highroads which overcame every obstacle threaded the whole district, now making use of hewn steps and now of levelled ravines, now passing through long tunnels and now over ingenious bridges. Peru taught the whole of Europe the principles of manuring—the introduction of guano has revolutionized our agriculture. Incomparable, too, was its textile art, which incidentally (by means of a complicated system of knotting that is still undeciphered) served also as writing. They were masters of carving, and they had a great drama. Their government was a sort of communism with an aristocratic superstructure and a theocratic apex, and it is probably no exaggeration to say that our own continent has never produced a form of government of like wisdom, justice, and benevolence. In their splendid irrigation system, in their religion, which honoured the sun as the highest god and the moon as his sister-wife, and in their mummy cult they remind us even more startlingly of the Egyptians than do the Aztecs.

The conquest of Peru is a more revolting story even than that of Mexico, a chain of the most infamous acts of treachery and bestiality. The name of the rascal Francisco Pizarro, who was not for nothing suckled by a sow, deserves to survive in the memory of posterity as the proverbial instance of treacherous meanness, shameless avarice, and bestial coarseness, as the basest term of abuse which one man can fling at another. The story of his "conquest" is briefly as follows. He arranged an interview with Atahuallpa, the Peruvian Emperor, to which the latter came with a large but unarmed escort; during the conversation Pizarro suddenly gave a sign, at which the soldiers pressed forward, cut down the whole of the imperial suite, and took Atahuallpa prisoner. He, like Montezuma, a man of such delicacy, gentleness, and nobility as was inconceivable in contemporary Europe, was at first thunderstruck by this foul deed, which would have been scorned by any moderately decent brigand captain; but, soon collecting himself, he so far maintained his calm and dignity that in his conversation with the Spanish rabble he even condescended to jesting remarks. Realizing very soon that the invaders were chiefly concerned with his treasures, he promised them as ransom a whole room filled with gold to the height of a man standing with arm upstretched. Pizarro agreed and carried off a colossal booty, such as had never been gathered in one heap in his native land. Then, once he had the gold, he caused the Inca to be strangled, on charges so trumped up, so ridiculous in their brutal stupidity, that some even of his own bandits protested. Such was the achievement of Christians in the year 1533, exactly fifteen hundred years after the crucifixion of their Saviour.

Pizarro ended his career like most murderers, being killed by one of his own boon companions. And all Spain had loss and not profit by his deeds of shame, for it fell more and more a victim to the enervating and stupefying habit of living on stolen goods, so that within a bare hundred years it lay as it has lain ever since, a soulless, mortifying corpse, gloomy, sullen, self-consuming, a victim of its own dullness of intellect, its own appalling barrenness of heart, its own fierce brutality. The rest of Europe, too, has fallen to the divine nemesis, for from the New World it imported not only maize and tobacco, tomatoes and bananas, cocoa and potatoes, vanilla and cochineal, but—gold and *syphilis*.

DOCUMENT 110

Aztec Sculpture

Despite the feverish Spanish concern for destroying works of the "Devil," which succeeded in depriving the world of numerous treasures of Indian art and writing, some objects could not easily be burned, melted down, or hacked to pieces. Among the surviving sculpture is the piece of Aztec sculpture of the period A.D. 1370–1520, that is reproduced in Plate 32, following page 334. It depicts a human head, and possibly represents a Pulque god. It is in the Chicago Natural History Museum.

DOCUMENT 111

"What Were They Like to Be With?"

The education of the young Nick Adams, the pro-
tagonist of many of Ernest Hemingway's earliest stories,
derived from both the natural and the human environment of the Michigan woods, as the following passage
from Hemingway's short story, "Fathers and Sons," first
published in the collection *Winner Take Nothing*,
pp. 231–42 (New York: Charles Scribner's Sons,
1933), reveals.

Nick's own education in those earlier matters had been
acquired in the hemlock woods behind the Indian camp.
This was reached by a trail which ran from the cottage
through the woods to the farm and then by a road which
wound through the slashings to the camp. Now he could
still feel all of that trail with bare feet. First there was the
pine needle loam through the hemlock woods behind the
cottage where the fallen logs crumbled into wood dust
and long splintered pieces of wood hung like javelins in
the tree that had been struck by lightning. You crossed the
creek on a log and if you stepped off there was the black
muck of the swamp. You climbed a fence out of the
woods and the trail was hard in the sun across the field
with cropped grass and sheep sorrel and mullen growing
and to the left the quaky bog of the creek bottom where
the killdeer plover fed. The spring house was in that
creek. Below the barn there was fresh warm manure and
the other older manure that was caked dry on top. Then
there was another fence and the hard, hot trail from the
barn to the house and the hot sandy road that ran down
to the woods, crossing the creek, on a bridge this time,

where the cat-tails grew that you soaked in kerosene to make jack-lights with for spearing fish at night.

Then the main road went off to the left, skirting the woods and climbing the hill, while you went into the woods on the wide clay and shale road, cool under the trees, and broadened for them to skid out the hemlock bark the Indians cut. The hemlock bark was piled in long rows of stacks, roofed over with more bark, like houses, and the peeled logs lay huge and yellow where the trees had been felled. They left the logs in the woods to rot, they did not even clear away or burn the tops. It was only the bark they wanted for the tannery at Boyne City; hauling it across the lake on the ice in winter, and each year there was less forest and more open, hot, shadeless, weed-grown slashing.

But there was still much forest then, virgin forest where the trees grew high before there were any branches and you walked on the brown, clean, springy-needled ground with no undergrowth and it was cool on the hottest days and they three lay against the trunk of a hemlock wider than two beds are long, with the breeze high in the tops and the cool light that came in patches, and Billy said:

"You want Trudy again?"

"You want to?"

"Un Huh."

"Come on."

"No, here."

"But Billy——"

"I no mind Billy. He my brother."

Then afterwards they sat, the three of them, listening for a black squirrel that was in the top branches where they could not see him. They were waiting for him to bark again because when he barked he would jerk his tail and Nick would shoot where he saw any movement. His father gave him only three cartridges a day to hunt with and he had a single-barrel twenty-gauge shotgun with a very long barrel.

"Son of a bitch never move," Billy said.

"You shoot, Nickie. Scare him. We see him jump. Shoot him again," Trudy said. It was a long speech for her.

"I've only got two shells," Nick said.

"Son of a bitch," said Billy.

They sat against the tree and were quiet. Nick was feeling hollow and happy.

"Eddie says he going to come some night sleep in bed with you sister Dorothy."

"What?"

"He said."

Trudy nodded.

"That's all he want do," she said. Eddie was their older half-brother. He was seventeen.

"If Eddie Gilby ever comes at night and even speaks to Dorothy you know what I'd do to him? I'd kill him like this." Nick cocked the gun and hardly taking aim pulled the trigger, blowing a hole as big as your hand in the head or belly of that half-breed bastard Eddie Gilby. "Like that. I'd kill him like that."

"He better not come then," Trudy said. She put her hand in Nick's pocket.

"He better watch out plenty," said Billy.

"He's big bluff," Trudy was exploring with her hand in Nick's pocket. "But don't you kill him. You get plenty trouble."

"I'd kill him like that," Nick said. Eddie Gilby lay on the ground with all his chest shot away. Nick put his foot on him proudly.

"I'd scalp him," he said happily.

"No," said Trudy. "That's dirty."

"I'd scalp him and send it to his mother."

"His mother dead," Trudy said. "Don't you kill him, Nickie. Don't you kill him for me."

"After I scalped him I'd throw him to the dogs."

Billy was very depressed. "He better watch out," he said gloomily.

"They'd tear him to pieces," Nick said, pleased with the picture. Then, having scalped that half-breed renegade and standing, watching the dogs tear him, his face unchanging, he fell backward against the tree, held tight around the neck, Trudy holding, choking him, and crying, "No kill him! No kill him! No kill him! No. No. No. Nickie. Nickie. Nickie!"

"What's the matter with you?"

"No kill him."

"I got to kill him."

"He just a big bluff."

"All right," Nickie said. "I won't kill him unless he comes around the house. Let go of me."

"That's good," Trudy said. "You want to do anything now? I feel good now."

"If Billy goes away." Nick had killed Eddie Gilby, then pardoned him his life, and he was a man now.

"You go, Billy. You hang around all the time. Go on."

"Son a bitch," Billy said. "I get tired this. What we come? Hunt or what?"

"You can take the gun. There's one shell."

"All right. I get a big black one all right."

"I'll holler," Nick said.

Then, later, it was a long time after and Billy was still away.

"You think we make a baby?" Trudy folded her brown legs together happily and rubbed against him. Something inside Nick had gone a long way away.

"I don't think so," he said.

"Make plenty baby what the hell."

They heard Billy shoot.

"I wonder if he got one."

"Don't care," said Trudy.

Billy came through the trees. He had the gun over his shoulder and he held a black squirrel by the front paws.

"Look," he said. "Bigger than a cat. You all through?"

"Where'd you get him?"

"Over there. Saw him jump first."

"Got to go home," Nick said.

"No," said Trudy.

"I got to get there for supper."

"All right."

"Want to hunt tomorrow?"

"All right."

"You can have the squirrel."

"All right."

"Come out after supper?"

"No."

"How you feel?"

"Good."

"All right."

"Give me kiss on the face," said Trudy.

Now, as he rode along the highway in the car and it was getting dark, Nick was all through thinking about his father. The end of the day never made him think of him. The end of the day had always belonged to Nick alone and he never felt right unless he was alone at it. His father came back to him in the fall of the year, or in the early spring when there had been jacksnipe on the prairie, or when he saw shocks of corn, or when he saw a lake, or if he ever saw a horse and buggy, or when he saw, or heard, wild geese, or in a duck blind; remembering the time an eagle dropped through the whirling snow to strike a canvas-covered decoy, rising, his wings beating, the talons caught in the canvas. His father was with him, suddenly, in deserted orchards and in new-plowed fields, in thickets, on small hills, or when going through dead grass, whenever splitting wood or hauling water, by grist mills, cider mills and dams and always with open fires. The towns he lived in were not towns his father knew. After he was fifteen he had shared nothing with him.

His father had frost in his beard in cold weather and in hot weather he sweated very much. He liked to work in the sun on the farm because he did not have to and he loved manual work, which Nick did not. Nick loved his father but hated the smell of him and once when he had to wear a suit of his father's underwear that had gotten too small for his father it made him feel sick and he took it off and put it under two stones in the creek and said that he had lost it. He had told his father how it was when his father had made him put it on but his father had said it was freshly washed. It had been, too. When Nick had asked him to smell of it his father sniffed at it indignantly and said that it was clean and fresh. When Nick came home from fishing without it and said he lost it he was whipped for lying.

Afterwards he had sat inside the woodshed with the door open, his shotgun loaded and cocked, looking across at his father sitting on the screen porch reading the paper, and thought, "I can blow him to hell. I can kill him." Finally he felt his anger go out of him and he felt a little sick about it being the gun that his father had given him. Then he had gone to the Indian camp, walking there in the dark, to get rid of the smell. There was only one person in his family that he liked the smell of; one sister. All the others he avoided all contact with. That sense blunted when he started to smoke. It was a good thing. It was good for a bird dog but it did not help a man.

"What was it like, Papa, when you were a little boy and used to hunt with the Indians?"

"I don't know," Nick was startled. He had not even noticed the boy was awake. He looked at him sitting beside him on the seat. He had felt quite alone but this boy had been with him. He wondered for how long. "We used to go all day to hunt black squirrels," he said. "My father only gave me three shells a day because he said that would teach me to hunt and it wasn't good for a boy to go banging around. I went with a boy named Billy Gilby and his sister Trudy. We used to go out nearly every day all one summer."

"Those are funny names for Indians."

"Yes, aren't they," Nick said.

"But tell me what they were like."

"They were Ojibways," Nick said. "And they were very nice."

"But what were they like to be with?"

"It's hard to say," Nick Adams said. Could you say she did first what no one has ever done better and mention plump brown legs, flat belly, hard little breasts, well holding arms, quick searching tongue, the flat eyes, the good taste of mouth, then uncomfortably, tightly, sweetly, moistly, lovely, tightly, achingly, fully, finally, unendingly, never-endingly, never-to-endingly, suddenly ended, the great bird flown like an owl in the twilight, only it daylight in the woods and hemlock needles stuck against your belly. So that when you go in a place where Indians have lived you smell them gone and all the empty pain killer bottles and the flies that buzz do not kill the sweetgrass smell, the smoke smell and that other like a fresh cased marten skin. Nor any jokes about them nor old squaws take that away. Nor the sick sweet smell they get to have. Nor what they did finally. It wasn't how they ended. They all ended the same. Long time ago good. Now no good.

And about the other. When you have shot one bird flying you have shot all birds flying. They are all different and they fly in different ways but the sensation is the same and the last one is as good as the first. He could thank his father for that.

"You might not like them," Nick said to the boy. "But I think you would."

"And my grandfather lived with them too when he was a boy, didn't he?"

"Yes. When I asked him what they were like he said that he had many friends among them."

"Will I ever live with them?"

"I don't know," Nick said. "That's up to you."

DOCUMENT 112

Relinquish . . . Relinquish

William Faulkner's "The Bear," which first appeared in the collection *Go Down, Moses* in 1942, is a story about men (red, white, and black), about land, and about a bear. Its meaning cannot be explained; it must be absorbed. The following passages from "The Bear" are taken from *Go Down, Moses and Other Stories*, pp. 191–94, 254–59 (New York: Random House, 1942).

I

There was a man and a dog too this time. Two beasts, counting Old Ben, the bear, and two men, counting Boon Hogganbeck, in whom some of the same blood ran which ran in Sam Fathers, even though Boon's was a plebeian strain of it and only Sam and Old Ben and the mongrel Lion were taintless and incorruptible.

Isaac McCaslin was sixteen. For six years now he had been a man's hunter. For six years now he had heard the best of all talking. It was of the wilderness, the big woods, bigger and older than any recorded document—of white man fatuous enough to believe he had bought any fragment of it, of Indian ruthless enough to pretend that any fragment of it had been his to convey; bigger than Major de Spain and the scrap he pretended to, knowing better; older than old Thomas Sutpen of whom Major de Spain had had it and who knew better; older even than old Ikkemotubbe, the Chickasaw chief, of whom old Sutpen had had it and who knew better in his turn. It was of the men, not white nor black nor red, but men, hunters, with the will and hardihood to endure and the humility and skill to survive, and the dogs and the bear and deer juxta-posed and reliefed against it, ordered and compelled by and within the wilderness in the ancient and unremitting contest according to the ancient and immitigable rules which voided all regrets and brooked no quarter;—the best game of all, the best of all breathing and forever the best of all listening, the voices quiet and weighty and deliberate for retrospection and recollection and exactitude among the concrete trophies—the racked guns and the heads and skins—in the libraries of town houses or the offices of plan-tation houses or (and best of all) in the camps themselves where the intact and still-warm meat yet hung, the men who had slain it sitting before the burning logs on hearths, when there were houses and hearths, or about the smoky blazing of piled wood in front of stretched tarpaulins when there were not. There was always a bottle present, so that it would seem to him that those fine fierce instants of heart and brain and courage and wiliness and speed were concentrated and distilled into that brown liquor which not women, not boys and children, but only hunters drank, drinking not of the blood they spilled but some condensa-tion of the wild immortal spirit, drinking it moderately, humbly even, not with the pagan's base and baseless hope of acquiring thereby the virtues of cunning and strength and speed but in salute to them. Thus it seemed to him on this December morning not only natural but actually fit-ting that this should have begun with whiskey.

He realized later that it had begun long before that. It had already begun on that day when he first wrote his age in two ciphers and his cousin McCaslin brought him for the first time to the camp, the big woods, to earn for him-self from the wilderness the name and state of hunter provided he in his turn were humble and enduring enough. He had already inherited then, without ever having seen it, the big old bear with one trap-ruined foot that in an area almost a hundred miles square had earned for himself a name, a definite designation like a living man:—the long legend of corncribs broken down and rifled, of shoats and grown pigs and even calves carried bodily into the woods and devoured, and traps and deadfalls overthrown and dogs mangled and slain, and shotgun and even rifle shots delivered at point-blank range yet with no more effect than so many peas blown through a tube by a child—a corridor of wreckage and destruction beginning back before the boy was born, through which sped, not fast but rather with the ruthless and irresistible deliberation of a locomotive, the shaggy tremendous shape. It ran in his knowledge before he ever saw it. It loomed and towered in his dreams before he even saw the unaxed woods where it left its crooked print, shaggy, tremendous, red-eyed, not malevolent but just big, too big for the dogs which tried to bay it, for the horses which tried to ride it down, for the men and the bullets they fired into it; too big for the very country which was its constricting scope. It was as if the boy had already divined what his senses and intellect had not encompassed yet: that doomed wilderness whose edges were being constantly and punily gnawed at by men with plows and axes who feared it because it was wilderness, men myriad and nameless even to one another in the land where the old bear had earned a name, and through which ran not even a mortal beast but an anachronism indomitable and invincible out of an old, dead time, a phantom, epitome and apotheosis of the old, wild life which the little puny humans swarmed and hacked at in a fury of abhorrence and fear, like pygmies about the ankles of a drowsing elephant;—the old bear, solitary, indomitable, and alone; widowered, childless, and absolved of mortality—old Priam reft of his old wife and outlived all his sons.

IV

then he was twenty-one. He could say it, himself and his cousin juxtaposed not against the wilderness but against the tamed land which was to have been his heritage, the land which old Carothers McCaslin, his grandfather, had bought with white man's money from the wild men whose grandfathers without guns hunted it, and tamed and ordered, or believed he had tamed and ordered it, for the reason that the human beings he held in bondage and in the power of life and death had removed the forest from it and in their sweat scratched the surface of it to a depth of perhaps fourteen inches in order to grow something out of it which had not been there before, and which could be translated back into the money he who believed he had bought it had had to pay to get it and hold it, and a reasonable profit too: and for which reason old Carothers McCaslin, knowing better, could raise his children, his descendants and heirs, to believe the land was his to hold and bequeath, since the strong and ruthless man has a cynical foreknowledge of his own vanity and pride and strength and a contempt for all his get: just as, knowing better, Major de Spain had his fragment of that wilderness which was bigger and older than any recorded deed: just as, knowing better, old Thomas Sutpen, from whom Major de Spain had had his fragment for money: just as Ikkemotubbe, the Chickasaw chief, from whom Thomas Sutpen had had the fragment for money or rum or whatever it was, knew in his turn that not even a fragment of it had been his to relinquish or sell

not against the wilderness but against the land, not in pursuit and lust but in relinquishment; and in the commissary as it should have been, not the heart perhaps but certainly the solar-plexus of the repudiated and relinquished: the square, galleried, wooden building squatting like a portent above the fields whose laborers it still held in thrall, '65 or no, and placarded over with advertisements for snuff and cures for chills and salves and potions manufactured and sold by white men to bleach the pigment and straighten the hair of Negroes that they might resemble the very race which for two hundred years had held them in bondage and from which for another hundred years not even a bloody civil war would have set them completely free

himself and his cousin amid the old smells of cheese and salt meat and kerosene and harness, the ranked shelves of tobacco and overalls and bottled medicine and thread

and plow-bolts, the barrels and kegs of flour and meal and
molasses and nails, the wall pegs dependant with plow-
lines and plow-collars and hames and trace-chains, and
the desk and the shelf above it on which rested the ledgers
in which McCaslin recorded the slow outward trickle of
food and supplies and equipment which returned each
fall as cotton made and ginned and sold (two threads
frail as truth and impalpable as equators yet cable-strong
to bind for life them who made the cotton to the land
their sweat fell on), and the older ledgers, clumsy and
archaic in size and shape, on the yellowed pages of which
were recorded in the faded hand of his father Theophilus
and his uncle Amodeus during the two decades before the
Civil War the manumission, in title at least, of Carothers
McCaslin's slaves:

'Relinquish,' McCaslin said. 'Relinquish. You, the direct
male descendant of him who saw the opportunity and
took it, bought the land, took the land, got the land no
matter how, held it to bequeath, no matter how, out of
the old grant, the first patent, when it was a wilderness of
wild beasts and wilder men, and cleared it, translated it
into something to bequeath to his children, worthy of be-
queathment for his descendants' ease and security and
pride, and to perpetuate his name and accomplishments.
Not only the male descendant but the only and last descendant in the male line and in the third generation,
while I am not only four generations from old Carothers,
I derived through a woman and the very McCaslin in my
name is mine only by sufferance and courtesy and my
grandmother's pride in what that man accomplished,
whose legacy and monument you think you can repudiate.'
and he

'I can't repudiate it. It was never mine to repudiate. It
was never Father's and Uncle Buddy's to bequeath me to
repudiate, because it was never Grandfather's to bequeath
them to bequeath me to repudiate, because it was never
old Ikkemotubbe's to sell to Grandfather for bequeath-
ment and repudiation. Because it was never Ikkem...
fathers' fathers' to bequeath Ikkemotubbe ...

Grandfather or any man because on the instant when Ikkemotubbe discovered, realized, that he could sell it for
money, on that instant it ceased ever to have been his
forever, father to father to father, and the man who bought
it bought nothing.'

'Bought nothing?' and he

'Bought nothing. Because He told in the Book how He
created the earth, made it and looked at it and said it was
all right, and then He made man. He made the earth first
and peopled it with dumb creatures, and then He created
man to be His overseer on the earth and to hold suzerainty
over the earth and the animals on it in His name, not to
hold for himself and his descendants inviolable title forever, generation after generation, to the oblongs and
squares of the earth, but to hold the earth mutual and intact in the communal anonymity of brotherhood, and all
the fee He asked was pity and humility and sufferance and
endurance and the sweat of his face for bread. And I know
what you are going to say,' he said: 'That nevertheless
Grandfather—' and McCaslin

'—did own it. And not the first. Not alone and not the
first since, as your Authority states, man was dispossessed
of Eden. Nor yet the second and still not alone, on down
through the tedious and shabby chronicle of His chosen
sprung from Abraham; and of the sons of them who dispossessed Abraham, and of the five hundred years during
which half the known world and all it contained was
chattel to one city, as this plantation and all the life it contained was chattel and revokeless thrall to this commissary
store and those ledgers yonder during your grandfather's
life; and the next thousand years while men fought over
the fragments of that collapse until at last even the fragments were exhausted and men snarled over the gnawed
bones of the old world's worthless evening until an acci-
dental egg discovered to them a new hemisphere. So let me
say it: That nevertheless and notwithstanding old Carothers did own it. Bought it, got it, no matter; kept it, held it,
no matter; bequeathed it: else why do you stand here re-
linquishing and repudiating? Held it, kept it for fifty years

until you could repudiate it, while He—this Arbiter, this Architect, this umpire—condoned—or did He? looked down and saw—or did He? Or at least did nothing: saw, and could not, or did not see; saw, and would not, or perhaps He would not see—perverse, impotent, or blind: which?' and he

'Dispossessed.' and McCaslin

'What?' and he

'Dispossessed. Not impotent: He didn't condone; not blind, because He watched it. And let me say it. Dispossessed of Eden. Dispossessed of Canaan, and those who dispossessed him dispossessed him dispossessed, and the five hundred years of absentee landlords in the Roman bagnios, and the thousand years of wild men from the northern woods who dispossessed them and devoured their ravished substance ravished in turn again and then snarled in what you call the old world's worthless twilight over the old world's gnawed bones, blasphemous in His name until He used a simple egg to discover to them a new world where a nation of people could be founded in humility and pity and sufferance and pride of one to another. And Grandfather did own the land nevertheless and notwithstanding because He permitted it, not impotent and not condoning and not blind, because He ordered and watched it. He saw the land already accursed even as Ikkemotubbe and Ikkemotubbe's father old Issetibbeha and old Issetibbeha's fathers too held it, already tainted even before any white man owned it by what Grandfather and his kind, his fathers, had brought into the new land which He had vouchsafed them out of pity and sufferance, on condition of pity and humility and sufferance and endurance, from that old world's corrupt and worthless twilight as though in the sailfuls of the old world's tainted wind which drove the ships—' and McCaslin

'Ah.'

'—and no hope for the land anywhere so long as Ikkemotubbe and Ikkemotubbe's descendants held it in unbroken succession. Maybe He saw that only by voiding the land for a time of Ikkemotubbe's blood and substi

for it another blood, could He accomplish His purpose.
Maybe He knew already what that other blood would be,
maybe it was more than justice that only the white man's
blood was available and capable to raise the white man's
curse, more than vengeance when—' and McCaslin

'Ah.'

'—when He used the blood which had brought in the
evil to destroy the evil as doctors use fever to burn up
fever, poison to slay poison. Maybe He chose Grandfather
out of all of them He might have picked. Maybe He knew
that Grandfather himself would not serve His purpose because Grandfather was born too soon too, but that Grandfather would have descendants, the right descendants;
maybe He had foreseen already the descendants Grandfather would have, maybe He saw already in Grandfather
the seed progenitive of the three generations He saw it
would take to set at least some of His lowly people free—'

Suggested Readings

The selections in this volume represent an introduction into the literature of the subject. For a more detailed approach to the literature, see *American Indian and White Relations to 1830: Needs & Opportunities for Study*, An Essay by William N. Fenton and A Bibliography by L. H. Butterfield, Wilcomb E. Washburn, and William N. Fenton (Chapel Hill: University of North Carolina Press, 1957). This book gives a guide to reference and bibliographical aids, ethnological literature, historical literature, serials, manuscript sources, documentary publications, as well as to various special topics such as portraiture, captivities, the Indian in literature and thought, etc.

Among the recent "literary" studies is Edmund Wilson's *Apologies to the Iroquois* (New York: Farrar, Straus & Cudahy, 1960), which details the story of the losing battle fought by the Senecas to prevent the State of New York from building the Kinzua dam (now under construction) on their treaty-sanctified territory.

One of the best studies of the influence of the Indian on the white man is A. Irving Hallowell, "The Backwash of the Frontier: The Impact of the Indian on American Culture," in Walker D. Wyman and Clifton B. Kroeber, eds., *The Frontier in Perspective* (Madison: University of Wisconsin Press, 1957).

William T. Hagan's *American Indians* in the Chicago History of American Civilization series (Chicago: University of Chicago Press, 1961), gives an excellent summary of American Indian and white relations and is a fine introduction to the field for the general reader.

A detailed account of governmental policy toward th

Indian is Francis Paul Prucha's *American Indian Policy in the Formative Years: The Indian Trade and Intercourse Acts, 1790–1834* (Cambridge, Mass.: Harvard University Press, 1962).

Frederick J. Dockstader's *Indian Art in America: The Arts and Crafts of the North American Indian* (Greenwich, Conn.: New York Graphic Society, 1961), is a profusely illustrated account of its subject.

The anthropological writings concerning the American Indian are legion. One of the best ways to survey the recent literature is to study the journal of the American Anthropological Association, the *American Anthropologist*. One of the great centers of research in the field of the American Indian is the Bureau of American Ethnology of the Smithsonian Institution, whose publications over the past three-quarters of a century provide a basic library in the field.

ANCHOR BOOKS

AMERICAN HISTORY AND STUDIES

ANCHOR BOOKS

8Ab

THE FUTURE OF CONSERVATISM—M. Stanton Evans, revised edition, A701

GOVERNING EDUCATION: A Reader on Politics, Power and Public School Policy—Alan Rosenthal, ed., A651

IMPERIALISM AND SOCIAL REFORM: English Social-Imperial Thought 1895–1914—Bernard Semmel, A618

THE JEFFERSONIAN AND HAMILTONIAN TRADITIONS IN AMERICAN POLITICS: A Documentary History—Albert Fried, ed., A464

KARL MARX ON COLONIALISM AND MODERNIZATION: His Dispatches and Other Writings on China, India, Mexico, the Middle East and North Africa—Schlomo Avineri, ed., A688

THE LAST LANDSCAPE—William H. Whyte, A717

LATIN AMERICAN POLITICS: Studies of the Contemporary Scene—Robert D. Tomasek, ed., A498

LAW AND PSYCHOLOGY IN CONFLICT—James Marshall, A654

LET THEM EAT PROMISES: The Politics of Hunger in America—Nick Kotz; intro. by Senator George S. McGovern, A788

MAIN CURRENTS IN SOCIOLOGICAL THOUGHT, Volume I: Montesquieu, Comte, Marx, Tocqueville, the Sociologists and the Revolution of 1848—Raymond Aron; Richard Howard and Helen Weaver, trans., A600a

MAIN CURRENTS IN SOCIOLOGICAL THOUGHT, Volume II: Durkheim, Pareto, Weber—Raymond Aron, A600b

A MAN OF THE PEOPLE—Chinua Achebe, A594

MAO TSE-TUNG ON REVOLUTION AND WAR—Mostafa Rejai, ed., A730

MARX AND THE INTELLECTUALS: A Set of Post-Ideological Essays—Lewis Feuer, A643

MARX IN THE MID-TWENTIETH CENTURY: A Yugoslav Philosopher Reconsiders K. Marx's Writings—Galo Petrović, A584

MAX WEBER: An Intellectual Portrait—Reinhard Bendix, A281

MAY MAN PREVAIL?—Erich Fromm, A275

MIRAGE OF HEALTH—René Dubos, A258

MOVEMENT AND REVOLUTION: A Conversation on American Radicalism—Peter L. Berger and Richard J. Neuhaus, A726

THE NAZI REVOLUTION 1933–35: Prelude to Calamity—Eliot Barculo Wheaton, A690

THE NEGRO AND THE AMERICAN LABOR MOVEMENT—Julius Jacobson, ed., A495

THE NEWCOMERS—Oscar Handlin, A283

A NEW HISTORY OF THE COLD WAR—John Lukacs, third edition, expanded, of A History of the Cold War, A533

NOBODY WANTED WAR: Misperception in Vietnam and Other Wars—Ralph K. White, revised and expanded, A612

THE OLD REGIME AND THE FRENCH REVOLUTION—Alexis de Tocqueville; Stuart Gilbert, trans., A60

ON INTELLECTUALS—Philip Rieff, ed., A733

THE PATH TO DICTATORSHIP, 1918–1933, Ten Essays by German Scholars—John Conway, trans., intro. by Fritz Stern, A547

ANCHOR BOOKS

HISTORY

JOHN CALVIN: Selections from His Writings—John Dillenberger, ed., A751

JOURNEYS TO ENGLAND AND IRELAND—Alexis de Tocqueville; J. P. Mayer, ed., A611

KARL MARX ON COLONIALISM AND MODERNIZATION—Shlomo Avineri, ed., A688

THE LAND TO THOSE WHO WORK IT: Algeria's Experiment in Worker Management—Thomas L. Blair, A734

LATIN AMERICAN POLITICS: Studies of the Contemporary Scene—Robert D. Tomasek, ed., new revised and updated edition, A498

LIFE IN MEXICO: The Letters of Fanny Calderón de la Barca with New Material from the Author's Private Journals—Howard J. Fisher and Marion Hall Fisher, eds., AO16

A MAN OF THE PEOPLE—Chinua Achebe, A594

MAO TSE-TUNG ON REVOLUTION AND WAR—Mostafa Rehai, ed., A730

MARX IN THE MID-TWENTIETH CENTURY: A Yugoslav Philosopher Reconsiders Karl Marx's Writings—Gajo Petrović, A584

THE MIND OF THE EUROPEAN ROMANTICS—H. G. Schenk, A655

MONT-SAINT-MICHEL AND CHARTRES—Henry Adams, A166

MOTHER EARTH AND OTHER STORIES—Boris Pilnyak; Vera T. Reck and Michael Green, trans. and eds., A625

MYTHOLOGIES OF THE ANCIENT WORLD—Samuel Noah Kramer, ed., A229

THE NAZI REVOLUTION 1933–35: Prelude to Calamity—Eliot Barculo Wheaton, A690

NEW DIRECTIONS IN BIBLICAL ARCHAEOLOGY—David Noel Freedman and Jonas C. Greenfield, eds., A753

A NEW HISTORY OF THE COLD WAR—John Lukacs, third edition, expanded, of A History of the Cold War, A533

NOBODY WANTED WAR: Misperception in Vietnam and Other Wars—Ralph K. White, A612

OBSTACLES TO DEVELOPMENT IN LATIN AMERICA—Celso Furtado, A747

THE OLD REGIME AND THE FRENCH REVOLUTION—Alexis de Tocqueville; Stuart Gilbert, trans., A60

THE PACIFIC ISLANDS—Douglas L. Oliver, revised edition, N14

THE PATH TO DICTATORSHIP, 1918–1933: Ten Essays by German Scholars—John Conway, trans.; intro. by Fritz Stern, A547

THE PHILOSOPHY OF HISTORY IN OUR TIME—Hans Meyerhoff, ed., A164

THE POLITICS OF CULTURAL DESPAIR—Fritz Stern, A436

POOR PEOPLE and A LITTLE HERO—Fyodor Dostoevsky; David Magarshack, trans., A619

QUEEN ELIZABETH I—J. E. Neale, A105

RECOLLECTIONS—Alexis de Tocqueville; J. P. Mayer and A. P. Kerr, eds., A749

THE RECORDS OF MEDIEVAL EUROPE—Carolly Erickson, ed., A770
9Cb

ANCHOR BOOKS

16Ab

History
Documents in American Civilization Series

The Indian and the White Man
Edited with an introduction by Wilcomb E. Washburn

From the description of the white man's first contact with the Indian as recorded in the journal of Christopher Columbus down to the "Declaration of Indian Purpose" prepared at the American Indian Conference in Chicago in 1961, this documentary history illustrates the most important aspects of Indian white relations and develops the larger theme of the Indian as part of the American experience. It is compiled, states the editor, from "a point of view strongly sympathetic to the American Indian."

32 Pages of Illustrations. Cover, Comanche Mounted War Party by George Catlin, Courtesy The Smithsonian Institution. Cover Design by Alain Duchamp.

 A Doubleday Anchor Original
ISBN: 0-385-01687-5